TEACHING CRITICAL PSYCHOLOGY

International Perspectives

This edited volume may be the 'definitive text' on methods and content in teaching psychology from an international and critical perspective. Chapters from internationally renowned contributors working clinically, educationally and in the community with a range of client groups, outline critical teaching by and for professionals and service recipients.

This timely book offers a unique, research-based and philosophically coherent approach to teaching psychology including teaching methods, the lecture content of radical approaches to modern psychology and debates as to whether the aim of teaching is to liberate or control. Themes include the nature of pedagogy, the importance of teaching and learning style, the relevance of context and content and the ways in which traditional teaching forms a part of the disciplinary rather than critical project.

Teaching Critical Psychology offers guidance in teaching pupils, students, peers and those on academic programmes at under-graduate and post-graduate level.

Craig Newnes is a Consulting Critical Psychologist, editor and author. He has published numerous works and is Editor of *The Journal of Critical Psychology, Counselling and Psychotherapy*. For 19 years he was the Editor of *Clinical Psychology Forum*, the in-house practice journal of the Division of Clinical Psychology of the British Psychological Society, and Director of Psychological Therapies for Shropshire's Community and Mental Health Services (NHS) Trust.

Laura Golding is Programme Director of the University of Liverpool's Doctorate in Clinical Psychology and chair of the British Psychological Society's Division of Clinical Psychology Conference Committee. Much of her career has been spent working in the National Health Service (NHS) in the North West of England with adults with intellectual disabilities.

TEACHING CRITICAL PSYCHOLOGY

International Perspectives

*Edited by Craig Newnes
and Laura Golding*

LONDON AND NEW YORK

First published 2018
by Routledge
2 Park Square, Milton Park, Abingdon, Oxon OX14 4RN

and by Routledge
711 Third Avenue, New York, NY 10017

Routledge is an imprint of the Taylor & Francis Group, an informa business

© 2018 selection and editorial matter, Craig Newnes and Laura Golding; individual chapters, the contributors

The right of the editors to be identified as the authors of the editorial material, and of the authors for their individual chapters, has been asserted in accordance with sections 77 and 78 of the Copyright, Designs and Patents Act 1988.

All rights reserved. No part of this book may be reprinted or reproduced or utilised in any form or by any electronic, mechanical, or other means, now known or hereafter invented, including photocopying and recording, or in any information storage or retrieval system, without permission in writing from the publishers.

Trademark notice: Product or corporate names may be trademarks or registered trademarks, and are used only for identification and explanation without intent to infringe.

British Library Cataloguing in Publication Data
A catalogue record for this book is available from the British Library.

Library of Congress Cataloging-in-Publication Data
A catalog record for this book has been requested.

ISBN: 978-1-138-28833-1 (hbk)
ISBN: 978-1-138-28834-8 (pbk)
ISBN: 978-1-315-20931-9 (ebk)

Typeset in Bembo
by Keystroke, Neville Lodge, Tettenhall, Wolverhampton

To Abigail, Milo and Rachel

CONTENTS

List of contributors — ix
Preface: on critical pedagogy — xv
Peter McLaren

1 Teaching psychology critically — 1
  David Fryer and Rachael Fox

2 Ten suggestions for critical teaching in psychology — 19
  John Cromby

3 Towards coherence in teaching critical Psy — 37
  Craig Newnes

4 Teaching disability, teaching critical disability studies — 64
  *Dan Goodley, Michael Miller and
  Katherine Runswick-Cole*

5 Fear and loathing in the education system — 82
  Robbie Piper

6 What can teachers of critical and community psychology
  learn from their learners? — 100
  *Olivia Fakoussa, Gemma Budge, Mandeep Singh Kallu,
  Annie Mitchell and Rachel Purtell*

7 Teaching Indigenous psychology: a conscientisation, de-colonisation and psychological literacy approach to curriculum 123
Pat Dudgeon, Dawn Darlaston-Jones and Abigail Bray

8 Teaching withdrawal of antipsychotics and antidepressants to professionals and recipients 148
Peter Lehmann

9 Psychiatry and the law: the Law Project for Psychiatric Rights' public education approach 170
Jim Gottstein

10 Human rights and critical psychology 195
Beth Greenhill and Laura Golding

11 Children's experiences of domestic violence: a teaching and training challenge 219
Jane Callaghan, Lisa Fellin and Joanne Alexander

12 Supervision: a principles-based approach 238
Sara Tai

13 Training that domesticates or education that liberates? Tensions and dilemmas related to teaching critical psychology in the context of UK clinical psychology training 259
Anne Cooke

Names index 278
Subject index 279

CONTRIBUTORS

Joanne Alexander is a Researcher in the Institute of Health and Wellbeing at the University of Northampton in the UK, and is currently conducting her doctoral research into the intergenerational transmission of family violence.

Dr Abigail Bray is a cross-disciplinary social scientist concentrating on critical psychology and critical theory. She has published numerous books and articles and is a Researcher in the School of Indigenous Studies at the University of Western Australia.

Gemma Budge is a third-year trainee Clinical Psychologist at Plymouth University in the UK. She is carrying out her doctoral research exploring the democratic approach of a mental health collective and has worked with charities representing the interests of marginalised groups, including people seeking asylum and the LGBT+ (lesbian, gay, bisexual and transgender plus) community.

Professor Jane Callaghan is at the University of Northampton in the UK where she leads the Centre for Family Life, the MSc Child and Adolescent Mental Health and the CYP IAPT programme. She is Secretary to the British Psychological Society's (BPS) Psychology of Women Section, and sits on the Ethics Committee as well as the Research Board of the BPS. She is Editor of the *Journal of Gender Studies*.

Dr Anne Cooke is Principal Lecturer, Department of Psychology, Politics and Sociology and Joint Clinical Director, Doctoral Programme in Clinical Psychology, Salomons Centre for Applied Psychology, Canterbury Christ Church University, UK.

Dr John Cromby is Reader in Psychology at the University of Leicester, UK. He is the co-author (with David Harper and Paula Reavey; Palgrave, 2013) of *Psychology,*

Mental Health and Distress, which won the 2014 BPS Book Award, and the author of *Feeling Bodies: Embodying Psychology* (Palgrave Macmillan, 2015).

Dr Dawn Darlaston-Jones is Associate Professor of Behavioural Science at the University of Notre Dame, Fremantle Campus, Western Australia. She has won several awards in the field of pedagogy including the inaugural ALTC/APS (Australian Learning and Teaching Council/Australian Psychological Society) Prize for Innovation in Teaching and Learning (2011). Her research interests lie in the area of critical psychology with a particular emphasis on resistance and emancipation, decolonisation and education.

Professor Pat Dudgeon is from the Bardi people of the Kimberley area in Western Australia. She is a Research Fellow at the School of Indigenous Studies at the University of Western Australia. She is a member of the Executive Board of the Australian Indigenous Psychologists Association (AIPA); the co-chair of the national ministerial Aboriginal and Torres Strait Islander Mental Health and Suicide Prevention Advisory Group; and chair of the National Aboriginal and Torres Strait Islander Leadership in Mental Health.

Olivia Fakoussa is a Clinical Psychologist who works in a Child and Adolescent Mental Health Services (CAMHS) Infant Mental Health Team offering support to some of the most vulnerable and voiceless in society.

Dr Lisa Fellin is Research Director of the Doctorate in Counselling Psychology programme at the University of East London in the UK. She is a Critical Clinical Psychologist and a Systemic Psychotherapist.

Dr Rachael Fox is a Senior Lecturer in Psychology at Charles Sturt University, New South Wales, Australia. She completed her PhD at the University of Stirling, Scotland, and specialises in research with young people.

Professor David Fryer is Professor Extraordinarius at the Institute for Social and Health Sciences, University of South Africa (Johannesburg), and at the South African Medical Research Council–University of South Africa's Violence, Injury and Peace Research Unit (Cape Town). He also teaches and supervises PhD students as Honorary Research Associate Professor at the School of Education, University of Queensland, Australia. Previously he was: Professor of Psychology and Head of Research and Academic Program Development at the Australian Institute of Psychology (a private sector higher education provider); Professor of Community Critical Psychology at Charles Sturt University, New South Wales; Reader in Psychology at the University of Stirling, Scotland. He is a Fellow of the British Psychological Society, a Fellow of the Society for Community Research and Action and an Associate Fellow of the Critical Institute. David is currently employed part-time on short insecure contracts in the School of Counselling at the Australian

College of Applied Psychology (part of private sector higher education provider, Navitas) to teach Master's students of Psychotherapy and Counselling about doing 'research'. He has attempted to teach psychology critically throughout his academic career, which explains why he is currently a member of the academic precariat.

Dr Laura Golding is Programme Director of the University of Liverpool's Doctorate in Clinical Psychology and chair of the British Psychological Society's Division of Clinical Psychology Conference Committee. Much of her career has been spent working in the National Health Service (NHS) with adults with intellectual disabilities. Her book publications include *Continuing Professional Development for Clinical Psychologists: A Practical Handbook* (co-edited with Ian Gray; BPS Blackwell, 2006).

Professor Dan Goodley is Professor of Psychology at the University of Sheffield, UK.

Jim Gottstein is President of the Law Project for Psychiatric Rights (PsychRights) and a US attorney at law (http://psychrights.org/about/Gottstein.htm). After 14 years working for PsychRights without pay, Jim has had to substantially curtail his efforts on behalf of PsychRights for financial reasons.

Beth Greenhill is a Clinical Psychologist and Cognitive Analytic Therapy practitioner working with people with learning disabilities in the Halton Community Learning Disability Team for the Five Boroughs Partnership NHS Foundation Trust in the UK. Beth is also a Senior Clinical Tutor for the University of Liverpool's Doctorate in Clinical Psychology programme. Beth has contributed to human rights education as project lead for the UK Department of Health's 'Human Rights in Healthcare' programme within her service, and has also led on collaborations with the Equality and Human Rights Commission, co-producing educational materials for trainees, professionals and experts by experience. Beth's research interests include applying human rights approaches in healthcare, clinical risk-sharing partnerships, and sexuality, primarily with people with learning disabilities.

Peter Lehmann was born in 1950 in Calw (Black Forest, Germany) and was educated in social pedagogy. He is a psychiatric survivor and activist and an independent publisher and author, based in Berlin. He published *Coming Off Psychiatric Drugs* in 2004, the first book in the world about the issue of successfully coming off psychiatric drugs (originally published in the German language in 1998). It has been translated into many different languages (see www.peter-lehmann-publishing.com/comingoff). On his website (www.antipsychiatrieverlag.de/info1/absetzen.htm), he offers a multilingual 'surview' of books, articles, websites, blogs, mailing lists, booklets and lectures relevant to the topic of coming off psychiatric drugs. In 2010, he was awarded the Honorary Doctorate degree of the Aristotle University of Thessaloniki, Greece; in 2011, he received the Order of Merit of the Federal Republic of Germany in acknowledgement of his service to the community by the

President of Germany. His latest book is *Neue Antidepressiva, atypische Neuroleptika – Risiken, Placebo-Effekte, Niedrigdosierung und Alternativen* (together with Volkmar Aderhold, Marc Rufer and Josef Zehentbauer, 2017); see www.peter-lehmann-publishing.com

Professor Peter McLaren is Distinguished Professor in Critical Studies, College of Educational Studies, Chapman University, California, where he is Co-Director of the Paulo Freire Democratic Project and International Ambassador for Global Ethics and Social Justice. He is also Emeritus Professor of Urban Education at the University of California, Los Angeles, and Emeritus Professor of Educational Leadership, Miami University of Ohio, United States. He is also an Honorary Director of the Center for Critical Studies in Education at Northeast Normal University, Changchun, China. His most recent book is *Pedagogy of Insurrection: From Resurrection to Revolution* (Peter Lang, 2015).

Michael Miller is a PhD student in the School of Education at the University of Sheffield, UK. Primarily focused on critical disability studies, Michael is thinking about and further developing (in)comprehensions of discontinuities of violence in/as education, asking what a crip refusal to reformative policies might become.

Annie Mitchell teaches clinical and community psychology at Plymouth University in the UK, works as a Clinical Psychologist in renal medicine at the Royal Devon and Exeter NHS Foundation Trust, is a mentor for the Point of Care Foundation's Schwartz Rounds programme and chair for the South West Division of Clinical Psychology of the British Psychological Society. She initiated the research programme Folk.us (Forum for Collaboration with Users in Research; www.folkus.org.uk) and now leads the qualitative arm of a National Institute for Health Research (NIHR) research programme exploring onward ripples of altruistic kidney donation. She is a Playback Theatre performer.

Craig Newnes is a Consulting Critical Psychologist, editor and author who has won two human rights awards for speaking out about the iniquities of the Psy complex. He has published numerous book chapters and academic articles and is Editor of *The Journal of Critical Psychology, Counselling and Psychotherapy*. He was, for 19 years, the Editor of *Clinical Psychology Forum*, the in-house practice journal of the Division of Clinical Psychology of the British Psychological Society (BPS), and Director of Psychological Therapies for Shropshire's Community and Mental Health Services (NHS) Trust.

He has edited five books and is Commissioning Editor for six volumes in the Critical Psychology Division series from PCCS Books. His latest books are *Clinical Psychology: A Critical Examination* (PCCS Books, 2014), as part of the new Critical Examination series for which he is also Commissioning Editor, and *Children in Society: Politics, Policies and Interventions* (PCCS Books, 2015). For Palgrave Macmillan, he has authored *Inscription, Diagnosis, Deception and the Mental*

Health Industry: How Psy Governs Us All (2016). He has been Honorary Professor at Murdoch University, Australia, and an Honorary Lecturer at seven UK universities.

Robbie Piper (BA, PGCE) teaches in a primary school in a deprived area of the North of England.

Rachel Purtell is a disabled woman and disability activist who holds a Master of Arts in Disability Studies. For 14 years, she was a Research Fellow at the University of Exeter in the UK, as Director of the Department of Health-funded Folk.us research programme (www.folkus.org.uk). She has been a freelance trainer in Disability Equality Issues using a Social Model approach rooted in the experience of disabled people. After taking medical retirement in 2014, Rachel now advises on involvement and disabled people's issues for a number of organisations, including the Division of Clinical Psychology of the British Psychological Society nationally and in the South West of England.

Dr Katherine Runswick-Cole is Senior Research Fellow in Disability Studies and Psychology at Manchester Metropolitan University in the UK. She locates her work in the field of critical disability studies.

Mandeep Singh Kallu attended the clinical psychology programme at Plymouth University, UK, where his clinical work focused on working with marginalised groups. His first experience of homelessness was at the age of 13, he left school without any qualifications, and at 16 years of age found himself homeless again for 4 years. Such experiences are crucial to the understanding of critical community psychology and the notion of 'lived experience'. Mandeep has developed several art projects and exhibitions that challenge societal perceptions for groups of people who find themselves on the fringes of society.

Dr Sara Tai is a Senior Lecturer in Clinical Psychology, Consultant Clinical Psychologist and Academic Director of the Doctorate in Clinical Psychology programme at the Faculty of Biology, Medicine and Health, School of Health Sciences, Division of Psychology and Mental Health at the University of Manchester, UK.

PREFACE

On critical pedagogy

Peter McLaren

Despite critical pedagogy's general discrediting by educational conservatives of every stripe—that it is anti-American, socialist, feminist and chock-a-block with political correctness and political demagoguery—critical pedagogy is thriving. But it is thriving more as a controversial approach to teaching than as an approach that has been fully vetted and implemented in school sites. At the very least, this remains the case in the United States. In Latin America, however, critical pedagogy has been taken up more systematically by educators, often under the rubric of what is called "popular education."

The benighted misconceptions surrounding critical pedagogy among conservatives in the United States which have equated it with social justice education and which, in turn, have equated social justice education with a conspiracy to destroy the country via the promotion of feminism, political correctness, economic equality, LGBT programs, etc., have kept critical pedagogy from making crucially important inroads into how we view knowledge construction and its relationship to teaching and learning. And while it is rare to find critical pedagogy programs fully implemented in public school sites, the field fortunately continues to proliferate in graduate programs in education.

Critical pedagogy has numerous trajectories. So many, in fact, that at times they press across the horizon in academic formation like armies on the march and vanish at the very point where you wish they would merge together in some kind of pedagogical decussation. While the yeasty challenges of their exponents to the obduracy and affordance of daily capitalist life have achieved little notice by mainstream education institutions and their official publication outlets, their unwavering and spritely efforts to take on the head honchos of corporate schooling, and to impugn the imprimatur that they have stamped upon their managerial, myopic and mechanistic approach to education, have been impressively robust if not, at times, uneven, unsettling and awkward. Critical educators, even those in their dotage, are, after all, prone to exuberant and irreverent heresies and more than inclined to believe that a failure to speak out against the primal sins of neoliberal capitalism is tantamount to a self-indicting embrace of the very system that prioritizes the victimizers of empire over its victims and enlists oneself in the systematic service of domination.

Within my own field of teacher education, many, if not most, advocates of critical pedagogy view themselves essentially as cultural workers fighting against societal injustices such as structural racism, social class inequality, homophobia, sexism, white supremacy and patriarchy. And many, if not most, critical educators would admit to being singularly influenced by the storied Brazilian educator and philosopher, Paulo Freire.

But critical pedagogy is far from being a homogeneous approach to education. For instance, some advocates of critical pedagogy approach (wrongly in my opinion) critical pedagogy as essentially a kit and caboodle of specific "how to" approaches to lesson planning, pedagogy and evaluation, and focus almost exclusively on developing classroom teaching methods. Other practitioners reject this "bag of tricks" approach (especially those working in the field of cognitive psychology) and are focused mainly on fostering critical thinking, while others, such as research practitioners of CHAT (cultural-historical activity theory), advance the contributions of Lev Semenovich Vygotsky and post-Vygotskian scholars and utilize concepts such as the "zone of proximal development." Still other critical educators (usually self-identified as belonging to the revolutionary left) are contributing to the development of a philosophy of praxis grounded in Marxist and Freirean epistemological approaches and embellished by their quest for social transformation.

It is a heartening sign that critical pedagogy now extends beyond graduate schools of education and teacher education. In addition to contributions from a transdisciplinary cadre located within the social sciences, English and comparative literature, cultural studies, psychology and the arts, critical pedagogy has incorporated politico-ethical appropriations from liberation theology. Interest in critical pedagogy is burgeoning in numerous academic and professional fields beyond teacher education.

My own work locates itself within a Marxist-humanist philosophy of praxis in which human subjectivity is seen as dialogical; that is, as forged in the "now" of our personal and collective self-presence as intersubjective beings in the immediate conversation we undertake with each other. The idea behind the development of a philosophy of praxis is that it can help to frame everyday life dialectically, enabling critical educators to identify, challenge and transform those asymmetrical relations of power that strengthen racist, sexist, homophobic, imperialist, white supremacist and other oppressive social, cultural and institutional formations. Other practices of critical pedagogy have developed into approaches such as feminist pedagogy, ecopedagogy, decolonial pedagogy, culturally relevant pedagogy, etc.

My articulation of critical pedagogical praxis falls under the category of "revolutionary critical pedagogy" in order to distinguish it from more politically domesticated instantiations of progressive pedagogy that often choose to list themselves under the rubric of critical pedagogy (and which in many ways do reflect some central aspects of critical pedagogy, albeit lacking the Marxist politics). Proponents of revolutionary critical pedagogy—which incorporates elements of many of the other critical approaches such as feminist pedagogy and ecopedagogy—decry the commodification and commercialization of everyday life and its Dante-esque integration into the macro-economy of capitalist globalization. Consequently, they have taken upon themselves the daunting task of placing themselves in diametric opposition to capitalism as a mode of production with its obscene and record-breaking levels of value production (value here meaning monetized wealth) and to its political ideology, neoliberalism. If we are to examine psychology and psychiatry seriously, we need to take seriously the crisis of the times described by Leonardo Boff (2016) as follows:

> The fury of capitalist accumulation has reached the highest levels of its history. Practically 1% of the wealthy population of the world controls nearly the 90% of its wealth. According to the reputable NGO Oxfam Intermon [International], in 2014, 85 members of the super-rich had the same amount of money as 3.5 billion of the poorest in the world. This level of irrationality and inhumanity speaks for itself. We are living [in] explicitly barbaric times.
>
> *(Boff, 2016, para. 3)*

Boff also names the two externalities produced by capitalism that remain central to any critical pedagogy:

> There are principally two of these: a degrading *social injustice* with high unemployment and growing inequality; and a threatened *ecological injustice* with the degradation of whole ecosystems, the erosion of biodiversity (with the extinction of between 30–100 thousand species of living beings each year, according to data of the biologist E. Wilson), the growing global warming, the scarcity of drinking water and general unsustainability of the life-system and of the Earth-system.
>
> *(Boff, 2016, para. 5)*

Critical educators give pride of place to the uncomfortable truth that we live as a society in a state of politico-economic trauma. Our demands come from the belly of the neoliberal state where we remain ensepulchered within a governing rationality through which everything is "economized" and in a very specific way. To quote Wendy Brown (interviewed by Shenk, 2015), neoliberalism is a process of governmentality (Foucault's term) in which

> human beings become market actors and nothing but, every field of activity is seen as a market, and every entity (whether public or private, whether person, business, or state) is governed as a firm. Importantly, this is not simply a matter of extending commodification and monetization everywhere—that's the old Marxist depiction of capital's transformation of

everyday life. Neoliberalism construes even non-wealth generating spheres—such as learning, dating, or exercising—in market terms, submits them to market metrics, and governs them with market techniques and practices. Above all, it casts people as human capital who must constantly tend to their own present and future value.

(Shenk, 2015, para. 4)

Expanding on Brown's concept of neoliberalism, I would also frame neoliberal capitalism as a world ecology, especially as this has been articulated by Jason W. Moore (2015). Moore writes that we need to grasp humanity-in-nature as a world-historical process, a dialectical unity among accumulation, power and the co-production of nature. Moore (Moore & Ahsan, 2015) argues that the problem of capitalism today

is that the opportunities of appropriating work for free—from forests, oceans, climate, soils and human beings—are dramatically contracting. Meanwhile, the mass of capital floating around the world looking for something to invest in is getting bigger and bigger.

(Moore & Ahsan, 2015, para. 24)

The instability of capitalism will intensify dramatically over the next several decades, as climate disaster, rising unemployment, increasing personal surveillance of the poor and powerless, and pollution turn our planet into a festering pattern of slums—conditions that are likely to contribute to increased instances of genocide, epistemicide and ecocide.

Yet the proliferation of a wide range of critical pedagogies over the last several decades has not led their main protagonists to water down their resolve nor veer from critical pedagogy's historical aim: to critique and transform asymmetrical relations of power and privilege that constitute and are constituted by the surrounding milieu of the classroom, school, culture and institutional and economic arrangements of society, those systems of mediation that negatively impact the academic success of students and, equally important, their ability to think critically and to develop the kind of protagonist agency necessary to transform the world in the interests of justice for the powerless and the oppressed. Examining instances of student failure in specific school settings, critical educators may uncover patterns of association that emerge among instances of social conflict related to class, gender or sexual orientation, to established cultural imperatives—even mythopoetic aspects of the culture—and to dominant social, institutional and politico-economic relations. However, to tack a lack of student creativity, or motivation, or work ethic onto a single supposed determinate factor, as behaviorists are apt to do, may cause educators to miss the culture-specific, latent and contemporaneous aspects of schooling that underlie manifest or structural content. Sometimes conflicts within the learner occur contemporaneously—perhaps even functioning as homologous processes within the home and the school—and will be more immediately important than those derived from the early life of the student, or the student's social class location, the institutional organization of the school or the social relations of production of the society at large. And sometimes it will be the other way around.

I will speak briefly about liberation theology since it informs my own approach to revolutionary critical pedagogy and is probably the least well-known approach to overcoming social relations of oppression. While now an interdenominational movement of significant international scope, the most widely known variants of liberation theology germinated within the Catholic Church in Latin America as early as the 1950s, with a strong—even frenzied—opposition from U.S. government administrations (McLaren, 1986; 2015). Liberation theology works from the premise of a "social gospel" and a "preferential option for the poor" which means prioritizing the social issues of widespread poverty and injustice throughout América Latina. Historically there has been a back-and-forth struggle between proponents of liberation theology within the Catholic Church and more orthodox bishops who, rejecting the notion of Jesus as a subversive political figure fighting injustice toward the poor, seek to dismantle it. Ronald Reagan launched a successful military strategy against liberation theology (with the strategic cooperation of Pope John Paul II) that saw a reversal of gains by anti-fascist guerrilla groups in El Salvador, Guatemala and Nicaragua. Catholic priests and proponents of liberation theology were sometimes viewed as sympathetic to guerrilla movements.

In one infamous event, the Salvadoran military, backed by the United States, murdered six Jesuits in El Salvador in November 1989: Ignacio Ellacuría, Ignacio Martín-Baró, Segundo Montes, Juan Ramón Moreno, Amando López and Joaquin López y López. Also brutally slain were their housekeeper and her teenage daughter. They were murdered by U.S.-trained troops of the elite Atlacatl Battalion in a heinous act of sophiacide (an attempt to destroy knowledge and wisdom) on the grounds of the University of Central America in San Salvador. Noam Chomsky described the attacks on liberation theology by the U.S. administration as punishment for "the crime of going back to the Gospels." He claimed that:

> The Church of Latin America had undertaken "the preferential option for the poor." They committed the crime of going back to the Gospels. The contents of the Gospels are mostly suppressed (in the U.S.); they are a radical pacifist collection of documents. It was turned into the religion of the rich by the Emperor Constantine, who eviscerated its content. If anyone dares to go back to the Gospels, they become the enemy, which is what liberation theology was doing.
>
> *(Chomsky, interviewed by Chaudary, 2007, n.p.)*

On a more cultural front, the CIA helped to bring into the living rooms of América Latina a depoliticized Protestant version of Christianity, courtesy of religious broadcast shows with the likes of Jimmy Swaggart, Pat Robertson, Jerry Falwell and Jim and Tammy Bakker. A book by one of the leading Jesuits slain by the Atlacatl Battalion, Ignacio Martín-Baró, entitled *Writings for a Liberation Psychology* (published posthumously in 1996 after his assassination), became a foundational text in developing the field of liberation psychology. The work of Mary Watkins, *Invisible Guests* (1986), and Watkins and Helene Shulman, *Toward Psychologies of Liberation* (2008), has more recently made a salutary impact in the field of critical psychology, not to mention the rediscovery of the work of the Frankfurt School theorists.

While my work in critical pedagogy has been very much informed by my mentor and friend Paulo Freire, it has also expanded into different theaters of struggle. For instance, my more recent work arcs in the direction of decoloniality, a perspective influenced by the thinking of Anibal Quijano, Ramón Grosfoguel, Walter Mignolo and Enrique Dussel, among others. Decolonial educators employ a meta-theoretical orientation that challenges the notion of discrete, autonomous, closed and isolated cultural, ideological and economic systems. The social totality is approached as a concrete material reality consisting of complex open systems integrated into various networks, structures and systems of intelligibility that are inescapably and irredeemably entangled. The emergent materialist reality is composed of heterarchies (i.e., multiple hierarchies) coeval with and co-constituent of a world divided into core and peripheral nations existing within an unjust international division of labor. A history of capitalist overproduction and accumulation by dispossession and an exportation of Eurocentric colonial relations have left a shameful legacy of economic inequality and alienated social relations of production, as well as heterarchical structures of sexual, gender, class, religious and racial discrimination and violence that have resulted in the exclusion and silencing of subaltern knowledges. Revolutionary critical pedagogy is a trans-modern response to U.S. imperialism—the coloniality of power, racism, sexism, white supremacy, patriarchy, ableism and economic inequality—which locates its politics of liberation on the subaltern side of colonial difference in solidarity with minoritized and oppressed groups. It seeks to develop a social universe outside of capitalist value production and in the pursuit of cognitive democracy, and economic, racial, gender and sexual equality. Revolutionary critical pedagogy attempts to move beyond the monologic, monotopic and inferiorizing discourses and epistemic practices of the capitalist world system and contemplates the struggle for social justice beyond the efforts of any single nation state. Those of us who are involved in this project envision a pluriversal world consisting of many ethico-political projects that are bound together through horizontal forms of dialogue and self-managed socialized production and distribution systems operationalized by communities of solidarity and reciprocity (McLaren, 2008).

The widespread inclination of contemporary progressive educators in the United States is to ignore or reject dialectical reasoning and this constitutes, in our view, a failure to take into account the most important processes that shape our empirical lives. We need to rupture that which sustains our ordinary sense of embodied selfhood; we need to reorient our default mode of neural pathways so we can discover more creative ways to resist the neoliberal empire, a new gradient, a new sense of direction, and not necessarily a final outcome, fixed terminus or grand omega point. We don't require blueprints, we require a new dialectical vision and a new consensus on how to move forward, a wider-than-customary range of alternative ideas. We need to re-tread our habit-sodden pedagogies congealed and crimped into the reports of blue-chip committees that we consider fixed and irrevocably complete—that we have falsely taken as axiomatic and exhaustively finalized by proponents of a narrow and reductive positivism—and realize that we have much to learn from the practical and spiritual insights of the popular majorities. It is important to note that critical consciousness does not arrive by divine fiat. It does not flood into our brainpans through the open-spigot eyes of a stained glass saint on a sun-drenched day, pulsating in ecstatic intimacy with a beatified intellect. No, it arrives not as an "ah ha!" moment, but humbly, out of a long-term commitment to and protracted engagement with popular constituencies caught in the messy web of daily life. Critical consciousness is not a precondition for transforming the world, but an outcome of a praxis of solidaristic engagement with others in which we are braided together as agents struggling for genuine, uncoerced communication and undamaged intersubjectivity.

I believe it is our task as educators to make socialist class consciousness possible, as an ideal to which current conditions of austerity must adjust themselves as we work to unify social movements on the left into a transnational socialist front. A step in this direction can be accomplished through what Martín-Baró (1996, p. 219) refers to as building historical consciousness through popular organizations and class practice. This does not mean that all critical educators need to follow a path to socialism. But it does mean that critical educators need to be attentive to the social, cultural and economic conditions that are responsible for the existence of such asymmetry in today's institutional relationships of power and privilege.

Teaching Critical Psychology is a book that further extends the scope and reach of critical pedagogy by addressing the type of teaching that is best suited for a critical psychiatry and psychology, and by adumbrating the contextual specificity of the individuals and communities being served in terms of a variety of standpoints that include race, gender, social class, sexual orientation and geopolitics. Its contributors write with an enlightened passion from a range of critical perspectives and within a variety of local, regional, national and international contexts. What they share in common is a deep engagement with psychology and psychiatry as a discipline and praxis that can effect profound and liberating changes in the lives of those who are suffering and who are likely to suffer. Here we can be grateful to the authors for their attempts to deprive systems of domination and alienation of their hegemonic power and to remove capitalism's raiment of legitimation that would bedazzle its victims with new manifestations of unfounded hope. It is a book whose time has come and whose pedagogical vision can be ignored only at our peril.

References

Boff, L. (2016). The Earth will defeat capitalism. *Tikuun*, January 5. Retrieved from www.tikkun.org/nextgen/the-earth-will-defeat-capitalism

Chaudary, A. (2007). On religion and politics, Noam Chomsky interviewed by Amina Chaudary. *Islamica Magazine, Issue 19*, April–May. Retrieved from https://chomsky.info/200704__/

Martín-Baró, I. (1996). *Writings for a liberation psychology*. A. Aron & S. Corne (Eds.). Cambridge, MA: Harvard University Press.

McLaren, P. (1986). *Schooling as a ritual performance: Towards a political economy of educational symbols and gestures*. New York: Routledge.

McLaren, P. (2008). This fist called my heart: Public pedagogy in the belly of the beast. *Antipode, 40*(3), 472–481.

McLaren, P. (2015). *Pedagogy of insurrection: From resurrection to revolution*. New York: Peter Lang Publishers.

Moore, J. W. (2015). *Capitalism in the web of life: Ecology and the accumulation of capital*. New York: Verso.

Moore, J., & Ahsan, K. (2015). Capitalism in the web of life: An interview with Jason W. Moore. *Viewpoint Magazine*, September 28. Retrieved from https://viewpointmag.com/2015/09/28/capitalism-in-the-web-of-life-an-interview-with-jason-moore/

Shenk, T. (2015). Booked #3: What exactly is neoliberalism? Interview with Wendy Brown. *Dissent*, April 2. Retrieved from www.dissentmagazine.org/blog/booked-3-what-exactly-is-neoliberalism-wendy-brown-undoing-the-demos

Watkins, M. (1986). *Invisible guests: The development of imaginal dialogues*. Hillsdale, NJ: The Analytic Press.

Watkins, M., & Shulman, H. (2008). *Toward psychologies of liberation*. New York: Palgrave Macmillan.

1
TEACHING PSYCHOLOGY CRITICALLY

David Fryer and Rachael Fox

What would it be to teach psychology critically?

We have both spent many years employed in Institutions of Higher Education (HEIs) in Academic Organisational Units (AOUs) of Psychology, Counselling, Nursing and Midwifery and Education as lecturers, teachers, tutors and supervisors. In those settings (and outside them at conferences, as members of discussion lists, in the community), we have attempted to enable students, colleagues and members of the public to learn about ways to engage in critical thinking (and to enable them to unlearn ways of engaging in critically problematic thinking and practice) in relation to 'psy'.

We use the term 'psy' as shorthand for the psy-complex, but also to flag up the point that our will to critique goes further than a will to critique the psy-complex. We use 'psy-complex' here in the sense of Rose (1999, p. vii) – that is, "the heterogeneous knowledges, forms of authority and practical techniques that constitute psychological expertise" – and we use it to refer not only to the psy-knowledges and psy-practices implicit in the various forms of the academic discipline of psychology which are taught in HEIs, colleges and schools around the Anglophone world (and other parts of the world intellectually colonised by the United Kingdom/ United States), but also to those forms of the psy-complex inscribed in: community education; counselling; education; psychiatry; psychotherapy; public health; social work; popular media and – since intellectually colonising psy-expansionism has progressed so far and so deeply – those forms of the psy-complex inscribed in 'common sense'.

As one or other or both of us have attempted to teach psychology critically within many of these settings over a long period, it would appear straightforward to write a chapter about teaching psychology critically: simply write an account of what we have done; how we have done it; why we have done it that way; and what the outcomes were. However, it is not straightforward for us because we position the teaching of psychology as a critical contradiction in terms in many respects.

Is teaching psychology critically a contradiction in terms?

Freire (1970, p. 45) classically positioned the "fundamentally narrative character" of the 'teacher–student relationship' as the profoundly problematic dominant discourse in relation to pedagogy, in which teachers are positioned as 'fillers' of students with content and students are positioned as "receptacles to be filled by the teacher". Freire (1970, p. 46) refers to: "the 'banking' concept of education, in which the scope of action allowed to the students extends only as far as receiving, filing and storing the deposits" although students are also, of course, expected to be able to withdraw what has been deposited on demand for examination by the depositor or their agents. Within this frame of reference, Freire (1970, p. 45) continues, "the more meekly the receptacles permit themselves to be filled, the better students they are" positioned as being within the dominant pedagogic discourse. Equally then, the more effectively teachers fill the passive receptacles, the better teachers they are positioned as being within the dominant pedagogic discourse.

Teaching is positioned, in dominant modernist discursive frames of reference, as involving: the intentional agentic building of interpersonal congruent relationships between skilled, authoritative teachers and enthusiastic blank-slate pupils; the inspiring, stimulating, motivating, creative-mentoring, etc. of pupils by teachers disseminating seminal ideas; and so on and so forth. Such dominant frames of reference within which teaching is constituted and practised are critically problematic. As Henriques, Hollway, Urwin, Venn and Walkerdine (1998) pithily put it:

> Discourses rooted in the notion of a unitary, rational subject still predominate in the social sciences in spite of the critiques which have shown such a concept to be untenable. These critiques have been developed from three standpoints, namely, critical theory and post-structuralist interrogations of the foundations of the discourses of modernity, feminist challenges to the phallocentric and masculinist model of subjectivity privileged in Western theory, and the 'post-colonial' questioning of the affiliations of the logocentric notion of the subject with the ideologies of racism and imperialism.
>
> (Henriques et al., 1998, p. ix)

Foucault wrote that he would:

> propose, as a very first definition of critique, this general characterisation: the art of not being governed quite so much . . . how not to be governed like that, by that, in the name of those principles, with such an objective in mind and by means of such procedures, not like that, not for that, not by them.
>
> (Foucault, 1978/1997, p. 46)

To engage in critical teaching of students would, thus, involve bringing it about that the students resisted the critical teaching in which one was engaging, refusing to be governed by and through the teacher's practices. The criterion for teaching critically successfully would be student resistance to and rejection of that critical teaching.

Teaching is dominantly discursively positioned as involving teachers making it easier for students to understand, whereas within the critical frame of reference being deployed in relation to this chapter: "to practise criticism is to make harder those acts which are now too easy" (Foucault, 1981/2000, p. 456). Teaching critically involves doing the opposite of teaching as simplifying and explaining.

Teaching is discursively positioned, in mainstream discourses, as about changing what people think, what they know, what they believe, the skills they can deploy and – in sum – what they are. Within the critical frame of reference within which this chapter has been constructed, re-subjectification (the re-constitution of the subject) is positioned as a form of obliteration of the subject. To teach a student is, within an acritical frame of reference, to promote a process of change 'within the person', but within the critical frame of reference being deployed in relation to this chapter, the process involves change *of the person*. Since critique involves resistance to re-subjectification and teaching involves the re-constitution of the subject, teaching critically involves doing the opposite of teaching.

Teaching psychology critically is, then, in many respects a contradiction in terms.

What do 'critical teachers' of psychology teach?

So far we have written about critical contradictions at the core of the notion of 'teaching critically', but what about content issues?

Many discursively position 'critical psychology' as a sub-component or core domain of psychology. The psychological 'establishment' appears to concur with this. For example, in relation to accreditation of undergraduate psychology programmes, the British Psychological Society (BPS) positions understanding of

> Conceptual and Historical Issues in Psychology e.g. the study of psychology as a science; the social and cultural construction of psychology; conceptual and historical paradigms and models – *comparisons and critiques*; political and ethical issues in psychology; integration across multiple perspectives
> *(British Psychological Society, 2010, p. 15; our italics)*

as a "core domain" of "the curriculum" which "accredited undergraduate and conversion programmes must deliver" (British Psychological Society, 2010, p. 15).

Some may attempt to meet this requirement by substituting critical psychology content for acritical psychology content. For those who try to do that there is a choice of textbooks. *Critical Psychology: An Introduction* (Fox, Prilleltensky, & Austin, 2009) is described on its back cover as "an essential text for undergraduate and postgraduate students studying critical psychology, conceptual issues, theoretical psychology" and is described as "compulsory reading" by a reviewer. *An Introduction* to *Critical Social Psychology* (Hepburn, 2003) is described on its back cover as: "essential reading for those studying critical social psychology or critical psychology and should be recommended on more mainstream courses where knowledge of these perspectives is required". *Critical Community Psychology* (Kagan, Burton, Duckett, Lawthom, & Siddiquee, 2011) is described on its back cover as "attractive to undergraduate and postgraduate students", lists among the highlights of the book "clear learning objectives", "activity questions . . . to be used as . . . class exercises" and advertises "additional resources for instructors" available via the publisher's website. Within our frame of reference, it is critically problematic to 'teach' critical psychology like any other core domain of psychology with simply an alteration to the content.

Bringing about situations in which students learn and regurgitate critical psychological subject matter is not teaching critical psychology, no matter what content is learned and regurgitated. Moreover, 'critical issues' is only one of eight domains which "accredited undergraduate and conversion programmes must deliver" (British Psychological Society, 2010, p. 15) and the others – biological psychology; cognitive psychology; developmental psychology; social psychology; individual differences; research methods; and empirical project – are in most respects critically problematic. The UK's Quality Assurance Agency for Higher Education (2010) insists that any "honours degree programme in psychology . . . should . . . aim to produce a scientific understanding of the mind, brain, behaviour and experience, and of the complex interactions between these" and that in covering "core topics, students will be exposed to standard information, traditional methods of scientific enquiry and sophisticated statistical analyses". Critical theory is only mentioned as one of "a range of the new developments in the field" of which students also need to be aware (Quality Assurance Agency for Higher Education, 2010, pp. 1–3). There is a contradiction in both insisting that students of psychology must uncritically swallow the problematic discipline of psychology hook, line and sinker, and also insisting that they are taught the ways in which psychology is critically problematic, until it is realised that many in mainstream modernist psychology systematically mis-use 'critical' to mean 'uncritical'. Writing about 'critical thinking', Halpern and Butler (2011, p. 30) claim that "researchers generally agree that it involves an attempt to achieve a desired outcome by thinking rationally in a goal-oriented fashion and reasoning in an open-ended manner". Citing one of themselves, they write:

> Halpern (1998, 2003) defines critical thinking as: . . . the kind of thinking involved in solving problems, formulating inferences, calculating likelihoods, and making decisions, when the thinker is using skills that are thoughtful and effective for the particular context and type of thinking task (p 6).
> *(Halpern & Butler, 2011, p. 30)*

Elsewhere – stating the absolute opposite of what we believe to be the case – Halpern and Butler (2011, p. 30) refer to "critical thinking, or thinking like a psychological scientist". For us, "thinking like a psychological scientist" is exactly what is in urgent need of critique, resistance and rejection.

What we actually do in practice with others in teaching: David

I am committed to critique in relation to teaching psychology, but what does that mean? One way to explicate this is through a reflection upon Horkheimer's positioning of 'critical psychology' as concerned with liberation of "human beings from the circumstances that enslave them" (Horkheimer, 1982, p. 244). Below, I will use this positioning as a device to describe and critique some of my attempts to teach psychology critically. It is a useful device because as soon as teaching psychology critically is discursively positioned as teaching to liberate from enslavement, there is an obligation to consider the questions of: how both 'enslavement' and 'liberation' should be understood; how each is constituted, re-constituted and is to be resisted; and the implications of all this for teaching in practice. It is also a useful device because it requires acknowledgement that the ways these questions have been answered, by me at least, have changed over time and those changes have been accompanied by changing implications for action. Finally, it is a useful device because, although there are similarities – in some respects – in the approaches to teaching psychology critically of Rachael and myself, there are also differences in other respects; this device allows us to make these clearer and, in turn, provides opportunities to consider what underpins differences and similarities.

In a commonly deployed frame of reference – for example, one dominant in community psychology – students are widely positioned as enslaved when their capacity for agentic self-determination as individual social and moral persons-in-context is restricted and disabled by powerful social forces, such as those operating through institutionalised psychology education.

I attempted to teach psychology critically within this frame of reference in the Psychology Department of a UK university where I set up a 12-week module in community psychology, which I coordinated, administered and in which I tried to facilitate critical thinking and practice. I also taught final-year electives on critical psychology and critical methodology (critically theorised research methods), supervised community-based undergraduate and postgraduate research, and taught community activists inside and outside the university. The context of my teaching at this time is important to indicate. I had the opportunity to write, teach and administer a completely new module (with no pre-existing organisational expectations of its content). I had almost complete autonomy, at first, with a supportive Head of Department and I was flying under the departmental radar as a new low-status staff member.

In this phase of my attempts to teach psychology critically, I attempted to promote critical reflection and participation by students in a new undergraduate community psychology module in relation to expertise. Through conventional teaching methods I would acquaint the students with the work of Cowen (1982) claiming that hairdressers used ways similar to mental health professionals to help people with moderate to serious personal problems; the meta-review by Durlak (1979) claiming that para-professionals were as clinically effective as professional therapists in helping people deal with such problems, and so on and so forth. In parallel, I would provide lecture platforms in the classes for survivors of mental health services who claimed that their 'lived experience' of psychological and psychiatric treatments was an oppressive part of the problem rather than a supportive part of the solution. I also provided this platform to a community activist who claimed that: architecture 'experts' who designed houses built in her community which were predictably destined to be damp; health 'experts' who blamed tenants' lifestyles for subsequent damp-related illnesses; and medical 'experts' who diagnosed depression and prescribed anti-depressants for people living in morbidly damp housing, were all part of the problem, combatants in the 'war without bullets' being waged against the poor.

I simultaneously adopted a conscious strategy of featuring as teachers both 'guest experts' who were highly credentialled (such as eminent professors George Albee, Donata Francescato, Jim Kelly, Jim Orford and Julian Rappaport, who kindly agreed to teach the class when visiting me) and 'guest experts' who were non-credentialled (speakers from People First, an organisation run by and for people with learning difficulties; representatives of tenants' groups, domestic violence projects, disabled activists, survivors of psychiatry, and so on) and to make no distinctions of expert status between them.

To support students doing the module, I employed undergraduates who had done the same module the year before as 'peer educators' to facilitate learning in student groups by blurring the 'disempowering' gap, as I then conceived it, in perceived expertise between students and academic staff. I also attempted to disrupt what I understood as the students' assumption that they themselves lacked sufficient expertise to critically evaluate the work of academic 'experts'. To do this, I negotiated a very short deadline (3 weeks into the term) for an assignment in which each student in the class was required individually to critically review the unit textbook. After marking each book review and giving feedback to individual student authors (as the exercise was also an assessment exercise), I produced a single 'merged' collective book review based on an analysis of all the reviews by class members, not a minor task as there were many scores of class members. With the class members' permission, I submitted the collective review for publication in a journal, with all class members listed as co-authors. At first, students expressed doubts about their capacity to evaluate the work of 'experts', but eventually they stood back, took up positions in relation to the whole textbook and made judgements as to how well the textbook achieved its objectives from the perspective of a student textbook user and – unusual for undergraduates in their penultimate year of study – they finished the community psychology module with a publication for their CV. Several collective student reviews of community psychology textbooks were published over a number of years.

As a second example, I co-facilitated, with 'artivists', members of a mutual aid group of survivors of psychiatry, who used arts as a form of anti-psychiatric activism, a module on 'critical psychology' for which the students received credit for a final-year module. Half of the meetings took place in the university (with the artivists visiting the Psychology Department to participate), and half the meetings took place in the artivists' community-based studio (with the students visiting the community to participate). Half of the sessions were led by students, who were tasked with explaining what they understood of critical psychology to the artivist survivors of psychiatry. Half of the sessions were led by artivist survivors of psychiatry who were tasked with explaining what they understood of surviving psychiatry to the students. Assessment was innovative and consisted of students writing a conventional essay in relation to a critical psychology issue, and also engaging collaboratively one to one with survivors of psychiatry in an artivist project. Both students and artivists were invited to write the essays to receive feedback from me upon them. The artivist projects were assessed collectively by the artivists themselves, who rank ordered the students' art work. After the module, an exhibition of the art work was mounted in the university library foyer, and students and artivists engaged passers-by, stopping to view the exhibits, in discussion about survival of psychiatry.

Within the critical frame of reference in which I currently work, this teaching was itself critically problematic. It reinscribed the modernist notion of a unitary, rational subject (and associated practices – support, respect, inclusion) which have been terminally critiqued by Henriques et al. (1998); it reinscribed power as something possessed by individuals and capable of being given away (whereas I was no more able to give away academic privilege than I was to give away white or male privilege); it positioned 'lived experience' as 'authentic' (rather than as just another manifestation of re-constituted subjectivity); it fostered new forms of compliance rather than resistance (with a different imposed assessment regime); it masqueraded as innovative, radical and locally relevant (but actually reinscribed a form of universalised conservative community psychology dominated by United States-ian [and secondarily European] intellectual colonialism); it was blind to community psychology being the new form of psy-complex ideal for neoliberalism (technology of the self/self as a project, etc.). Nevertheless, although much of the detail of these attempts at critical teaching was below the departmental radar, there were repeated attempts to close the module down and I spent a great deal of time and energy – and enlisted the help of external supporters – resisting these attempts, before having to accept the inevitable.

In another common frame of reference for critical teaching, students are positioned as enslaved by capitalism – or, in current parlance, neoliberalism. Some critical teachers teaching within that frame of reference draw upon historical materialism or Marxism for the means of liberation. Referring to the work of "the Frankfurt School of Marxist intellectuals concerned with questions of culture and its relation with society (e.g. Adorno, Horkheimer, Marcuse, Fromm, Habermas)", Kagan et al. (2011) write in their textbook (*Critical Community Psychology*):

> here what is meant by the term 'critical' is an approach that tried to understand a social reality through introduction of another, more penetrating

frame of reference, one that has to do with a general theory of human society (or at least late capitalist society) understood in terms of contradictions between different social interests and economic processes of exploitation, capital accumulation, and so on.

(Kagan et al. 2011, p. 12)

In the second phase of my attempts to teach psychology critically, I maintained attempts to teach critically in process, but focused more on content chosen to facilitate students' critical reflection upon the interrelations between psychology and the neoliberal forms which capitalism was then taking. At a time when clinical psychology was overwhelmingly focusing on individual intra-psychic interventions to change dysfunctional individual cognitions and behaviours, individualistically emphasising the aetiological role of personality and biography in 'well-being', I emphasised 'social causation' of 'psychological problems' through destructive labour market experience (unemployment, insecure employment, strain-inducing employment, etc.). This emphasis gradually extended to cover the relationship between psychological states and poverty, social class, and then societal inequality in addition to adverse labour market experience, and soon all were presented as consequences of manifestations of neoliberal austerity policies. The shrinking of the State and the erosion of social services were also consistent with the inclusion of emphasis on the social model of disability and its implications for effective intervention, the roots of domestic violence in patriarchy and male privilege, and of racism in white privilege. This focused upon what I then thought of as the psychological consequences of the policies of the neoliberal Right and was naively intended to be conscientising.

Within this critical frame of reference, psychology was positioned as myopic and individualising, but psychological research and other knowledge work were positioned as basically sound. In teaching about the statistically sophisticated longitudinal research using standardised reliable and valid measures following people in and out of employment, and persuading students that this demonstrated that unemployment caused mental health problems rather than the reverse, or in explaining the epidemiological work of Wilkinson and Pickett (2009) demonstrating that less equal societies were less healthy than more equal societies, I assumed it was possible to mount a persuasive evidence-based case that the social and economic policies of the Right led to mentally and physically unhealthy communities, and the social and economic policies of the Left led to mentally and physically healthy communities.

During this phase, the concern with process evident in Phase 1 continued, with, for example, workshops for students run by women in the community who had established themselves as a domestic violence intervention project. They used drama to communicate with the (largely female) students not only about how the project challenged domestic violence and supported women who had been assaulted by partners, but also, in line with the Duluth model and power wheel (DAIP, n.d.), how to recognise the controlling behaviours and other manifestations of male privilege which, in their experience, had so often been the early unheeded warning signs of the driving in of the thin edge of the intimate partner assault wedge.

On another occasion, a film fresh from triumph at the Edinburgh Film Festival[1] was screened which drew graphic but insightful parallels between the social and economic apartheid being waged in South Africa and that being waged in the West of Scotland as part of the 'war without bullets' against the poor and marginal. The witness to both, Scottish community activist Cathy McCormack, attended the screening, took questions and facilitated critical debate. As another example, apart from teaching about the social model of disability and emancipatory disability research, disabled activists addressed the students directly.

Separately, as part of her PhD research, Adele Laing set up a module, of which I was officially the coordinator as only a staff member could serve in that role, in which students from several Scottish universities were able to enrol and receive credit. The teaching in this module was designed to facilitate students in coming to understand the, then current, Disability Discrimination Act (DDA), the social model of disability, emancipatory disability research and how to evaluate a university's compliance or otherwise with the DDA. The module members' assignments reported those evaluations (Laing, 2008) and were potentially deployable as political intervention.

Within the critical frame of reference in which I now work this teaching was critically problematic too. It embraced a Marxist notion of power and Marxist notions of false consciousness which I now reject in favour of a Foucauldian approach to power and governmentality; it took seriously psychological states like 'depression'; it took seriously modernist science and particularly the notion of 'cause' and 'effect', which I now reject in relation to subjectivity and social power; it accepted uncritically the new Left acritical orthodoxy relating to inequality and neoliberalism; it positioned critical teaching as being about endorsing the 'good' and denouncing the 'bad' rather than as underlining the contingency of what 'is the case' and the possibility of otherness.

In the third phase of my attempts to teach psychology critically, my focus is increasingly upon facilitating resistance, especially in relation to governmentality; that is, to promote "the art of not being governed quite so much" (Foucault, 1978/1997, p. 46).

The context for this attempt at critical teaching is private sector Higher Education Institutions (HEIs), where HEIs are first and foremost run as profit-making companies compliant with 'industry standards' under the surveillance and control of management acting as proxies for external accreditation bodies and shareholders, and students are positioned as customers/consumers who expect to receive services (teaching) and products (credentials) in return for payment. In line with scientific management principles, teaching material is mostly written, marking criteria established, etc. by a small cohort of relatively secure 'faculty', but taught and marked by a quite separate cohort of precarious academic teachers employed on insecure short-term part-time contracts (whether or not they are in agreement with content or criteria). Much of the teaching is delivered online with all class-space content under surveillance, and any perceived questioning of teaching material, pedagogic practices or organisational policies is likely to be positioned as 'anti-government activity' and result in non-renewal of contract. The neoliberalisation of Higher Education is most fully advanced and thoroughly achieved in such private sector HEIs, but public sector HEIs are being subjected to the same processes and academics' experiences in both sectors are converging (Lorenz, 2012). The challenges involved in trying to teach psy critically in such a context where the learning objectives, the assessment criteria, the mode of delivery of teaching material and the content of teaching material are all determined by others and policed by management are many and profound.

I try to set up conditions within which students are better able to resist governmentality, in the sense of Foucault: "the techniques and procedures which are designed to govern the conduct of both individuals and populations at every level not just the administrative or political level" (www.michel-foucault.com/concepts/index.html). Teaching critically within this frame of reference is to facilitate the acquisition and deployment of "the art of not being governed quite so much".

The facilitation of critical pedagogic process, as illustrated by earlier phases above, is effectively impossible in the brave new neoliberal world of 'Higher Education'. Within the frame of reference in which I attempt to teach critically in this third phase, critique involves "showing that things are not as obvious as people believe, making it so that what is taken for granted is no longer taken for granted. To do criticism is to make harder those acts which are now too easy" (Foucault, 1981/2000, pp. 456–457).

I thus try to make understanding things harder rather than easier. This involves giving large amounts of exacting critical feedback upon what students write, say and do. As this is often experienced by students as anything but supportive, but rather as hostile criticism of the author, it is necessary to try to pre-empt this by clarification that critique eschews individualism and that its intention is the facilitation of critical reflection in relation to systems of ideas and practices rather than in relation to the individuals who inscribe them in particular cases.

It is essential within my critical frame of reference not to endorse any particular epistemological frame of reference, not because none is less problematic than others, but because it is critically important that the focus of teaching is on processes of warranting and on resistance to processes of warranting, rather than on what is warranted (or not).

More generally, teaching critically from my perspective involves always focusing on process rather than content. My aim is that my students will leave my courses knowing less about 'what' than when they started, and knowing more about 'how not to' and 'why not to do so'.

More broadly, I intend as a critical teacher to: prevent foreclosure on key issues; shield the student as far as possible from surveillance and control; resist neoliberal agendas in relation to the student; shield the student from forces working to dumb down teaching; promote (or try to) increasingly radical critique; and set in train never-ending iterations of critique of the results of critique which are sustained long after the teaching finishes.

Within this frame of reference, students are positioned as enslaved by being rendered compliant through the broader project of governmentality. As Foucault (1978/1997) put it:

> to not want to be governed is of course not accepting as true . . . what an authority tells you is true, or at least not accepting it because an authority tells you that it is true . . . critique finds its anchoring point in the problem of certainty in its confrontation with authority.
>
> *(Foucault, 1978/1997, p. 44)*

I aspire, as a critical teacher, to my students refusing to be "governed like that, by that, in the name of those principles, with such an objective in mind and by means of such procedures, not like that, not for that, not by them" (Foucault, 1978/1997, p. 46) generally; but specifically, I aspire, as a critical teacher, to my students refusing to be governed like me, by me, in the name of my principles, with my objectives in mind and by means of procedures set up and policed by me. Accordingly, I do not want my students to accept that what I say is true, to accept my 'truthing' practices, to position me as an authority, to accept what I say because I say it.

My approach is then increasingly to try to resist, sabotage, unsettle, destabilise, undermine, deconstruct and destroy mainstream psy and its associated claims, methods and assumptions without instructing others what to think, do or be instead, to demolish the old to create a space for different ways of thinking, doing and being, but not to endorse any specific new way of thinking, doing or being in a similar way as an atheist might aspire to undermine the credibility of a religion without trying to substitute a different one. My approach is to then subject any new ways of thinking, doing and being to critique. Critique is never completed.

What we actually do in practice with others in teaching: Rachael

I am committed to critique in relation to teaching psychology, but what does that mean?

Deconstruction

Deconstruction is one of the principle challenges I take to be vital for teaching critical psychology. The extent to which dominant knowledge can be deconstructed, reconstructed or transformed is a moot point, but my aim in any event is to disrupt and challenge, in a directed fashion. That direction involves attempts at problem-posing and challenging taken-for-granted, dominant knowledges which otherwise go unchallenged. Additionally the aim is to make more complex that which is usually reductive, to question the overly simplistic 'truthing', in both psychology and the teaching of psychology.

In a compulsory third-year unit in which I engage psychology undergraduate students, one of the ways I attempt to disrupt this indoctrination is to problematize positivism as an epistemology and to reveal the consequences it has on research and knowledge production. To even present positivism as a theory is something which students find novel – in their third year, undergraduates often appear to be hearing of it for the first time and seem unaware of its dominance. In the unit, titled 'Qualitative Research Methods', positivism is contrasted with social constructionism over several weeks at the start of the semester, for the types of knowledge they produce and their consequences for theory and practice. Presenting, for example, the generalisability of positivism against the specificity of social constructionism is acritical in that it is polarising and essentialising in similar ways to mainstream teaching, but this does position positivism as a visible theory rather than an invisible innate constant.

The second way in which I attempt to disrupt is to engage with students in thinking about the 'self' as a psy-construct which has problematic consequences for knowledge production, particularly in research. In the Qualitative Research Methods unit, one of the key topics is subjectivity. Against dominant assumptions in positivism which pose objectivity as both possible and desirable, subjectivity, positioned as an opposite, is framed as a personal bias which limits the fidelity of the research. Parker (1994) further adds a useful note:

> Objectivity and subjectivity are always defined in relation to one another, and the mistake that positivists make is to assume that the relationship is like a conceptual zero-sum game in which a diminution of one, the erasure of subjectivity, will lead to an increase in the other, the production of a fully objective account.
>
> *(Parker, 1994, p. 13)*

While positivism positions subjectivity as bias, phenomenology, hermeneutics, even to an extent social constructionism and social psychological forms of discursive research, also position subjectivity in problematic ways which have consequences for knowledge produced. The discursive and pervasive nature of the 'self' as psy-construct, which assumes an individualising, discrete, autonomous construct, goes unquestioned and mediates these understandings of subjectivity (Henriques et al., 1998; Rose, 1996; Stainton-Rogers, 2003). This creates problems for engaging critically with students in relation to subjectivity. The topic therefore requires an extended engaging with the concept of the self as theorised most predominantly by Rose (1996; 1999). Introductory material from the subjectivity topic of the unit argues that:

> Psychology contributes to our understandings of 'self' as discrete, uniform individuals – this is what Henriques, Hollway, Urwin, Venn, and Walkerdine (1998), mean when they say psychology has helped constitute our modern

individuality. Psychology is not the only thing that has played a part but it is one field which has: this idea means that rather than just recording and describing what individuals are (involves realist, positivist assumptions), psychology has helped shape what they are; it has been productive in the process.

(Materials from the subjectivity topic of the unit)

The topic deals with dominant assumptions of self, before moving on to theories on poststructural positioning and intersubjectivities. These are considered for their consequences in research and knowledge production, and are engaged with directly when students collaborate on a research project. In the research project, they participate simultaneously as both researchers and participants, on research into their own subjective experiences in Higher Education and psychology, which creates a space for more complex reflection around subjective intersections.

These attempts at disrupting regimes of truth and practice in relation to 'self' and subjectivity are perhaps the most difficult and least achieved. The powerful discourse of 'self' as a unitary, rational, autonomous, discrete subject is pervasive at every level of our lives. I spend much of my academic life reflecting upon it and continue to alter my position, so unsurprisingly, it is very difficult for students to reflect on and engage with it. Lack of reflection in the academic community compounds this: good theoretical writing is sparse, and in published research, deeper understandings of subjectivity go unreflected on, and dominant discourses of 'self' go unchecked.

Making things uncomfortable

"To practise criticism is to make harder those acts which are now too easy" (Foucault, 1981/2000, p. 456). To make more difficult, to complicate, is suggestive of creating space to critique in a way that should be necessarily uncomfortable. In teaching critical psychology, the experience is not just uncomfortable for students, it is uncomfortable for the teacher. Not just because the aim is to discomfort, and that aim is intended to be all encompassing, but also because the Higher Education space in which teaching critical psychology is being attempted makes the act *more* uncomfortable. In a space which is increasingly neoliberal, regimes of practice in relation to 'learning' are increasingly intended to be easy and comfortable for students. The underlying aim is often to produce a positive experience for students, which translates into a positive evaluation in evaluation surveys, which is ultimately of economic benefit to the HEI.

In the teaching of the third-year Qualitative Research Methods unit, I aim to make space for an uncomfortable process where possible. What is achieved is very minimal – explanations of phenomena are not straightforward, students are engaged with in complex ways when they ask a question (a straightforward answer is not given), and the contradictions and hypocrisies of academic research are examined and problematized rather than being ironed over. This process of making things uncomfortable is conducted with a simultaneous attempt at some sort of 'safe space'. While this is difficult critically, it involves the understanding that students are positioned in a very tenuous place, with a lot to lose, and understandably find discomfort very challenging. Developed ideas of social justice, disability and marginalisation inform an approach which attempts to be strong on challenging ideas and strong on social support.

While the windows of opportunity to make things uncomfortable are small, feedback from students suggests that they find the approach very uncomfortable and unsettling. The strength of the reaction suggests that they do not experience this approach elsewhere. From a student subject position, the minimal level of discomfort argued here is, at times, argued to be quite the opposite: "The extreme (often ignorant, and sometimes dangerous) views posted by the subject coordinator encouraged me to be more communicative. This unit should not be compulsory. The extreme views of the main lecturer are of great concern" (Student Evaluation Survey, 2012). While a comment like this feels like a proud achievement for a critical psychologist, it requires consideration of the assumptions and positions it reinscribes. It would be problematic to simply argue that my views are extreme, although they could be said to be so in some frames of reference, but the important implication is that they are experienced as extreme in comparison to other teaching practices in psychology education. The level at which a pretty minimally challenging unit can be positioned as 'dangerous' is interesting and concerning. It is also valuable to reflect on the way that this comes not directly from Higher Education, but from a student. Resistance to my (usually flawed and contradictory) teaching from students would be most welcome. In fact, I almost never get this sort of challenge to my face. Rather than a dialogue between a student and myself, this resistance can be argued not to arrive unfettered from the student. The evaluation survey is a very small window of opportunity that Higher Education has opened up to position students to speak in very limited ways, which serve the HEIs' interests. Furthermore, in this very limited space, dialogue is not possible, but what is possible are negative consequences for teachers who are increasingly put under surveillance and disciplined using these surveys. In this way, students become the surveillers, the discipliners. To make teaching critical psychology uncomfortable therefore has increasingly negative consequences for teachers, as students are brought into the regime of discipline. In fact, each year the unit tends to receive very positive survey feedback and scores from students – numerical scores are consistently above the department average. This is not to suggest that the unit is 'good'. Rather, the positive scores may provide some sort of 'buffer' to being prevented from teaching this way. This creates a difficult juxtaposition whereby really great critical teaching could be scored very poorly and prevented, and the system keeps in place only very weak, minimal critical teaching. On the other hand, it does potentially suggest, in spite of the anxiety of a neoliberal system aiming for a 'nice' comfortable experience, that the uncomfortable, unsettling experience is often positioned positively by some students as something they enjoy and benefit from.

Different relationships

Teaching critical content while performing critical practice is still diminished if deeper ways of being, assumed to be fundamental to 'teaching', are not critiqued. The assumption that the expert teacher should be in control and should transfer knowledge in one direction to the grateful, passive students, incorporates the psy-complex assumption of 'expert' and the power imbalance inherent in teacher–student relationships. Authoritatively telling students to think critically is not consistent with critical praxis. Thus, in engaging students in teaching critical psychology, an attempt is made to disrupt this traditionally assumed power imbalance. In theory, this should involve disrupting the traditional relationship, and simultaneously reflecting overtly with students on the attempts at disruption as a more critical form of learning. This should involve using dialogical, problem-posing, connected experiences where deconstruction of assumptions and resistances to authority *move in more than one direction*.

In teaching with third-year psychology students, this has included collaborating on research which investigates the students' own positions and experiences in Higher Education and psychology. The students do all the fieldwork, interviewing each other, which moves my position as teacher or chief investigator further away from the interview conversation. This process invites students to think beyond the teacher–student relationship, to the institutional, cultural, political contexts which *produce* the teacher–student relationship. The following are insights from students about their positions in Higher Education and the institutional context for their experiences:

> I sort of see participation as a joint, um, commitment between students and the university. I think that, definitely the onus is on the student to engage fully or as fully as they can. But I think it's mediated by the university systems and there are facilitatory systems as well as systems that obstruct.
> *(Viv, third-year student, 2012)*

> I think the current grading system is – they talk about wanting people to participate but they don't actually facilitate that participation as well as they could, and I think even with the grading system that we have at the moment, everybody is graded on a bell curve. So basically what that means is that the emphasis is on not on knowing the subject [unit], the emphasis is actually on knowing the subject [unit] better than the person next to you because you're in direct competition with them all the time.
> *(Dawn, third-year student, 2012)*

(Dawn and Viv are pseudonyms chosen by the students, who gave permission for dissemination of the research and for their interviews to be quoted).

This research collaboration goes some way, in addition, to making knowledge production and our interrelationships more dialogical as I learn (a version of) what Higher Education looks like today from the students' standpoints.

Opportunities to disrupt power imbalance are very limited. When I did my undergraduate degree, I took part in a unit (coordinated by David) where the assessment deadlines were voted on by students. Today, before I meet a class of students, I have to produce a legalistic document which sets out in minute detail the deadlines, readings and activities, and in even more minute detail, the exact things which will and will not get students marks in assessments. A colleague teaching English who was trying to insert ambiguity into his marking rubrics for a Creative Writing course, was prevented from inserting the following:

> Note: These are not here to undermine your creativity but to give you some indication of the kinds of things that markers may generally look for in your work. The uni makes us write these. They aren't necessary for a good grade (for example you can submit amazing HD [first class] pieces of writing without them). Nor are they sufficient for a good grade (for example, you can have all these things and still have a piece of writing that isn't great).

Higher Education positions the lecturer firmly in control, although control, of course, is an illusion – an 'in control' lecturer cannot today decide to alter what went into the unit outline, or to award the same marks to all their students. The student is again positioned as discipliner and is invited to police this relationship. There have been times when my attempts at collaborative relating, rather than an authoritarian approach, have been positioned by students as 'weak', or positioned me as a bad teacher, disorganised or lacking in knowledge. This positioning of my practice may well intersect with my female gender. It is also interesting to note that as I have spent more time engaged in lecturing, I have received this sort of repositioning less – potentially as I age, I am more naturally seen as an 'expert' no matter what I do. I also question the extent to which my voice and performance have changed to a more authoritarian approach the longer I have been embedded in the system, and potentially the extent to which the last 5 years have seen an increase in systemic control and surveillance which makes it more difficult for me to disrupt power relations.

Conclusion

While spending our academic careers engaging with critical ideas as scholars and researchers, we have found ourselves to be afforded opportunities, and, indeed, have been required, to engage as teachers with others; students, colleagues and community members. However, we have increasingly found that teaching critically inside neoliberalised HEIs, saturated by dominant discourses from enforced problematic subject positions, could never be satisfactorily realised. We have concluded that 'teaching psychology critically' in Higher Education in contemporary neoliberalised academia in the metropole as opposed to the periphery, a useful binary distinction made by Connell (2007, p. 212) to call up "the long-lasting pattern of inequality in power, wealth and cultural influence that grew historically out of European and

North American imperialism", is not only in many respects a contradiction in terms in theory, but an impossibility in practice. 'Higher Education', during the time we have been teaching in it, has become increasingly preoccupied with engineering passive compliance of students and academic staff with the 'real world', that is, the world as it is constituted to be (but could be other), which serves the interests of those benefiting from the oppressive status quo and is decreasingly tolerant of teaching which challenges the status quo inside education or outside it. Freire (1970, p. 47) foresaw this four decades ago, writing: "The oppressors use their 'humanitarianism' to preserve a profitable situation. Thus they react almost instinctively against any experiment in education which stimulates the critical faculties".

Note

1   *At the sharp end of the knife*, documentary, BBC World, RUV Netherlands, http://truetvandfilm.co.uk/product/at-the-sharp-end-of-the-knife/

References

British Psychological Society. (2010). *Accreditation through partnership handbook: Guidance for undergraduate and conversion psychology programmes.* Leicester: British Psychological Society. Retrieved from www.bps.org.uk/sites/default/files/documents/undergraduate_accred 2010_web.pdf

Connell, R. (2007). *Southern theory.* Crows Nest, NSW: Allen and Unwin.

Cowen, E. (1982). Help is where you find it: Four informal helping groups. *American Psychologist, 37,* 385–395.

DAIP (Domestic Abuse Intervention Programs). (n.d.). Wheels. Retrieved from www.theduluthmodel.org/wheels/

Durlak, J. (1979). Comparative effectiveness of para-professional and professional helpers. *Psychological Bulletin, 89,* 566–569.

Foucault, M. (1978/1997). What is critique? In S. Lotringer (Ed.), *The politics of truth* (pp. 41–81). Los Angeles: Semiotext(e).

Foucault, M. (1981/2000). So is it important to think? In J. D. Faubion (Ed.), *Power: The essential works of Foucault 1954–1984. Volume 3* (pp. 454–458). New York: New Press.

Fox, D., Prilleltensky, I., & Austin, S. (2009). *Critical psychology: An introduction* (2nd ed.). London: Sage.

Freire, P. (1970). *Pedagogy of the oppressed.* London: Penguin Books Ltd.

Halpern, D., & Butler, H. (2011). Critical thinking and the education of psychologically literate citizens. In J. Cranney & D. Dunn (Eds.), *The psychologically literate citizen: Foundations and global perspectives* (pp. 27–40). Oxford: Oxford University Press.

Henriques, J., Hollway, W., Urwin, C., Venn, C., & Walkerdine, V. (1998). *Changing the subject: Psychology, social regulation and subjectivity.* London: Methuen.

Hepburn, A. (2003). *An introduction to critical social psychology.* London: Sage.

Horkheimer, M. (1982). *Critical theory.* New York: Seabury Press.

Kagan, C., Burton, M., Duckett, P., Lawthom, R., & Siddiquee, A. (2011). *Critical community psychology.* London: Wiley.

Laing, A. (2008). *Changing disabling places* (Thesis submitted in partial fulfilment of the degree of Doctor of Philosophy). University of Stirling, Stirling, UK. Retrieved from http://hdl.handle.net/1893/7148

Lorenz, C. (2012). If you're so smart, why are you under surveillance? Universities, neoliberalism, and new public management. *Critical Inquiry, 38*(3), 599–629.

Parker, I. (1994). Qualitative research. In P. Banister, E. Burman, I. Parker, M. Taylor, & C. Tindall (Eds.), *Qualitative methods in psychology: A research guide* (pp. 1–16). Buckingham, UK: Open University Press.

Quality Assurance Agency for Higher Education. (2010). *Subject benchmark statement: Psychology 2007* (3rd ed.). Retrieved from www.qaa.ac.uk/en/Publications/Documents/Subject-benchmark-statement-Psychology.pdf

Rose, N. (1996). *Inventing ourselves: Psychology, power and personhood.* Cambridge: Cambridge University Press.

Rose, N. (1999). *Governing the soul: The shaping of the private self* (2nd ed.). London: Free Association Books.

Stainton-Rogers, W. (2003). *Social psychology: Experimental and critical approaches.* London: Open University Press.

Student Evaluation Survey (2012). *Student Evaluation Survey from subject titled Qualitative Research Methods.* Wagga Wagga, NSW: Charles Sturt University.

Wilkinson, R., & Pickett, K. (2009). *The spirit level: Why more equal societies almost always do better.* Bury St. Edmunds, UK: Allen Lane.

2
TEN SUGGESTIONS FOR CRITICAL TEACHING IN PSYCHOLOGY

John Cromby

There have recently been two major international publications in critical psychology: the encyclopaedia edited by Teo (2014) and the handbook edited by Parker (2015). In this context, it may seem odd to ask whether there is still a living critical psychology in the UK. But it is many years now since the last national or international conference on critical psychology was held here; the *International Journal of Critical Psychology* has mutated into the social science journal *Subjectivity* – a fine publication, but nevertheless one with a distinctly different focus from its predecessor; and the notable institutional concentrations of critical psychologists that were visible at UK universities in the early 2000s have mostly either dispersed (or been dispersed), have re-badged themselves – for example, as psychosocial studies – or have migrated into other disciplines.

To be sure, there are still many critical voices in UK psychology, there are still many psychologists who are critical of mainstream conceptual and methodological presumptions, and there are still many who reject the naïve notion that – because psychology presents itself as objective science – its findings must somehow be objective. But this is not the same thing as claiming that, in the UK, there is still something called critical psychology that exists as a coherent alternative or sub-discipline.

This change has not occurred in a vacuum, nor of its own accord. Recent years have seen profound changes to the organisation and funding of the UK universities where psychology is taught. These changes have included increased pressures upon staff to publish in mainstream 'high impact' journals that debar the critical perspectives which they recognise, quite accurately, as challenging their core precepts. Partly as a result of these pressures, anxious reactions from within psychology to the rise of alternatives to the quantitative individualistic orthodoxy have gained traction. The combined effects of these and other pressures have been experienced by many critically oriented scholars as a mixture of flavourless carrots and managerial bludgeons. Some have responded to these incentives and penalties pre-emptively, and perfectly understandably, in order to safeguard their careers, wellbeing and livelihoods, by shifting either their institutional location, research strategy or publishing focus, and in the process, frequently discarding any overt allegiance to critical psychology.

This chapter is responsive to this context in two ways. First, its primary emphasis is upon teaching psychology critically rather than upon teaching critical psychology. While the suggestions presented owe much to insights and evidence garnered within the ambit of critical psychology, they are in many ways applicable to the teaching of mainstream perspectives as critical ones. And second, these suggestions are themselves contextualised with respect to critical debate and relevant evidence concerning wider social and material conditions, the character of contemporary mainstream psychology, the political economy of the UK university, and the needs and desires of psychology students who – as predominantly young people – are consistently amongst the biggest actual and potential losers from the neoliberal policies currently being implemented.

Economic, social and material circumstances

In his book *Capitalist Realism*, Mark Fisher characterised many of his students as being prey to what he called "depressive hedonia", a state "constituted not by an inability to get pleasure so much as by an inability to do anything else *except* pursue pleasure" (Fisher, 2009, p. 22). In the social relations of contemporary late capitalism – the world of 'there is no alternative' and 'we're all in this together', of privatisation, modernisation, efficiency, surveillance and precarity, of EU-sponsored coups of its own member-states, and of the deep penetration of business 'logic' into quite literally every sphere of everyday life – in this peculiar world, we often have a sense that 'something is missing', yet cannot quite articulate what that something might be. In these conditions, it makes considerable sense to seek indulgent comfort from the ubiquitous meaninglessness of exploitation by immersing oneself in meaningless entertainment, by trying to constantly anaesthetise, divert and moderate the senses, or – as the band Pulp (Banks et al., 1995) once so eloquently put it – to "dance, and sing, and screw, because there's nothing else to do".

Fisher argues that students' structural position within these social relations leaves them stranded between the disciplinary regimes Foucault identified and the subsequent societies of internalised and diffused control that Deleuze posited. In more immediate educational contexts, the contradiction between these imperatives gets played out within economic conditions where to fail a student contravenes the business logic that now regulates the institution, and where there is considerable ambiguity as to whether the 'product' of this business is the student per se, the educational process to which they are subject, or the educational qualification they (conditionally) purchase. Further, these multiple ambiguities arise in contexts where staff are over-regulated and subject to continuous surveillance within what Fisher characterised as a form of 'market Stalinism'. Here, the *appearance* of educational competence and success – an appearance generated by National Student Survey (NSS) ratings, standardised learning objectives, module feedback, module review, programme review, and soon the promised 'Teaching Excellence Framework' – sometimes comes to matter more than the actual task of producing students who are genuinely capable of independently thinking, evaluating, researching, synthesising, questioning and writing: students, in short, who are capable of being critical. I was once firmly admonished by a senior colleague that my job as a psychology lecturer was absolutely not to encourage students to ask 'difficult' questions: instead, I should simply provide them with a technical training in psychological methods, and familiarise them with the 'canon' of established psychological knowledge.

Under such social and material conditions, both staff and students are prone to what Fisher (2009) called *reflexive impotence*. Since in absolute terms they are relatively powerless, in the proximal sphere of immediate social relations – where they can exert some slight influence – they frequently strive to assert what little power remains to them. Some staff assuage their alienation and disempowerment in small acts of resistance, rebellion and minor bureaucratic sabotage; others attempt to recoup some power by aligning themselves ever more precisely with bureaucratic imperatives, in the process becoming enthusiastic promoters – or, indeed, enforcers – of the spectacular regimes they constitute. 'Spectacular' is meant here in the quite specific sense that these regimes instantiate social relations that prioritise the mere appearance of coaching in intellectual inquiry, but these relations tend to supplant and obscure those where genuine learning is the goal – c.f. Debord (1967/1987). Meanwhile, students under these social and material conditions tend to quickly realise that minimal attendance and mere lip service to regulations and assessment is usually enough to get by. Many respond to this freedom "not by pursuing projects but by falling into hedonic (or anhedonic) lassitude: the soft narcosis, the comfort food oblivion of Playstation, all-night TV and marijuana" (Fisher, 2009, p. 23).

In characterising staff and students in these ways, Fisher is not describing anything so rigid, static, (supposedly) determinate and therefore unhelpful as personality types. Rather, they are more akin to what I (Cromby, 2015) have elsewhere called *sensibilities*: socialised and enculturated organisations of felt, embodied, unfinished potentials, built up through experience, and primed to be called out and enacted in relevant circumstances. With this in mind, Fisher's insightful analysis can usefully be further nuanced to reflect prevalent differences in social class (Charlesworth, 1999; McKenzie, 2015), the markedly and increasingly unequal concentrations of financial, social, cultural and material capital. In critical psychological terms, differences in social class may also be associated with differences in what Klaus Holzkamp called the *subjective possibility space* – the space of imagination that defines what is experienced as accessible, legitimate, feasible, practical and therefore thinkable:

> The life world of the mine owner is literally different to that of the miner ... they perform different functions in the division of labour ... they occupy different positions in society and thus experience different life

> situations. This is bound to have significant effects upon subjectivity . . . [the real, objective, quantitative differences in their situations] are experienced subjectively in their respective life situations as distinctly larger or smaller subjective possibility spaces.
>
> *(Tolman, 1994, p. 113)*

In short: we might primarily emphasise the felt or affective dimensions of lived, socially classed and stratified experience, and talk then of sensibilities; or we might primarily emphasise its sensory and intellectual dimensions, and talk of subjective possibility spaces. In both cases, we will necessarily attend to persistent and pervasive power relations that produce corresponding constellations of opportunities and resources, both material and immaterial, together with the entwined synergistic effects of exposure and access to these opportunities and resources. In both cases, too, we must recognise that social class hierarchies do not end as the higher education system starts: rather, that system is one of the most prominent mechanisms by which those hierarchies are reproduced.

The students of whom Fisher wrote were predominantly those in UK colleges of Further Education: institutions disproportionately occupied by students from disadvantaged backgrounds who, in some cases, will have entered further education in large part to shield themselves for a little while longer from the grim actuality of zero-hour contracts that awaits them in the world of paid servitude. Higher up the academic food chain, however, in universities ranked as among the 10 or 20 best in the country (and note that for all but a handful, this is a fluid ranking that *necessarily* varies, both between indicators and across time), things are often a little different. Staff here are no less intensively regulated and controlled than in the FE colleges: indeed, arguably more so, since their policing extends to compulsory engagement with both research and 'enterprise' as well as with teaching. At the same time, these staff are frequently differently and better incentivised: on average, their salaries are typically higher, they are often accorded a little more status and respect by managers; and they have the possibility to wield at least some control over aspects of their work by conducting research that maps, at least in part, onto their own desires or interests.

The sensibilities of the students are also, on average, a little different. Some, often privately educated before coming to university, have a ready sense of their own presumed future importance, a sometimes disproportionate self-confidence that may infuse their academic work with a continuous (if sometimes misplaced) certainty. Others, predominantly from more aspirant backgrounds, throb with the pervasive anxiety induced by an acute, inculcated need to succeed – or, at least, appear to do so – at almost any cost. And others still lapse into a state that superficially resembles the hedonic lassitude that Fisher describes: although in their case, this is frequently not because there is no conceivable positive future for them to imagine and strive for, but in fact for the precise opposite reason. These more privileged students can *always* imagine that things are going to work out well for them, that reasonable comfort and a modicum of success are ultimately all but guaranteed, that (to quote Pulp again), "when you're laid in bed at night watching roaches climb the wall, if you called your dad he could stop it all" (Banks et al., 1995). For such students, the highly ranked university becomes a kind of middle-class holiday camp – complete with exercise and leisure facilities, all the alcohol that can be consumed and a regulatory and attendance regime that doubles up as a weekly calendar of social engagements.

In such circumstances, it might seem that students are united only by their diversity. Indeed, recognising and working with diversity is now an acknowledged and in many cases audited challenge for university staff (a circumstance clearly demonstrating how the mere recognition of these diverse backgrounds is far from sufficient for teaching to actually become critical). But within this diversity, students frequently do have some common concerns, notably (1) getting an acceptable grade on the award for which they are studying; and (2) getting 'value for money', receiving what they deem an acceptable educational service in return for the significant fees they now must pay. And at the same time, albeit perhaps less frequently, consistently or visibly than in the past, many students genuinely do also have concerns (3) to find out more about, or to better understand, themselves and their worlds, to engage critically with the information presented to them, and to strive to use it for what are often progressive purposes. These three concerns, each in their turn, lead to three initial suggestions for critical teaching in psychology.

The *first* suggestion involves making explicit the connections between getting a good grade for a degree in psychology and the network of contingencies that determine what counts as a recognised psychology qualification. Here, students can be invited to reflect upon what mainstream psychology omits, ignores or even ridicules in order to constitute itself as an apparently viable discipline. Psychoanalysis, characterised by Parker (1997) as psychology's 'repressed other', the already-existent practice that mainstream psychology had to ignore, bypass, cover over and replace in order to constitute itself as a coherent discipline, is perhaps the most obvious example that can be used to spur such discussions. Conversely, students might be invited to reflect upon the taken-for-granted hierarchy of mainstream psychology, the hierarchy whereby cognitive or biological/neuroscientific explanations, backed up with quantitative evidence, are for the most part deemed 'automatically' superior to other explanations – regardless, it seems, of their fit with the questions being answered. Research methods in psychology also have a presumed hierarchy, and students might also be invited to reflect upon this.

The *second* suggestion involves inviting students to reflect upon the economic, social and material conditions within which their learning of psychology is taking place. This will initially involve supplying information that the debate about fees for the most part failed to emphasise: notably, that the 2012 increase in student fees to £9000 per year did not result in a massive influx of money to universities because it was accompanied by a simultaneous cut in the Higher Education Funding Council for England (HEFCE) block grant of around 85%; a funding reduction applied divisively, as almost all such reductions have recently been applied, so that so-called STEM (science, technology, engineering and mathematics) subjects continue to be supported more generously than others. Experience shows that most students are very surprised to learn that the fees they now pay in fact mostly replace funding that was formerly provided by central government. This understanding not only fosters critical reflection upon why they are now expected to pay fees; it also has the additional advantage of explaining why staff–student ratios have not dramatically improved, and why staff are no more able than before to offer individualised or one-to-one supervision or support. Further explaining that many staff were opposed to the introduction of fees (as evidenced by consistent union opposition) can also be helpful in some circumstances. More fundamentally, such discussion can form part of a burgeoning awareness that psychology at every level, including the very basic level of its teaching, is already permeated with and structured by networks of competing interests, networks that shape the potentials and constraints that dynamically shape its character, content and delivery.

The *third* suggestion involves, at least in the early stages, some very general reflection on the nature of mainstream psychology and its consonance, or otherwise, with the experiencing subjects that students find themselves to be. Such reflection is of course continuously central to any practice of teaching psychology critically and will re-appear, in various guises and contexts, throughout the process of teaching. Students can be invited to reflect upon the various models of the human that are presupposed within dominant psychological paradigms – the human-machine of behaviourism, the software programme of cognitive psychology, the individualised 'brainhood' of contemporary biological psychology and neuroscience – and explore gaps and contradictions between their own experiences and these implicit and reductive notions of the person.

Individualising psychology

One of the most recurrent tropes in the critical psychological literature concerns the status of the discipline as a putative science of the individual. Mainstream psychology is predicated upon an implicit notion of persons as isolated monads, whose actions are directed, on the one hand, by some complex set of hidden mechanisms (cognitive, biological or – somehow – both at once); and on the other hand, by social or environmental forces from which these individuals are presumed to be meaningfully separable. In mainstream psychology it is as though there actually existed individuals whose opinions, actions and feelings would be comprehensible and sensible without the sociocultural resources that continuously co-constitute them: as though anyone's experiences would be remotely sensible, even to themselves, without their prior and continuous embedding in dynamic fields of relationships, material affordances, social goals, cultural norms, words and other symbols.

In its theories, and perhaps even more so in its methods – where seemingly innocuous practices of 'operationalising variables' serve to instantiate and quite literally real-ise this fiction of the isolated individual – mainstream psychology not only produces individualism, it also depends upon it: both for its own apparent coherence, and for its differentiation from other disciplines. I have argued (Cromby, 2015) that mainstream psychology is unified by its emphasis upon a largely unexamined notion of 'the individual', and this focus separates it in one direction from the more social disciplines (economics, sociology, human geography, cultural studies, etc.) and in the other direction from the more biological ones (today, mostly the neurosciences). Yet this unification is no more than superficial because the individual posited in cognitive psychology, which typically looks something like a software flowchart, differs in almost every important respect from the individual posited in biological psychology, which typically looks like a brain or some subsystem thereof. The individual in social psychology, by contrast, is mostly hollowed out and prone to incessant buffeting by external forces that selectively gain traction by means that are nevertheless rarely specified. In short, mainstream psychology's emphasis upon the individual works, first, to the extent that it seemingly renders concrete economic, social and material circumstances as mere separable context: and second, to the extent that in so doing, it is able to posit an internal world of experience with its own supposedly sovereign dynamics and processes. These observations in their turn lead to another three suggestions for teaching psychology critically.

The *fourth* suggestion involves sensitising students to the many ways in which their activities, concerns, interests, attitudes, feelings and intentions are made possible and constituted by the very economic, social and material circumstances that mainstream psychology encourages them to treat as somehow optional. One way of doing this involves a version of an exercise sometimes used in disability studies to educate the temporarily able-bodied (TAB) about the pervasive restrictions of choice, power and control that typically accompany disability. For a given day, students are asked to make an hour-by hour record of their activity: for each hour, to make a brief diary note of what they were doing, where they were, and who they were with. Students bring these diaries to a meeting where they compare and contrast them. In disability studies, they might then be presented with a diary from a typical user of services that displays quite starkly how, compared to TABs, people with disabilities are much more often dependent upon the whims and imperatives of others. In psychology, these diaries can be used in a parallel fashion to highlight how, at every moment of the day, what students did and how they felt were inextricable from the projects that engaged them, the places they were and the people with whom they were relating. The exercise can be given considerable critical force by presenting students with the (if necessary, fictionalised) diaries of others in quite different circumstances – the call-centre worker, the single parent, the member of the Royal family, even the person with disabilities – so as to emphasise how the possibilities we can viably realise never actually float free from the social and material circumstances within which we live.

The *fifth* suggestion is a thought experiment that involves posing a very simple challenge which illustrates for students the fictional status of the isolated monad of mainstream psychology with its own internal dynamics and processes. Students are asked to identify and briefly describe an experience that they have had – just one – that was entirely free of social and cultural influence. They will find this peculiarly difficult, so the exercise tends to work best if the question is posed one week and the answers requested a week or so later. From the perspective of critical psychology, where experience is continuously co-constituted by society and culture, the students are, of course, being asked to do something that is impossible. This, indeed, is what my own experience of using this exercise in teaching demonstrates: I have been posing this question to large groups of students for over a decade now, and so far not one of these many hundreds of students has managed to produce any experience that cannot quickly be shown to bear at least some trace of social relations, cultural norms, technological, material or economic resources or capacities. Moreover, the putative examples they come up with are almost without exception trivial, fleeting and non-consequential: blinking, breathing, feeling weightless while swimming and so on. This is highly relevant in itself because from the perspective of mainstream psychology, where individuals are, in principle, separate from their social and cultural contexts such that their 'inner' experiences and dynamics can apparently be meaningfully studied in isolation from them, it seems like there should be a limitless supply of answers to this question.

Of course, students also derive their assumptions about the existence and central importance of this pristine and discrete inner world of experience from other sources than psychology, including cultural presuppositions of mind–body or Cartesian dualism, tendencies to individualise achievement and ability, religious precepts, and ideological pressures associated with neoliberal capitalism. These influences are able to gain traction, to instil within psychology students a common-sense understanding of an inner world very precious to them, largely because the feelings, memories, intentions and desires that constitute it loom so subjectively large – even though, in the overall scheme of things, they are almost immeasurably transient and insignificant (Smail, 2005). Consequently, the exercise can provoke determined efforts to find exceptions, although these can invariably be shown to be invalid: neural activity is not part of experience, although it is necessary for experience to occur; breathing is usually not only automated, but also outside experience, and in fact only tends to enter experience when it acquires some significance beyond itself, and the same goes for blinking; to the extent that we experience ourselves sleeping, we are dreaming, and dreams invariably invoke images, feelings, people and situations from the waking world (and this remains true even if we do not tell anyone else about the dream); and so on.

A *sixth* suggestion that also reveals for students the already-shared origins of their experiences is to engage them in a memory work group. Memory work (Haug, 1987) is a research method associated with German Critical Psychology that involves a collective discourse analysis of written accounts of memories produced by group members. Fuller details of the method are available in sources including Willig (2001) and Crawford, Kippax, Onyx, Gault and Benton (1992), but in brief, it involves first jointly agreeing a prompt to which the memories respond: for example, 'getting angry'. Group members then each write a memory following a specific format:

1. choose the earliest relevant memory possible;
2. write in the third person;

3. with as much detail as possible, even seemingly irrelevant material;
4. without any explanation or justification (the word 'because' would never appear).

The written memories are circulated among the group for a week or so. The group then meet to discuss the memories which are first examined individually and then cross-sectionally. These discussions identify clichés, gaps, contradictions, the taken-for-granted, inconsistencies, absences and ambiguities. This can take a while, so multiple meetings are frequently required. When memory work is used within research projects, the data consist of both the written memories and the conclusions from the group discussions (which would typically be audio-recorded): for teaching purposes, more informal or partial summaries of these discussions would be adequate and recording would not be necessary. The procedure reveals how individual memories are consistently positioned and interpellated (i.e. how their reactions, feelings and actions are 'called out') by social positions and relations, and how they are shaped by resources (both conceptual and material) and in accord with normative expectations of culture.

The customer is always right

Free market economies are ostensibly organised according to the principle of consumer sovereignty, a principle which states that the desires and needs of consumers control the output of producers. As we have seen, under the business regime that now dominates higher education there is some ambiguity about what the actual product is. This ambiguity has not prevented the National Student Survey (NSS) and its associated rankings from gaining massive influence upon university teaching, largely because this – and now the proposed Teaching Excellence Framework – are necessary aspects of the covert privatisation of higher education that has already been enacted (and to which – perhaps because the government has studiously avoided the 'p' word – many university teachers still seem surprisingly oblivious). As Collini (2012) notes, the public debate about increasing student fees to £9000 largely failed to consider the more fundamental change imposed by this policy. The Browne Report (Browne et al., 2010), upon which the policy was based, in fact inaugurated a profound shift from public funding of a public and social good (societies thrive more when their citizens are better educated) to a purely instrumental and economic view of higher education where "students . . . have the opportunity to choose between institutions on the basis of price and value for money", choices that will primarily be made on the basis of "the employment returns from their courses" (Collini, 2012, p. 182).

The various ramifications of this fundamental transformation in the nature of higher education are still working their way through the institutions affected by it. Many of the fundamental contradictions it forces lecturers to negotiate can be stated quite simply: the customer is always right, even though it is often our job to tell them when and how they are wrong; the customer expects free choice, but at university their choices are necessarily restricted by disciplinary and other constraints; consumption is about satisfying desires, but education is about inculcating sometimes difficult knowledge and skills. These contradictions continue to play themselves out at multiple levels during learning, quite simply because students do not materially cease being consumers once they have enrolled on their chosen degree. Understandably, the annual basis of the £9000 fee encourages them to continuously expect for their payment something like the kinds of responsiveness to customer desire that, say, a supermarket might provide. For some, at least, it can foster the presumption that there should be an all but limitless choice of modules, just as there is choice in the supermarket. At the same time, it is equally the case that lecturers must sometimes teach students material that they would rather not study: that good teaching sometimes involves explaining to students that and how they are mistaken about something; that effective teaching often begins by challenging taken-for-granted truths, and some students can find this disconcerting; and that there is frequently a considerable difference between what students *want*, as consumers, and what they *need* to be competent psychologists (or, indeed, mature and thoughtful citizens of an equitable and caring society).

This leads to a *seventh* suggestion for teaching psychology critically which is, quite simply, to make these contradictions explicit. I have done an exercise with students where they are first asked to list and second to rank order, in terms of their influence, up to five reasons why they chose to study psychology. They are then asked to discuss these influences and the rankings that they gave to them. Invariably when they do this, it emerges that many of the reasons for their choices are not simply – and often not even primarily – economic or commercial. Alongside desires to occupy high-paid professional jobs there sit desires to better understand one's self, to be better at relationships, to help others who are less fortunate or in some way vulnerable, to contribute to education, and even to produce new knowledge. Drawing out and reflecting upon these different kinds of reasons is therefore a way of making explicit for students, in the context of their own experience, the profound contradiction between students as mere consumers and students as (potentially) engaged learners. It can, of course, lead on to further discussion of the social role of psychologists: are we disinterested technicians neutrally documenting human nature and implementing value-free interventions to transform it in accord with uncontroversial notions of the common good? Or alternately – as the mere existence of ethics committees and codes of professional conduct would seem to imply – are things of necessity considerably more complex, value-laden and more problematic than this?

Totally wired

Mandell, Thompson, Weintraub, DeStefano and Blank (2005) report that between 1989 and 2000 in the United States, diagnoses of Attention-Deficit Hyperactivity Disorder (ADHD) increased by 381%. Timimi and Taylor (2004) show how we need not endorse psychiatric presumptions of genetically impelled or neurally caused disease processes as the root cause of this increase (presumptions in any case frankly implausible, given the notable absence of the nuclear radiation event needed to cause the background rate of mutation to increase at the exponential rate necessary to explain such an increase on biologically determinist grounds). They list instead a series of changes in children's environments and associated changes in the ways in which children's behaviour is understood, and argue that this combination of changes in fact accounts for the increase. Their list includes dietary changes (more sugar, more fast food); more dual-parent working, and more parents working longer hours; changed lifestyle norms (more TV, more channels, more advertisements, shorter programmes; less exercise, less outdoors play); changes in education (more testing; more emphasis upon self-direction); changed cultural norms (more surveillance, fewer shared values and rules, less authority granted by parents to teachers and schools); more 'hands off' parenting; the increased influence of the pharmaceutical industry; and the forcible imposition of more selfish, individualised norms of conduct and a corresponding decline in notions of collective responsibility, an imposition neatly summarised by Margaret Thatcher's now infamous assertion (from Keay, 1987) that "there is no such thing as society. There are individual men and women, and there are families".

Timimi and Taylor's analysis (2004) clearly provides a sound basis for critically informed teaching in mental health that draws out both the individualising, medicalising effects of psychiatric diagnosis and the profound peculiarity of 'solving' the problems that this complex of social, relational, cultural and material changes has produced by simply drugging those children most obviously affected. In the present context, its wider relevance is simply that today's psychology students are, for the most part, young people who have grown up and been educated in just such conditions. While we might bemoan their seemingly short attention spans, their dependence upon TV programmes, their constant availability for and monitoring of social media, and while we might despair of the innervated yet exhausted, totally wired yet enormously tired states they sometimes end up in, as lecturers we can do almost nothing to change these circumstances (although this does not mean we should not, in very small ways, try: I will return to this point later).

This actuality leads to an *eighth* and in some ways more conventional suggestion which is to make use of TV, film and documentaries in teaching psychology critically. We are fortunate in psychology (by comparison with some other disciplines) that there is, relatively speaking, a great wealth of material freely available online that students can be directed towards. I have experimented successfully (i.e. with good feedback from students, and some – admittedly limited and impressionistic – evidence of positive impacts upon learning) with methods of using online resources within what I have called 'virtual seminars'.

Virtual seminars consist of three elements: (1) a reliable link to an appropriate online source; (2) a document explaining why this source is relevant, appropriate or interesting, and posing a set of questions about its content; and (3) a document containing my answers to these questions. These three elements are made available to students via the university server, together with some general instructions. These instructions explain that the content of each seminar links to a particular week's teaching, or alternately to a particular theme in the module. Students are thus advised that while they can attempt the virtual seminar at any time during the module, they may find it more rewarding and valuable to wait until at least the basic relevant information has been introduced in lectures. They are advised that subject to these considerations, they can study for the virtual seminar at any time of day or night that suits them: all they need is a suitable networked device. The procedure is simple: they first read, and perhaps print, the framing remarks and questions; they watch the programme, making notes as they do so in order to answer the questions that are set; then they compare their own answers with those provided. Importantly, the instructions also explain that no marks or penalties are attached to these virtual seminars: they are an invitation to self-directed learning purely for its own sake.

Virtual seminars allow totally wired students to engage in learning at the time and in the circumstances of their own choosing. They work with, rather than against, key elements of the hyperactive consumer culture that today's students occupy, and since they are not marked or judged, it is impossible to fail at them. At the same time, they supply opportunities for gentle subversion of mainstream psychological precepts: in the content of what is studied, in how it is framed, and in the questions and answers supplied. I have used very mainstream teaching aids – for example, programmes showing studies in biological psychology – and raised critical questions about them; I have used online excerpts from the comedy *Peep Show* to prompt reflection upon the Vygotskian account of the origins of inner speech and the validity of cognitive psychological models of experience; and I have used Adam Curtis's cult documentary *The Century of the Self* (2002) to introduce more intrinsically critical material in a disarming and relatively accessible manner.

The death of the text

Poststructuralist philosophers such as Derrida have famously been associated with proclamations of the 'death of the author' and that 'there is nothing outside the text', perspectives that have been taken up in critical psychology to de-centre the unitary self that is presumed by the mainstream, to challenge its apparent coherence by demonstrating the necessary gaps it must paper over in order to achieve its apparent consistency. My present concern with the death of the text is more prosaic and simply refers to the apparent recent decline of reading as an activity, and the possible consequences of this for critical teaching in psychology. A recent study by the UK National Literacy Trust, which surveyed the reading habits of 21,000 young people, showed that between 2005 and 2012, the numbers reading in their own time fell significantly. Outside of class, the most commonly read items were text messages, the proportion of children who read magazines declined from 75% to 54%, and more than 20% said that they never read in their own time (Vasager, 2012). A key reason often given for the apparent decline in reading is the increasing availability and use of digital media and entertainment, including computer games. Students today, including psychology students, spend far longer online than did those from previous generations, and this includes time accessing academic material. In this regard, Liu (2005, p. 700) found that the self-reported character of reading changed when it was conducted online, so that it came to consist of "more time spent on browsing and scanning, keyword spotting, one-time reading, non-linear reading, and reading more selectively, while less time is spent on in-depth reading, and concentrated reading. Decreasing sustained attention is also noted."

We must remain careful, when interpreting the results of such work, not to lapse into doom-laden neuro-babble along the lines of Susan Greenfield's unsupported claims that computer games cause brain damage (Goldacre, 2009). Computer games, and computer-mediated reading, are likely to represent and facilitate new forms of literacy alongside the old, to encourage new skills of information retrieval and synthesis at the same time as they might sometimes mitigate against sustained engagement. Nevertheless, when teaching psychology critically, there is something to be said for encouraging deep reading, reading that demands sustained engagement, commitment and some degree of effort. In part, this is because the effort required to read or understand something can be correlated with its perceived value. In part, too, it is because the domination of capitalism, the extent of its colonisation of everyday life, is such that only sustained and detailed arguments, backed up with copious quantities of evidence, are now likely to prove persuasive. In part, then, it is also because critical perspectives have been so thoroughly marginalised in many areas of life that they will be largely unfamiliar to many students. And in part, it is because being critical fundamentally requires skills of reading, analysis and synthesis that can be developed in many different ways, but the development of these skills will often benefit from the disciplined engagement that careful and sustained reading demands.

The *ninth* suggestion for teaching psychology critically is therefore to compel students to read a relevant book. Experience suggests that, unfortunately, compulsion is often necessary: on a third-year mental health module I taught, a very short (126-page) book by Smail (2005) was required reading. But it quickly became apparent – from responses to questions posed during lectures, from the pattern of exam answers, and from the content of other assessments – that almost no students were actually reading, or even merely scanning, this book. So the assessment was changed from an essay to a 2000-word review of this book, with the instruction that relying upon or quoting from published reviews would result in penalties. Effectively, this made reading the book compulsory, and the slew of sometimes bitter complaints this generated confirmed the suspicion that, previously, most students had simply not read it. While the majority, it is fair to say, simply got on and did the reading, a substantial and vocal minority each year would complain: some about the length ("what – all of it?!"); some about the language and terminology ("impossible to understand"); some about the book's political values ("it should be neutral, like our other reading"). Astonishingly, perhaps, on a third-year degree-level module, one student even compared the book unfavourably – in terms of content and readability – to the Harry Potter novels.

There is, of course, no way of knowing what longer-term effects reading this book produced. The overall pattern of the reviews – which were frequently of strikingly good quality – suggested that, for many, the reading had simply confirmed whichever biases (for or against biological explanations for distress, for or against analyses emphasising social and material influences) they already held. But for smaller numbers of others, there was a clear sense of insight, of transformation, of recognising that the experience of reading something different and slightly challenging had opened up for them new and valuable perspectives above and beyond those provided in their lectures and seminars.

Dismantling authority

A colleague once described the fantastic way in which he delivered his lecture on the Milgram experiments to first-year psychology students. His first lecture slide was densely covered in text that described in considerable detail the context of and background to the experiment. Upon presenting this slide, he would say, "Please copy all of this material down immediately, word for word". As soon as it seemed that most students had done this, he would immediately advance to the next slide, which was similarly densely packed with text, and give the same instruction. Typically, one or more students would begin to question why this was necessary; he would respond by simply and calmly saying, "Please carry on", "You must carry on" or "It is necessary that you continue". Eventually, perhaps by the time they got partway through copying the fourth slide's dense descriptions, a substantial proportion of the students would have realised what he was getting them to do: the majority, though, would still be desperately trying to write.

As this example shows, there is something paradoxical about encouraging – perhaps, requiring – students to question authority and received wisdom, while using one's own position of authority to do so. The passive and unthinking acceptance of the status quo, what Fisher (2009) called interpassivity, is a barrier to critical thought in every discipline. This inculcated passivity has consequences that are of particular relevance in psychology, which for all its many faults, nevertheless often attracts students who feel that they would like to better understand themselves and others. Cushman (2012) describes how psychology teaching in America that presents the discipline as a STEM subject and is therefore imbued with scientism – the view that the only understandings worth having are those produced using 'scientific' methods and which are based upon 'hard' evidence – not only fails miserably to produce the enhanced understandings it promises, but also deadens the minds and aspirations of students:

> I see their young faces, I watch as they catch the subtle demands that lead them to become
>
> 1. scientists in the physical science tradition;
> 2. professionals in the American business tradition; and
> 3. humorless, managerial bureaucrats in what Max Weber called the Iron Cage.

I see the growing deadness in their eyes as they come to realize that they are being called upon to think of themselves as knowledgeable mechanics, expert followers of detailed rules and manuals. And worse yet, I begin to detect the frightened, angry defensiveness that comes when they realize that they are required not only to act like bureaucratic automatons, but to like it, to believe in it, to swear by it, to stake their adult identities on it. I see them accommodate to the endless rules, fill out the never-ending forms, bend to the soulless regulations, conform to the mind-numbing requirements, follow the multitude of manualized behaviors and procedures. I see them tolerate the institutional surveillance they are put under, avoid noticing the self-surveillance they adopt to survive (just as Foucault, 1977, predicted). Above all, they have to learn how to turn a blind eye to the consequences of the self-righteous surveillance they practice on others, all in the name of a soulless ethics that has little political commitment or moral vision apart from the necessity of carrying out one's orders with efficiency and effectiveness.

(Cushman, 2012, p. 264)

Cushman shows how submission to power – whether enforced by discipline or insinuated by control, whether made explicit or whether coded in the form of ostensibly 'neutral' disciplinary presumptions and methodological requirements – undermines critical thinking by imbuing it with a pervasive yet ineffable feeling of being somehow wrong, unacceptable, marginal, ludicrous, threatening, perhaps even dangerous. Experience shows that this can happen in relatively surprising ways: more than once when female psychology students have pursued dissertation topics related to gender, and I have suggested that they search for relevant papers in the (peer-reviewed, highly regarded) journal *Feminism & Psychology*, they have responded by asking, "But . . . is that even allowed?"

This leads to a *tenth* suggestion of (at least partially) dismantling or subverting authority during teaching. In previous generations, this could be done in more radical ways; for example, by empowering students to mark their own or their peers' work: perhaps surprisingly, lecturers who experimented with this found that students' own assessments typically mirrored fairly faithfully those the lecturer would have given, but were on average up to ten percentage points harsher. While this degree of subversion seems unthinkable, almost immoral, in the contemporary university, a strategy that is still acceptable in most institutions is to ask students to write their own essay questions.

Students can first be given a handout explaining what a good question would look like: it must be relevant to the module themes; an adequate answer to it could not be merely descriptive; answers have to be achievable within the remit of the coursework (in terms of length, resources, focus and presumed prior competencies); it must be neither too specific nor too general; and it must include a verb from a list of relevant terms – compare, contrast, synthesise, evaluate, critique and so on. The handout can be presented in Week 1 of the module and a two-stage process initiated: beginning from the start of Week 3, students are asked to email the lecturer with a draft of their question (if desired, using a specific subject line in their emails to enable filtering into a dedicated folder). They receive feedback on their draft question, enabling them to further develop it in order to produce something answerable and appropriate. A suitable deadline for completion of these revisions and for final approval of all individual essay questions is set – say, end of Week 5. Students are then given a further deadline, towards the end of the module, by which to submit their answers.

Reflections

In this chapter, I have presented suggestions for critical teaching in psychology that respond to various aspects of contemporary culture, social and economic conditions, student life and experience. None come with guarantees, and perhaps all should come with warnings: one year when I asked students to write their own essay titles, they complained to the staff–student committee that I wasn't doing my job properly because it is the lecturer's task to set essay questions. The complaint was summarily dismissed: that some students ever thought it acceptable to complain is nevertheless telling. It illustrates again how these suggestions are themselves situated in history and culture, how their viability is in large part a function of the circumstances to which they speak. Maybe, by the time the complaint was made, the scholarly value of writing one's own essay question, the freedom it bestowed to identify and then research your own perspective upon a topic, was already too threatening, too alien, too seemingly irrelevant to the instrumental workings of the degree-factory culture into which it fell.

Sadly, perhaps, it seems that at least some of these suggestions will continue to be relevant for some time yet to come. The majority of psychologists aligned with the mainstream do not seem imminently likely to be reconsidering their fundamental presumptions and methods, any more than it seems probable that they will suddenly realise how their ostensibly value-neutral stance necessarily converts into implicit support for, and reproduction of, the ever more reactionary status quo.

In the face of this challenge, we might do well to remind ourselves that, in many senses (and despite occasional appearances to the contrary), teaching university students is still a privilege. Bracket off, momentarily, the ongoing slew of edicts, policies, standards, objectives, criteria and new uses of technology (for example, compulsory recording of lectures) that will ultimately serve primarily to deaden, standardise and homogenise teaching, to render it bland, compliant and uninspiring. With this maelstrom pushed, however fleetingly, into the background, we might again sense how our work continues to provide an irreducible opportunity to awaken and inspire the imaginations of (predominantly) young people. University teaching provides occasions for lecturers to temporarily enlarge the subjective possibility spaces of their students, to interpolate ('call out') and encourage different and more questioning sensibilities than those legitimated by the orthodoxy, to validate minority viewpoints, to legitimate 'awkward' questions, and so to nurture, sustain and give rigour and direction to the curious, questioning and critical impulses that many students still experience.

Neither psychology lecturers nor their students got to choose the economic, social and material circumstances that organise most current psychology teaching. Very few even had any significant say over these circumstances. To judge by the expressions of disappointment and dismay on both sides, if such choice or influence had been available, it seems likely that psychology teaching – indeed, psychology itself – might be very different. In this context, each of the suggestions here aims – in one way or another, and to some small degree or other – to infuse psychology teaching with a distinct critical impulse. In turn, this criticality might engender future challenges: both to the toxic effects of the individualising mainstream of psychology, and to the damaging economic, social and material circumstances with which it is co-dependent.

References

Banks, N., Cocker, J., Doyle, C., Mackey, S., Senior, R., & Webber, M. (1995). Common people. On *Different class* [CD]. UK: Island Records.

Browne, J., Barber, M., Coyle, D., Eastwood, P., King, J., Naik, R., & Sands, P. (2010). *Securing a sustainable future for higher education: An independent review of higher education funding and student finance*. Available at www.gov.uk/government/publications/the-browne-report-higher-education-funding-and-student-finance

Charlesworth, S. (1999). *A phenomenology of working class experience*. Cambridge: Cambridge University Press.

Collini, S. (2012). *What are universities for?* London: Penguin.

Crawford, J., Kippax, S., Onyx, J., Gault, U., & Benton, P. (1992). *Emotion and gender: Constructing meaning from memory*. London: Sage Publications.

Cromby, J. (2015). *Feeling bodies: Embodying psychology*. Basingstoke, UK: Palgrave.

Curtis, A. (Director). (2002). *The century of the self* [Moving picture]. UK: RDF Media.

Cushman, P. (2012). Defenseless in the face of the status quo: Psychology without a critical humanities. *The Humanistic Psychologist, 40*, 262–269.

Debord, G. (1967/1987). *Society of the spectacle*. London: Rebel Press, AIM Publications.

Fisher, M. (2009). *Capitalist realism*. Ropley, Hampshire, UK: Zero Books.

Goldacre, B. (2009). Chilling warning to parents from top neuroscientist. Retrieved from http://www.badscience.net/2009/05/professor-baroness-susan-greenfield-cbe/

Haug, F. (1987). *Female sexualisation: A collective work of memory* (Erica Carter, Trans.). London: Verso.

Keay, D. (1987, 23 September). Interview with Margaret Thatcher. *Woman's Own* magazine.

Liu, Z. (2005). Reading behavior in the digital environment: Changes in reading behavior over the past ten years. *Journal of Documentation, 61*(6), 700–712.

Mandell, David S., Thompson, William W., Weintraub, Eric S., DeStefano, Frank, & Blank, Michael B. (2005). Trends in diagnosis rates for autism and ADHD at hospital discharge in the context of other psychiatric diagnoses. *Psychiatric Services, 56*(1), 56–62. doi:10.1176/appi.ps.56.1.56

McKenzie, L. (2015). *Getting by: Estates, class and culture in contemporary Britain*. Bristol: Policy Press.

Parker, I. (1997). *Psychoanalytic culture*. London: Sage Publications.

Parker, I. (Ed.) (2015). *Handbook of critical psychology*. London: Routledge.
Smail, D.J. (2005). *Power, interest and psychology: Elements of a social materialist understanding of distress*. Ross-On-Wye, UK: PCCS Books.
Teo, T. (Ed.) (2014). *Encyclopaedia of critical psychology*. New York: Springer-Verlag.
Timimi, S., & Taylor, E. (2004). ADHD is best understood as a cultural construct. *British Journal of Psychiatry, 184*, 8–9.
Tolman, C. (1994). *Psychology, society, subjectivity: An introduction to German Critical Psychology*. London: Routledge.
Vasager, J. (2012, 7 September). Number of children reading for fun has fallen since 2005, study reveals. *The Guardian*. Retrieved from www.theguardian.com/society/2012/sep/07/children-reading-fun-fallen-study
Willig, C. (2001). *Introducing qualitative research in psychology*. Buckingham, UK: Open University Press.

3

TOWARDS COHERENCE IN TEACHING CRITICAL PSY

Craig Newnes

Long before I knew of the discipline of critical psychology, I found myself teaching 'A' level psychology to keen mums attending night classes in a variety of Lincolnshire villages. Such knowledge as I had of parenting was limited to getting my middle brother off to sleep when I was about ten and driving my youngest brother through red stop lights on the way to hospital after he had jumped from a first-floor window; I knew that parenting was tiring. The mums wanted to know more; how should their children be developing? How to deal with temper tantrums? I was grateful to pass as expert, reading up on Piaget the day before each presentation. Gesell wasn't on my radar and ADHD (attention-deficit hyperactivity disorder) had yet to be invented. Passing as expert is now ubiquitous for everyone from climatologists to economists and members of Psy. The fact that climatologists can't *change* the weather, economists aren't necessarily rich and Psy professionals can be pretty fucked up only seems a problem to those branded cynics and naysayers. The complexity – contextual and personal – of being human is acknowledged by some psychologists and all novelists. As Ruth Rendell (1994, p. 153) has her Detective Inspector acknowledge in *Simisola*: "With human nature you could only guess – and try to guess right."

Psy professionals must, however, pass as experts and, as professionals, the disciplinary process is ubiquitous. This chapter will discuss that process as it relates to almost 40 years of teaching, researching and practising clinical psychology and psychotherapy. I shall also highlight the distal and proximal powers that impact on a retrospective reflection on the endeavour as an attempt is made to bring some coherence (in itself a concept fraught with the demands of a kind of Whig view of history).

In the militaristic jargon of business speak, there are elements in this chapter that might be read as "strategic." The use of concepts such as referent power does more than hint at Machiavellian conduct. An alternative title might be "Stumbling towards a retrospective coherence. . . ." Such a title suggests less deliberation in the forms and methodology of "teaching" outlined. In fact, much of what follows, from time scale to content of the teaching and publication endeavour described, was thought through strategically, though the aim, to prevent death in human services rather than directly cause it, is diametrically opposed to the object of actual warfare.[1]

A history of formal teaching

Foucault (1975/1977) cites the Gobelins school (established via an edict in 1667) as the first documented guild – where "domestic service is mixed with a transference of knowledge" (p. 156). The school was the start of "the development . . . of a new technique for taking charge of the time of individual existences." The professional discipline of teaching, rather than the tradition of teaching via individual tuition as employed by the aristocracy since the Roman Empire, starts here. Specifically, "The disciplines, which analyse space, break up and rearrange activities, must also be understood as machinery for adding up and capitalizing time" (p. 157) and, "The disciplines function increasingly as techniques for making useful individuals" (p. 211).

By the mid-eighteenth century, the schools "became a sort of apparatus of uninterrupted examination that duplicated along its entire length the operation of teaching . . . a perpetual comparison of each and all that made it possible to both measure and judge" (Foucault, 1975/1977, p. 186). The Brothers of the Christian Schools, for example, wanted pupils to be examined on every day of the week; on the first day, spelling, the second, arithmetic, the third, catechism and handwriting and so on. Further, "The examination that places individuals in a field of surveillance also situates them in a network of writing; it engages them in a whole mass of documents that capture and fix them" (p. 189). Such documentation now takes the form of lesson plans (see Piper, Chapter 5, this volume), marked essays, performance "targets" and teaching "objectives." Millions "fix" themselves (at least as far as they want to be seen) via blogs, family photographs, selfies and a seemingly endless supply of bumper stickers disguised as philosophy on Facebook.

The drive to efficiency in the teaching project becomes part of an overall system of surveillance and competition between individuals, institutions and their staff: "in order to extract from bodies the maximum time and force, the use of those overall methods known as time-tables, collective training, exercises, total and detailed surveillance" (p. 220). It may seem ironic that in following a system for disciplining the uneducated and uncontrollable peasantry and military, it is just such internalised discipline that enables the modern independent Doctoral candidate and qualified Psy practitioner to succeed.

In the eighteenth century,

> First, the hospital, then the school, then, later, the workshop were not simply "reordered" by the disciplines; they became . . . apparatuses such that any element of objectification [the exam, the norm] could be used in them as an instrument of subjection.
>
> *(Foucault, 1975/1977, p. 224)*

"[I]t was this link . . . that made possible within the disciplinary element the formation of clinical medicine, psychiatry, child psychology, educational psychology, the rationalization of labour" (p. 224). Disciplinary power has become integrated within psychology and psychiatry:

> its appearance in the form of tests, interviews, interrogations and consultations is apparently in order to rectify the mechanisms of discipline: educational psychology is supposed to correct the rigours of the school, just as the medical or psychiatric interview is supposed to rectify the effects of the discipline of work. But . . . these techniques merely refer individuals from one disciplinary authority to another.
>
> *(Foucault, 1975/1977, p. 226)*

In what follows, the reader will find elements of the disciplinary project as outlined by Foucault in the work of psychological therapists and academics and, by virtue of the intrinsic demands of institutionalised teaching, will discern how supposedly *critical* educational praxis retains all the features of the panopticon.

Integrating teaching and Psy practice

During clinical psychology training, I had organised a couple of teaching days. One had involved a small group of academics and fellow trainees sitting in more or less silence at the front of an audience. The group represented my then weekly attempts to help in-patients at a Lincoln health unit to converse. The groups were marked by long, psychotropic-induced silences interrupted by the occasional, quite reasonable attempts by patients to leave the room. The audience was equally silent, but after half an hour of mute "learning," several voices were raised in protest at what was seen as a mockery – of the patients and of the kind of directive groupwork in vogue at the time. Undirected groups of ordinary folk tend to chat a little, and then leave. Undirected groups of analytically minded professionals assume something mysterious is going on and – at the Tavistock Clinic large groups, for example – frequently explode into rage; leaving is seen as even more rageful. For the highly disciplined audience at the presentation, a group leader not intervening in a "helpful" way was seen as unprofessional.

The second teaching day was for an audience of psychotherapists at a Lincoln therapy interest group. This time I sat with a patient and conducted a conversation not, on the face of it, so different from our therapy meetings. The audience was quiet throughout and asked respectful questions of the patient afterwards. Several therapists thanked her for her "courage." None commented on the power differential involved in her agreement to sit in front of a group of strangers and "perform," though an analyst raised a concern about counter-transference in a private conversation with me later. At our next session, she claimed the experience had been "helpful." In hindsight, it would be possible to examine the public session in terms of part of the disciplinary project; both participants were under the gaze, both unsure of what might occur and at least one of us acutely aware of "performing." Indeed, a member of the audience wondered (again in private) if the *patient* was an exhibitionist; he had clearly not met me before. Perhaps, it was all just entertainment (see below).

I didn't repeat the experience, instead, having moved jobs to Berkshire, limiting myself to organising conferences on family therapy and Normalisation.

From 1989, for almost 20 years, as Director of the Department of Psychological Therapies in Shropshire, I – along with some colleagues – maintained a kind of assault on modernist psychiatry and, increasingly, modernist psychology. A fairly consistent stance was maintained through teaching, supervision, consultancy, research, publication and an approach to patients emphasising the importance of context over concepts like will-power or "cure." Teaching usually involved people designated service users acting as consultants or seminar leaders (and an acknowledgement that "service recipient" was a more accurate construction – see Newnes, 2005). Uniquely, at the time, service recipients were also employed – with a majority vote – on interview panels for Psy staff (Long, Newnes, & MacLachlan, 2000; Newnes, Long, & MacLachlan, 2001). The views of service recipients were also an integral part of the departmental research programme.[2] The teaching programme spread rapidly; first locally in the form of conferences, seminar series and the Internet (previously www.shropsych.org), and later nationally via conferences and international conference organisation and participation. Teachers on Shropshire courses and, later, the Staffordshire University Doctoral programme included service survivors such as Viv Lindow and Peter Lehmann (ex-chair and founder of the European Network of (ex-)Users and Survivors of Psychiatry – see, for example, Lehmann [2015] and ENUSP website[3]) and critical voices from within Psy; for example, Lucy Johnstone and Peter Breggin. Breggin's debate with the then president of the Royal College of Psychiatrists proved something of a "lamb to the slaughter" event, with Breggin sticking to the known research and the president using various rhetorical devices to unsuccessfully counter his adversary.

The Department helped to found the Staffordshire Clinical Psychology Doctorate, a programme that started with a first series of seminars so critical of current Psy praxis and theory that the course director doubted that the British Psychological Society would accredit it.

Resistance both from within the Department and externally was considerable, resistance I had tried to allay by establishing a well-respected staff counselling service (Newnes, 1992a). Many local psychiatrists and other colleagues saw the Department as at best an irrelevance and at worst something to challenge as publicly as possible: the Antipsychiatry placement for clinical psychology trainees came under particular scrutiny (Newnes & MacLachlan, 1996). The placement was established in 1994. Its aims included examination of the psychiatric system and clinical psychology's place within it (via reading, discussion, video material, research, supervision, and membership of Shelton's patients' council). Publication was highlighted; at least two papers were to be published or sent for review within 6 months. No therapy was given by trainees on the grounds that there is poor evidence of its efficacy.

For colleagues tasked with working alongside psychiatrically trained staff, the existence of the placement could sometimes add to a sense that they were unwillingly part of a renegade group in the process of reducing their opportunity to get along with those same psychiatrically trained staff. In community mental health team meetings and hierarchical rituals, "getting along with" colleagues remains crucial. Perpetual self-monitoring (a universal social panopticon) ensures that politeness is monitored as much as intelligent argument and woe betide a colleague seen as too passionate about the matter under discussion. Colleagues' roles in psychiatrist-led teams were made no easier by a continuous published critique of psychiatry's addiction to prescription (Newnes, 2011a; Baker, Newnes, & Myatt, 2003; Newnes & Holmes, 1996; Newnes, 1990a).

Although local Psy practitioners enjoyed the opportunity to attend critical seminars or conferences, the topics under review didn't offer them much hope of being seen as "traditional" therapists. From "Professional power" (British Association for Behavioural Psychotherapy Symposium) in 1991, to "How does clinical psychology harm people?" (Bangor Clinical Psychology Doctoral Course) in 2005, the critique seemed relentless.[4] The teaching was further supported via the establishment of a library for use by anyone within the organisation, supervision and a proficient publication endeavour.[5] Films critical of Psy praxis available for loan included *Welcome to Happy Valley* (Sapin, 1994) and *We're Not Mad, We're Angry* (MadFilmsByMadPeople, 1986). Both are as relevant today as they were when they were made; one of the frustrations within Psy is that so-called breakthroughs or developments in technique are non-existent or minor and never pivotal while the harmful excesses remain a constant.

From a *strategic* perspective, the Department's teaching programme makes interesting reading. To underline our legitimate power, courses were offered on less provocative topics; for example, "Basic counselling skills," "Service quality," "Group and family therapy" and "Psychology for medical trainees."[6] As part of an attempt to make the lecture programme available to all staff, a series of presentations on the service wounds, counselling and harmful effects of medication were given to nursing staff on night shift. The seminars started at midnight and ran until 2 am – for me, horribly reminiscent of pre-professional days working at Birds Eye and in a rope factory. The hours from 3 am until 4.30 am are a dead time for all but ravers and lovers; nursing staff sensibly preferred the talks to finish at 2 am.

For the first few years, the Department's job advertisements began, "This is a socialist department," a statement that, on reflection, seems naïve. The line was eventually removed at the insistence of the Director of Mental Health Services who, despite a lifetime affiliation to the Labour Party, regarded public political positioning as potentially counter to equal opportunities. No doubt, more ground-level political activists would have regarded the statement as a version of *champagne socialism*. Members of the Department were, however, politically active and involved in local work; for example, as members of the governing boards of schools, in union activity and, in one case, almost daily involvement in the establishment and management of a children's play group.[7]

Clinical psychology training

Experiences of managing play groups or union activity add to the referent power of individual qualified practitioners, but are not generally considered as relevant at the level of applications for clinical psychology training. As noted by Fakoussa et al. (Chapter 6, this volume), the standard qualification for acceptance for training is a psychology degree and experience in some kind of paid helping role, often as an assistant psychologist. Experiences such as caring for an elderly relative, parenthood, surviving a life-threatening illness, employment in non-social-care jobs, *un*employment or voluntary work as a local councillor are considered at the interview on some Doctoral programmes, though to me, it seems another aspect of the disciplinary process that life experience must compete with academic qualification. Although training courses pay some lip service to community and critical psychology, the role of such courses is to produce individually focussed practitioners rather than agents of social change. A programme with a social change agenda may struggle to maintain its funding.[8]

Clinical psychology courses in the UK retain many of the unquestioned features of the earliest training programmes. For example, trainees are expected to experience an ever burgeoning series of lecture topics squeezed into 1 day per week of a 3-year programme. The remainder of the working week is frequently devoted to practical experience of one-to-one therapy sessions. Here, trainees are exposed to the disciplinary nature of appointment diaries, are inducted into their role in the Gaze (Foucault 1975/1977) and must spend a considerable portion of their time coping with the proximal distress of strangers called either patients or clients (see Newnes, Hagan, & Cox, 2000). This might be contrasted with the critical psychiatry and psychology placements (internships) popular in Shropshire (see above).

Course content is slowly becoming more adventurous, if not actually critical. This is, in part, due to a change in the type of course director appointed. They are increasingly women and, unlike the first 30 years of training programme directors, have no connection with the course based at the Institute of Psychiatry; the Institute produced the majority of course directors between 1952 and 1980 (Dabbs & Newnes, 2000).

Critical praxis?

Within the Department, the majority of psychological therapists conducted themselves (at least in terms of what they said they did) along conservative lines. Quite reasonably, they wanted well-paid jobs to support their families that gave them the freedom to practise the mainstream therapies that had taken time, effort and money to learn. Variants of cognitive behavioural therapy (CBT), person-centred counselling and some psycho-dynamic notions were to the fore in many one-to-one meetings with patients. For some members of the Department, research was anathema, something to be practised elsewhere (in the Academy). Meanwhile, modernist (scientific) research was criticised in print (Newnes, 2004a) *and* used to establish essentially disciplinarian local services (Cureton & Newnes, 1995).

All patients were offered a degree of informed consent via a pre-appointment opt-in form and description of the therapist they would meet – one way of not developing a waiting list is to inform people of your limitations (Newnes, 1988). At a first meeting, patients were asked how they would describe a successful outcome to therapy. Despite this, for several years, only *one* local clinical psychologist actually published a piece on therapeutic outcome (Holmes, 2003). Departmental counsellors, however, had no resistance to completing outcome measures with patients – a position that could be read in many ways. Perhaps some felt obliged to comply due to the legitimate power of the hierarchy, perhaps some were intrigued. Even those just as capable as the clinical psychologists of critiquing the research methodology asked patients to complete the questionnaire.

Until recently in the UK state system, patients attending clinical psychology appointments were not routinely given access to personal files. Thus, incorrect factual information could easily remain unchecked for as long as files were held (even this is a grey area: various rules exist for the destruction of psychiatric and similar records, but I am unaware of anywhere which has a system in place for acting on the destruction policy). Ironically, the collection of files on deviant individuals is one area where the gaze is at its most inefficient – records are kept, but rarely read and frequently lost; rather like CCTV cameras, it only appears that Big Brother is watching. Whatever ultimately happens to those records, it is a condition of employment in the NHS that clinical psychologists record details of the patients seen and any assessments or treatment attempted. The BPS *Professional Practice Guidelines* (British Psychological Society, 1995) offer advice on the types of notes to be kept, security, confidentiality and more. In the United States, notes on diagnosis and treatment are used to form reports for insurance companies underwriting the costs. In a series of seminars on record keeping over some 15 years, I encouraged groups of clinical psychologists to discuss the advantages and disadvantages of such praxis. The latter have consistently outweighed the former even though all the participants (in the region of 500 practitioners) kept clinical notes; frequently, the justification was along the lines, "I think I have to." None of these practitioners knew how long such records were kept by their employers (Newnes, 1995). In the National Health Service (NHS), the electronic record has become synonymous with staff dissatisfaction as computer systems are found not to "talk" to each other, it is claimed that staff pay is based on patient contact (thus every contact is recorded) and staff find ways of recording even less information than in the original paper record. Here, the gaze is passed to unknown people who can access these records and check that professional staff are turning a disciplinary eye on patients.

These are not idle concerns. If assessments and accompanying diagnoses are held on record and made available to later staff who have no direct experience of the patient, those records will be used to add substance or detract from contemporary theorising about the patient's predicament. The written word has a tendency to be reified. A 10-year-old IQ assessment or Beck Depression Inventory score and subsequent diagnosis may be challenged, but as a critical practitioner may not be on hand to offer an alternative, the patient's mark will be used to justify fresh attempts to ameliorate the patient's so-called disorder.

And being personal . . .

For all its fetishising of "the individual," "Psy" is quietly taken aback when confronted with a personal approach to its subject matter. Articles published in mainstream journals in order to garner cultural capital should be referenced accordingly; unreferenced articles are rejected or dismissed as "personal opinion" (see my article on "References": Newnes, 1992b). Published articles using personal experience to illustrate factors in, for example, Psy service delivery, can be ignored as "unrepresentative" or heralded as "brave" (see Newnes, 2006).

For many, a personal style can promote a volume into the "must read" category. For me, David Smail's work exemplified this (e.g. Smail, 1978). Ian Parker remarks (reviewing in the *Journal of Critical Psychology, Counselling and Psychotherapy*) on how in *Inscription, Diagnosis and Deception in the Mental Health Industry: How Psy Governs Us All* (Newnes, 2016a), the chapter notes reporting on what music was listened to and which substances ingested while writing add a "sensuality" usually absent from Psy texts (for interested readers, I am drinking pastis and listening to *Manassas* [Manassas, 1972] while writing this paragraph[9]). Faith in the normally reified written word can, however, be challenged if readers grasp that a book review uses the well-known format to critique a *non-existent* book.[10]

Similarly, professional attendees at seminars are surprised when asked to keep their mobile phones switched *on* and less than sanguine in lectures which promote privileging ordinary acts of collaboration (giving money or rides in cars) over the latest therapy. In the context of formal teaching, this approach can be seen as arrogant rather than serious in intent. The humour can be lost altogether. Psy takes itself far too seriously to joke about itself, though there are numerous dry volumes devoted to the "Psychology of Humour." Yet, in 2006, during a review session by clinical psychology trainees summarising their views on the first semester's critical psychology teaching, the best (by popular acclaim) presentation was a video of three students rewording some of the teaching whilst in a bath and wearing snorkelling gear.

Professional psychology is not entirely devoid of humour. The *Journal of Polymorphous Perversity* first appeared in 1984. Its first article, "Psychotherapy of the dead," led the Freudians at the American Psychoanalytic Association at their annual convention to ban the publication on the basis that humour was "inappropriate" (Ellenbogen, 1992). Now defunct, the journal initially went from strength to strength and three anthologies appeared. They should be compulsory reading for Psy professionals. One article captures – all too painfully – the inherent demands of publication: the need to reference everything, the importance of quoting "great" psychologists (in this case, Frankl is selected at random) and the place of the footnote in credibility enhancement: "footnotes suggest that the author has penetrated some phenomenon more deeply than is reasonable to expect an ordinary reader to follow" (Gilbert, 1990, pp. 20–21).

My own CV includes humorous – it is hoped – (though profound) articles on references (Newnes, 1992b), diagnosis (Newnes, 2007a), a Derrida-style stab at what might be read/understood/meant through and by reading (Newnes, 2007b), group therapy for commuters on trains (Newnes, 1987) and the spaces between words (Newnes, 1998). A bibliography (Newnes, 1994a) of Psy publications all critical of the status quo appeared under the innocuous title "Bibliography I: Psychiatry" and was duly attacked in the correspondence pages of *Clinical Psychology Forum*. As an editor, it seemed incumbent on me to make my own position on language clear (another impossibility) via publication (see Baker & Newnes, 2005; Newnes, 1994b; Newnes, 1989). Even the title of my first published article was, at the time, risqué (Newnes, 1981) and my last had a certain alliterative appeal (Newnes, 2016b). I might add that this chapter includes image-enhancing references to Foucault and, crucially (*pace* Marshall [1996] – don't you just love the "*pace*"?), mention of the most recently feted demagogue, Žižek.

A few jokes and clever word play can be found in the final chapter of *Inscription, Diagnosis, Deception and the Mental Health Industry: How Psy Governs Us All* (Newnes, 2016a) but – as an ex-director of PCCS Books might say – "Craig is just showing off." Georges Perec wrote a memoir in which words containing the letter e never appear. Imagine a Psy text with no words with the letter p – no pathology, psychosis, phenothiazine, Stroop test, aptitude assessment, psychiatry or personality. As ever, references to the poor, passion and peace would be thin on the ground; there are some notable exceptions to this including the work of David Smail, some social and community psychologists (e.g. Newnes, 2011b; Holmes and Newnes, 2004), and Godsi's (2004) *Violence and Society*. Without the letter p, overnight the psychology of depression would become the sighchology of sadness.

Wittgenstein, however, claimed that, "A serious and good philosophical work could be written consisting entirely of jokes."[11] True to form, Slavoj Žižek (2014) duly produced a volume consisting of numerous jokes illustrating philosophical points of interest (to him). He can be found on YouTube reading from the book.[12]

Then . . .

A near-fatal road traffic accident in 2003 ultimately freed me from the proximal influences of structured employment (see Newnes, 2006). The demands of gardening and fatherhood came to the fore. My presentations, conference organisation and publication focussed more on critique of my own profession, clinical psychology and the barely plausible claims and theories of psychology itself. "Recovery" turned to discovery and, no doubt partly fuelled by a desire to focus on the real, the scientific illusions of the psy-disciplines have been readily deconstructed.

These presentations now include the ubiquitous PowerPoint slides; a form central to the disciplinary process which can simultaneously act as a reflexive tool for examining that process while ostensibly questioning Psy professionals' role. For example, one slide asks:

> Have any of your placement supervisors:
> - Routinely researched clinical outcomes for their own work?
> - Made integral links with local user and advocacy groups?
> - Suggested you read *Discipline and Punish, Germinal, The Human Comedy,* poetry, *Clinical Psychology: A critical examination* or *Insanity: The idea and its consequences*?
> - Regularly given examples of their own fears or mistakes?
> - Encouraged you to research and publish?
> - Handed you their waiting list?
> - Modelled research and publication?
> - Invited you to critique your clinical sessions from a position privileging race, sex and sexuality, income or class?
>
> *(Slide presented to final-year Liverpool Clinical Psychology Doctorate candidates, 2015)*

Another makes explicit the links between psychology and eugenics:

> - "Dullness seems to be racial – psychologists and their IQ tests are the beacon light of the eugenics movement." (Terman, 1924, p. 300)
> - "Our data indicate clearly the intellectual superiority of the Nordic race group." (Brigham, 1923, p. 192)
> - "[T]he vast majority of humans are obsolete, the earth will be choked with the more primitive forerunners unless a way is found to eliminate them – genthanasia." (Cattell, 1972, quoted in Mehler, 1997, p. 154)
>
> *(Slide presented to University of Stirling Critical Psychology Master's Degree students, April 2008 and various Clinical Psychology Doctoral programmes)*

In June 2012, my presentation included slides of comments requested from colleagues about the absence of any women speakers at the event – the launch of the East Anglian branch of the Division of Clinical Psychology:

> Dear audience the problem lies before you, gaze upon the representation of clinical psychology in the UK. Look around you, the world is gendered, our profession is gendered, the issues people present with are gendered – we cannot ignore the social structures which surround us, shape what we think and how we act but we do. The future of clinical psychology is dry, dusty and for me dead unless we put more effort into understanding what creates and maintains inequality and educating those in power positions to make more sensible decisions.
>
> *(Jan Burns, 12 June 2012)*

This last conference had featured the late Professor Mark Rapley, at the time undergoing treatment for cancer, as a fellow speaker. A year later, I organised a memorial conference for Mark, and at that event, offered a presentation in part based on discussions with my late friend. "Going mobile: The end of psychology" included a favourite quotation: "Psychology has yet to establish a *single* fact about human behaviour" (Beloff, 1973, p. 64).

At the memorial conference for David Smail, a slide proposed some new "Guerrilla tactics" (see Reicher, 1993):

- Develop shyness groups for people who are too assertive – bankers, chief executives, politicians, journalists, Psy professionals, etc.
- Picket leadership seminars.
- Follow employer guidelines *exactly* (on the assumption that monitoring systems are now so haphazard and disconnected that no time will remain for seeing patients if every updated computer recording scheme – with consequent training days – is routinely adopted and every *Health and Safety* course attended).

(Newnes, 2016c, p. 61)

The majority of presentations start with a review of the "wounds" to service recipients that clinical psychologists either actively participate in or say nothing publicly about.

- Rejection/exclusion, being moved, losing relationships, isolation/congregation, lacking security/control, being "marked", being confused with others, being poor, blamed, subject to case conferences, invaded without consent, referred without consent, denied help, given aversive or useless "treatments", being hidden in institutions, subjected to the gaze.

(Wolfensberger, 1987)

All presentations and several of my publications now include the following:

- Think small
- Be kind
- Share children's clothes/baby-sitting
- Celebrate achievement
- Encourage criticism
- Practise what you preach
- Seek allies
- Aim carefully.

In the context of the disciplinary endeavour, this brief list of recommendations is fraught with contradiction. Practising "what you preach" might imply partaking of a modernist therapy while also delivering it; "achievement" might include publishing an acritical account of that same therapy in a mainstream journal. I shall return to "contradiction" later.

Now . . .

Augustine declared that "now" cannot exist; by the time you have said the word, it is gone. We live in a kind of perpetual past with an unknown future – for all the attempts by existential therapies and pseudo-philosophical bumper stickers urging us to "grasp the present."

Shortly after my car accident, I was offered, and accepted, the CCHR International (Citizens Commission on Human Rights) Human Rights award for 20 years of speaking out about Psy (Newnes, 2001). Within months, a letter to *The Psychologist* reminded readers that CCHR is funded by Scientology, an organisation I had long thought extinct (having no television is one way of missing "news" about the antics of Tom Cruise). It was, in fact, my second award, having received the "Golden Sparkle" prize from a local psychiatric survivor group in 2002. The number of awards exactly matches the number of serious death threats of which I have been the beneficiary (see, for example, Newnes, 1990b); speaking out can be a risky business (Newnes, 2001).

A life-time of work (starting aged eight – see Newnes, 2014) has led to what some find as an exhaustion-by-proxy degree of discipline in my own life. Subsequent to the road traffic accident, I was assessed for a new work station at home as I couldn't easily travel to the office – buses are not wheelchair-friendly; two push-chairs and one wheelchair make a sacrifice inevitable. The assessment concluded that I worked 75 hours per week in my director role. Had all that teaching and discipline made a difference? I was away from the position of Director of Psychological Therapies for 9 months. A patient arriving for an early January appointment to find me absent assumed I was dead – I hadn't been late once for sometimes thrice-weekly consultations in 12 years. Another visited me – comatose – in hospital. The work of the Department continued. Some colleagues and supervisees came to take me out to disability-friendly pubs, others just carried on. The Staffordshire Doctoral Course moved seamlessly towards incorporating CBT in its programme despite a first semester that had denied the *possibility* of CBT. The teaching stopped for a year – I was learning the nature of irrelevance.

Having spoken at over half the Clinical Psychology programmes in the UK over the years, invitations are now, at best, annual: clinical psychologists want a guide as to how to survive discussions with patients where they must pretend to expertise, not an examination of the power inequalities inherent in disciplinary praxis offered by myself and a dwindling band of others.

A deconstructive turn has led to some presentations where I attempt to deconstruct my own writing (see Newnes, 2016c and the final sentence in Newnes, 2014). For the Liverpool Doctoral Programme in 2015, I attempted to deconstruct a paper that the more critically inclined students had much admired (see Newnes, 2004b). This seems an exercise so clearly anti-hubristic that it was, in itself, hubristic, not unlike the so-called "reflective diaries" on which trainees are now *assessed* (a more explicit example of disciplinary praxis would be hard to find).

Since 2004, I have conducted writing seminars. The aim has been to enable Psy professionals to publish their work. Whether such work *should* be published is a moot point – in the UK, state-employed clinical psychologists are contracted to research and publish. Although the median publication rate for this branch of Psy remains at zero, the seminars have been designed to buck the trend (Newnes, Blofield, & Morris, 2005; Newnes & Jones, 2005; Newnes, 2004c).

As Editor of *Clinical Psychology Forum* (for a time rebranded as *Clinical Psychology*), the job was to edit and publish accounts of the current state of the profession. This was problematic in several ways. Calling ourselves a collective rather than a board raised many objections from the then Division of Clinical Psychology (DCP) committee, a group that had already threatened censoring editorial freedom after an article criticising the profession for the absence of any criticism of electroconvulsive therapy (Newnes, 1991). The committee disputed the quality of the published articles; the publication wasn't scientific (in the committee's terms, scientific) enough. In fact, few articles were written in a non-scientific way and most were based on local projects where the author(s) failed to note the importance of context. Despite this, the committee was embarrassed at the lack of modernist science in the finished product and concerned that the journal gave an unfavourable (though accurate) picture of the state of the profession.

Editorship placed the Editor in the (un)enviable position of keeping abreast of developments in a profession for which he had little sympathy, but did offer the opportunity to understand the editorial and writing process. The writing seminars thus were examples of the use of legitimate power (French & Raven, 1959). Simultaneously, editorship of *The Journal of Critical Psychology, Counselling and Psychotherapy* and both the Critical Psychology Division series and Critical Examination series for PCCS Books continues to enable me to (a) earn money, (b) appreciate the efforts of some Psy professionals to escape the disciplinary project (though, for them, like me, they may find that, in Leonard Cohen's terms, the disciplinary project "sentenced me to twenty years of boredom for trying to change the system from within" [Cohen, 1988]). Further, commissioning special issues that add some balance to scientistic and professional rhetoric has not been demanding.[13]

Power, teaching and coherence

> We are what we pretend to be, so we must be careful about what we pretend to be.
> (Vonnegut, 1961/1979, p. vii)

Teachers, therapists, experts, all of us, pretend. Politicians, at the mercy of the press, have pretentions stripped away on a daily basis. None of us can know if such public revelation makes politicians (or anyone else within the panopticon) *bad*, as badness, like goodness, is in the eye of the behold*en*.

French and Raven (1959), in examining social power, found referent power (i.e. the perception that the other person is essentially similar to you in status or culture) as the most influential. Undeniably, for psychiatric patients, reward power and the legitimate power of authority are vested in the consultant's ability to discharge the patient, but in day-to-day life on the wards, referent power is key; hence the influence of domestic staff of a similar cultural or social background to patients.

For teachers, reward and legitimate power are inherent in the role. The simple fact that a lecturer, PowerPoint prepared, is standing in front of an audience gives the lecturer some credibility. Within the Academy, power is enhanced if the lecturer is also an examiner or supervisor. Whatever the ups and downs of referent power in such sessions, legitimate power is assured.

What we do and describing what we do are processes dictated by proximal and distal power, an idea that led to the development of power-mapping (Hagan & Smail, 1997).[14] Proximal power refers to immediate influences. In the case of a patient, such influence might be the presence of a professional deemed an expert with the power to diagnose, prescribe, incarcerate, allow access to financial and other help or interpret what the patient says from an authoritative position implying insight. For the professional, the proximal power of the patient can range from describing experiences to which the professional cannot personally relate, to more physically present factors like size, gender, race and class or an earnings differential.

The proximal power of a lecturer may be enhanced or undermined by appearance; as with patients, however, it is unknown how a lecture group will react to hair style, clothing, height, etc. In offering proposed objectives for teaching sessions during the 1990s, I would sometimes suggest that students might "Learn that lecturers may still be sensible despite wearing leather trousers." Course directors were, generally, not amused. But, in teaching, "The thing you gotta know is, everything is show-biz" (Brooks, Sanger, & Stroman, 2005).

Style (within the parameters set by "professionalism") is important (leather trousers excepted). At a departmental conference organised by Helen Jones at the Lilleshall Sports Complex, Professor Steve Baldwin memorably used PowerPoint to include animation and photographs. Asking questions of the audience like "Who is this?" Steve showed pictures of, amongst others, Bini and Cerletti (see Newnes, 2016a, Chapter 5). His style of response to some younger trainees was equally memorable: polite and invariably starting with, "I'm glad you asked that," or, "Good point," Steve would return to his theme (a searing critique of biological psychiatry) as if the questions were planned in advance. His technique echoed the way Scientologists are advised to smile and deflect if they are challenged, a style Tom Cruise has yet to master.

Might the ways in which teaching, management, research, writing and clinical work are outlined above be described in terms of a coherent strategy? Integrating recommended reading – particularly when the recommended texts are the lecturer's own – within lecture series is one way in which Psy professionals garner cultural capital. The *fact* of publication adds legitimacy to whatever is being presented.

For local seminars, the provision of a library featuring numerous critical volumes added to a sense that some kind of "stand" was being made. The process of teaching, however, might be regarded as acritical, even formulaic. As a disciplinary praxis, that process included many disciplinary turns; the "expert" lecturer and students and trained professionals are expected to *listen* as well as question and otherwise participate. There were no examinations, but there was the inevitable attendance register. Doctoral trainees participating in the first semester's programme were expected to produce essays for *assessment* and, if involved in research, produce articles for submission to peer-reviewed journals. The academic gaze was in place.

The proximal influence of the students comes, in part, from lecturers having an idea of the audience's expectations. This power is increased if lecturers are concerned about student response. Students are simultaneously pressed by other proximal influences – from hangovers to the need to meet with a colleague during the break. For the lecturer, proximal power is enhanced if she or he has some grasp of the subject matter and ways of *engaging* the audience. In my own case, legitimate and reward power for some came from being positioned as a grandee within the profession and a potential employer.[15] In this context, *finding* referent power is more difficult; we may be wise and "successful," but we are *old* and Psy professional audiences are no less ageist than the general population. Being officially disabled, however, brings with it a certain respect from professional audiences and referent power with service recipient groups.

The nature of the teaching venue is often ignored. Rooms are used because they are free, available, reasonably well heated and big enough. Many of the Shropshire courses used the Gateway learning centre close to Shrewsbury railway station, a venue valued by the community, wheelchair-friendly and not associated with health services. Thirty years ago at Westminster Hall, Dorothy Rowe talked to an audience of some 800 people, half of whom watched her talk relayed by video to an upstairs room away from the main lecture theatre. In the 1970s, a friend, Diane Weissman, attended lectures during the University of Chicago undergraduate psychology course based at Champaign, Illinois, where over 1000 sophomores watched speakers on closed-circuit television because the lecture theatre seated fewer than 300.[16] The size of many cohorts for undergraduate psychology degrees now makes electronic transmission of lectures inevitable and students can watch replays at their leisure.

Television, and now YouTube, are positioned as educational media. Television has presented the Open University for 40 years. *Ouch*, a monthly Internet radio and blog service, reports that since 2010 many young people inscribed as disabled have used videos and interviews broadcast on YouTube. The format is the same – someone talking into a camera about what life is like for a young disabled person. The "share" facility on the BBC News page allows reports of the various posts (from the UK to Australia) to be accessed on Twitter and Facebook accounts (Hawkins, 2015).

The web is a rich source of conflicting "educative" material. For every statement criticising Psy and its products, there are dozens supporting a modernist and scientistic position. There are, for example, 6000 websites critical of Psy in the United States and numerous Facebook groups (e.g. The Network Against Psychiatric Assault). TED Talks on Psy are presented as fact (with various celebrities queueing up to come out as "bi-polar" or "depressed"), and on YouTube you can learn how to starve yourself or cut yourself without doing too much damage.

The resources at Psy's disposal ensure a constant diet of educational material conducive to the profit motive. The *Psychiatric Times*, for example, appears daily, replete with "breakthroughs," "advances" and other motifs replaying the psychiatric credo. A recent phenomenon is the suggestion of "spectrum" disorders, now to include schizophrenia.[17] A "special report" from the *Psychiatric Times* on advances in schizophrenia spectrum treatment advises that the writer is "Clinical Professor, Psychiatry and Behavioral Sciences, Stanford Medicine, Stanford, CA," and, "He reports no conflicts of interest concerning the subject matter of this Special Report." The notion of conflict of interest is usually employed to mean no financial conflict. The notion of *no* conflict of interest, however, would elevate professionals to sainthood.

The physical context of learning is ignored; the audience participation and reflective critique possible in small university lecture theatres is not reproducible watching a documentary in your own sitting room or bedroom. The proximal influences for trainee clinical psychologists attending lectures are different from those experiencing the regular interruption of TV shows by children wanting something from the fridge or dogs demanding to be walked. The filmed lecturer is influenced by the presence of cameras and lights in a way distinct from the proximal influence of an audience of possibly familiar trainees or fellow professionals.

An immediate proximal influence for clinical psychology trainees is the pressure of meetings arranged in between lectures – frequently at the supposed lunch break. This is mirrored for staff in schools and universities and part of a pattern of work to be found everywhere from banks to boardrooms. Professionals, like business people, are inducted into a system of discipline where notional times for relaxing or eating are replaced by meetings or the "work" of getting to the gym or shopping for the evening meal. As a worker at both Birds Eye and a rope factory, I was expected to punch a clocking-in card. The physical demands of the jobs made voluntarily giving up break times unlikely. Now, "zero-hour" contracts for shop workers mean that someone may be told to work through a break or stay on "after" work to pack shelves or clean the store. For universities, an ever expanding demand to include more and more lectures is used as justification for both staff and students to forego breaks. In addition to whatever learning occurs during lectures, what is being taught is the *nature* of professional working life; that is, effortful praxis. The Gobelins school timetable has now expanded to include events that invoke *self*-discipline beyond the prospectus.

Teaching is thus a political enterprise, an aspect of Psy praxis made explicit by some critical thinkers. What, why and how teaching is offered often sits within a predominantly white, Northern Hemispheric, explicitly deterministic frame. Burton (2013) has remarked that it is very difficult – if not contextually impossible – to import critical Psy from, for example, Latin America. Psy trainees and practitioners may find the importance of language and context powerfully persuasive, but they are practising as therapists, not politicians. And they are constrained and influenced by the same proximal and distal powers as their patients, patients who present distress rather than an obvious need for politicisation. Holland's work in the 1970s is an example of enabling people to move from an individual position of immediate distress to a politicised collectivist stance. Her work stands out because it is *unusual* (Holland, 1992).

And next . . . entertainment

How might legitimate power be affected by falsehood? Psy lecturers face inevitable accusations of at least bad faith, if not dishonesty. Promoting a particular form of therapy may involve citing research disproving the efficacy of other therapies with no acknowledgement of the difficulty of researching relationships, the vested interest of researchers or, ironically in a discipline devoted to the importance of the individual subject, the uniqueness of every therapeutic encounter. Such uniqueness should point to the impossibility of replication in therapy studies. An inherent contradiction in this chapter is the revelation that I have published reviews on non-existent books. Does it matter? For Pessoa, a writer (or writers) who invented many identities (heteronyms) with complete biographies (Pessoa, 2001), probably not. Can the reader believe what I write? I was once asked my age at a job interview because the interviewing psychiatrist could not accept the extent of my curriculum vitae, and that was over 30 years ago; before much of the teaching and writing practice outlined above and in the references below. Perhaps it is all invention.

A second contradiction is the impossibility of understanding analysology (Fryer & Easpaig, 2013). For a therapist bound to highlight certain motifs during a consultation or a trainee assessed via a reflective diary, the subject (therapist/trainee) cannot *stand outside* their subjectivity in order to grasp why this or that motif or aspect of the session is privileged. An analysis of this chapter in terms of distal influence is equally difficult. Why teach or write at all? Is it relevant that I had an uncle who taught arts and wrote a well-received adventure yarn about pirates (Symonds, 1960)? Four great aunts were also teachers at a time when the choice for women was between marriage, service or teaching. My father, a factory employee, had a deep suspicion of the idle middle classes; a category that included hard-pressed teachers. Perhaps my qualifications and professional trajectory are teenage rebelliousness. Does it matter that I still remember the name of a primary school headmaster (Mr. Etheridge) because he said I could write? Is there distal power at work that means I highlight family history rather than other factors? Do I think teaching or writing makes a *difference* and if I do, do I *want* to make a difference?

Four possibilities as "explanation" for working as a lecturer and author come to mind. The first, money, holds water as a good enough reason to be a professional – though hardly justification for adding teaching and publication to the burden of clinical work and management. The second is familial; expected to become either a doctor or a rabbi, I became something of both. The third? Well, you have to do *something*. And teaching and learning are reciprocal processes. To stop learning is to die. Last, I seem to have known some extraordinary teachers.

My own training included supervision with Freudian and Horneyan analysts, *the* leading Personal Construct Therapist (Dottie Rowe – G-d bless her), the Cardiff Family Institute, the Institute of Group Analysis, the Boston Psychoanalytic Society and Institute, a PASS course sponsored by CMHERA (Community and Mental Handicap Research Association), a Master's degree in Psychopathology, Doctorates in Clinical Psychology and History and a psychodrama training courtesy of Marcia Karp (a disciple of Zerka Moreno, wife of the founder of psychodrama). Was I learning? I understood that some lecturers could be inspiring while being funny, others could be dull as ditch-water (possibly with something to say, but who knows?) and some "supervisors" could be silent for weeks on end. Wolfensberger taught that any teaching concerning the distantiated should start with their service wounds – a lesson that back-fired when leading a Normalisation seminar at my local psychiatric hospital in Shelton (an early base for the Psychology Consultancy Service, renamed later as the Department of Psychological Therapies) in the late 1980s; it's not a good idea to inform psychiatric nurses that they are responsible for killing patients. The teaching (style and content) of these experiences saturated my life – from lecturing to protesting about disabled facilities on buses. Then, a near-fatal road accident taught me that recovery is in the eye of the beholder and life for disabled folk can be terrible – we are disabled by society's need for speed, not our intrinsic difficulties.

After one of the gorier scenes about halfway through the film *Gladiator* (Scott, 2000), Maximus, appalled at the bloodthirstiness of the baying crowd, angrily yells, "Are you not *entertained*?" The circus master is quick to put him right, pointing out that if he is to get back to Rome as a gladiator, then he must get the audience on his side.

The concept of entertainment brings a certain distance to proceedings. For those that suffer at the hands of well-meaning professionals, Psy treatment is far from entertaining, but for those same professionals arguing about the causes of suffering and means to alleviate it, it is a well-paid and frequently intellectually stimulating activity. Blogs, websites and Facebook groups evidence the depth of self-interest involved. Similarly, mass media provide opportunities to debate, ridicule or provoke. I am on a continuous DVD loop at a Los Angeles Human Rights museum discussing the barbaric and eugenic legacy of Nazi psychiatry. It is tempting to ask viewers, "Are you not *entertained*?" Facebook has an anonymously authored page (Psylies) that uses (steals) quotations from my work in a consciously entertaining way. The page "is about how we are all complicit in the bamboozlement of everyone by Psy, its professionals and its links to business and governmentality."

For some, the idea of teaching as entertainment is nihilistic. After all, audiences may expect to *learn* something relevant to the subject at hand and a lecturer who simply told jokes, despite the best efforts of Žižek, would certainly have to *be* Žižek to get away with it.

For me, approaching a teaching session doesn't seem to have changed a great deal and isn't so different from how I approached being taught, the numerous meetings I had when designated a therapist or, perhaps, life itself. Amidst the supposed goals of education and therapy, there remains a bottom line – to survive. Whichever "self" predominates in my "community of selves" (Mair, 1977), the one which stands out – as evidenced by how I feel after performing any given professional role – is the one that can say, in retrospect, "I made it – again." Perhaps it's the same child who couldn't wait to get out of primary school classes in order to play football (unless they were sports classes). This kind of reflection is not encouraged by schools of education or therapy. There is a "by your fingertips" element to it that goes against praxis dominated by ideas of control and discipline. "Targets," "learning objectives" and "therapy goals" all become subsumed within a kind of existential dread: "Will I be found wanting?"; "Will I be liked?"; "Will I be discovered to be fraudulent?"

Such preoccupations don't seem to diminish with time or experience. As I write this (in a warm study with Humble Pie's *Performance: Rockin' the Fillmore* [1971] in the background), I am aware of a day's teaching coming up in a couple of weeks. Thirty clinical psychology Doctoral trainees have received a couple of papers and a print-out of a PowerPoint presentation to read in advance and have been asked a question: "What do you particularly want to learn from the session?" Perhaps, like me, they haven't considered the question. Perhaps they just want to survive the day in a relatively convivial atmosphere and go about their business. It seems unlikely that trainees learn much from lectures and seminars that will be of any practical value when sitting with patients. Learning about consultancy or therapy is, rather, an absorption of a certain style and the kinds of things to say. These aspects come from reading, supervision or personal therapy. Mythic ideas about "typical" consultants (possibly funny and wise stereotypes) or therapists (the controlling cognitivist, the laid-back humanist, the bespectacled analyst) are as likely to come from television or YouTube as from a one-off seminar or series of lectures on any particular aspect of Psy. And if one can manage to survive a day's teaching or an hour's therapy, perhaps the sense of relief says more about the purpose of that teaching or therapy than any prescribed targets or goals. The money helps; and for UK clinical psychology trainees paid £20,000 annually, enjoyable or thought-provoking talks must be something of a bonus.

So-called feedback questionnaires give some idea of the consensus around the purpose of post-graduate education. "Feedback" was a term originally used to describe a particular process in inorganic, often electrical systems (Bertalanffy, 1968). For 50 years, it has been used as a term describing the process whereby we let people know what we think of their efforts. Frequently the process is *via* electronic means, but no longer *part* of electronic systems. The system used at Liverpool is Qualtrics and an email from the Programme Administrator informs prospective speakers that, "In recent years trainee completion of feedback has been low, however, we are mindful that the majority of teachers find feedback useful," and, "In order to maximise completion of the feedback we would be grateful if you could remind trainees at the end of the session to complete the feedback through the online system." In what way feedback is found to be "useful" isn't explained; many lecturers are invited back a full year later to talk with a different audience. The feedback is another incarnation of the gaze as course organisers only look at extremes, inviting back those who score well and refusing to issue return invitations to those who do poorly (Golding, 2017).

Full circle

In the interests of closing the loop, readers might like to refer back to the first paragraph to help make sense of this last section. I now know something of the sub-discipline of critical psychology (Newnes, 1997; Newnes, 1996). Critical psychology is, however, caught in the same disciplinary nexus as other aspects of Psy. Courtesy of two of my children, I know a good deal more about 'A' level psychology, a subject that shamelessly inducts young people into a world of guesses disguised as knowledge and theories presented as facts. The fact that about 20% of the students are seeing counsellors or taking psychoactive medication adds a certain irony to their lecturers' claims that psychology can be "objective." My children have also helped me dispense with Piaget (for a more considered critique of Piaget, see Newnes, 2016a); any reader interested in the work of Gesell as an element of governmentality is directed to Rose (1989). Six children later, I still know that parenting is tiring and have, at various times, helped each of them off to sleep or driven them to hospital. Temper tantrums? Vodka helps enormously. ADHD? Just another diagnosis beginning with the letter A (Newnes, 2016b). The loop is closed, the last paragraph almost coherent. Are you not entertained?

Dedication

This chapter is dedicated to Guy Holmes who taught alongside me many times and who has the distinction of being the *first* guest lecturer on the Birmingham Clinical Psychology Doctoral Programme some 30-odd years after its foundation to mention the C word – capitalism.

Notes

1 Death-making – the idea that treatment of distressed and "marked" individuals is designed to kill either the body or the spirit (or both) under the guise of aid. Wolfensberger saw this as a largely unconscious process; though there are practitioners who set out to harm, one should hope that the majority espouse more charitable motivations. See: Wolfensberger, W. (1987); and "The service wounds," Chapter 2 of Newnes, C. (2016a).
2 See: Newnes, C. (2001) Clinical psychology, user involvement and advocacy. *Clinical Psychology Forum, 150*, 18–22; Newnes, C. (2001) The commitments? Advocacy and clinical psychology. *Openmind, 107*, 14–15; Goodwin, I., Holmes, G., Newnes, C., & Waltho, D. (1999) A qualitative analysis of the views of inpatient mental health

service users. *Journal of Mental Health*, 8(1), 43–54; Holmes, G., Dawson, O., Waltho, D., Beaty, J., & Newnes, C. (1998) User views of two psychiatric day hospitals. *Psychiatric Bulletin*, 22, 362–364; Newnes, C. & Shalan, D. (1997) Fear and loathing in patients' council visitors. *Clinical Psychology Forum*, 110, 10–12; Booth, H., Cushway, D., & Newnes, C. (1997) Counselling in general practice: Clients' perceptions of significant events and outcome. *Counselling Psychology Quarterly*, 10(2), 175–187; Trinder, H., Mitchell, S.A., Newnes, C., & Todd, L. M-K. (1994) Valuing patient feedback II: Shelton Hospital's rehabilitation wards. *Clinical Psychology Forum*, 74, 21–25; Williams, A., Harris, K., & Newnes, C. (1994) The patients' council: Shelton Hospital. *Clinical Psychology Forum*, 73, 30–32; Turner, I. & Newnes, C. (1993) Inpatient views of the service at Shelton psychiatric hospital. *Clinical Psychology Forum*, 56, 23–29; Bond, J., Newnes, C., & Mooniaruch, F. (1992) User views of the inpatient psychiatric service at Shelton Hospital. *Clinical Psychology Forum*, 49, 21–26.

3   European Network of (ex-)Users and Survivors of Psychiatry (http://enusp.org). The webmaster was originally Peter Lehmann, publisher, writer and survivor. The site includes articles, links, commentaries and information generated by survivors on the various iatrogenic effects of psychiatry. The information appears in over 50 languages. The translations are provided by survivor activists around the world: one of my own contributions appeared in Japanese, Arabic and Finnish within days of it being posted.

4   *Conferences/courses/seminars organised and facilitated:* I can see for miles: Memorial conference for Prof. Mark Rapley (UEL, 2013); Prescribing rights for non-medical staff (Belfast, 2005; Leicester, 2005); Writing for publication (Shropshire PCT and Stafford Foundation Trust, 2004–2005); Society and context (Clinical Psychology Doctorate, Keele/Stafford, 2004–2005); Mental health awareness and occupational stress (Shropshire HA, 2001); The artist practitioner (Birmingham Clinical Doctorate, 2002–2003); How does clinical psychology harm people? (Bangor Clinical Course, 2005; Leicester Clinical Course, 1993; Birmingham Clinical Doctorate, 1995– 2003; SE Thames CP course, 1999–2001; N Thames course, 1999, 2000; Queens University, Belfast course, 2001; Liverpool Doctorate, 1998–2001); Thinking about psychiatry (Shropshire Community and Mental Health Services Trust [CaMHT], 22 seminars, 1997); Dilemmas in professional relationships (1995, 1996); Empowerment and de-institutionalisation (Shropshire Social Services, 1992–1995); Alternatives to psychiatry (Shropshire CaMHT, 20 seminars, 1993); Clinical psychology and the NHS (DCP Study day, 1993); Hurt, harm and clinical psychology (DCP/BPS Conference, 1993); Group theory and practice (1992, 1993); What is mental health? (1991, 1992, 1993); Gender issues and mental health (Shropshire Social Services 1992, 1993); Advocacy in action (Regional Study day, 1992); The seven deadly sins (Shropshire MHS, 1992); Handling waiting lists (Mersey Region, 1992); Daring to be human despite professional training (PPA Conference, 1992); Making people listen (Introduction to advocacy study day, 1991); Death and dying (PPA Conference, 1990). Seminars organised also include: User empowerment; Values in services to adults and elderly people; How services harm people; Sloth; Breaking bad news; De-institutionalisation; The history of psychiatry, etc.

5   See: Newnes, C. (2016a). Newnes, C. (Ed.) (2015) *Children in society: Politics, policies and interventions*. Ross on Wye, UK: PCCS Books. Newnes, C. (2014). Newnes, C., & Radcliffe, N. (Eds.) (2005) *Making and breaking children's lives*. Ross on Wye, UK: PCCS Books. King-Spooner, S., & Newnes, C. (Eds.) (2001) *Spirituality and psychotherapy*. Ross on Wye, UK: PCCS Books. Newnes, C., Holmes, G., & Dunn, C. (Eds.) (2001) *This is madness too: A further critical look at mental health services*. Ross on Wye, UK: PCCS Books. Newnes, C., Holmes, G., & Dunn, C. (1999) *This is madness: A critical look at psychiatry and the future of mental health services*. Ross on Wye, UK: PCCS Books. Newnes, C.D. (Ed.) (1991) *Death, dying and society*. Hove, UK: Lawrence Erlbaum Associates.

Commissioned volumes: Smail, D. (2005) *Power, interest and psychology.* Ross on Wye, UK: PCCS Books. Lynch, T. (2004) *Beyond Prozac: Healing mental distress.* Ross on Wye,

UK: PCCS Books. Godsi, E. (2004). Hansen, S., McHoul, A., & Rapley, M. (2003) *Beyond help: A consumers' guide to psychology*. Ross on Wye, UK: PCCS Books. Joseph, J. (2003) *The gene illusion: Genetic research in psychiatry and psychology under the microscope*. Ross on Wye, UK: PCCS Books. Chadwick, P. (2003) *Personality as art; Artistic approaches in psychology*. Ross on Wye, UK: PCCS Books.

Book chapters: Newnes, C. (2015) Children and childhood constructed. In. C. Newnes (Ed.), *Children in society: Politics, policies and interventions*. Monmouth, UK: PCCS Books. Newnes, C. (2015) Children and electroconvulsive therapy. In. C. Newnes (Ed.), *Children in society: Politics, policies and interventions*. Monmouth, UK: PCCS Books. Newnes, C. (2014) The Diagnostic and Statistical Manual: A history of critiques of psychiatric classification systems. In J. Moncrieff, J. Dillon, & E. Speed (Eds.), *Demedicalising misery II*. Basingstoke, UK: Palgrave Macmillan. Newnes, C. (2011) Toxic psychology. In M. Rapley, J. Moncrieff, & J. Dillon (Eds.), *Demedicalising misery*. Basingstoke, UK: Palgrave Macmillan. Newnes, C. (2010) Ilusion, individuality and autonomy. In P.J. Barker (Ed.), *Mental health ethics: The human context*. London: Routledge. Newnes, C. (2009) Clinical psychology and ADHD. In S. Timimi & J. Leo (Eds.), *Rethinking ADHD: From brain to culture*. London: Palgrave Macmillan.

6 Other courses offered included: Counselling and psychotherapy (Shropshire HA 1-Year Course, 1991–1996); Psychology for General Practitioners (Shropshire GP Scheme, 1991); Group psychotherapy (Mersey Clinical Psychology Doctoral Course, 1989, 1990, 1991); Systems theory (Oxford Clinical Course, 1989); Psychology for GP trainees (Macclesfield GP Trainee Course, 1989; Shropshire GP Scheme, 1993–1997).

Seminars organised also included: Psychotherapy and counselling; Basic counselling skills; Getting published; Service quality; Normalisation; Group and family therapy; Psychology for medical trainees; Burnout; Organisational change; Alcohol use and abuse; Systems theory; Facilitating management; Organisational stress; Time management; Stress management; Negotiating skills; Complaints; Psychiatric rehabilitation services.

7 The widening expert gaze before the First World War set the context for the establishment of child guidance clinics in the 1920s and the emerging disciplines of child, educational and developmental psychology. All three were boosted by the advent of the Second World War and the opportunity to study the effects of evacuation from the major English cities of nearly one million unaccompanied children and half a million mothers with pre-school children to non-industrial areas less likely to be bombed. These studies led to John Bowlby's theory of attachment. The combination of Psy theory and increasing guilt in mothers has led to a current praxis where the original intention that play groups would free up busy mums to have a break or go out to work instead has been replaced by monitoring of the parents and a disciplinary endeavour reminiscent of the Gobelins school – this time with children aged from 2 years upwards.

8 It is hard to understand why the University of Stirling closed a profitable Master's programme in the sub-discipline (see Chapter 1, this volume); what did the administration think was going to happen, world revolution?

9 Much of this chapter was written in France – complete with pastis and the occasional cigarillo. For breaks, I have maintained a DVD habit – Michael Caine in *The Eagle Has Landed* and *Half Moon Street* (based on Paul Theroux's novel, *Doctor Slaughter*), *Delicatessen*, and the Laurence Fishburne (2005) version of *Assault on Precinct 13*. No doubt by its end, I shall have watched, for the umpteenth time, *Knight and Day* (with Tom Cruise – ha!). I also have *France Musique* in the background and occasionally mute the radio in preference for the last Sandghosts' CD – if I believed in the "self," this chapter might, perhaps, be better entitled "Advertisements for Myself" (Mailer, 1992).

10 Examples of reviews of non-existent books include Newnes, C. (2014) Review of D. Green and K. Green (2013) *Book reviewing: A guide for reviewers*, in *The Journal of Critical Psychology, Counselling and Psychotherapy*, 14(1), 58–59; and Newnes, C. (2016) Review of Andy Lied (Ed.) (2016) *A thousand psychology books you shouldn't read before you*

die, in *The Journal of Critical Psychology, Counselling and Psychotherapy, 16*(1), 74–75. The non-existence of the volumes under review neither prevented the reviews including valid discussion, nor journal readers enquiring why the books weren't available via Amazon. The tendency to reify concepts within Psy can be traced to Freud's use of a tri-partite division of the mind. It is generally ignored that the impulse for tri-partite schema from id, ego and superego to cognitions, emotions and behaviour had already been established in Germany during the nineteenth century (Richards, 1992). Freud, however, believed that the id would eventually be discovered as a part of the primitive brain rather than concluding that the idea originated in his own teaching at his rabbi grandfather's knee (see Berke, 2015). Reification can, however, become absurd: asked where "love" was located in the brain, one neuropsychologist in a group of qualified clinical psychologists once confidently responded, "In the pineal gland." When asked to define "love," the group offered five different definitions. The pineal gland has a lot to answer for. Reification works because it can be useful; one intellectually lazy, but simple way to "explain" war is the notion of a death instinct. Explanations that include the arbitrary concept of "nation" or the profit agenda of the arms industry are readily available to the majority, but explanations based on political or macro-economic theory do not suit the vested interest of the Psy industry.

11 Ludwig Wittgenstein, as quoted in "A view from the asylum" in Dribble, H. (2004) *Philosophical investigations from the sanctity of the press*, iUniverse, p. 87.

12 Slavoj Žižek's jokes. Retrieved 20 November 2016 from www.youtube.com/watch?v=rLKYOb1xS3c

13 Newnes, C. (Ed.) (2001) Involving service users. Special issue: *Clinical Psychology Forum, 150*; Newnes, C. (1996) Schizophrenia. Special issue: *Changes: An International Journal of Psychology and Psychotherapy, 14*(1); Newnes, C. (1992) Morality and method III. Special issue: *Changes: An International Journal of Psychology and Psychotherapy, 10*(2); Marzillier, J. & Newnes, C.D. (1991) Morality and method II. Special issue: *Changes: An International Journal of Psychology and Psychotherapy, 9*(4); Marzillier, J. & Newnes, C.D. (1991) Morality and method I. Special issue: *Changes: An International Journal of Psychology and Psychotherapy, 9*(2); Barkham, M. & Newnes, C. (1995) Outcome in psychotherapy. Special issue: *Changes: An International Journal of Psychology and Psychotherapy, 13*(2); Newnes, C.D. (1990) The harm that services do. Special issue: *Changes: An International Journal of Psychology and Psychotherapy, 8*(1); Newnes, C.D. (1989) Gender issues. Special issue: *Clinical Psychology Forum, 22*; Newnes, C.D. (1989) Politics. Special issue: *Clinical Psychology Forum, 20*; Newnes, C.D. (1988) Developing community services. Special issue: *Clinical Psychology Forum, 16*.

14 Power-mapping can be subjected to the criticism that those involved, subject to similar distal powers (culture, the macro-economy, etc.) are still responding to the proximal power of each other. The distal power behind the "expert" in the room makes it likely (though not inevitable) that the expert analysis will be privileged.

15 *Legitimate and reward power:* Director of Psychological Therapies, Shropshire County PCT, including responsibility for the Psychology Consultancy Service, Staff Counselling Service, GP Personal Therapy and Support Service, Eating Distress Service, Centres for Psychological Therapy (Chaddeslode and Dawley), Mental Health Liaison Service, Prison In-reach and Primary Care Counselling Service, a total of 85 staff. Vice-chair, Patient Council Support Group; Supervisor and Honorary Lecturer, University of Birmingham; Supervisor, Keele, Surrey, Staffordshire and Liverpool universities; Director responsible for www.shropsych.org; Module co-ordinator and co-founder, Staffordshire Doctorate in Clinical Psychology. Professionally, I was a member of the Division of Clinical Psychology National Committee, a member of the Psychology and Psychotherapy Association National Committee and ex-chair of the Psychotherapy Section of the British Psychological Society. Also, Editorial Board member of the journal *Ethical Human Sciences and Services*.

16 This kind of public speaking spectacle began with Dickens, who read and performed his oeuvre to hundreds in specially hired halls. His first readings were for charity, beginning with two performances of *A Christmas Carol* before a crowd of 2000 working-class people in Birmingham. The author turned professional performer in 1858. Almost a decade later, between December 1867 and April 1868, he earned over £19,000 (the equivalent of £855,000), far more than he was earning from his published works. The comparison holds true today – former prime minister Tony Blair is paid considerably more for his lecturing than he receives from his various memoirs, and bands such as U2 earn more from touring than music sales.

17 Advances in schizophrenia in 2016, *Psychiatric Times*, 11 November. Retrieved from www.psychiatrictimes.com/schizophrenia/advances-schizophrenia-2016?GUID=E7BD9D7E-A63B-41ED-A97F-34FCBFAAE3D6&rememberme=1&ts=29112016

References

Baker, E., & Newnes, C. (2005). What do we mean when we ask people to take responsibility? *Forensic Psychology Update, 80*, 23–27.

Baker, E., Newnes, C., & Myatt, H. (2003). Drug companies and clinical psychology. *Ethical Human Sciences and Services, 5*(3), 247–254.

Beloff, J. (1973). *Psychological sciences.* London: Staples.

Berke, J.H. (2015). *The hidden Freud: His Hassidic roots.* London: Karnac Books.

Bertalanffy, L. von (1968). *General system theory: Foundations, development, applications.* New York: George Braziller Inc.

Brigham, Carl C. (1923). *A study of American intelligence.* Princeton, NJ: Princeton University Press.

British Psychological Society (BPS). (1995). *Professional practice guidelines 1995: Division of Clinical Psychology.* Leicester, UK: BPS. Retrieved from www.bps.org.uk/sites/default/files/documents/professional_practice_guidelines_-_division_of_clinical_psychology.pdf

Brooks, M. (Producer), Sanger, J. (Producer), & Stroman, S. (Director) (2005). *The producers* [Motion picture]. United States: Columbia Pictures/Universal.

Burton, M. (2013). A second psychology of liberation? Valuing and moving beyond the Latin American. *Journal of Critical Psychology, Counselling and Psychotherapy, 13*(2), 96–107.

Cohen, L. (1988). First we take Manhattan. On *I'm your man* [CD]. New York: Columbia Records.

Cureton, S., & Newnes, C. (1995). A survey of the practice of psychological therapies in an NHS trust. *Clinical Psychology Forum, 76*, 6–10.

Dabbs, A., & Newnes, C. (2000). Histories of clinical psychology training. Special issue: *Clinical Psychology Forum, 145.*

Ellenbogen, G.C. (Ed.) (1992). *Freudian Encounters for the Jung at Heart: Still More Readings from the* Journal of Polymorphous Perversity. New York: Norton.

Foucault, M. (1975/1977). *Discipline and punish: The birth of the prison.* New York: Random House.

French, J.R.P., & Raven, B. (1959). The bases of social power. In D. Cartwright & A. Zander (Eds.), *Group dynamics* (pp. 150–167). New York: Harper & Row.

Fryer, D., & Easpaig, B.N.G. (2013). Critical analysology: The critical theorising of analysis. *Journal of Critical Psychology, Counselling and Psychotherapy, 13*(2), 67–72.

Gilbert, S.J. (1990). Scholarly image enhancement through a meaningless publication. *Journal of Polymorphous Perversity, 7(1),* 20–21.

Godsi, E. (2004). *Violence and society: Making sense of badness and madness*. Monmouth, UK: PCCS Books.

Golding, L. (2017). Conf. comm.

Hagan, T., & Smail, D. (1997). Power-mapping I. Background and basic methodology. *Journal of Community and Applied Social Psychology, 7*, 257–267.

Hawkins, K. (2015, 2 February). The new breed of "vloggers" here to challenge people [*Ouch Blog*, BBC News]. Retrieved 2 February 2017 from www.bbc.com/news/blogs-ouch-30803000

Holland, S. (1992). From social abuse to social action: A neighbourhood psychotherapy and social action project for women. *Changes: An International Journal of Psychology and Psychotherapy, 10*(2), 146–153.

Holmes, G. (2003). An audit: Do the people I see get better? *Clinical Psychology, 24*, 47–50.

Holmes, G., & Newnes, C. (2004). Thinking about community psychology and poverty. *Clinical Psychology, 38*, 19–22.

Humble Pie (1971). *Performance: Rockin' the Fillmore*. New York: A&M Records.

Lehmann, P. (2015). Securing human rights in the psychiatric field by utilizing advance directives. *The Journal of Critical Psychology, Counselling and Psychotherapy, 15*(1), 1–10.

Long, N., Newnes, C., & MacLachlan, A. (2000). Involving service users in employing clinical psychologists. *Clinical Psychology Forum, 138*, 39–42.

MadFilmsByMadPeople (Director) (1986). *We're not mad, we're angry* [TV film]. UK: Channel 4, Eleventh Hour Production. Retrieved from www.youtube.com/watch?v=qD36m1mveoY

Mailer, N. (1992). *Advertisements for myself*. Cambridge, MA: Harvard University Press.

Mair, M. (1977). The community of self. In D. Bannister (Ed.), *New perspectives in personal construct theory* (pp. 125–137). London: Academic Press.

Manassas. (1972). *Manassas* [CD]. New York: Atlantic Records.

Marshall, J.R. (1996). Science, "schizophrenia" and genetics: The creation of myths. *Clinical Psychology Forum, 95*, 5–13.

Mehler, B. (1997). Beyondism: Raymond B. Cattell and the new eugenics. *Genetica, 99*(2–3), 153–163.

Newnes, C. (2016a). *Inscription, diagnosis, deception and the mental health industry: How Psy governs us all*. Basingstoke, UK: Palgrave Macmillan.

Newnes, C. (2016b). Autism, Alzheimer's and angst. *Clinical Psychology Forum, 284*, 23–28.

Newnes, C. (2016c). What then shall we do? *The Journal of Critical Psychology, Counselling and Psychotherapy, 16*(1), 54–64.

Newnes, C. (2014). *Clinical psychology: A critical examination*. Ross on Wye, UK: PCCS Books.

Newnes, C. (2011a). Medication, psychotherapy and the right to know. *The Journal of Critical Psychology, Counselling and Psychotherapy, 11*(3), 173–186.

Newnes, C. (2011b). Psychology and poverty. *The Journal of Critical Psychology, Counselling and Psychotherapy, 11*(2), 92–102.

Newnes, C. (2007a). Are we all mad? *The Journal of Critical Psychology, Counselling and Psychotherapy, 7*(3), 191–194.

Newnes, C. (2007b). Postscript: On reading. *Clinical Psychology Forum, 172*, 42–43.

Newnes, C. (2006). Reflecting on recovery from head injury. *Clinical Psychology Forum, 159*, 34–40.

Newnes, C. (2005). Constructing the service user. *Clinical Psychology, 50*, 16–19.

Newnes, C. (2004a). The evidence game. *Openmind, 122* (July/Aug.), 14–15.

Newnes, C. (2004b). Psychology and psychotherapy's potential for countering the medicalization of everything. *The Journal of Humanistic Psychology, 44*(3), 358–376.
Newnes, C. (2004c). On writing. *Clinical Psychology, 45,* 44–45.
Newnes, C. (2001). Speaking out. *Ethical Human Sciences and Services, 3*(1), 135–142.
Newnes, C. (1998). What we don't much write about. *Clinical Psychology Forum, 117,* 35–36.
Newnes, C. (1997). Teaching critical psychiatry and clinical psychology. *Clinical Psychology Forum, 109,* 37–40.
Newnes, C. (1996). The development of clinical psychology and its values. *Clinical Psychology Forum, 95,* 29–34.
Newnes, C. (1995). On note taking. *Clinical Psychology Forum, 80,* 31–36.
Newnes, C. (1994a). Bibliography I: Psychiatry. *Clinical Psychology Forum, 69,* 30–31.
Newnes, C. (1994b). Defining mental health. *Nursing Times, 90,* 19, 46.
Newnes, C. (1992a). The three Cs of staff counselling. *Employee Counselling Today, 4*(3), 4–6.
Newnes, C. (1992b). References. *Clinical Psychology Forum, 42,* 27–29.
Newnes, C.D. (1991). ECT, the DCP and ME. *Clinical Psychology Forum, 36,* 20–24.
Newnes, C.D. (1990a). Psychiatric short-cuts. *What Doctors Don't Tell You, 4,* 8.
Newnes, C.D. (1990b). Who will rid me of this turbulent clinician? *Community Psychiatric Nursing Journal, 10*(1), 20–21.
Newnes, C.D. (1989). Lingua obscura. *The Psychologist, 2*(2), 52–53.
Newnes, C.D. (1988). A note on waiting lists. *Clinical Psychology Forum, 13,* 15–18.
Newnes, C.D. (1987). Letting the strain take the train: Group therapy using public transport facilities. *Changes, 4*(2), 348–349.
Newnes, C.D. (1981). Black stockings and frilly caps. *Nursing Mirror,* 28 October, 28–30.
Newnes, C., Blofield, A., & Morris, P. (2005). The writing group. *Clinical Psychology, 48,* 30–33.
Newnes, C., & Jones, H. (2005). More on writing. *Clinical Psychology, 46,* 8–10.
Newnes, C., Long, N., & MacLachlan, A. (2001). Recruits you sir? Involving service users in interview panels. *Openmind, 108,* 12.
Newnes, C., Hagan, T., & Cox, R. (2000). Fostering critical reflection in psychological practice. *Clinical Psychology Forum, 139,* 21–24.
Newnes, C., & Holmes, G. (1996). Medication: The holy water of psychiatry. *Openmind, 82,* 14–15.
Newnes, C., & MacLachlan, A. (1996). The antipsychiatry placement. *Clinical Psychology Forum, 93,* 24–27.
Pessoa, F. (2001). Text 23 (Absurdity). In F. Pessoa, *The book of disquiet.* (Richard Zenith, Trans.). London: Allen Lane/Penguin Press.
Reicher. S. (1993). Policing normality and pathologising protest: A critical view of the contribution of psychology to society. *Changes: An International Journal of Psychology and Psychotherapy, 11*(2), 121–126.
Rendell, R. (1994). *Simisola.* London: Hutchinson.
Richards, G. (1992). *Mental machinery: Part 1, The origins and consequences of psychological ideas 1600–1850.* London: The Athlone Press.
Rose, N. (1989). *Governing the soul: The shaping of the private self.* London: Routledge.
Sapin, P. (Producer) (1994). *Welcome to Happy Valley* [TV documentary]. UK: Everyman BBC Production.
Scott, R. (Director) (2000). *Gladiator* [Motion picture]. United States: Universal Studios.
Smail, D. (1978). *Psychotherapy: A personal approach.* London: Dent.

Symonds, D.M. (1960). *Highwayman's holiday*. London: Warne.
Terman, L.T. (1924). Autobiography of Lewis M. Terman. In C. Murchison (Ed.), *History of psychology in autobiography (1930, vol. 2)* (pp. 297–331). Worcester, MA: Clark University Press.
Vonnegut, K. (1961/1979). *Mother night*. St. Albans, UK: Triad/Panther Books.
Wolfensberger, W. (1987). *The new genocide of handicapped and afflicted people*. New York: University of Syracuse.
Žižek, S. (2014). *Žižek's jokes (Did you hear the one about Hegel and negation?)*. Cambridge, MA: The MIT Press.

4

TEACHING DISABILITY, TEACHING CRITICAL DISABILITY STUDIES

Dan Goodley, Michael Miller and Katherine Runswick-Cole

Introduction

In the spirit of reflexivity and with a nod to critical pedagogy, our chapter adopts a personalised and politicised approach towards the teaching of disability studies. We split the chapter into three parts and each take a turn at tackling what we see as the promise of disability studies to help develop more critical psychologies and, crucially, to enhance critiques of psychology. We share some starting assumptions. We think that the history of psychology is one that has done a tremendous amount of damage to disabled people. We know, too, that some contemporaneous psychological theories and interventions continue to pathologise human diversity. Markers and marks of disability are key to the progression of many different fields of psychology. Indeed, without disability, a lot of what we know as psychology might never have existed. But we also acknowledge that critical psychologists and their work can be allies to disabled people and their politics.

Section 1: Dan's exploration of teaching disability

Much of my teaching involves connecting with students around generic psychology and education course materials. Psychological theories of learning, sociological critique of educational institutions and qualitative research methods are just some of the topics on which I work with learners. I have taught, in the past, specific tailored undergraduate and postgraduate courses on disability studies. These courses are enjoyable because they permit students and teachers to drill down to the nuanced complexities of disability theory. There is something very exciting about getting students to develop theoretical thinking about disability. My recent engagements with more general education and psychology courses raise another set of interesting considerations. These include getting students to think about disability – sometimes for the first time – in different ways. Most students are literate in mainstream psychological and educational theories where disability is often brought in as a pathology of human life. This knowledge is a challenge to educators who seek to enhance the achievements of learners when disability seems to stifle such development. My teaching aspires to push students out of their comfort zones; to think again about disability as a phenomenon of social life. Thinking about my teaching, I think disability comes to be known in three different, though interconnected, ways.

Disability is a problem

Disability comes to be known in psychology, like it is in society, as a problem. We know from leading disability studies scholars in the 1990s, such as Mike Oliver, that disability-as-problem is a well-worn concept with a long history (Oliver, 1990). Many religions have understood disability as a punishment from God, though the dominant discourse of disability-as-problem of the last 100 years belongs to medicine or at least the process of medicalisation. Our bodies often come to be known through powerful medical discourses. And when our bodies and minds fail to function in ways that we and others would expect, then these failings are quickly conceptualised by medical narratives. And when these narratives become the central ways through which we think of our bodies and minds, then we have made unconscious deals with medicalisation. One of the first topics of teaching that I choose to tackle with students relates to our shared understandings of the workings of medicalisation. This powerful discourse threatens to draw common-sense and everyday understandings of disability into its essentialised web of meanings. Disability becomes known only as a deficit of the person's body and/or mind. And in working through medicalisation, we eventually find psychologisation. This latter process is one where we come to understand our bodies and minds through those reductive methods and theories of psychology that individualise bodily, cognitive and emotional failings (Goodley, 2016). Take depression. A psychologising gaze only understands this pathological condition as a failing of the individual mind. Depression is a consequence – a product – of a mind that is not working rationally. Depression is a metaphor for human failing. Depression is understood as a disease of the individual, caused by failing within the individual. Here, then, depression is very much an individualised phenomenon. One of the key tasks of teaching disability relates to unpacking and problematizing the individualisation of disability. And to help us to do so, we can stick with the notion of disability-as-problem but consider the problem from a very different epistemological position.

One such position is found in the social model of disability. This counter-narrative to medicalisation, individualisation and psychologisation asks to what extent disability is a problem of society? Oliver's (1990) seminal text laid out the building blocks of the social model. This was a very British and entirely Marxist model. Resonating with the left-wing and Union politics of the late 20th century, the social model of disability made a simple but powerful argument: that people with sensory, physical or cognitive impairments faced discrimination in their everyday lives because of the widespread existence of physical, cultural and attitudinal barriers. Hence, wheelchair users have historically faced stairs and steps that deny them access, Deaf people are subjected to an oralist culture devoid of sign language, and people with intellectual disabilities are not accommodated or assimilated into mainstream forms of schooling. Disability is a social, political, cultural and economic phenomenon. The social model was and remains a powerful example of counter-hegemonic thinking, an ontological shift in thinking about the reality of disability that then demands a new epistemological home and associated forms of methodological inquiry. To re-situate disability, as a political concern, demands different kinds of question and types of intervention. Hence, a disabled learner's failings in school are no longer dismissed as the result of failings within their body or mind, but instead are understood as a failing of education, schools and teachers. Educational failing is not an individualised trait, but a marker of the inadequacies of educational systems and types of pedagogy. Disability-as-problem actually says more general things about the problems of society. The inabilities of school systems to cope with the participation and involvement of disabled children can be understood as a form of educational apartheid that excludes disabled children and supports only those non-disabled students who implicitly and explicitly fit the demands of education.

In teaching disability and teaching psychology, I would want to ask how psychology is historically implicated in this educational apartheid? Psychology has a shameful history in relation to the sifting out and segregating of disabled students from mainstream educational settings. As Tom Billington (2014) documents, the profession of educational psychology is but one example of this shameful past, where scientifically questionable ideas associated with intelligence were foisted onto different populations by psychologists and others, feeding into contemporary movements associated with eugenics and psychological hygiene in the early to middle parts of the 20th century. In the present day, an immediate task of educational psychology is rethinking the profession's relationships with those sectors of the population that the profession has historically marginalised (see Williams, Billington, Corcoran, & Goodley, 2016). This would include disabled people and gay, transgender or working-class individuals, as well as women and people of colour.

Teaching disability and teaching psychology therefore demands critical pedagogies. As I have recently argued (Goodley, 2016), disability has the potential to energise a particular kind of critical pedagogy that addresses a key question: who is included in our teaching and who is excluded? When disciplines such as psychology constitute disabled people simply as objects of theory and subjects of study – and the ensuing understandings of disability pathologise disabled people – then such disciplines are in severe need of overhauling and reconfiguring. Moreover, when the idealised human being of systems of psychology and education is assumed to be non-disabled and 'normal', then these systems are clearly working from and peddling narrow curricula and forms of engagement. Education-as-problem and teaching-as-problem are important hooks on which to hang our critical pedagogies.

Disability is an opportunity

How might we know disability or think again of it as a phenomenon that opens up debates, poses different questions and offers moments of reconsideration? This conceptualisation of disability is very much in line with more affirmative theories of disability. One of these – crip theory – refers to a broad emerging form of critique and activism that repositions disability as something that we might desire (McRuer, 2006). What might desiring disability mean? One way in which disability becomes something that is desired relates to an event or moment when disability disrupts the normal ways in which we live our lives. Hence, in the teaching of psychology and education, we might ask – in what way does the presence of a disabled child in a classroom necessitate a new way of thinking about how that classroom is managed, ordered or facilitated? Similarly, how might a child with the label of intellectual disabilities – now a key member of the mainstream classroom – urge a reconsideration of curriculum and the kinds of pedagogy that take place in that classroom? At the heart of crip theory is potentiality. Disability has an enduring potential to get us thinking differently about the world. And this thinking about the world includes, of course, psychology. An encounter with disability – and disability studies literature such as that of crip theory – makes me ask about the usefulness and relevance of psychology. In a recent newspaper article by the South African critical psychologist Wahbie Long (2016), he argues that psychology too often reflects the middle-class interests of psychologists who live and work in the Global North. Mimicking C. Wright Mills's critique of sociology in 1959, Long suggests that psychologists need to spend more time attending to the intersections of class, race, gender and poverty, thus giving psychology to communities who might use its methods and theories to build a better world. This reconfiguration of psychology as a discipline of the people has clear links with community psychology (Kagan, Burton, Duckett, Lawthom, & Siddiquee, 2011). This is a burgeoning field of activists and practitioners that re-situate psychology in different community spaces which require psychological, political and cultural work in ways that increase the health and well-being of community members. Clearly, disabled people and their allies may well draw on alliances with community psychologists to address the material barriers that many disabled people continue to face. This is especially the case today, in the UK and elsewhere, where disabled people are facing cuts to welfare and essential services as a consequence of austerity measures. One could argue that a politicised psychology – and the teaching of this – has never been more needed.

One example of politicising our teaching of psychology through the teaching of disability relates to desiring disability. Clearly, when disability is individualised as a pathology, then it is hardly the most desirable of human artefacts. Crip theory reclaims disability as something that one might desire – as the difference that disability makes (Michalko, 2002). Rather than considering low intelligence or the presence of intellectual disabilities as characteristics of human deficiency, we carefully consider the differences that are made by the entrance of intellectual disability into our culture. So, a person with profound intellectual disabilities (who might not talk or walk) demands profoundly responsive forms of human relationships, support and care. The interdependencies of our human condition are magnified by the presence of profound intellectual disability. We are encouraged to think about how we might emphasise our interdependencies on one another and to think, for example, how our education systems might promote interdependencies. In a time when our planet's sustainability is in question, one could argue that all we have in responses are our reliances on one another. Disability rekindles our emphasis on mutuality and connection.

Disability necessarily disorientates

Hitherto, we have seen that disability works in contradictory ways: as problem and opportunity. Teaching disability studies requires us to become disorientated with psychology. Jill Smith's recent doctoral work makes a convincing case for disorientation (Smith, 2016): the notion that we permit ourselves to be troubled by the object of our study (to think again about how we might orient ourselves to that object) after a period of disorientation (a process of rejecting what we already know about that object). Teaching disability studies troubles our taken-for-granted understandings of (and perhaps alliances with) psychology and demands disorientation; to take time to find new kinds of personal, professional and ethical relationships with psychology.

- Do we need psychology?
- How might psychology be serviced by disability studies?
- To what extent can psychologists contribute to a politics of disability?
- What would it mean to teach psychology with disability present, in the classroom, as an ally rather than an object of study?
- How might we emphasise the subject(ivity) of disability?

Disorientation invites other moments of affect, including disengagement (where we reject psychology) and disavowal (where we might want to push against psychology, but also are drawn to its potential to further, say, an affirmative reading of disability). Disorientation is a key element of teaching disability. Yet perhaps it would be more accurate to talk of teaching disability studies rather than simply teaching disability. Indeed, as I have tried to outline in a recent text (Goodley, 2016), disability studies constitutes an interdisciplinary body of knowledge with the potential to challenge established disciplinary knowledges around disability. One of these disciplines, clearly, is psychology, and there remains a pressing need to contest the impairment-obsessed, pathologising tendencies of much of what passes as mainstream psychological research (see Goodley & Lawthom [2005] for an overview). Disability is so much more than simply being a convenient object of psychological study. And disabled people are far more than simply subjects of research and investigation.

Section 2: Michael's exposure to un/learning disability

As a student of critical disability studies, my conceptualisation of the field and the vast, nuanced implications of my engagement, is incomplete. I have no intention of ever finding myself, or critical disability studies, static in a (seemingly) fully formed framework. The potential opportunities, as I perceive them, exist in the risks of remaining incomplete and in an ongoing process of dismantling naturalised notions of what disability is and how it is measured, defined, taught and learned in order to create a place for constant reimagining.

I've come to understand the learning process as an exploration of how and why we know what we know of ourselves and the world. We could think of engaging in disability studies critically as a process of getting to know oneself and one's world, offering an opportunity to get to know and work to engage in a process of transformation. This potential transformation (of self, community, etc.) is an exploration of dominant, exclusionary and violent institutions and social systems that are taught, among other places, in the classroom and reproduced in often subtle, unintended ways.

There is no how-to guide for recognising and dismantling the oppressive thoughts and behaviours we've accepted as natural, nor should there be. But there are people and organisations which are actively engaging in the messiness and instability of reimagining and enacting new ways of knowing. Facilitating and fostering an understanding of theories along with critique and reflection is a flexible undertaking. A critical approach to teaching (disability studies) necessarily works to ground theory in practice in a reciprocal, ongoing process of exposing and exploring individual and collectively accepted beliefs and naturalised systems of oppression. Education then is constantly remade in the process of praxis – action and reflection of the self to change the self, and of the world to change the world (Freire 1970/2000). Here I see it is necessary to clarify what I have titled un/learning disability – a jumbled, blended process of learning new knowledge of and about oneself and one's world while simultaneously acknowledging accepted indoctrinations and, importantly, collectively and reflexively imagining new ways.

Un/learning myself

My engagement with critical disability studies was, and continues to be, a disorientating process, beginning when I was an undergraduate student of mainstream psychology. My focus was in behavioural neuroscience, which is what led me to volunteer for a brain scan. I had intended to play a few mind-games and do my small part in contributing to the next great discovery in science. Instead, the great discovery was of a tumour in my right cerebellum. My educational process from that point on was at times frighteningly illuminating – from the practicalities of navigating hospital visits and health insurance, to the uncertainties and fears I had and which were expressed to me by others, I learned a lot in a short amount of time.

What led me towards critical disability studies was not an intellectual awakening, but an awakening of deep-seeded fears and insecurities. I was confronted with an unexpected brain tumour, and along with it, what I would later recognise as the implicit ableist attitudes and normative desires of someone who understood disability in the way it was taught – as an undesirable pathology. After the tumour was removed and it was discovered to be benign, I was further challenged by my feelings of relief, which exemplified the instilled and accepted ableist fears of living on the other side of the dis/ability divide. Confronting and reflecting on these fears and insecurities, along with a commitment to change, informs my studies and analyses.

I conceptualise the teaching and learning of disability studies as a challenge to the mainstream education system and the roles we (who are in it) play in the reification and distribution of 'normal'; a critical lens that encourages considerations for alternative ways of learning and knowledge creation. Although engaging in a challenge often means seeking to produce solution(s), I reject this and reassert prefigurative positions that creatively and critically reimagine the world.

Un/learning education

Appreciating the messiness and vulnerabilities in teaching disability critically offers a necessary opportunity to do more than impart information about a subject. Rather, it can get us – students and teachers – to (re)consider the foundations of our education, our positions within it, and what we've come to know as normal. Incorporating critical disability studies into a psychology curriculum gives space to those engaging with it to consider the ordinary and the complex, the interactions and interconnectedness of our education and conceptions of the world, each other and ourselves. Thinking beyond stories of Phineas Gage or HM as insightful case studies and troubling dominant discourses of disability as a topic of study, we realise that disabled people have been treated as that – topics of study. These observations of ab/normality have been bound up in books of psychology's history, dismissed as a dark, distant past that led to the discovery (see: creation) of normative functioning through the study of so-called abnormal functioning. Examining the complexities in the seemingly mundane interactions we have with studying disability, we can start to see the violence that we are complicit in, as well as opening up other questions and connections about 'the possible cultural, structural and historical foundations that give rise to that [mundane] moment' (Goodley, 2014, p. 74).

A classroom has the opportunity to do more than be a place of depositing and storing information (Freire, 1970/2000). Shifting the dynamics to facilitate conversations on our heuristics of disability and people with disabilities can unexpectedly open up concepts that, at the core, question all that we know and how we came to that knowledge. Fraser and Lamble (2015) give us much to consider in their insights and modelling of how a transformative process of teaching can expose one's own normalised desires and how they came to be shaped. Queering normative desires and understandings exposes the neoliberal frameworks seamlessly woven into classroom curriculum – from what is taught, what is expected, to how value is defined and measured. Foundational conceptions of naturalised behaviours and systems are challenged when approaching education in a critical way such as queer theory offers. Anarchist frameworks for challenging hegemonic power also provide practical support, such as working to fundamentally change the dynamics between teacher and student (Spoto, 2014), or encouraging schools to employ disabled teachers (Greenstein, 2015). How we are taught and, in turn, teach dominant understandings, from the ordinary to the complex and wide-ranging, start to become disorientated.

Compulsory education, for example, is a more overt form of the many compulsory behaviours, identities and actions that are taught and reified in schools. These cultural and societal expectations have become naturalised creations that, to anyone unable or unwilling to meet these standards, manifest themselves through various forms of punishment and violence. However, punitive measures that justify and perpetuate violence are actively being challenged and alternatives offered through the work of community-based interventions and transformative justice organisations (e.g. in the United States, Save the Kids [n.d.], Bay Area Transformative Justice Collective [n.d.]). As stated above, the open reflexivity of working towards change (of self, community, systems) does not come with an anti-oppression checklist, nor does ableism occur in isolated instances separate from other socially constructed categorisations of people who cannot – or will not – conform to dominant expressions of normativity. However, from the collaborative and continuing critical work of many people and organisations, there are toolkits and guides such as the *Creative Interventions Toolkit: A Practical Guide to Stop Interpersonal Violence* (Creative Interventions, 2012) that are not instructions, but instead serve as practical, grounded resources based on years of experiences, sharing successes and failures, in a connected process of transformation.

Un/learning norms

Considering the process of naturalised normative expressions within disability studies, I quickly turn to address what Robert McRuer refers to as 'compulsory able-bodiedness' (2006, p. 2), a term indebted to Adrienne Rich's 'compulsory heterosexuality' (1980/2003). But before going any further, I'm attentive to Alison Kafer's call to emphasise and engage with that which cannot be exclusively described through physical disability, and work to include 'compulsory able-mindedness' (2013, p. 16). Identifying these compulsories within a standard curriculum quickly reveals the centring of heteronormativity and able-bodiedness/able-mindedness in classroom study and dialogue where differences are exploited at the expense of anyone displaying (or not) qualities deemed undesirable, with the creation of and allegiance to an 'us' and a 'them'. Incorporating mad studies into Psy curricula would further offer a needed tension between the dominant and the disruptive. A classroom incorporating mad studies would benefit from many examples of past and ongoing alternative ways to help each other that don't reduce people to symptoms, but help understand them 'within the social and economic context of the society in which they live' (Menzies, LeFrançois, & Reaume, 2013, p. 2).

As with other socially imposed beliefs, the expectations of an able body and mind are understood as something so natural that the 'compulsory' is an unnecessary component that need not be considered. That is, until disabled bodies and minds expose and disrupt the ontological insecurities of non-disabled people's own psyche, body and culture. Or further, when the able-bodied/able-minded are confronted with the possibility of disability. Here is a vulnerable space where deep-seeded fears and insecurities can be exposed, one's desires challenged, ableist feelings brought up. Here is a space to really get to know one's self. Here is where an experience like discovering a brain tumour can bring about a structural shift.

Schools market themselves as hubs of diversity and inclusion, but as Davis (2011) points out, this only goes so far. The label of disability remains as a steadfast barrier between what is desired and disavowed. As long as the dominant narrative of disability and students with disabilities remains within the medical model, a normative human existence will remain, as will the necessary and necessarily undesired Other. This is exemplified inside and out of the classroom, and an approach to disrupting these narratives is to reject the continued use of the same standard course materials and media that study disabled people, and instead utilise work created by disabled people, valuing scholarly work as well as other platforms (e.g. blogs, books, films, performances).

Inclusion is too often conditional, with the terms set by the very same systems and people in power that initially created and enforced exclusion. Inclusion into a hegemonic institution like the education system requires assimilation of the disabled student, rather than a change of the disabling institution (Erevelles, 2014; Goodley, 2014). The limited and often unfulfilled guarantee of reasonable adjustment and accommodation in schools portrays disability as a problem of and in the person, instead of in socially imposed barriers which are taught in schools both within and outside a formal curriculum. This doesn't even address the 'quagmire of hurdles and stigma' of applying for, proving the need for and actually acquiring one's rights of adjustments/accommodations – which further doesn't address their quality and consistency once acquired (crippledscholar, 2016, n.p.).

Un/learning rights

A long history of disability activism has brought immeasurable accomplishments. The rights gained (such as inclusion into mainstream education) and benefits granted for people with disabilities have happened because of the organised actions of disabled activists and advocates (e.g. It's Our Story [n.d.]). But with every celebration, there must be a critique. Writing of mad movements, Louise Tam calls in bell hooks' demands for systemic resistance and warns that necessary critiques and reflections 'not be viewed as antithetical to our movements ... because rigorous critique is a gesture of respect and love' (2013, p. 285). The fact that rights such as inclusion are still fought for, that protests against cuts are still happening, are indicators that the reforms being made to the systems being fought are means of necessary but limited changes. Measures of reform uphold the systems and power in (seemingly fixed) place, while appearing to be solutions of suffering. New tactics are needed not only in our dissent, but directed towards what kind of future we want.

These rights and reforms are granted by people representing the very same institutions and social systems that oppressed and indeed constructed the disabled person as Other, profiting from this social construction and remaining generally unaffected by the very real, violent outcomes these largely unquestioned social norms perpetuate. Relying on an education system that privileges certain identities and expressions, what is presented as 'normal', while punishing students deemed 'abnormal' is not actual recognition of the rights and lives (and indeed the right to, and a certain quality of, life) of disabled students labelled as Other.

With every new political season come calls for more cuts in government spending, with schools and disabled people's movements among the many that suffer from the swaying charity extended. When charity is the dominant model for support – for example, financial, social, emotional, access – (disabled) people's livelihood is at the mercy of those in power, deciding according to their current interests in the neoliberal order.

Seeking alternatives, I echo Mia Mingus's call for us all to shift from dominant discourses of access and an equality-based model of sameness towards one that 'embraces difference, confronts privilege and challenges what is considered "normal" on every front' (Mingus, 2011, n.p.). While not abandoning the ongoing reforms and rights achieved by the countless and ongoing struggles of disability rights activists in and out of education, reform is not the end goal. A new formation into disability justice would extend these struggles and work towards dismantling current systems rather than assimilating and integrating into them. For an 'unreasonable' reading on sameness which necessitates an 'us' without disability at the expense of a 'them' with disability, I recommend *Youth and Disability: A Challenge to Mr Reasonable* (Slater, 2016).

These alternatives are not concrete sets of directions, nor are they ambiguous utopian dreams. People have organised and implemented strategies that seek a different way of teaching and learning, in and out of the classroom, and continue to do so. A call to incorporate disability studies into Psy curricula is a call to incorporate radical teachings that reimagine how we come to know ourselves and each other.

Teaching norms, teaching violence

The classroom is an incubator of understandings, and because of this, we must be critical of what we as teachers/learners are engaging with and upholding. The classroom is a single example of the larger society and societal idea(l)s, a designated space for fostering a certain type of expression. Yet this dominant institution is also dominating – these legal measures and non-binding agreements to inclusive education and reasonable accommodation/adjustment are not just (contestably) guaranteed in the Global North. The education-for-all rhetoric gets 'fabricated in the global North and transferred to the global South, with little or no alertness to context or culture, or how this discourse is framed, applied (or otherwise) or even resisted in practice' (Grech, 2014, p. 130). Disability and people with disabilities are becoming more frequently featured in declarations and treaties, yet so long as charity remains the driving force and the medical model is the presiding lens with which to perceive disability, it will remain only discourse.

Un/learning violence

An un/learning of normal will lead us to a recognition of the violence that these 'normals' do not just facilitate, but actually necessitate. The 'us' needs a 'them', and ableism is foundational to maintaining a normal, dominant order. Ableism describes the prevailing dominant 'notions of whose bodies [and minds] are considered valuable, desirable, and disposable' (Mingus, 2011, n.p.). These notions are learned, and through recognition and reflexive work they can be unlearned, but the naturalised place that ableist desires occupy in classroom curriculum don't set us up for support.

The violence validated by an ableist education manifests in any number of forms when the classroom isn't a space to challenge dominant conceptions of 'normal' students and the necessary, undesirable opposite, 'abnormal' students. Though the language used has largely changed, this acceptance and distinguishing of naturalised norms simultaneously reinforce 'normal' and punish 'abnormal' (behaviours, desires, bodies, minds, etc.). Indeed, the classroom remains a space where violence is taught, where differences are exploited and measures of value and worth are reduced to strict and ever narrowing categorisations evaluated by an increasingly assessment-based school system. A critical conceptualisation of ableism identifies disability as intersectional, with various overtly and covertly pathologised, criminalised, marginalised differences that are removed from historical contexts, individualised, and depoliticised in curricula (Fabris & Aubrecht, 2014). The reification of socially constructed ab/normalities and the manifested forms of violence are not always obvious. Being aware of the violence that one is inflicting and being inflicted with is not a necessary component in the process of perpetuating it (for example, those whom Freire called 'well-intentioned bank-clerk teachers' [1970/2000, p. 75], and Slater's 'Mr Reasonable' [2016]). But becoming aware is a beginning in the process of un/learning.

Section 3: Katherine's exploration of intersectionality

I came to disability studies as a postgraduate student studying in a Department of Education. My early encounters with disability studies were shaped by engagement at undergraduate level with ideas from (critical) psychology. The emerging, and sometimes troubled, relationship between disability and psychology (Goodley & Lawthom, 2005) has continued to be an area of focus and interest for me, prompting me to question, among many other things, the construction and function of diagnostic labels in people's lives (Runswick-Cole, Mallett, & Timimi, 2016).

In the past, I've had the pleasure of teaching disability studies courses to undergraduates on a Disability Studies and Education degree, although now, working in a Faculty of Health, Psychology and Social Care, I often find myself teaching 'disability' to a range of practitioners in training, including: physiotherapists, teachers, social workers and psychologists. As a student and teacher of critical disability studies, I regard this as an opportunity to reflect upon taken-for-granted assumptions and to begin to reimagine our relationships with this thing called 'disability' as well as with one another as human beings in the world.

As Dan and Michael have so clearly demonstrated, critical disability studies require those of us who engage with them to expose and challenge everyday disablism. Teaching disability studies draws on a host of theoretical resources from a wide range of literature. In other words, disability studies are always an intersectional inquiry as they demand that we pay attention to the ways in which disablism is connected with other forms of marginalisation, including: racism, (hetero)sexism, poverty and colonialism. Teachers and students of critical disability studies may start with disability, but they should never end there (Goodley, 2013).

Let's be clear; teaching and learning critical disability studies through an intersectional lens does not require an abandonment of the social model of disability that Dan outlines above; rather, it offers an opportunity to theorise disability and disablement by drawing on a range of critical resources. As Mallett and Runswick-Cole (2014, p. 17; emphasis in original) suggest, in this way, it is possible 'to move *on, with* and *through* the social model of disability to expose and challenge the oppression of disabled people'. Critical disability studies, then, have need of an intersectional analysis through which to interrogate issues of social oppression and marginalisation in the lives of disabled people. Indeed, ideas from feminism, queer theory and postcolonial theory are written through and in critical disability studies (as we have already seen in this chapter), and are part of what we describe above as our personalised and politicised approach towards the teaching of disability studies.

An intersectional approach to critical disability studies refers to an interdisciplinary methodology that pays attention to the connections between different social identities and the systems of oppression and discrimination that touch people's lives. An intersectional lens is crucial to understanding complex forms of oppression resulting from intersecting minority identities (Crenshaw, 1991; McCall, 2005).

For example, Frohmader and Meekosha (2012) found that disabled women face a 'double disadvantage' because of their membership of two oppressed identity groups: women and disabled people. And yet, an intersectional lens offers more than simply a bringing together of these markers to suggest that there is some sort of cumulative effect; rather, it offers the opportunity to consider how each supports the co-constitution of the other (Goodley, 2011).

At the same time as asserting the value of an intersectional approach to the study of disability, it is worth noting that disability studies have often been marginalised within cultural and sociological study. Mallett (2007) argues that race, gender and sexuality have often been theorised without reference to disability, and Davis (1995) too has noted the absence of disability in analysis of class and poverty. Feminist, critical race and postcolonial literature, like psychology, often has a troubled relationship, to say the least, with disability (Sherry, 2007). Too often, a critical approach to the theorising of disability is the absent presence within psychological, sociological and cultural teaching, learning and analysis.

So, what does an intersectional approach offer to the teaching of critical disability studies? How might we draw on feminism, queer theory and postcolonial theory as resources to inform the theorising and practices of critical disability studies?

Feminism

The contribution of feminist thinking to the development of critical disability studies cannot be underestimated. Feminists have demanded that the gendered nature of disability be acknowledged (Thomas, 1999). As Lloyd (2001, p. 726) has suggested, the social model emerged in ways which privileged the concerns of 'white, middle-class, professional, physically disabled men'. This has led to the prioritisation of issues like paid work over seemingly more private matters such as sexuality, personal relationships and caring. In response to Marxist materialist accounts of social oppression (Oliver, 1990), feminists, including Thomas (1999) and Morris (1992, 1993), have challenged the idea that disability studies must maintain the distinction between 'public issues' and 'private troubles'. By calling for a focus on the subjective experiences of disabled people, feminists have also insisted that disability studies pay attention to the ways in which people experience their bodies.

Feminists like Thomas (2007) and Reeve (2008) have cleared a space within the teaching of critical disability studies to think about emotions. While always seeking to avoid the disabling processes of psychologisation that Dan outlines above, they share an interest in thinking about the 'barriers in here' that determine what 'disabled people can be' rather than what 'disabled people can do' (Reeve, 2008, p. 1). 'Barriers in here' are often ignored by those who follow a 'hard' social oppression model of disability and who continue to be more focused on the 'barriers out there' as the subject of inquiry. Crucially, the psycho-emotional register that Thomas and Reeve invoke allows for a much-needed exploration of in/direct forms of disablism (Reeve, 2008, p. 1; see also Thomas, 2007, p. 72). They describe this form of oppression as psycho-emotional disablism (Thomas, 2007; Reeve, 2008).

Queer theory

Just as critical disability studies owe much to feminism, queer theory has also drawn on feminism to distinguish between the biological and the social (sex and gender). Queer theory has been associated with radical writings around sexuality; queer is both a practice and an ambition, focused on unsettling, disturbing and challenging the 'norm' (Goodley, 2011). Queer theory's rejection of the idea that there are 'essentialist' identities has been crucial in the development of 'constructionist' ideas of identities. Constructionist approaches to identities challenge the notion of identity as something fixed and immutable, seeing identity (sexuality, gender, disability), instead, as something that is in constant formation and fluid (Mallett & Runswick-Cole, 2014).

As we have seen above, these ideas from queer theory have been taken up within teaching critical disability studies to theorise difference and non-normativity, and to expose the processes through which normalcy is demanded and enforced (Mallett & Runswick-Cole, 2014). Michael has described the ways in which queer theory might trouble and expose the normative desires and understandings that underpin the neoliberal frameworks written into classroom curricula. This problematization of the idea of 'normal', using a queer theory lens, has been described as 'compulsory heterosexuality', and in turn, McRuer (2006) has borrowed from queer theory to talk about 'compulsory able-bodiedness' in the same way. In effect, McRuer names compulsory able-bodiedness as an agent and product of neoliberal capitalism. He defines neoliberal capitalism as the dominant economic and cultural system, driven by market forces, which has conceived of and constructed idealised identities that exclude and marginalise queer and disabled people. In response, queer theory and critical disability studies always seek to dismantle the idea that the ideal neoliberal subject is an able-bodied subject, one whose identity is not compromised by either disability or queerness (Goodley, 2011).

As Goodley (2011) argues, to be queer is to be subversive. And so, engagement with critical disability studies is an opportunity to queer contemporary societal norms. Queer theory and disability theory have become increasingly and productively entangled with one another to mount a challenge against the hegemony of the norm.

Postcolonial theory

Postcolonial theory, too, offers a challenge to dominant views. Postcolonial thinkers critique notions of both 'disability' and 'colonised people' that have traditionally emanated from the Global North. However, just as feminists have critiqued disability studies as the product of white, middle-class, Western, male academic concerns, postcolonial thinkers have also questioned the relevance of Global North models of disability for the Global South. They also challenge the assumption that ideas and values concerned with disability in the Global North are inherently more advanced than understandings emanating from the Global South (Mallett & Runswick-Cole, 2014).

Often, majority world issues are either excluded from mainstream disability studies thinking and teaching or included in tokenistic or piecemeal ways (Ghai, 2002; Grech, 2009). Nevertheless, the histories of disability and race are inevitably entangled (Goodley, 2011) and black and disabled people have historically been viewed as less than fully human (Connor, 2008). And yet, despite these entanglements, the practices of neoliberal global capitalism mean that disability studies are still dominated by Western theorists (Grech, 2009). It is crucial, then, that teachers and students of critical disability studies must strive to avoid falling unself-critically into Western-centric accounts in their teaching and learning.

Working in the context of the Global North, my teaching and learning in critical disability studies have been greatly influenced by new (to me) knowledges emerging from the Global South. Much of my teaching and research has focused on the lives of disabled children, young people and their families (Curran & Runswick-Cole, 2013; Goodley, Runswick-Cole, & Liddiard, 2015; Runswick-Cole, Curran, & Liddiard, in press). Despite attempts to queer(y) normative models of child development (Curran & Runswick-Cole, 2014), it remains the case that accounts of the developing child continue to privilege 'normal development' and to implicate parents, or more usually, those who take the mothering role, in ensuring and maintaining normative development. The relationship between mother and child becomes the key site of scrutiny and control when a child's development is deemed to be 'non-normative'. Postcolonial writers remind us of the cultural contexts of such Global North practices by offering alternative accounts. For instance, Chataika and McKenzie (2013, p. 158) describe African cultures in which the mother–child relationship is not the primary focus of concern. They describe *ubuntu*: 'Whatever happens to the individual happens to the whole group, and whatever happens to the whole group happens to the individual. The individual can only say: "I am, because we are; and since we are, therefore I am"' (Mbiti, 1992, p. 109, cited in Chataika & McKenzie, 2013, p. 158).

Writings from the Global South, then, as we have also seen above, demand that we reimagine Western cultural norms that seek to individualise parenting practices and highlight what it means to be part of a bigger whole in extended families and communities (Runswick-Cole & Goodley, in press). The contribution to teaching and learning in critical disability studies of postcolonial thinkers is crucial to developing understandings.

Conclusions

We finalise the finishing touches to this chapter the day after Donald Trump was made President of the United States. Teaching disability is more important today than it was this time last week. Disability demands that we think about our connections with others and our reliance upon other people in order that we might live as human beings. Disability studies politicises everyday life and challenges a cultural emphasis on independence and isolation. Disability asks us to think about what it means to be human. And in these political times of uncertainty, we need disability.

References

Bay Area Transformative Justice Collective (n.d.). https://batjc.wordpress.com

Billington, T. (2014). Changing the subject: The past, present and future of educational psychology. In T.D. Corcoran (Ed.), *Psychology in education: Critical theory-practice*. Rotterdam: Sense Publishers.

Chataika, T., & McKenzie, J. (2013). Considerations for an African childhood disability studies. In T. Curran & K. Runswick-Cole (Eds.), *Disabled children's Childhood Studies: Critical approaches in a global context* (pp. 152–163). Basingstoke, UK: Palgrave MacMillan.

Connor, D.J. (2008). Not so strange bedfellows: The promise of disability studies and critical race theory. In S. Gabel & S. Danforth (Eds.), *Disability and the international politics of education* (pp. 201–224). New York: Peter Lang Publishers.

Creative Interventions. (2012). *Creative interventions toolkit: A practical guide to stop interpersonal violence*. Retrieved from www.creative-interventions.org/wp-content/uploads/2012/06/CI-Toolkit-Complete-Pre-Release-Version-06.2012-.pdf

Crenshaw, K. (1991). Mapping the margins: Intersectionality, identity politics and violence against women of colour. *Stanford Law Review, 4*(3), 1241–1299.

crippledscholar. (2016, January 15). So you've made progress in expanding rights to academic accommodation . . . But do you really deserve it? Retrieved from https://crippledscholar.wordpress.com/2016/01/15/so-youve-made-progress-in-expanding-rights-to-academic-accommodation-but-do-you-really-deserve-it/

Curran, T., & Runswick-Cole, K. (Eds.) (2013). *Disabled children's Childhood Studies: Critical approaches in a global context*. Basingstoke, UK: Palgrave Macmillan.

Curran, T., & Runswick-Cole, K. (2014). Disabled children's Childhood Studies: An emerging domain of inquiry? *Disability & Society, 29*(10), 1617–1630.

Davis, L.J. (1995). *Enforcing normalcy: Disability, deafness, and the body*. New York: Verso.

Davis, L.J. (2011, 25 September). Why is disability missing from the discourse on diversity? *The Chronicle of Higher Education, 25*. Retrieved from http://raceandfaith.com/uploads/3/3/7/2/3372898/disabilities_left_out.pdf

Erevelles, N. (2014). Crippin' Jim Crow: Disability, dis-location, and the school-to-prison pipeline. In L. Ben-Moshe, C. Chapman, & A.C. Carey (Eds.), *Disability incarcerated* (pp. 81–99). New York: Palgrave Macmillan US.

Fabris, E., & Aubrecht, K. (2014). Chemical constraint: Experiences of psychiatric coercion, restraint, and detention as carceratory techniques. In L. Ben-Moshe, C. Chapman, & A.C. Carey (Eds.), *Disability incarcerated* (pp. 185–199). New York: Palgrave Macmillan US.

Fraser, J., & Lamble, S. (2015). Queer desires and critical pedagogies in higher education: Reflections on the transformative potential of non-normative learning desires in the classroom. *Journal of Feminist Scholarship, 7*, 61–77.

Freire, P. (1970/2000). *Pedagogy of the oppressed* (30th anniversary ed.). New York: Continuum.

Frohmader, C., & Meekosha, H. (2012). Recognition, respect and rights: Women with disabilities in a globalised world. In D. Goodley, B. Hughes, & L.J. Davis (Eds.), *Disability and social theory: New developments and directions* (pp. 287–307). Basingstoke, UK: Palgrave Macmillan.

Ghai, A. (2002). Disability in the Indian context: Post-colonial perspectives. In M. Corker & T. Shakespeare (Eds.), *Disability/postmodernity: Embodying disability theory* (pp. 88–100). London: Continuum.

Goodley, D. (2011). *Disability studies: An interdisciplinary introduction*. London: Sage.

Goodley, D. (2013). Dis/entangling critical disability studies. *Disability & Society, 28*(5), 631–644.

Goodley, D. (2014). *Dis/ability studies: Theorising disablism and ableism*. London: Routledge.

Goodley, D. (2016). *Disability studies: An interdisciplinary introduction* (2nd ed.). London: Sage.

Goodley, D., & Lawthom, R. (Eds.) (2005). *Disability and psychology*. London: Palgrave Macmillan.

Goodley, D., Runswick-Cole, K., & Liddiard, K. (2015). The dishuman child. *Discourse: The Cultural Politics of Education, 37*(5), 770–784. doi: 10.1080/01596306.2015.1075731#.Vh-V2844RDE

Grech, S. (2009). Disability, poverty and development: Critical reflections on the majority world debate. *Disability & Society, 24*(6), 771–784.

Grech, S. (2014). Disability, poverty and education: Perceived barriers and (dis)connections in rural Guatemala. *Disability and the Global South, 1*(1), 128–152.

Greenstein, A. (2015). *Radical inclusive education: Disability, teaching and struggles for liberation.* London: Routledge.

It's Our Story. (n.d.). https://youtube.com/user/itsourstoryproject

Kafer, A. (2013). *Feminist, queer, crip.* Bloomington, IN: Indiana University Press.

Kagan, C.M., Burton M., Duckett P.S., Lawthom R., & Siddiquee, A. (2011). *Critical community psychology.* Oxford: Wiley–Blackwell.

Lloyd, M. (2001). The politics of disability and feminism: Discord or synthesis? *Sociology, 35*(3), 715–728.

Long, W. (2016, 9 October). Op-Ed: The recolonising danger of decolonising psychology. *Daily Maverick.* Retrieved on 14 October 2016 from www.dailymaverick.co.za/article/2016-10-09-op-ed-the-recolonising-danger-of-decolonising-psychology/#.WAR745MrIU3

Mallett, R. (2007). *Critical correctness: Exploring the capacities of contemporary disability criticism* (Unpublished PhD thesis). University of Sheffield, Sheffield, UK.

Mallett, R., & Runswick-Cole, K. (2014). *Approaching disability: Critical issues and perspectives.* London: Routledge.

McCall, L. (2005). The complexity of intersectionality. *Signs: Journal of Women in Culture and Society, 30*(3), 1771–1800.

McRuer, R. (2006). *Crip theory: Cultural signs of queerness and disability.* New York: New York University Press.

Menzies, R., LeFrançois, B.A., & Reaume, G. (2013). Introducing Mad Studies. In B.A. LeFrançois, R. Menzies, & G. Reaume (Eds.), *Mad matters: A critical reader in Canadian Mad Studies* (pp.1–22). Toronto, ON: Canadian Scholars' Press.

Michalko, R. (2002). *The difference that disability makes.* Philadelphia, PA: Temple University Press.

Mingus, M. (2011, February 12). Changing the framework: Disability justice. *Leaving Evidence.* Retrieved from https://leavingevidence.wordpress.com/2011/02/12/changing-the-framework-disability-justice/

Morris, J. (1992). 'Personal and political': A feminist perspective on researching physical disability. *Disability, Handicap and Society, 7*(2), 157–166.

Morris, J. (1993). Feminism and disability. *Feminist Review, 43,* 57–70.

Oliver, M. (1990). *The politics of disablement.* London: Palgrave Macmillan.

Reeve, D. (2008). *Negotiating disability in everyday life: The experience of psycho-emotional disablism.* (Unpublished PhD thesis). Lancaster University, Lancaster, UK.

Rich, A.C. (1980/2003). Compulsory heterosexuality and lesbian existence. *Journal of Women's History, 15*(3), 11–48.

Runswick-Cole, K., Curran, T., & Liddiard, K. (Eds.) (in press). *A Handbook of disabled children's Childhood Studies.* Basingstoke, UK: Palgrave Macmillan.

Runswick-Cole, K., & Goodley, D. (in press). 'The disability commons': Re-thinking motherhood through disability. In K. Runswick-Cole, T. Curran, & K. Liddiard (Eds.), *Palgrave handbook of disabled children's Childhood Studies.* Basingstoke, UK: Palgrave Macmillan.

Runswick-Cole, K., Mallett, R. & Timimi, S. (Eds.) (2016). *Re-thinking autism.* London: Jessica Kingsley Publishing.

Save The Kids. (n.d.). http://savethekidsgroup.org

Sherry, M. (2007). (Post) colonising disability. Special issue: *Wagadu, Journal of Transnational Women's and Gender Studies, 4* (Summer), 10–22.

Slater, J. (2016). *Youth and disability: A challenge to Mr Reasonable.* London: Routledge.

Smith, J. (2016). *The talking, being and becoming of Autism, childhood and disability* (Unpublished PhD thesis). University of Sheffield, Sheffield, UK.

Spoto, S. (2014). Teaching against hierarchies: An anarchist approach. *Journal of Feminist Scholarship, 7*(8), 78–92.

Tam, L. (2013). Whither indigenizing the Mad Movement? Theorizing the social relations of race and madness through conviviality. In B.A. LeFrançois, R. Menzies, & G. Reaume (Eds.), *Mad matters: A critical reader in Canadian Mad Studies* (pp. 281–297). Toronto, ON: Canadian Scholars' Press.

Thomas, C. (1999). *Female forms: Experiencing and understanding disability.* Buckingham, UK: Open University Press.

Thomas, C. (2007). *Sociologies of illness and disability: Contested ideas in disability studies and medical sociology.* Basingstoke, UK: Palgrave Macmillan.

Williams, A., Billington, T., Corcoran, T., & Goodley, D. (Eds.) (2016). *Critical educational psychology: Research and practice.* Oxford: Wiley–Blackwell.

Wright Mills, C. (1959). *The sociological imagination.* Oxford: Oxford University Press.

5
FEAR AND LOATHING IN THE EDUCATION SYSTEM

Robbie Piper

I was halfway through the English lesson when the drugs started to kick in.[1] Earlier in the day I had spoken to this particular child when he was fidgety, mischievous and particularly defiant.[2] This was behaviour that I had come to recognise over the first term or so, behaviour that I found both intensely disruptive to the 'learning environment' and that had come to define him as a person. He was naughty, but he was lively, and cheeky and funny as well. When I spoke to him, asking about the weekend and looking for clues to see if anything had happened at home, I talked to him about his behaviour and what I expected and what was appropriate. His reply was, 'I can't help it, my pills haven't kicked in yet.' These pills were Ritalin. They were prescribed by a child psychiatrist who was gossiped about by teachers as giving out Ritalin 'like M&Ms'. Another child in the class, who was not on them at the time, said his mum called them his 'naughty pills'. To return to the child in question: he had been getting used to the 'small' original dosage, so his dose had been increased. He was right – for some reason, they had taken a while to kick in. He was a nightmare in Mathematics, the first lesson, and no one around him got much learning done. But halfway through English, he had started to mellow and calm down. By lunch time, he was very calm – docile is more accurate. The child I was beginning to know and like (despite his behaviour) was disappearing. In his place was a different child. How he felt about this was very hard to tell: he did not smile as easily as he used to, but he was also less angry and upset, and did not act so frustrated with his difficulties in learning. From my point of view, he was definitely easier to have in the classroom. I sighed with relief and felt ashamed at my relief. The boy was 6 years old.

During my teacher training, I attended a lecture by Dr Neil Hopkin (2013), a progressive headteacher, and blogger.[3] He introduced me to Paulo Freire's *Pedagogy of the Oppressed* (Freire, 1970/1996). It was the most influential thing I read during my training. I will use this book alongside my own experiences to demonstrate what teaching in primary school encompasses. I will show the difficulties and challenges that teachers face and how these lead to a culture where children's difficulties are constructed as defects. Peter Breggin states that usually ADHD (attention-deficit hyperactivity disorder) results 'from boring and poorly disciplined classrooms' (Breggin, 2015, p. 147). Although his research and papers on the effects of these drugs are important, his analysis of the cause is as reductive as saying it is the result of chemical imbalances in the brain. This is not a chapter solely about ADHD, and I do not profess to have any psychological expertise; I do, however, see the diagnosis of children as suffering from ADHD, ASD (Autism spectrum disorder), or some other acronym, as symptomatic of a larger malaise within primary education. This chapter uses the research of others, experiences of teacher training and teaching, and theories of pedagogy. It will show how educational psychology, children's behaviours, pressures from Government and Ofsted,[4] the culture and education of teachers, children and children's parents combine to create an environment of fear and loathing that is primary education in England today.

I have been interested in special educational needs (SEN) for a while and specialised in this during my PGCE.[5] Dorothy Rowe's chapter on ADHD in *Making and Breaking Children's Lives* was illuminating to me as a trainee teacher (Rowe, 2005). Rowe writes that adults are simply frightened of acknowledging that children are terrified. Rowe mentions this in terms of how we see children with 'ADHD'; several other critics have detailed the detrimental effects of prescribing drugs to children for a disorder that is potentially spurious (Breggin, 2015; Jackson, 2009; Timimi, 2009). I was surprised to find how many of my student contemporaries were not as sceptical as I was about whether children with SEN statements were different enough from other children to warrant diagnosis and prescription.[6] When I quoted statistics which showed how before 1990 there were 'barely 5000 children in the UK diagnosed with ADHD. [By 2005] there are over 200,000' (Newnes & Radcliffe, 2012, p. iv), the educational psychologist who marked my essay put exclamation marks in the margin and wrote, 'I didn't know that – that's shocking'. During my teacher training, the only critical lectures we had were from the aforementioned Dr Neil Hopkin: one of his main points was that Ofsted and Government ministers do not know or do what is best for children.[7] Additionally, there was an optional post-5pm lecture that gave a detailed history of 'Special Educational Needs within Education' by Dr Garry Squires (2013). The lecture was aptly summarised by a tentative question from an audience member at the end who said, 'You seem to be saying that SEN is a construct of society. . .'. Whereupon Squires raised his hands and said, 'Yes! That's exactly what I'm saying!' Given that this lecture was 'optional', several of my contemporaries who felt they already knew all they needed to know about SEN did not attend.

The educational system in the UK is necessarily implicated in both the apparatus for diagnosing psychiatric disorders and the prescription of appropriate behaviour and academic achievement. The move towards a social-educational definition of 'maladjustment' has been suggested as the reason for the term becoming 'a catch-all for many different types of emotional and behavioural difficulty, such as delinquency, mental illness, and social deprivation' (Squires, 2012, p. 13; c.f. Laslett, 1998; Visser, 2003). In 1944, the Butler Education Act considered some children to have 'a disability of mind' not just if they were deemed 'incapable of receiving an education in school', but also, 'with respect to ability and aptitude', if the opinion of the local education authority, teachers or 'other persons' was that it would be 'expedient that he should be educated in association with other children in his own interests or in theirs'. This disability was to be confirmed by 'a medical officer of the authority' in line with the Mental Deficiency Act of 1913 (HMSO, 1944, sections 34 and 56–57). The vagaries of these disabilities, which were the object of judgment for various professionals surrounding the child, were given more detail in the 1945 Handicapped Pupils and School Health Service Regulations (Ministry of Education, 1945; as quoted in Squires, 2012, p. 12). These new regulations now included children who were blind, partially sighted, deaf, partially deaf, delicate, diabetic, educationally subnormal, epileptic, maladjusted, physically handicapped, or had speech defects.

The Underwood Report in 1955 stated that the spectrum of maladjustment ranges from 'introverted and withdrawn children' to disruptive children who 'have a bad effect on himself or his fellows' and, crucially, require expert help to remedy the diagnosis (Underwood Report, 1955, p. 22). The government policy of mixing identifiable disabilities, such as blindness, with subjective disabilities such as being delicate, introverted or a bad influence, meant that children were coming increasingly under the gaze of the professionals who were there to help them. Furthermore, it was at this time that the first *Diagnostic and Statistical Manual* was produced (APA, 1952), which described 112 different diagnostic categories. This was an increase on the 22 groups of mental disorder put forward by the American Medico-Psychological Association in 1918, and therefore broadened the remit for diagnosing a person with a disorder (Newnes, 2013). Squires notes that the Act of 1944 was to lead 'to a definition of special education needs that has had a lasting impact . . . repeated in government policy documents and Education Acts for the next 60 years' (Squires, 2012, p. 12). The rise in medical diagnosis along with the development of the language used to define special educational needs provides an ouroboros structure with circuitous logic: children need to be professionally diagnosed – children are difficult to teach – children have something wrong with them.

Changes in the education system and a rise in diagnosis seem closely linked: the 1981 Education Act introduced Statements of Special Educational Need for children with severe learning needs. It defined children with special educational needs as children who have 'significantly greater difficulty in learning than the majority of children his age' or 'having a disability which prevents or hinders him from making use of the educational facilities' (HMSO, 1981, section 1). The Act made the teacher responsible for identifying and providing for special educational needs. This gave teachers an excuse, an incentive and a wider range of disorders based on subjective evidence of behaviour to identify difficult children as having an SEN difficulty or disorder. In 1987, the *DSM-IIIR* (APA, 1987) was published and the number of disorders increased to 292. A year later, the 1988 Education Reform Act saw the introduction of national compulsory education, League Tables, and SATs[8] to measure school performance based on attainment, consequentially returning the education system back to the Payment by Results system of nearly a century before (Squires, 2012). This, unsurprisingly, led to a rise in statements of SEN to compensate for poor results and increase a school's value-added score (Office for Standards in Education, 2010). The rise in the number of children having SEN and therefore a mental disorder categorised through behaviour, with little or no emphasis on the context or the pressures that this behaviour is a reaction to, is likely to continue. The *DSM-5* (APA, 2013) has 365 categories of mental disorders. For all of the most common SEN categories, assessment is based on behaviour. In the *DSM-5,* the remit for diagnosis of ASD has now changed to 'difficulties adjusting behaviour to suit different social contexts' (APA, 2013, p. 88). It is hard to think of children or adults who would not fit into this category at some point. The British Psychological Society's response to *DSM-5* notes concern 'that clients and the general public are negatively affected by the continued medicalization of their natural and normal responses to their experiences' (quoted in Allan, 2011, n.p.). The philosopher Heisenberg's (1927, quoted in Jackson Brown, 2005, p. 40) uncertainty principle is relevant to this debate: 'What we observe is not nature in itself, but nature exposed to our method of questioning'; if we see a child as a problem, we will find a problem with the child.

I have not been teaching many years, but in my experience, one in ten teachers are openly critical of the widespread diagnosis of ASD and ADHD; a significant proportion of others appear uncomfortable with giving children medication that has to be signed for when dispensed because it is essentially an illegal drug. Special Education Needs Coordinators (SENCos) in the local cluster group of schools which the psychiatrist mentioned above (who gave out Ritalin like M&Ms) served, have banded together in an attempt to form a strategy to stop the over-prescription of drugs to children in Grades 1 through to 6. Yet teachers are constrained by several factors. Although I am critical of diagnosing children, I am inextricably involved in the process. The Government released its new national curriculum in July 2014 which increased the academic expectations for each year group. Teachers' pay is indexed to whether they can either show progression in children's learning or make them reach a certain standard by the end of the year. If targets are not met, Ofsted can fail schools and schools can turn into privately controlled academies. Children who find it too difficult to meet these targets have to be excused, explained or accounted for in some other way . Children need to be prevented from disrupting others through statements that help to pay for extra support, medication or expulsion. Or it is the fault of teachers and the school. It is a legal obligation for Primary Mental Health Workers in Education (read teachers) to act as a bridge between CAMHS[9] and schools: it is our job to promote 'good emotional health, preventing mental health problems developing and identifying mental health problems early' (Atkinson, Lemon, & Wright, 2010, p. 2). If I do not identify and help to prevent mental health problems from developing, I would be failing in my duty of care. Parents also have their own expectations of what you should be doing for their child. Some want you to bring back the cane, others want extra homework, still others want you to pick their child up from home in the morning because they cannot get them into school. When you are not supportive of a child's diagnosis with SEN, some parents feel glad, others feel frustrated and judged. All these pressures and problems get passed along until they end up heaped upon the children. The question that is often left for the teacher is, 'What are you going to do about it?'

What do teachers actually do?

Apart from having 12 weeks off a year, working 9am to 3pm, and being the stooge of society and scapegoat of governments, teachers actually work quite hard. I teach English, Mathematics, French, Computing, Geography, History, Science, Music, Art, Design and Technology, Religious Education, Physical Education, Guided Reading, Philosophy and Personal, Social and Emotional Health. There are also several other issues that arise throughout the year, such as interventions for children who are falling behind and need to be pushed further or need some extra emotional or social support. The majority of these lessons are differentiated at least four ways for the spread of ability within one class of 30 children. The lessons are planned to form a sequence and to cross and overlap as much as possible in order to reinforce what they have learnt in other contexts. They are designed to inspire and enthuse the children and centre on real-life context or problems to enhance other non-core curriculum skills because, we are told, 'the teacher who sets out to work *with* the learning process of children's daily lives, in sum total, seeks to reap continually a harvest he has not sown' (Rosen & Rosen, 1973/1975, p. 12).

Along with Breggin, Freire also critiques boring lessons that do not engage with people's natural understanding of the world. Freire's 'boring lessons' are a symptom of what he calls 'banking education' (Freire, 1970/1996, pp. 56–62), where abstract or seemingly irrelevant facts are taught and have to be repeated back. It is a type of education that is also referred to in Ken Robinson's popular TED talk (2006) on how education kills creativity, which was used on my teacher training course and was recommended viewing in the application process for Teach First.[10] Despite criticism, however – and epitomising the ambivalent forces affecting education – this type of teaching model has both receded and intensified in recent years. The current (early 2017) Government has shown an interest in testing children at an early age: the SPAG (spelling, punctuation and grammar) test in the final year of primary school, which is an important factor in the school's published statistics, has been introduced for 6 and 7 year olds as well.[11] Progress and achievement are measured through these results, and there is increased pressure to teach facts in the style of banking education. However, although the national curriculum targets have been made more challenging, in many subjects, the language has been designed to encourage teachers to move away from traditional schemes of work, to teach creatively and incorporate the targets with the children's own experiences and interests. Caught between two different models of educating, teachers are equally expected to create engaging lesson plans that are nevertheless not so exciting that they prevent sensible working habits.

An English lesson, looking at one element of a novel or genre, for example, might run as follows: a starting activity that allows the teacher to assess the children's understanding of a previous concept or skill; main teaching input that refers back to previous learning and links in spelling and grammar (which are also taught discretely), where children are aware of the objective of the task and how they can measure their own level of achievement of the task; a task for children differentiated four or five ways; a review session where teacher and children review the success so far; a second task that progresses the learning, also differentiated four or five ways; and finally a plenary which either allows children to demonstrate how they understand they have achieved the objective of the lesson or challenges their thinking in applying what they have learnt further or in a different context. This process is repeated four or five times a day, five times a week. Work is marked, feedback given, children respond to feedback, teachers respond to children's feedback. I am not moaning about this; it is what I am paid to do. Issues arise when you then have to plan and deliver all this while also spotting and preventing mental health issues.[12] The problem is further increased when these young people have incredibly complex and difficult lives: some are on the run from abusive fathers, some are born addicted to drugs, some live in care because their siblings died of starvation, some spend the first years of their life tied to a cot. They obviously have mental health issues. Who wouldn't? What are we, as teachers, meant to do about it? Flagging concerns seems pathetically ineffectual. My main tactic, which I haven't found in any literature, is simply to be consistent and show them that I care.

The immediate problem with preventing and identifying mental health problems is the difficulty of defining what mental health problems actually are. As mentioned previously, during my teacher training, there was very little information provided about the merits/credibility of different diagnoses. Most teachers do not have the time or inclination to read articles or the latest *DSM*, so awareness is dependent on whatever colleagues talk about or what the media represents. I do my best to be a role model for the children and promote 'good emotional health' like happiness, resilience, positive self-esteem. These are values I think are particularly relevant for the children I teach; although I am also aware that my own life experiences have been very different to theirs.[13] The children whom I teach have difficult lives; so do their parents. As I teach these children, I am aware of my responsibilities to them, but also of the pressures and expectations that I am under from the Government or society at large. I am aware that I am a Foucauldian 'teacher-judge' (Foucault, 1975, p. 304). I am obliged to deal with, document and inform higher management of any behaviour that I deem to be inappropriate or unhealthy. Although a professional, I am not an arbiter of truth and morality. During in-job training on these issues, covering which behaviours I should report and on what type of form, I raised this issue.[14] The answer was a vague rebuttal, 'You must do what you think is right' – deflecting the responsibility onto the teacher and their moralist judgment on the child. With the added caveat of 'if in doubt, write it down and pass it on' up the chain of responsibility, meaning that critical awareness of your role is not encouraged; if you are selective, you could miss something that endangers a child's life – the result being a paradoxical image of a nervous automaton judging everything indiscriminately. The fear of being the one who missed something in one of the horror cases that every year or so get reported is such that the children, their personalities, behaviour, language, appearance, even their smell, are all under intense scrutiny. The duplicitous teacher-judge has to be a warm, friendly authoritarian figure that the children respect while also analysing them and their families because I cannot trust that their parents will look after them adequately.

What children (should) do

Teacher training courses suggest that children naturally love learning. Babies and infants seek out the experiences that their bodies and brains need in order to develop. They learn through trial and error. Mistakes are fundamental and teachers should aim to give opportunities to learn in this manner. Children should love learning: the idea that this is 'natural' creates a moral imperative that schools are expected to reinforce. By the time they reach primary school, children should show behaviour that demonstrates they love learning. This is then translated into: they should be able to listen attentively, follow several instructions, work on new activities, be sensitive to others, understand and follow rules (Standards and Testing Agency, 2014a–2014e, p. 1). There are two main problems that teachers face when attempting to implement this training or assuming this philosophic/pedagogic view: first, children have frequently missed out on vital experiences in their formative years, and for various reasons, resent the constraints and pressures of school from an early age. Second, the pressures from Government and Ofsted mean that teachers cannot afford to allow children to make mistakes,[15] or to exhibit anything other than exemplary classroom behaviour.

The fact that some children miss vital experiences in their infant years creates a significant obstacle in the teacher's attempt to build a relationship with them, where they are supposed to be intrinsically motivated to love learning. Children with whom I have worked have had significantly below age-expected levels of language capability. When they have gained an age-expected level of language, much of what they say is often judged inappropriate; that is, shouting, aggressive and swearing.[16] They have also had what is termed by teachers, in teacher-judge mode, as 'pramitus' – where key years spent confined to and pushed around in a pram have resulted in impaired physical development. Additionally, where physical restraint has disempowered children from discovering and learning for themselves, a learned dependency has been fostered.[17] Early Years teachers do extraordinary work with these children, covering a huge amount of lost ground and helping the children achieve their 'Early Learning Goals'. Further up the school, however, focus on gross and fine motor-skills has to be sacrificed as curriculum targets take priority. Early on in my teaching career, I had some training on the physical development of children run by two women who were very nice, but had no understanding of the pressures and expectations we were under. They talked about how children's brain development is linked to their bodies. Without the exposure to the sorts of activities that children needed to develop, children wouldn't be able to progress from the 'reptilian part of their brain' and wouldn't be able to sit and concentrate for any extended period of time. Their advice was that if children needed to roll around on the floor when I was teaching, I should not stop them because I was stopping their brains developing. They make an excellent point: some children need learning experiences that our current education system does not offer, especially the children we were teaching. If, however, I was observed by the Local Authority (who at the time were a constant presence due to the school's poor performance in SATs) or Ofsted and this behaviour was going on, I would immediately be judged an inadequate teacher.[18] This would mean more scrutiny and training and extra work, or possibly a pre-emptive career move. The 'behaviour for learning'[19] in the classroom would be deemed too chaotic for children to reach their learning goals, which would be bad for their academic education, and for any hope for me in moving up the pay scale. Depending on results and how important that particular year group was for the overall statistics, it could be a contributing factor in the school being forced into becoming an academy and people losing their jobs. There is quite a lot riding on children doing what 'we' have decided they should be able to do.

That children cannot sit still or are not motivated to learn is not evidence of mental health problems. It signifies nothing other than that they cannot sit still and are not motivated to learn. In my experience, a major influence in either helping or hindering the teacher's attempts to build a relationship with a child is the background and attitude of their immediate culture and family. When training in inner-city schools, the cohorts were always around 50% white British, 50% other ethnicity (primarily Asian). Often it was closer to 80% non-white British. When teaching in these schools or talking with parents who were first- or second-generation immigrants, their respect for the education system was clear; the work that teachers put in and what we were trying to do were valued by both parents and children. Although there were children with challenging behaviour, the respect for education within these communities made learning to teach in these schools enjoyable. One girl who joined my Grade 2 class of 6–7 year olds in Manchester halfway through the school year came from Iraq. She was obviously a bright child and wanted to do well in school, make friends and improve her English. She was always critically thinking about what it was she was being asked to do. She was curious as to how she could build on what she had already learned because she trusted that I was trying to take her logically from one step to another. This was my first experience of what intrinsic motivation looks like. She even said, 'I just love learning things.' Her improvement was visible every day and her parents were always incredibly grateful for any extra support I gave her or even if I was just doing my job. Gratitude is inevitable, perhaps, when you come from a war-torn country and you arrive in a place with decent housing and opportunities. In terms of teaching critically, children who have recently moved from another country have often been the most interesting to teach.

I have also taught a girl who had started school locally, but due to her parents' work, had also had experience of non-western schooling. Building a relationship with her was easy: she was respectful of school and behaviour and she was keen to learn and to show off what she knew.[20] More pertinently, she was never afraid to ask questions about what we were learning, or how I had explained it. Sometimes it would become clear that I had explained it in some way that was indeed confusing, misleading or had used the wrong terminology. At other times, she would explain why it was not right that I had said her answer was wrong; for example, when she'd marked quarter past on the clock as half past, she explained it was still half past, just half past in a different direction. These are only two stand-out examples of how changing education systems can result in children automatically thinking more critically about what they learn and how they are taught. It is also an example of how cultural differences have an effect on my own attitudes to children; as a teacher, I am more likely to be sympathetic towards children and parents who value the education I am providing. In this respect, these children are more similar to me than many others whom I have taught.

My first paid teaching roles were within schools serving council estates notorious for crime, gangs and drugs. Statistics showed that people on any type of out-of-work benefits in the town as a whole represented 11.5% of the population – 0.5% below the national average.[21] The sample size of the particular areas relevant to my experience, however, is too small to merit official Government statistics. The estates which my schools served have had a significant number of low-income families or families on out-of-work benefits: at my current school, 35.3% of all pupils qualify for free school meals, which is more than double the national average of 16.3%.[22] As I got to know the families in areas like these, I realised how interconnected they all were: step siblings, step cousins, half this or that, children removed from their mothers to other relatives. It reminded me of an idea in Plato's *The Republic* (fourth century BC/1992) where children are not the single responsibility of their birth parents but of the wider community. This is not necessarily a 'bad' social model, but the fact that I was reminded of a book written more than 2000 years ago and the fact that some of these parents' reading and writing abilities were being surpassed by those of their young children, does little to mitigate the social, cultural and educational gap between me and them and justifies, to an extent, their anger at my interference. I was trying to get onside and instil them with a sense of hope for their children's future, but as a childless, upper-working-class, educated man from the suburbs of Birmingham, I had no idea what I was doing.

When talking with parents about the aggressive behaviour of their children, they vehemently disagreed with the sanctions I had put in place and said I did not understand what it was like on a council estate: they wanted the children to be able to fight; otherwise, they would not survive. My opinion was that they did not have to be on the council estate forever, but could do well at school, go on to further/higher education and move away to another area with more jobs where being physically tough was not a primary concern. Diagnosis of ADHD is linked to social environment: research published in 2015 found that 'in almost every year studied' between 2004 and 2013, 'incidence rates were highest among the most deprived patients and lowest among the least deprived patients' (Hire, Ashcroft, Springate, & Steinkel, 2015, p. 4). This report concludes that 'in the United Kingdom, ADHD may be associated with socioeconomic deprivation' (Hire et al., 2015, p. 8); equally, behaviour associated with ADHD is also that associated with the poorest socio-economic groups: children with ADHD may develop 'significant conduct problems and antisocial behaviours (such as fighting, early substance experimentation and adverse driving outcomes) and increased risk of developing oppositional defiant disorder (ODD) and conduct disorder (CD)' (Peasgood et al., 2016, p. 1218, citing Pliszka, 2000). According to these descriptors, the violence that parents see as necessary to survival is deemed pathological.

Furthermore, so many of the children I have taught do a lot of sitting around playing computer games, or on iPads or iPhones, and eating poor-quality food – it must be noted that this is not unique to certain social classes. This makes me question the training I was given about how children naturally love learning and will seek the experiences they require to develop. Sitting around, not really thinking or interacting with the world, and eating unhealthy processed food is not good for children. It certainly is not good in terms of their behaviour in school – I have taught a lot of pent-up children, without basic physical and interpersonal skills, who exhibit 'antisocial behaviours'. One child I taught had not yet been diagnosed with anything.[23] He was a nightmare to teach, however. It was not that he was unintelligent academically, but emotionally, it was like trying to teach a violent and angry 2 year old. His emotional and behaviour difficulties were extremely difficult to manage, especially as an inexperienced teacher. I was meant to teach him the complexities of phonics and the various phonemes that one grapheme can represent and how to form letters correctly in line with the school handwriting policy. My lesson would struggle to be more exciting than shooting people and stealing cars; equally, it was difficult to build a relationship with this child when he seemed to have difficulties distinguishing the virtual world from reality. It is a common theme that I have encountered: many children spend long hours playing computer games that are rated above their age or spend their time watching YouTube videos – living inside what Grace Jackson calls a 'dromosphere' (Jackson, 2005, p. 91). They then come to school tired, restless and irritable, and definitely not exhibiting their 'natural' love of learning. However, all is not lost; when reading the brilliant *Invention of Hugo Cabret* (Selznick, 2011), albeit projected onto a screen, a restless and difficult class would sit for hours listening in rapt attention, or quietly and urgently discussing the book with each other lest they miss out on anything. This shows that the children in my class diagnosed/diagnosable with ADHD, but not on medication, can sit and concentrate for an extended period of time without chemical intervention and with one simple way of competing with the dromosphere of their everyday lives.

What do teachers do when children don't do what they're supposed to do?

Behaviour management is a continual preoccupation for teachers. It is no coincidence that good behaviour 'management' is necessary for a good Ofsted score, and that children's mental health issues are identified primarily as a result of disruptive and aggressive behaviour. I mentioned I was doing this chapter to a headteacher and he gave me a book called *Teach Like a Champion* (Lemov, 2010) which had all sorts of different 'Behaviour for Learning' tips. A colleague of mine told me that her favourite teaching book was *Getting the Buggers to Behave* (Cowley, 2010). As mine was *Pedagogy of the Oppressed* (Freire, 1970/1996), it perhaps explained why I was not seen as the 'go to' authoritarian in the school. A resource I use to organise the wealth of teaching aids you can find online is Pinterest, a kind of virtual notice board. It is a website where pictures or websites are 'pinned' onto one of your boards; others can view your boards and follow any updates you do, 'like' it, share it, or re-pin something you found onto their own board. One of the boards I have is 'classroom management', on which is my most re-pinned item. It is a short blog called '5 Quick Classroom-Management Tips for Novice Teachers' by Edutopia website editor Rebecca Alber (2012). This illustrates the main pressure felt by teachers – classroom behaviour – as well as a desire for 'quick wins' and simple solutions. The five quick tips are:

1. Use a normal, natural voice ...
2. Speak only when students are quiet and ready ...
3. Use hand signals and other non-verbal communication ...
4. Address behavior issues quickly and wisely ...
5. Always have a well-designed, engaging lesson.

(Alber, 2012, n.p.)

Tips 1 and 2 are about your presence in the classroom, the general environment you are trying to create, but fundamentally, it is about the relationship you are trying to build with the children. In terms of behaviour, this is the most important – do you want the children to do what you've asked because they fear the consequences if they don't; or because they respect you and need your praise to validate them? Tip 3 is about both saving your voice and having a system so you do not have to shout, which helps the learning environment and enables you to avoid hypocrisy when dealing with loud/aggressive children. It is also about dealing with 'attention seeking behaviour' without giving attention or disrupting your lesson. Tip 5, the need for well-designed lessons was examined earlier; Tip 4 is partly obvious, but the 'wisely' part is more complex. It is to do with 'psychologising' the children, giving them power over their behaviour through language. I will mention more on this later.

Diagnosis can also provide a quick fix to behavioural difficulties – although filling in the associated forms when children have been referred is a time-consuming, frustrating job. They are designed so that various professionals can extrapolate quantitative data from the behaviour of a complex, troubled child. This behaviour is exhibited in a high-pressured, demanding and unnatural classroom environment, and subsequently categorised and reduced to a statistic by a teacher with various pressures to negotiate, who is required to professionally put aside any frustrations with the particular child and view them and their behaviour 'objectively'. Here is a selection of ridiculous questions I had to answer in regard to children, aged 6–10, where you tick one of: '0: not true at all, seldom'; '1: just a little true or occasionally'; '2: pretty much true, often, or quite a bit'; '3: very much true, very often, very frequently'.

> 14 Uses a weapon (bat, brick, bottle, knife, or gun)
> 27 Steals while confronting a person (mugging, purse snatching, armed robbery)
> 28 Is perfect in every way
> 60 Avoids or dislikes things that take a lot of effort and are not fun
> 68 Gets into trouble with the police
> 90 Has broken into someone else's house, building or car
> 101 I cannot figure out what makes him/her happy
> 109 Is hard to motivate[24]

At first, I was shocked that Questions 14 and 27 were included in a questionnaire about children so young. However, several children have used 'weapons' in the form of classroom or playground equipment to dominate or hurt other children. It is not an uncommon sight in nurseries around the country – again, there is not necessarily a social class judgment being made here; as a child, I was guilty of behaviour like this. According to the terms of the statement, their behaviour is then considered as parallel to knife and gun crime and armed robbery. I have yet to meet a child who is perfect in every way. This statement is loaded with my notion of what a 'perfect' child is – in the context of the classroom, it is often one who can be quiet, or alternatively, inquisitive and engaged, when required. Most of the children I have taught are hard to motivate and dislike and avoid any task that is difficult and not fun. It is my job to motivate, inspire and break down and differentiate problems so they are achievable. If I were to tick 3 (very much true, very often, very frequently) for Questions 60, 101 and 109, it is not clear whether I am commenting on my own inability to teach or their inability to be taught. When completing the questionnaire, the incongruence of Question 101 is striking, overtly asking about your ability to understand a child – again, is this a question about the child, or about my capacity to be an understanding teacher? I have only taught one child who was in trouble with the police – allegedly, he was used by his older siblings and cousins to break into houses through small windows. Having difficulty sitting still in lessons was the least of his worries. If they are getting into trouble with the police at the age of six, promoting drug dependency does not seem a sensible approach to helping these children, although it may well change their behaviour in the classroom.

Both Breggin's idea (2015) that boring and poorly disciplined classrooms contribute to ADHD diagnoses, as well as this bizarre questionnaire, are examples of an inherent problem in education. There is a structure of 'perfect sages' and 'utter ignoramuses', with psychologists and governments at the top, children at the bottom and teachers somewhere in the middle, filling in forms, making judgments and planning lessons that try to prioritise both children's engagement and behaviour management.[25]

Addressing behaviours wisely

Freire (1970/1996) describes an ideal pedagogy in which both the oppressed and the oppressor are liberated from their limiting roles. Fear is a central motivator in both of these roles: 'The oppressed are afraid to embrace freedom; the oppressors are afraid of losing the "freedom" to oppress' (pp. 28–29). Freire notes that prescription is a basic element of the oppressed–oppressor relationship. Written before the rise and rise of ADHD, prescription refers to instruction, although Freire's description serves as a useful analysis of the ongoing impulse to pathologise and medicalise children's behaviour:

> Every prescription represents the imposition of one individual's choice upon another, transforming the consciousness of the person prescribed to into one that conforms with the prescribers' consciousness. Thus, the behaviour of the oppressed is a prescribed behaviour, following as it does the guidelines of the oppressor.
>
> *(Freire, 1970/1996, pp. 28–29)*

Freire's argument has a sad relevance to my profession where we have a duty of care for the children in our schools, but if they cannot behave as we demand, there must be something wrong with them. Inscribing a label or diagnosis onto these children is a type of invasion: '[preventing] individuals from engaging in the process of inquiry is one of violence . . . to alienate human beings from their own decision making is to change them into objects' (Freire, 1970/1996, p. 66). An example of this was noted at the start of this chapter, where a boy who was simply too difficult was made easier to manage. The only positive outcomes of this type of inscription which I have encountered are to create a kind of shorthand in the praxis of professionals for describing types of personalities. As already noted, it is fraught with difficulties, rendering it largely futile on any meaningful level. Discussing a particularly difficult child with the educational psychologist and another teacher, I was given a questionnaire that aimed at determining whether the child had attachment issues or Autism. I asked what the point of it was and one of the answers I was given was, 'it will help us understand the child better', which we all knew was nonsense. The second answer was that it is easier to get diagnosed with these things earlier in life, and that in the long run, one diagnosis would be better than the other: a diagnosis of attachment issues now leads to a diagnosis of psychosis in adult life, which is potentially more damaging than a diagnosis of Autism now. *'Oh God, I shouldn't have asked'*, I thought, although as it turned out, the child was too complex to fit either pigeon hole sufficiently. Obviously the child never knew, but the same child did give me a 'thank you' card before I left.

As mentioned previously, Rowe (2005) states that ADHD is a result of adults' fear of frightened children. The praxis of addressing behaviour, however, shows that this is not necessarily a revelation to teachers: the acknowledgement that children are scared is deeply embedded in how teachers think about children in general. Alber's blog post (2012), discussed above, suggests using neutral language that does not make children defensive, emphasising that the teacher should '*act* as if you do care' (2012, n.p.; my emphasis). During my training, I was given conversational scripts to run through with difficult children where you psychologise the child's behaviour. My training was explicit in explaining that you separate the child from their behaviour, to the extent where 'that behaviour' is preferable to 'your behaviour' and never simply, 'you'.[26] The aims are various: not to damage self-esteem (which is probably already low, hence the bad behaviour); empower the children to take responsibility for the behaviour (if it is separate, it is not a part of them that cannot be changed); and also to make the children think that the teacher 'gets' them (i.e. that behaviour tells me you are worried that you won't do well and people will laugh at you if you try and fail, so you . . .). Teachers are not scared of acknowledging that children are terrified – they readily do so. Although, of course, this does not mean that Rowe is wrong: the idea that children are scared is still a frightening one. Behavioural teaching praxis shows that teachers use what the fear shows them of the child's personality to build a relationship and trust with the child, to appear knowing and wise, in order to manipulate their behaviour. Some teachers share their practice of being 'a complete psychobitch' for at least the first few weeks, so the fear is increased and the children are desperate to please you.

Diagnoses such as ADHD revolve around fear. The symptoms are synonymous with fear and agitation (Rowe, 2005), the children are fearful of the oppressive system and are using their most effective weapon: misbehaviour (Freire, 1970/1996, p. 28); the adults are fearful that their profession is violent in nature, so choose to view their failures as a result of a mental illness in the child (Freire, 1970/1996, p. 136) as well as other possible factors such as diet, exercise, home environment, self-esteem, boring classrooms and poor classroom management (Breggin, 2015). We are right to be scared. In an increasingly automated and technologically advancing society, I do not know what jobs I am training my students to do. I despair at the lack of practical jobs at which some children I have taught would excel, though they found learning and remembering difficult. With talk of a Universal Income Benefit gaining traction, the old idea of training a workforce is perhaps obsolete. The world in which compulsory education was originally formed has radically changed, as has the culture that the children grow up in. The American Dream that anyone can achieve anything if they try has permeated UK society to the extent that our education system reflects this, even if reality does not. As a result of the fact that more students are achieving A grades than ever before, they have had to create an A★, in an attempt to differentiate between candidates. The number of graduates achieving Firsts at university has more than doubled in a decade. And yet global tables show that British students are falling behind other countries in core areas of the curriculum. What is education for – a liberating force that teaches people to transform their world, or an oppressive one that transforms people so that they fit the world? Perhaps I should concentrate on teaching values such as to be considerate, to be happy, to not be fearful, to do good, to not do harm, to be kind to those with less power than you. Good lessons for many professionals. In this struggling education system, although the children lack the communication skills of adults, I would like to start a genuine dialogue with these 'essentially communicative creatures' (Freire, 1970/1996, p. 109) where the power is shared and 'there are only people who are attempting, together, to learn more than they know' (Freire, 1970/1996, p. 71). I am trying. Don't tell Ofsted.

Notes

1. Credit to Hunter S Thompson (2005, p. 3).
2. 'Unsettled' is the word that I immediately think of, but that is a very 'teachery' word. We have a whole thesaurus to dip into for parents' evenings, phone calls, etc. You get it when you qualify. I will try to steer away from these words as they seem deliberately diluted – designed to not irritate parents, but still tick boxes that you have raised the issue with parents. They are coated with blandness and duplicity.
3. For his blog, see: https://neilhopkin.wordpress.com/; his Twitter account, @neilhopkin
4. Office for Standards in Education – independent ombudsman for education.
5. Post-Graduate Certificate in Education: a year-long teacher training course.
6. Around one-third to half of them, it seems, were getting into teaching in order to try and become educational psychologists. Having a little knowledge about how difficult that profession was to get into, it seemed to me worrying that so many uncritical thinkers would fail in this elusive goal and then become potentially disgruntled, pseudo-psychologising teachers.
7. For instance, research was published in the UK over 25 years ago stating that there was no evidence that marking had an effect on children's achievement, and yet Ofsted still insist that lengthy comments are required in order for teachers to be considered 'Good' or 'Outstanding' – when teaching younger children, I have had to write comments in their books knowing that some of them cannot spell their own names, let alone read the comments. The revolutionary research in 1998 by Paul Black and Dylan Wiliam's *Inside the Black Box* (1998) is still waiting to gain momentum. An example of a school that does know what is best is @thehappiestschoolonearth aka Three Bridges Primary School, Southall, London: see www.theguardian.com/education/2016/mar/22/teaching-crisis-school-what-keep-them
8. An abbreviation that has become one word meaning one or all of: Standard Assessment Tasks when introduced, but also Statutory Assessment Tests, Standard Assessment Tests or Standard Achievement Tests, etc.
9. Child and Adolescent Mental Health Services.
10. Teach First: a graduate teacher training programme designed to reduce inequality in education and provide future leaders in business.
11. Ministers had to make a u-turn on their plans for all 4 year olds to be assessed: see www.independent.co.uk/news/education/education-news/baseline-tests-for-four-year-olds-ministers-forced-to-make-humiliating-u-turn-after-admitting-they-a6973886.html. See also consultation on education reform www.gov.uk/government/news/government-to-consult-on-reforms-to-primary-assessment-system, which has the potential to alleviate some of the internal pressures of the current system, if teachers are critical of themselves and the profession and the Government responds accordingly.

12 Ironically, it is teachers' mental health that is currently in the news: see www.bbc.co.uk/news/education-35900499
13 There is a worldwide scheme that promotes teaching through certain values (www.valuesbasededucation.com/). There is also a Government requirement to teach 'British Values'. These are: Mutual Respect and the Tolerance of Those with Different Faiths and Beliefs; Democracy; Rule of Law; Individual Liberty.
14 My question only pre-empted the plan of the training, which was to state the laws and then discuss our interpretations of where we 'draw the line'. The training is an example of the self-awareness of the profession: as teachers are on the front line of child services, essentially we have to 'act' as arbiters of truth and morality.
15 Unless these are quickly addressed and only a limited number of mistakes is permissible.
16 I once heard a girl in reception class (age 4 to 5) when playing on a telephone, say to an imaginary person, 'You're really fucking me off now'.
17 I am not trying to judge the parents here, although there is obviously a judgment implied in the coined term 'pramitus'. Numerous 'how to parent' books are one example of the difficulties and complexities involved in raising children. The Government closures of initiatives such as Sure Start aimed at helping parents is one of many contributing factors in making a difficult problem harder. The respite of a pram is obvious.
18 I should note that as it is never the child who is bad, but their behaviour and their choices which are bad, it is never the teacher who is inadequate, but their teaching, that particular lesson or that choice in how they responded or behaved to the child. Obviously, neither child nor teacher seems particularly fooled by this linguistic device and I will mention more on the idea of liberating through praxis later.
19 Behaviour for Learning or B4L is a concept which emerged from a review aimed at improving Initial Teacher Education and was incorporated into a variety of Government educational policy and guidance. Initially, it came from Powell and Tod (2004).
20 When we discussed different consequences of breaking class rules as a class, she would sometimes suggest a physical punishment that she had obviously come across in a non-UK school. Although she took the line that good behaviour brought its own satisfaction, she did like to see misbehaviour sanctioned. This provides worrying evidence, if evidence was needed, that obedience and a dutiful attitude to learning are underpinned by an element of fear of the educators. Tied to this is the current Government's highlighting of outcomes in countries where this fear is used as a teaching tool.
21 Statistics obtained from NOMIS, Office for National Statistics (www.nomisweb.co.uk). Statistics relate to the period of 2014–2015.
22 Statistics obtained from the Department for Education (2016). The national average is from 2014 which reduced slightly from the previous year. I cannot find an accurate current average as the Government is changing how money for 'free school meal' children is distributed. The Ofsted report from 2015 confirms that this school is well above the national average in terms of low-income families.
23 The following year he was diagnosed with ADHD and other behavioural and emotional difficulties, and prescribed medication for this, but I no longer had the task of teaching him. He had forgotten or forgiven past grievances and greeted me cheerily in the corridor when our paths crossed.
24 Confers 4th Teachers' Questionnaire.
25 It is worth noting that my students behave best when I read stories to them. They particularly love the writings of Brian Selznick. Unfortunately, there is not much time in the week which I can spend on 'just' reading.
26 There is a worrying parallel with the *Northern Lights* trilogy of Philip Pullman (1998) where children are separated from their daemons or exterior manifestations of their soul. In an environment where children are disempowered to such an extent that their misbehaviour is their only expression of their freedom, teachers resemble Pullman's horrific oblation board or Freire's camouflaged 'invader assuming the role of a helping friend' (1970/1996, p. 134).

References

Alber, R. (2012, 13 March). 5 Quick Classroom-Management Tips for Novice Teachers. *Edutopia*. Retrieved 22 April 2016 from www.edutopia.org/blog/classroom-management-tips-novice-teachers-rebecca-alber

Allan, C.A. (BPS) (2011). *Response to the American Psychiatric Association: DSM-5 Development*. British Psychological Society. Retrieved from www.scribd.com/document/125773578/DSM-5-2011-BPS-Response

American Psychiatric Association (APA). (1952). *Diagnostic and Statistical Manual of Mental Disorders*. Washington, DC: APA.

American Psychiatric Association (APA). (1987). *Diagnostic and Statistical Manual of Mental Disorders-IIIR*. Washington, DC: APA.

American Psychiatric Association (APA). (2013). *Diagnostic and Statistical Manual of Mental Disorders-5*. Washington, DC: APA.

Atkinson, M., Lemon, E., & Wright, B. (2010). *NFER Review: The Role of Primary Mental Health Workers in Education*. Slough, UK: National Foundation for Educational Research.

Black, P., & Wiliam, D. (1998). *Inside the Black Box*. London: GL Assessment Limited.

Breggin, P. (2015). The Rights of Parents and Children in Regard to Children Receiving Psychiatric Diagnoses and Drugs. In C. Newnes (Ed.), *Children in Society: Politics, Policies and Interventions* (pp. 145–161). Monmouth, UK: PCCS Books..

Cowley, S. (2010). *Getting the Buggers to Behave* (4th ed.). London: Continuum.

Department for Education. (2016). Statistics available at www.compare-school-performance.service.gov.uk/

Foucault, M. (1975). *Madness and Civilization: A History of Insanity in the Age of Reason*. New York: Vintage.

Freire, P. (1970/1996). *Pedagogy of the Oppressed*. (2nd revised ed.). London: Penguin Books.

Hire, A.J., Ashcroft, D.M., Springate, D.A., & Steinke, D.T. (2015). ADHD in the United Kingdom: Regional and Socioeconomic Variations in Incidence Rates amongst Children and Adolescents (2004–2013). *Journal of Attention Disorders, 19*(11), 915–996.

HMSO (His Majesty's Stationery Office). (1944). *Education Act 1944*. London: HMSO.

HMSO (Her Majesty's Stationery Office). (1981). *1981 Education Act*. London: HMSO.

Hopkin, N. (2013). Introduction to Religious Education lecture.

Jackson, G. (2005). Cybernetic Children: How Technologies Change and Constrain the Developing Mind. In C. Newnes & N. Radcliffe (Eds.), *Making and Breaking Children's Lives* (3rd ed.; pp. 90–104). Ross-on-Wye, UK: PCCS Books.

Jackson, G.E. (2009). The Case against Stimulants. In S. Timimi & J. Leo (Eds.), *Rethinking ADHD, From Brain to Culture* (pp. 255–286). Basingstoke, UK: Palgrave Macmillan.

Jackson Brown, F. (2005). ADHD and the Philosophy of Science. In C. Newnes & N. Radcliffe (Eds.), *Making and Breaking Children's Lives*. Ross-on-Wye, UK: PCCS Books.

Laslett, R. (1998). *Changing Perceptions: Emotional and Behavioural Difficulties since 1945*. Maidstone, UK: AWCEBD.

Lemov, D. (2010). *Teach Like a Champion*. San Francisco, CA: Jossey-Bass.

Newnes, C. (2013). The Diagnostic Statistical Manual: A History of Critiques of Psychiatric Classifications Systems. In J. Dillon, J. Moncrieff, & E. Speed (Eds.), *De-medicalizing Misery* (pp. 211–225). Basingstoke, UK: Palgrave Macmillan.

Newnes, C., & Radcliffe, N. (2012). Introduction. In C. Newnes & N. Radcliffe (Eds.), *Making and Breaking Children's Lives* (3rd ed.). Ross-on-Wye, UK: PCCS Books.

Office for Standards in Education. (2010). *The Special Educational Needs and Disability Review: A Statement Is Not Enough*. Manchester: Ofsted.

Peasgood, T., Bhardwaj, A., Biggs, K., Brazier, J.E., Coghill, D., Cooper, C.L. . . . Sonuga-Barke, E.J.S. (2016). The Impact of ADHD on the Health and Well-being of ADHD Children and their Siblings. *European Child & Adolescent Psychiatry, 25*, 1217–1231. doi:10.1007/s00787-016-0841-6

Plato. (fourth century BC/1992). *The Republic* (A.D. Lindsay, Trans.). London: Everyman's Library.

Pliszka, S.R. (2000). Patterns of Psychiatric Comorbidity with Attention-Deficit/Hyperactivity Disorder. *Child and Adolescent Psychiatric Clinics of North America, 9*(3), 525–540.

Powell, S., & Tod, J. (2004). *A Systematic Review of How Theories Explain Learning Behaviour in School Contexts*. In Research Evidence in Education Library [search engine]. London: EPPI-Centre, Social Science Research Unit, Institute of Education.

Pullman, P. (1998). *Northern Lights* (3rd ed.). London: Scholastic Ltd.

Robinson, K. (2006). *Do Schools Kill Creativity?* [video]. Available at: www.ted.com/talks/ken_robinson_says_schools_kill_creativity.html (Accessed 22 April 2016).

Rosen, C., & Rosen, H. (1973/1975). *The Language of Primary School Children*. Harmondsworth, UK: Penguin Books Ltd.

Rowe, D. (2005). ADHD: Adults' Fear of Frightened Children. In C. Newnes & N. Radcliffe (Eds.), *Making and Breaking Children's Lives* (3rd ed.; pp 71–74). Ross-on-Wye, UK: PCCS Books.

Selznick, B. (2011). *The Invention of Hugo Cabret*. New York: Scholastic Press.

Squires, G. (2012). Historical and Socio-Political Agendas around Defining and Including Children with Special Educational Needs. In D. Armstrong & G. Squires (Eds.), *Contemporary Issues in Special Educational Needs: Considering the Whole Child* (pp. 9–24). New York: Open University Press.

Squires, G. (2013). Introductory lecture for the Inclusion Pathway.

Standards and Testing Agency. (2014a). *EYFS Profile Exemplification for the Level of Learning and Development Expected at the End of the EYFS: Communication and Language: ELG01 – Listening and Attention*. Coventry, UK: STA.

Standards and Testing Agency. (2014b). *EYFS Profile Exemplification for the Level of Learning and Development Expected at the End of the EYFS: Communication and Language: ELG02 – Understanding*. Coventry, UK: STA.

Standards and Testing Agency. (2014c). *EYFS Profile Exemplification for the Level of Learning and Development Expected at the End of the EYFS: Personal, Social and Emotional Development: ELG06 – Self-Confidence and Self-Awareness*. Coventry, UK: STA.

Standards and Testing Agency. (2014d). *EYFS Profile Exemplification for the Level of Learning and Development Expected at the End of the EYFS: Personal, Social and Emotional Development: ELG07 – Managing Feelings and Behaviour*. Coventry, UK: STA.

Standards and Testing Agency. (2014e). *EYFS Profile Exemplification for the Level of Learning and Development Expected at the end of the EYFS: Personal, Social and Emotional Development: ELG08 – Making Relationships*. Coventry, UK: STA.

Thompson, H.S. (2005). *Fear and Loathing in Las Vegas*. London: Harper Perennial.

Timimi, S. (2009). Why Diagnosis has Increased So Rapidly in the West: A Cultural Perspective. In S. Timimi & J. Leo (Eds.), *Rethinking ADHD: From Brain to Culture* (pp. 133–159). Basingstoke, UK: Palgrave MacMillan.

Underwood Report. (1955). *Report of the Committee on Maladjusted Children*. London: HMSO.

Visser, J. (2003). *A Study of Children and Young People Who Present Challenging Behaviour*. London: Ofsted.

6

WHAT CAN TEACHERS OF CRITICAL AND COMMUNITY PSYCHOLOGY LEARN FROM THEIR LEARNERS?

Olivia Fakoussa, Gemma Budge, Mandeep Singh Kallu, Annie Mitchell and Rachel Purtell

Learners of applied psychology, in many ways, are reflecting a similar challenge that service users face, which is the 'right to participate'. Although learners perhaps speak more from a position 'on the side lines looking in', rather than an 'outside looking in' position, learners are moving towards an 'in' position, which presumably is where they aspire to be. If learners are to come out of training knowing both how to support and work with individuals and to be ready to challenge and change the systems and structures that oppress, they need teaching and placement experiences that enable and encourage them to develop and retain a critical focus and foster reflexivity on the systems they operate within. How to provide such teaching is, of course, the subject of this entire book.

Far too frequently, applied psychologists can find themselves inadvertently perpetuating the very issues that they set out to redress, as a result of moving within systems which have power imbalances built into their core architecture. We wish to challenge the still far too common practice of psychologists developing services for people wanting help, with little to no input from service users themselves. Similarly, the idea of developing and progressing the curricula of critical and community psychology, without input and considerations from learners (who will, after all, be the ones later subjected to this teaching), would be ill-fitting to a critical psychology framework.

In line with critical psychology's aim to challenge hierarchical structures and redistribute power, this chapter is written primarily by current (Gemma Budge and Mandeep Singh Kallu) and recent (Olivia Fakoussa) clinical psychology trainees, in collaboration with a lecturer in clinical and community psychology (Annie Mitchell) and a service user with an academic research background (Rachel Purtell). The perspectives of 64 other clinical psychology trainees (gathered by us via a brief survey, distributed to all 31 training courses for clinical psychology in the UK) have been incorporated, to include a broader range of voices, otherwise left unheard in the corridors of those already imbued with more power to speak and write than are learners themselves. The survey themes are illuminated by direct quotes from the survey respondents and complemented by our own reflections of learning, teaching and working with clinical psychology through training. We conclude our chapter with 12 key recommendations for teachers of critical and community psychology, forged from the experiences of learners.

We hope to ignite discussion and reflection on the opportunities and challenges of teaching and learning about critical approaches to practice. While our experiences are drawn from learning, teaching, studying and using clinical psychology, we hope that our conclusions and recommendations may also be relevant for other applied disciplines within psychology and psychiatry.

Our understanding of critical, community and clinical psychology

We have come to understand critical psychology as a movement that opposes the application of psychology as a means, directly or indirectly, by which to perpetuate oppression and injustice (Parker, 1999). In equal measure, we identify with critical psychology as an approach that seeks to apply psychology for the promotion of emancipation and social justice (Parker, 1999) and that functions as "psychology with its eyes open" (Morss, 2000, p. 103). More specifically, we have learned about community psychology as a set of perspectives that emphasise the importance of social context in people's lives (Orford, 2008) and seek to challenge the individualistic approach of Western psychology. In this sense, critical consideration of commonly accepted practices and perceptions is a core component of community psychology. We recognise that critical and community psychology approaches, while often overlapping, have different emphases. We see critical psychology as particularly concerned with challenging and changing the structural power dynamics and social and economic injustices that determine health outcomes and inequalities. We see community psychology as also concerned with the social relationships and broader environmental determinants of our individual and collective well-being and resilience. For the purposes of this chapter, we will focus on teaching and learning that are informed by community psychology ideas, characterised in particular by the promotion of social support, valuing inclusivity, active partnership with service users, carers and other citizens, inter-disciplinarity and participatory research methods, and based on critical reflection with an emphasis on always trying to shift power towards those who have least.

We recognise that the discipline of clinical psychology is viewed with scepticism by many critical and community psychologists. As a profession, clinical psychology has been seen to decontextualise human misery and to promote individualising solutions. Its over-emphasis on therapy and its promotion of individual lifestyle changes have been critiqued as distracting from action on fundamental social, political and economic determinants of distress and ill-health (see, for example, Rapley, Moncrieff, & Dillon, 2011). Along with other professions, clinical psychology also acts as a closed shop, potentially bamboozling the lay public into a sense that there are 'specialist' others, who know better than they do about what really matters in living satisfying lives. In addition, with relatively well-paid and apparently privileged and secure roles in the healthcare economy, in the UK, clinical psychology practitioners can appear arrogant and professionally self-serving.

Nevertheless, we clinical psychology learners who have chosen this particular career pathway with a keen interest in social justice and a community-psychology-informed understanding of mental health, feel hopeful and optimistic that the detrimental understandings and narrow professional focus described can shift in a positive and community-psychology-orientated direction. We know that many people who use our services wish to champion us as professionals who have sometimes been able to help them to achieve their goals, live life as they wish and contribute to broader society to make the world a better place for others too. We believe that community psychological ideas can inform and support our camaraderie with others who want to promote social justice, and that clinical psychology will be a more socially useful profession the more it opens up to community psychology and other critical perspectives.

Indeed, we have evidence, from our survey findings, from the most recent British Psychological Society Division of Clinical Psychology conferences (Boyle, 2015; Dillon, 2015; Johnstone, 2015) and from some aspects of recent changes to the clinical psychology accreditation criteria (British Psychological Society, 2015), that a shift towards incorporating community perspectives is already afoot on a national scale. The role that social inequality plays in influencing our mental and physical health (Marmot, 2010) has finally become too significant, too unequivocal, too widespread and toxically detrimental for clinical psychologists to continue to ignore it.

Context: an overview of clinical psychology training

For readers who may not be aware of the UK clinical psychology training pathways, we will briefly outline the commitments of clinical psychology training in the UK, to provide context to survey findings which form the basis for the rest of the chapter.

In the UK, an undergraduate degree in psychology and relevant work experience are required in order to gain a training place on a postgraduate course in clinical psychology. Competition for the approximately 600 training places per year is high, with only one in six applicants successfully gaining a place. There are inequalities in access to training: people from ethnic minority backgrounds, disabled people and men are currently under-represented in the profession. There are no data on social class, but it is widely recognised that the complex and uncertain route to training can be more readily navigated by those from more financially privileged backgrounds, whose families can afford to support them in taking on short-term, low-paid work or unpaid voluntary internships to gain relevant experiences. The 3-year doctorate training has historically been fully funded (and salaried) by the National Health Service (NHS) (itself funded by the taxpayer), but at the time of writing, there is some uncertainty about this, following the UK government Spending Review and

Autumn Statement in 2015, which saw a shift away from central funding to individual loan funding for training nurses and allied health professionals. If salaried funding for clinical psychology training is lost, courses will face huge risks around ensuring fair access and widening participation. Training in clinical psychology requires substantial placement practice in a range of health and social care contexts, working with service users across the life-span (hitherto usually within the NHS, but as the NHS fragments, increasingly now in private, voluntary and independent settings). Trainees conduct doctoral-level research and evaluation and a range of academic tasks that require broad-ranging teaching, learning and independent study.

Within clinical psychology training, there is an increasing tension between focussing on ameliorative work, aimed at addressing personal suffering, and transformative work, aimed at preventing suffering in the first place by addressing the economic, social, political and environmental conditions that give rise to inequality, disadvantage, neglect, trauma and consequent distress. Ameliorative models prevail, with individualistic approaches remaining dominant. This issue stems from outside the individual training courses and is promoted by the British Psychological Society (BPS). The BPS provides standards for the accreditation of clinical psychology training programmes (British Psychological Society, 2015). The most recent criteria put increasing emphasis on teaching the cognitive behavioural therapy (CBT) model, stating that "courses have freedom to choose which approach they teach *in addition to CBT*" (British Psychological Society, 2015, p. 57). Identifying CBT as a compulsory model for training clinical psychologists reinforces the dominant discourse of CBT as a panacea for all psychological ills (which will no doubt be overtaken in due course by new and more fashionable models, since the history of persuasion shows us that therapeutic fashions change and evolve in line with broader social forces). On the other hand, other changes to the accreditation criteria indicate a move to address complexity within individual work and incorporate competencies which pertain more to preventative work. For example, learners must acquire "in addition . . . the ability to utilise multi-model interventions, as appropriate to the complexity and/or co-morbidity of the presentation, the clinical and social context and service user opinions, values and goals" (British Psychological Society, 2015, p. 12).

We wish to briefly reflect here on use of language within professional documents and the profession. All language can be contested (Purtell & Gibson, 2011, p. 71) and has often been used to denote differences in power and to reinforce prejudices. Although professional language about distress is gradually shifting away from pathologising terminology, some infelicities, such as "co-morbidity" regrettably do still remain in training documents. While critically examining professional language, some service user voices also remind us that service users and carers may be just as guilty as professionals of using language to gain power and exclude others. Terms such as 'lived experience', when examined, surely represent all experience, unless there is a 'dead experience'? 'Expert by experience', while accurately conveying that we are all experts in our own experience, becomes almost meaningless when we consider that this applies to every human. The term 'service receiver' is often preferred over 'user', but what does this mean? The implications are that people receive some great gift from the state! There are significant challenges in finding inclusive and respectful language that fairly reflects the many varied and different voices of those who engage with psychology.

Returning to the accreditation criteria: learners are also expected to acquire "knowledge of and capacity to conduct interventions related to, secondary prevention and the promotion of health and well-being" (p. 12). They must "understand the impact of differences, diversity and social inequalities on people's lives, and their implications for working practices" (p. 14). This last point may be a key area of focus for training courses, given that currently, the vast majority of people accepted onto clinical psychology training courses are white, female, non-disabled, single and under 30.

The implicit assumption running throughout even the newly revised accreditation criteria is that most of the work conducted by clinical psychologists will comprise ameliorative work. We still have a long way to go before there is a strong public health, socially transformative emphasis within the training of clinical psychologists.

It is hoped that, for readers previously unaware, the above has served as a sufficient overview of clinical psychology training.

Opportunities and challenges related to learning critical and community psychology during clinical psychology training

If, as we feel, and as the previously mentioned shifting landscape denotes, critical and community psychology approaches are essential and pertinent for clinical psychology trainees' learning and practice, how best can these approaches and such content be taught? The previous and subsequent chapters discuss this question in great detail and from numerous interesting perspectives. We offer here an account based largely on learners' own perceptions and suggestions.

In order to write this chapter using mainly learners' own perceptions and suggestions, we sent a brief survey to clinical psychology trainees on all 31 training programmes in the UK, asking them what had been their experience of critical and/or community psychology through training. We received 64 responses, from trainees across all 3 years of training – from ten different course centres. Trainees from five courses stated having had no community or critical psychology teaching so far. Trainees from the other five courses reported experiencing between 2 and 30 hours of critical or community teaching over the 3 years.

We conducted a thematic analysis of their narrative responses and identified 16 key themes pertinent to the opportunities and challenges of learning critical and community psychology from a learner perspective. Obviously, 64 trainees (from an estimated 1800 trainees at any one time) from just 10 of 31 courses may well not be a representative sample, but then those of us writing the chapter were hardly representative either! Certainly those who responded raised interesting and significant issues which both challenged and amplified our own thinking, and which feel important to address in future teaching and learning about critical and community approaches.

TABLE 6.1 Learners' perceptions of opportunities and challenges related to critical and community psychology teaching

Opportunities	Challenges
1 Teaches principles and values in addition to content/promotes positive social values and a caring professional identity.	1 Opportunities are restricted by the limitations within the clinical training process/course requirements.
2 Develops critical thinking and reflection on teaching, practice and personal/political agendas and values.	2 Leaves a sense of hopelessness/disillusionment without sufficient knowledge of or opportunity for application.
3 Challenges assumptions.	3 Creates additional uncertainty during a time of great existing uncertainty as a learner.
4 Raises awareness of external influences on 'the individual': enhances formulation/reduces diagnosis.	4 Can create distance/alienation/isolation from others.
5 Connects people: professionals/service users/communities/learners.	5 Can result in an uncomfortable process of feeling professional and personal identity is challenged/destabilised.
6 Encourages and permits working in a preventative and politically active way as a psychologist.	6 Lack of cultural and social diversity within clinical psychology trainees can result in mixed responses to this paradigm.
7 Amplifies otherwise unheard voices.	7 Challenging the current paradigm and powerful elders.
8 Encourages development of holistic curiosity and a move towards novel and flexible approaches within shifting service contexts.	8 Lack of opportunity to integrate these perspectives into research.

For clarity, the themes are listed, in isolation, in Table 6.1. Thereafter, the themes are detailed with illustrative quotes from respondents. This section is followed by our own reflections on learning critical and community psychology during clinical psychology training at Plymouth University, linking with the survey data. In the final section of this chapter, the findings and reflections culminate in our recommendations for teachers of critical and community psychology.

Learners' perceptions of opportunities arising from critical and community psychology teaching

1 Teaches principles and values in addition to content/promotes positive social values and a caring professional identity

Respondents expressed appreciation of the role of critical/community psychology in allowing them to retain their personal values within their professional practice:

"One of my concerns about joining a Clinical Psychology programme was that I may feel a 'giving up' of my values and ethics. The community/critical psychology elements of the course have been very reassuring."

Others spoke about critical/community psychology perspectives being important, due to their supporting the development of a professional identity based around responsibility and care for others: "having a bigger responsibility to help people/society – using the power we have for the greater good."

2 Develops critical thinking and reflection on teaching, practice and personal/political agendas and values

Respondents felt that learning critical/community psychology was: "Important so we can have a critical understanding of our discipline and we don't just rely on discourses that are imbedded in unequal relations of power."

In addition, learners felt that the teaching was helpful for supporting them to question the narratives commonly circulated in society and their therapeutic work: "Useful in thinking about psychological theory, but also about stories that are told in our society, media and in the therapy room."

Although some may think it is illusory, learners in our survey showed an appreciation of the power they felt they would hold in their qualified positions within the current system, and were grateful for the reflective space that critical/community psychology teaching offered them to decide how they wished to use this power: "As psychologists we are imbued with a lot of power, whether we would want to choose this or not. We need time to reflect and make decisions about how we position ourselves with respect to this."

Trainees further identified the benefits of being able to explore their own role in relation to a larger context as a result of critical/community psychology teaching: "I think it's useful to critically examine our own role within the wider system."

3 Challenges assumptions

Respondents were aware of some of the assumptions inherent and often unquestioned within the profession of clinical psychology and how critical/community psychology teaching can help to challenge these: "I think this (critical/community psychology teaching) goes some way to challenge the implicit assumption of the 'expert' position of psychologists."

They further expressed feeling that it was relevant to be encouraged, through critical/community psychology teaching, to challenge their own implicit assumptions:

> I think we should be encouraged to question current practice and challenge our own beliefs and assumptions. I think an important part of our role is to understand our own beliefs/biases/assumptions and where these come from and how they have been shaped.

4 Raises awareness of external influences on 'the individual': enhances formulation/reduces diagnosis

Learners felt critical/community psychology teaching offered an opportunity to prevent inadvertent collusion with oppressive perspectives of psychological distress: "Without this, we would be colluding with the oppressive ideology of attributing all distress to personal failures, which clouds our perspective on how we understand distress."

Others expressed the feeling that critical/community psychology perspectives enabled less reliance on diagnostic frameworks: "I think it fits with a BPS approach of moving away from diagnostic labels."

They felt that in situations where diagnoses were still used, critical/community psychology teaching offered them the opportunity to contextualise and question these: "Considered in a critical realist perspective where we would have to use diagnoses within teams, but teaching us how to help teams critique and understand backgrounds to diagnoses."

5 Connects people: professionals/service users/communities/learners

Respondents felt that the critical/community psychology teaching encouraged the connection of psychologists with the wider society they serve and with a range of different professionals: "Helps us to connect with wider society" and "In critical psychology I encounter other professionals' perspectives, which I really value (e.g. social workers, academics, sociologists, ethnographers)."

Others identified critical/community psychology teaching as a protective source of connection to other learners who shared this, sadly, still far too rare a perspective: "It's been relevant for me particularly as a source of support, as I find myself sometimes quite alone in questioning mainstream practice of clinical psychology."

6 Encourages and permits working in a preventative and politically active way as a psychologist

Many respondents indicated that critical/community psychology teaching provided them with permission and encouragement to be socially responsible and politically active clinicians: "Feeling encouraged that as psychologists we may have a voice that can go some way in influencing the broader structures in society, which are harmful[,] and [is] helpful in individual and collective mental distress"; "It fostered a greater interest in political and cultural movements and how this impacts on distress"; "I think it's important to think about different ways of working and maybe the political side of things"; and "I think critical psychology is linked to activism and a desire to produce positive social change for communities where traditional methods of psychology are not apt, suitable or liked by the clients themselves."

7 Amplifies otherwise unheard voices

Respondents identified community psychology teaching as a positive way to "bring volume" to people's voices which are often "deleted":

> I was drawn to psychology as a means of listening to people whose voices or stories are often reduced, unheard or deleted. The community psychology teaching we have had has helped bring volume to these voices and increase my curiosity and skills such that, hopefully, I can listen and help lesser heard voices be heard.

8 Encourages development of holistic curiosity and a move towards novel and flexible approaches within shifting service contexts

Learners described the influence of critical/community psychology teaching on encouraging a broader curiosity about human distress and supporting them to be more flexible in their use of approaches which might not fit within the 'mainstream': "Important in light of the changing NHS climate and our increasing need to be flexible practitioners and take novel approaches to difficulties which might not fit under current umbrella therapies or theories."

Learners' perceived challenges of critical and community psychology teaching

In addition to the numerous positive opportunities perceived by learners to be presented by critical and community psychology teaching within training, learners also identified several challenges that it is crucial for teachers of these approaches to be aware of and to take into account, if they are to be prevented from becoming barriers to learning.

1 Opportunities are restricted by the limitations within the clinical training process/course requirements

Some learners found critical/community psychology teaching "interesting, but not relevant", due to the fact that there were: "No opportunities to work this way within NHS placements, plus the fact [that] very little services do work in this way."

And the skills taught within this perspective: "are not valued in the context in which we practise."

One respondent felt that spending money on critical/community teaching during training, which could not be applied in clinical placements, was not a good use of NHS funds:

> Given that working in this way is not facilitated by services we work in or are likely to work in, [and it] is only applicable to a very small proportion of the client groups, I do not think it is cost effective to work this way or spend lots of our training teaching us about it when there are lots of other more relevant things to learn.

Learners further cited the 'competencies' all trainees are required to acquire during training and felt that critical and community psychology perspectives did not marry up well with these: "It doesn't neatly fit into the competencies – NHS services are stretched and critical psychology is sometimes interpreted as an alternative or unusual approach that doesn't obviously fit into commissioners' plans or priorities."

Finally, learners expressed anxiety that the course requirements, which stipulate that a certain number of hours of direct psychotherapeutic work in various models needs to be evidenced by trainees over the course of training, provide a challenge to devoting clinical time to the provision of community psychology work, without the risk of failing the course: "Unlikely to meet (course) requirements if you work in this way (e.g. number of therapy hours/CBT hours/client hours)."

2 Leaves a sense of hopelessness/disillusionment without sufficient knowledge of or opportunity for application

Crucially, many respondents reported feeling left "overwhelmed" and unsure how to apply the teaching, following exposure to critical/community psychology ideas in teaching, without examples of or opportunities for applying this new learning:

> It can feel a bit overwhelming. After our class, it felt like we came out with big ideas and then realising how we were only a small part of the profession and society, it felt like too big . . . a challenge to take on!

Learners also said: "After the teaching people generally felt somewhat hopeless/overwhelmed, because if the systems are what are getting people down, and systems are difficult to change, what does that mean about our ability to help people and make a difference?" and "It was too general and abstract – it would be good if a critical psychologist came and told us about their work."

3 Creates additional uncertainty during a time of great existing uncertainty as a learner

Learners not previously aware of critical/community psychology perspectives reflected on the difficulty that being asked to question so many previously held perspectives/assumptions can pose at such a vulnerable and anxiety-provoking time as training: "It also involves questioning what one is learning – which can be difficult to do when one is already anxious about not knowing what one is meant to know (training is a time of great uncertainty)."

Others pointed out the difficult contradiction in being asked/trained to be 'clinical leaders' by the professional body while being challenged by critical/community psychology perspectives to question everything they are being taught:

> The challenge is that we are striving to gain confidence in a way of working, and the temptation is to want to hold an expert position, because this masks our vulnerability of not knowing. It's difficult for trainees to be told "there is

no right way to understand mental health . . . but you'll have a doctorate and will be in a senior position in mental health teams and expected to offer expert advice".

4 Can create distance/alienation/isolation from others

Many respondents noted the risk of isolation that accompanied learning about and aligning oneself to the critical/community psychology perspective during training: "It felt quite distancing – also, becoming so politically aware has meant that I struggle to tolerate different political ideas that could potentially alienate me from others." Another trainee said:

> I think, in some ways, exploring oppressive political systems can be divisive of trainees and I am aware that some have felt wary of voicing their political views/opinions, as they have felt that these may be seen to be 'wrong'.

Also, "It can feel quite isolating being on a training course that doesn't genuinely support alternative approaches."

5 Can result in an uncomfortable process of feeling professional and personal identity is challenged/destabilised

Learners described critical/community psychology teaching as particularly challenging to their professional identities as 'helpers':

> Our identity as clinical psychologists in training is challenged by an approach that says that clinical psychologists and all that they do may be part of the system that makes things worse for some people. Being faced with that idea was something that people found particularly difficult to accept.

Furthermore, "A lot of trainees seemed to have never thought about such things (and were) offended by the idea that they weren't as powerful as [they] thought or that they weren't the cure to someone's problems."

6 Lack of cultural and social diversity within clinical psychology trainees can result in mixed responses to this paradigm

Respondents reflected on the composition of the trainee population and how this may interact with responses to critical/community psychology perspectives:

> I think training courses are becoming more elitist, rather than recruiting individuals who can offer more than the luxury of affording a good education. This is essential of course, but degree level or masters should be sufficient and perhaps more people with clinical experience should be considered. I would love to see more diversity within the profession.

7 Challenging the current paradigm and powerful elders

Some respondents reported feeling wary of critical/community psychology perspectives, explaining that during training they are mainly: "Trying not to be too 'controversial', i.e. not challenge thinking too much, in order to get by and meet the course requirements."

8 Lack of opportunity to integrate these perspectives into research

Respondents noted that even where there is the opportunity to use critical/community psychology perspectives during placements, these opportunities are not always provided in the research component of the course: "There is encouragement to think about these values on placements, but then a difficulty in bringing these in to the research elements of the course."

Conclusions

Overall, regardless of whether community and critical psychology teaching had been part of the training curricula, the vast majority of respondents reported feeling that it was a worthwhile and important perspective for clinical psychologists to understand. However, the challenges that were highlighted seem highly pertinent for training providers and teachers of critical and community psychology perspectives to take into account for future planning. In particular, they should note the risks involved in offering teaching on these perspectives within a training environment lacking in opportunities to apply the teaching during placements or research, and inadvertently leaving learners feeling subsequently overwhelmed and hopeless.

There are also important learning points for clinical psychology training providers, regarding the messages they send to trainees around being trained to be future 'leaders' within the NHS and beyond; recognising that from community or critical psychology perspectives, being a leader should mean widening inclusivity, holding complex and uncertain understandings, and drawing on community psychology skills, including critical reflection, networking and facilitation. We would challenge the inadvertent messages that trainees apparently take from the new emphasis on leadership that being a 'leader' excludes them from holding more complex and uncertain understandings. Surely, the reverse should be the case: leadership roles should require us to celebrate and embrace complexity and the kind of "safe uncertainty" advocated by the family therapist Barry Mason (Mason, 1993).

Interestingly, those who had not had access to any critical or community psychology teaching expressed disappointment about the lack of something which they felt was "crucial" and "essential" to the role of a clinical psychologist. Indeed, one respondent suggested it should become mandatory for all clinical psychology courses to include critical and community psychology in the syllabus.

Of course, we cannot discount the possibility that only those learners who feel that learning critical and community psychology is important took the time to respond to a survey on its subject, though several respondents did voice critical views about critical psychology.

The findings showed that trainees positively recognised community psychology's potential to support them in challenging their own implicit assumptions (Opportunities, No. 3). However, uncovering and exploring these assumptions, many of them deeply embedded in an eco-political landscape veiled in order not to be swiftly seen (see, for example, Smail, 1983; Newnes, 2016), may prove more challenging than we might like to believe.

Trainees' concerns that working in a community-psychology-orientated way would make it unlikely for them to meet course requirements (Challenges, No. 1) leaves room for the development of more appropriate placements. Some courses have already been offering and valuing critical placements for some time. Craig Newnes, for example, has been offering alternative placements for third-year clinical psychology trainees on the Birmingham clinical psychology training course since 1994. In these placements, trainees are able to work alongside service users and work to acknowledge what they experience, with allocated "space and time to think about the system" (Newnes & MacLachlan, 1996, p. 26) and without the expectation that they need to "cure anyone" (Newnes & MacLachlan, 1996, p. 25).

When considering learners' reflections on the destabilising impacts of learning about critical psychology perspectives and issues of expertise and power while training as psychologists (see Challenges, No. 5), perhaps it is important to acknowledge and discuss the need for learners to accept that they have, to some extent, chosen a career path which is about taking power in the form of expert knowledge – after all, they have not chosen to wipe bottoms as careers (although many may have worked in such roles while gaining experience in the caring and mental health field before commencing clinical psychology training). Trainees clearly want to have expertise and this is not a bad thing in and of itself. Individuals who are being seen by trainees, will, one assumes, want the learners to know how to help and have knowledge. There is little that frustrates people more than the person who is being paid to deliver a service knowing less than the people who are using or receiving the service. However, this does not in any way mean that the particular knowledge that a learner has is more important than the service users' own knowledge – they are equal and simply different.

Challenge No. 2, relating to the sense of hopelessness often experienced by learners when faced with the 'wider picture', emphasises that perhaps it is a mistake to think that learning is always utilitarian – when, in fact, it can just as easily be 'damaging' to students' emotional well-being. Nonetheless, it is right that learners are challenged to think widely about the world in which they will practise. The people they will see as part of their practice have to exist and negotiate that world 24 hours a day. All learning, to some extent, is a game to be played according to some set of rules. The challenge lies in determining that the rules followed are not damaging to those with least power. The strength of community and critical psychology lies in instilling learners with a sense of responsibility and response-ability once they have proven that they can play the game (i.e. graduated and got a job) and can make influential decisions about how they wish to apply their professional power.

When faced with feelings of hope- and helplessness, it is always worth remembering that simply acknowledging and empathising with someone about the injustice that they are experiencing is a truly valuable practice. Understanding is just as important as changing and challenging something. The obsession with 'impact' and 'value' has become quite damaging. In Patient and Public Involvement (PPI) in health research, the emphasis on showing impact is in danger of destroying meaningful involvement, as there is a continually growing requirement to know what the involvement will bring before people are involved (Purtell & Wyatt, 2011). That is anathema to the very essence of involving people – involvement needs to happen precisely because it will bring something different and unpredicted – that is the point.

Our personal experiences of learning critical and community psychology during clinical psychology training at Plymouth University: disparities and connections to other learners' reflections

We have divided this section into four categories which incorporate most of the experiences of clinical psychology training: 1) research, 2) teaching and learning, 3) practice and 4) critical reflection, which underpins the other three categories.

1 Research

As some survey respondents highlighted, while opportunities to apply critical and community psychology teaching within services remain frustratingly rare, opportunities to do so within the research element of training are even scarcer.

Aside from conducting research into topic areas pertinent to critical and community psychology, using research methodology aligned with community psychology values can also be possible during clinical psychology training, and should be taught to trainees.

However, trainees should also be prepared by teachers to understand that proposing and conducting a project using, for example, participatory research methodology, may not be as easy to have accepted by a course team. Dentith, Measor and O'Malley (2009) explain such an experience, when they reflect that research which seeks to empower the mass, as opposed to privilege the few, poses a threat to the status quo (including the power of academia), so that research with critical aims will inevitably face opposition from those in positions of comfort.

Mary Boyle (2015, n.p.), in her address to the 2014 Division of Clinical Psychology Annual Conference, spoke about clinical psychology's fear to "speak truth to power", which may result in a fear-driven, unconscious drive to prevent more critical research projects from being encouraged within clinical psychology settings. Critical research processes with real sharing of power require true partnership, in which those who have a stake in the topic being researched either themselves act as commissioners and controllers of the research activity, or at least have clear direct influence on the research topics, questions, methodology, analysis and dissemination. Negotiating this level of partnership can be hugely complex. University examination constraints can limit how much partnership can be achieved. Research supervisors themselves may unfortunately resist or misunderstand or minimise the complex nature of partnership processes.

We have had experiences of this during our own training journeys. For example, in efforts to have a project using participatory research methodology to explore adolescents' experiences of outdoor learning accepted by members of the course team in Plymouth, it became evident that there was strong opposition from some academic staff and a lack of understanding about the nature and value of such research. The trainee in question (Olivia) had to submit several revisions of the project proposal and was faced with questions such as "How is this relevant to clinical psychology?" The initial proposal, which was interested in exploring adolescents' experiences of climate change, was never accepted, as the relevance of climate change to clinical psychology and wellbeing in the broader sense was not understood by some staff.

Common to all partnership approaches is a value base which sees people as 'subjects' and 'actors', rather than research 'objects' and recognises and values people's own expertise in their own lived experience (Hall, 1992). For truly: "what is the point of findings that are 'true' if they have been produced in circumstances that disempower people, that distort social relations, and add to the monopoly power of dominant groups?" (Reason, 2000, p. 2). For clinical psychologists, just as for any other practitioners purporting to improve the lives of others, the question of how to conduct research is as crucial as how to conduct therapy. Particularly when one acknowledges perspectives such as Freire's (1970, p. 73) that "any situation in which some men prevent others from engaging in the process of inquiry is one of violence" and considers the role of 'expert researchers' in disempowering people to take seriously the conclusions of their own methods of knowledge inquiry.

Participatory research is aligned to critical and community psychology in its aims to redistribute unequally held power and should have its place within critical and community psychology teaching and be acknowledged and appreciated within clinical psychology research practices. Unfortunately, as briefly discussed previously, we have found that while some fellow practitioners and researchers are favourable to and supportive of conducting inclusive and empowering research, many still find their positions of power in the heights of ivory towers too severely challenged by such notions and resist such practices.

Teaching on participatory research practices needs to go hand in hand with preparation for the level of defence students and researchers are likely to encounter, from all areas of society, when challenging assumed hierarchies and offering power and microphones to the many people in society previously held silent and powerless for the benefit of the few.

Nina Browne, a trainee clinical psychologist at University College London, is one exception and is currently conducting her research (supervised by Professor

Chris Barker, Dr Kat Alcock and Dr Sally Zlotowitz) into clinical psychologists working at a policy level, with her project entitled: "Practice to policy: Clinical psychologists' experiences of macro-level work". Nina has shared her experiences of proposing and conducting a community-psychology-centric project within her course. While she experienced the process of planning a macro-level project as initially overwhelming, it provided her with the opportunity to learn about the social, political and historical context around community psychology, research and action. Overall, the project has helped her to build a much broader professional network and exposed her to ideas and debates that were not covered in the curriculum. She also said it was an opportunity to develop a professional identity that aligned with both community and clinical psychology, and encourages other trainees to express their interest to as many people as they can and take the risk of doing something different.

It is important to note that it would be false to promote the idea that there is only one research methodology that involves people best (Rickard & Purtell, 2013) – all methods can involve people well. However, involving people in research during training, while learners are required to learn, show and prove a set of research skills and prove they can 'play the game' proficiently, will be difficult. Once learners are qualified and 'proven', the scope for partnership in research is huge. Good partnership in research always requires a good balance in contribution from both parties and mutual respect.

2 Teaching and learning

Learning from experts by experience: the Service Receiver and Carer Consultative Group

Plymouth University's Clinical Psychology and Social Work programmes are fortunate to benefit from the involvement of the Service Receiver and Carer Consultative Group. This consultative group process, dating back to work at the University of Exeter in 2004 (Curle & Mitchell, 2004) involves service receivers and carers sharing their time, knowledge and expertise by experience with students on the two courses through involvement in various activities, including selecting candidates for training, designing and moderating meaningful assessments, contributing to teaching sessions and facilitating reflective mentoring groups and conversations for learners.

As learners, having exposure to the honest reflections of people directly affected by the services we are training to later provide, offers truly invaluable insights and critical reflections and ensures that theory remains humanised and relevant to the people it seeks to benefit and support, rather than to the practitioners applying the theories, or worse, to the systems surrounding both service users and practitioners (for example, using psychological assessment for decisions around work and benefits).

Re-contextualising distress through interdisciplinary learning: The Bridges Project

While individualistic notions of psychological difficulties have become prominent over the life-course of clinical psychology, there is a counter movement afoot to try and contextualise human suffering more accurately. The training course at Plymouth University endeavours to teach an integrative approach to mental health and learners receive teaching on systemic, psychodynamic, cognitive and social constructionist/ community psychology approaches. However, many learners have still felt unsatisfied with the limited models of distress incorporated in the course, and we have sought to enrich our understanding by learning with and from other health and social care learners at the university. Due to bureaucratic difficulties which make it challenging for the courses to implement inter-disciplinary learning into the curriculum, a group of different health and social care learners started a steering group to form our own extra-curricular learning events for inter-disciplinary students and staff. After attending a staff-led conference (marking the launch of Health and Well-being Boards in 2013), nursing, medicine, social work and clinical psychology learners were startled to realise that this was the first time we had ever met and worked together on campus. We saw the potential value of pre-qualification shared learning (challenging assumptions and prejudices about different professions before they harden) for improved team work, for kinder and more integrated patient and client-centred care, and for collectively influencing the social determinants of health. We formed the view that mutual understanding – giving each other an insight into the roles, expectations and demands of different health professions (and beyond to housing, politics, business and the arts) – might lead to new ways of improving the culture of health and social care (and beyond). And we could see that entrenched attitudes, pragmatics and institutional barriers stopped staff from implementing good inter-professional learning processes. So we seized the initiative and together set up and implemented a series of regular meetings, seminars, workshops and learning events, dedicated both to promoting our own understanding across disciplines and to urging staff to work harder and better on this agenda. All this is done after classes and out of placement activity – extra hours dedicated to values-based shared learning. This resulted in the university's first learner-led inter-disciplinary conference and now continues with regular clinical skills days, such as a day organised around cardiac arrest, which brought medical, social care and psychology learners together to consider the physical, emotional, psychological and social aspects of having a heart attack.

Many learners have reported that the sessions, generally held once a month in the evenings, supported their understanding of additional and more holistic factors influencing a person that they would previously not have considered, and felt the sessions would make working collaboratively with other health and social care workers, as well as service users and carers, more intuitive in their future practice.

3 Practice

Many barriers to critical and community psychology thinking and practice stem from institutional processes and structures. As many survey respondents describe, we too have felt the frustrations of learning community psychology principles during teaching, and then being faced with service or research structures unable (or unwilling) to accommodate application of such thinking.

Critical psychology not only acknowledges that it is a value-based enterprise, but also advocates the value-based application of its theories (Fox & Prilleltensky, 1997). Without action, critical psychology theories remain, at best, redundant in their intentions; and at worst, complicit in the systems they have been derived to challenge and transform. If learners are not encouraged to apply critical and community psychology teaching, through the facilitation of opportunities – on campus or in placements – then presenting its theories, in isolation of possible action, seems ineffectual at best, and at worst, damaging to learners' esteem (see challenges elicited from the survey).

Various UK training programmes, including those at Hull, Lancaster and Liverpool, are finding new ways to provide community psychology, public health or primary care placements. For example, in Hull, community psychology placements are provided in Year 1, prior to NHS placements, to enhance trainee understanding of contextual factors in well-being. The Lancaster programme has been gradually building its capacity (with support from a grant from the Division of Clinical Psychology) to offer what they describe as "innovative placements". These placements have been primarily outside the NHS, in areas of unmet need. Examples include services for veterans, the homeless, and looked-after children. Overseas placements have also been offered, and the programme now has strong links with services in Uganda and Malawi. After completing part of a final-year placement in Malawi, two trainees went on to set up a charity (The Umoza Trust) and now act as supervisors to trainees going to Uganda. As part of the innovative placement agenda, leadership placements in the NHS and public health have also been offered. The Lancaster programme is still very much in its infancy with this work, but community approaches are very much a part of the programme's long-term thinking. At Plymouth, we are piloting new long-term community inter-professional placement opportunities across the 3 years, within open-minded statutory and charitable sector services, to enable interested trainees to explore opportunities aligned with community psychology principles and to learn with and from voluntary sector colleagues and partners. These innovative opportunities have prevented, for some, the sobering experience of learning community psychology ideas and values, but feeling stifled and helpless to apply these in one's work as a clinical psychologist.

Here, we briefly outline two examples of how collaborating with third-sector agencies and working in primary care can enhance clinical psychology placements and offer opportunities for the application of community psychology principles by clinical psychology trainees.

A clinical psychology placement in a local refugee support charity

The collaboration with a local charity offering practical support to people who have recently gained refugee status in the city of Plymouth has enabled trainee clinical psychologists from the Plymouth course to undertake placements within the service. The placement offered an occupational therapist working within the charity as a supervisor, with a course staff member offering overarching clinical psychology supervision every 6 weeks. Such an opportunity has enabled a rich exchange and led to research being undertaken with and for the charity, as well as the carrying out of mental health and well-being related projects that very much take into account people's social and economic circumstances, and the power of place and community for people's psychological well-being. One example is a listening project that was conducted by a trainee with people from various asylum-seeker and refugee (ASR) support agencies from around the city, which ultimately led to a successful funding bid to allow people from the ASR community to develop their own peer-mentoring support service, influenced by their own values and needs, rather than a further service developed for them by well-meaning but presumptuous others.

A placement spanning the statutory and charitable sector: fruitful and creative collaborations in the interest of service users

A placement opportunity was provided to offer psychology support to a GP service specifically targeting one of the most deprived areas within the city of Plymouth. Creative freedom was given by the GP practice and the course to the trainee on placement, to enable a better understanding of what type of psychological formulation and support would truly be helpful to people living in this area.

The placement commenced with a period of critical reflection on the power of the application of labels, such as 'deprivation', for example; their benefit of directing much-needed resources to individuals in the area, but also their diminishing of the positive qualities and resourcefulness of the communities that reside in such 'labelled' areas. The trainee worked in particular with the homeless population in the area around the GP practice, and in doing so, worked in collaboration with a number of homeless charities working to support people in the same region.

Supporting service users with appealing their benefit sanctions, writing letters to MPs, using creative therapeutic tools such as 'walking and talking' (the process of therapeutic conversation while walking within the community in which people reside), or facilitating a men's mental health group which involved fishing in the surrounding natural environment all became 'interventions' which felt meaningful and useful to service users and were informed by collaborative formulations which incorporated power, social context and community aspects into understanding a person's 'psychological' experiences.

Using teaching days for concrete action

Bringing a practical element of community psychology into a clinical psychology training course doesn't just have to remain restricted to placement opportunities. Suzanne Elliott and Peter Beardsworth, who teach disempowerment, gender and social action to clinical psychology trainees on the University of Leicester training course, have blogged about their experiences of using their teaching days to take social action together with trainees, rather than just lecturing on it (Elliott & Beardsworth, 2016). For them, this took the shape of collecting stories through conversation with members of the local community accessing various support agencies around the issues affecting their lives. The themes of these collated stories were found to largely cluster around the five "austerity ailments" described by the Psychologists against Austerity in their briefing paper (McGrath, Griffin, & Mundy, 2015): (1) increasing fear and mistrust; (2) increasing humiliation and shame; (3) increasing instability and insecurity; (4) increasing isolation and loneliness; and (5) increasing experiences of feeling trapped and powerless. The stories were later handed over to the Shadow Minister for Mental Health at Westminster in a meeting with others.

4 The crucial role of critical reflection

In their chapter on "Community approaches, social inclusion and user involvement", Mitchell and Purtell (2009) identify "critical reflection" as a key competency for community psychologists. Indeed, it has been our experience through training and beyond, that the capacity (and the space!) to reflect critically on what one is learning, observing and practising is fundamental to an inclusive and questioning approach to psychology. Mitchell and Purtell (2009) define critical reflection as the capacity to question whose interests are being served by the work we do, to make connections between our intentions, actions, outcomes and reflections and to consider our own values and experiences in our work. As highlighted in the survey data, these processes, particularly at such a vulnerable and stressful time as training, are not always easy to attend to and can create numerous psychological tensions for trainees. For many, being critically reflective within placement and education systems which promote mainstream thinking and practice and discourage critical and independent thought poses not only a challenge, but a real risk of 'failure' when being constantly 'assessed' by 'elders'. In addition, as described by survey respondents, being encouraged to reflect critically on one's own identity, values and the consequences of one's own practice, within a training system which encourages new learners to roll almost instantaneously into 'leadership' positions within teams, can create an almost 'freeze-like' state of contradictory uncertainty. Brookfield's (1994) creative exploration of postgraduate education students' journeys in critical reflection stresses the importance of questioning the majority position. As many survey respondents found, this can be a frightening thing to do from the bottom of a hierarchy, while one is dependent on having the doors of one's own future unlocked by gatekeepers whose whole careers have been, and remain, invested in the majority position.

Given its significance for teaching, learning, research and practice, teachers of applied psychology must be thoughtful and well-informed about how to foster and encourage an atmosphere of critical reflection in learners and enable this skill in all facets of learners' work. The recommendations we have drawn out of our own reflections and the considerations provided by our survey respondents will, it is hoped, provide teachers with useful avenues by which to achieve this.

Recommendations for teachers of critical and community psychology

1. Offer practical opportunities/recommendations for translating theory into action to avoid feeling overwhelmed and despondent.
2. Offer space for reflection and discussion of the impact of theory on personal identity.
3. Provide opportunities/links/resources for learners to connect with others interested in community psychology and the promotion of social justice in order to avoid isolation.
4. Encourage placement providers to be interested in/encouraging of community psychology ideas: help them see that trainees can be a resource to spearhead new creative and more inclusive ways of working.
5. Provide teaching and supervision around community psychology research topics and methods.
6. Encourage and promote the role of psychologists in political and social activism/ provide opportunities for learners to collectively engage in social/community activism locally or nationally.
7. Make it rewarding and permissible to challenge ways of thinking and working in the learning and clinical environment.
8. Support students to tolerate difficult and complex feelings including frustration, fear of failure, disappointment, anger in the face of social injustice and grief in the face of suffering.
9. Work together in partnership with people who use services: explore models of co-production of change.
10. Think from a public health perspective.
11. Explore and promote opportunities to work together with the voluntary sector.
12. Own our own privilege and put this to good use (step up!): power, of itself, is not bad, it is necessary and useful − it is how power is used and applied that is the crucial issue.

Questions to take forward into the future

We hope that the findings from our survey, our reflections on our own learning and the subsequent recommendations for teaching can provide a good basis for reflection and can perhaps make a contribution − even if just a small one − to progressing the curricula of critical psychology and psychiatry.

While our findings have provided us, as authors, with novel and interesting insights, we have, as is common when one seeks answers, also been left with some new questions following our work. We would like to share these with you here, in the hope that they can ignite further consideration, debate, discussion and critical reflection among like-minded and interested individuals.

1. Does critical psychology teaching have to start much earlier in order to be most effective – in A-level and undergraduate psychology, for example? If so, how can this be developed?
2. The potential strength of community and critical psychology lies in what learners do once they have qualified. However, beyond the world of training, newly qualified practitioners are faced with huge pressures for efficiency, speed and 'value for money' that can seem de-humanising, exhausting and that can be hard to bear and yet hard to resist. How can teachers of critical and community psychology support learners in making the transition from learner to qualified practitioner while helping them to retain a determination to engage critically with systems and sustain their own well-being in tough environments?
3. How can clinical psychology learners truly be supported to both sit and develop within a system while simultaneously critically appraising it from the outside? Is it perhaps the case that the healthcare and training systems themselves (and their broader political and economic contexts), which can be criticised so heavily, need changing? If so, who is responsible for instigating these changes and how can they be made? What partnerships can we forge to build a better world?

References

Boyle, M. (2015). Is clinical psychology fearful of social context? Speech presented at BPS Division of Clinical Psychology Annual Conference, Glasgow, 2014. Retrieved from BPS Media Centre: www.youtube.com/watch?v=Kt4JcTDPUoc

British Psychological Society (2015). *Standards for the accreditation of Doctoral programmes in clinical psychology*. Leicester, UK: BPS. Retrieved from www.bps.org.uk/system/files/Public%20files/PaCT/clinical_accreditation_2015_web.pdf

Brookfield, S. (1994). Tales from the dark side: A phenomenography of adult critical reflection. *International Journal of Lifelong Education, 13*(3), 203–216.

Curle, C., & Mitchell, A. (2004). Hand in hand: User and carer involvement in clinical psychology training. *Clinical Psychology, 33*, 12–15.

Dentith, A., Measor, L., & O'Malley, M. (2009). Stirring dangerous waters: Dilemmas for critical participatory research with young people. *Sociology, 43*(1), 158–168.

Dillon, J. (2015). The lived experience and meaning of power and threat, Hearing Voices Network England. Paper presented at the BPS Division of Clinical Psychology Annual Conference, London.

Elliott, S., & Beardsworth, P. (2016, 9 March). Taking social action with trainees: Walking and talking in the name of social justice. *Psychology Cultures* blog, University of Leicester. Retrieved on 10 May 2016 from https://psychologycultures.wordpress.com/2016/05/09/taking-social-action-with-trainees-walking-and-talking-in-the-name-of-social-justice/?blogsub=confirming#blog_subscription-2

Fox, D., & Prilleltensky, I. (Eds.) (1997). *Critical psychology: An introduction*. London: Sage.

Freire, P. (1970). *Pedagogy of the oppressed*. London: Penguin Press.

Hall, B. (1992). From margins to centre? The development and purpose of participatory research. *The American Sociologist, 26*(1), 15–28.

Johnstone, L. (2015). Beyond diagnosis to meaningful patterns in emotional distress: The Power/Threat/Meaning framework. Symposium, BPS Division of Clinical Psychology Annual Conference, London.

Marmot, M. (2010). *Fair society, healthy lives*. London: The Marmot Review.

Mason, B. (1993). Towards positions of safe uncertainty. *Human Systems: The Journal of Systemic Consultation and Management, 4*, 189–200.

McGrath, L., Griffin, V., & Mundy, E. (2015). The psychological impact of austerity: A briefing paper. Retrieved from https://psychagainstausterity.files.wordpress.com/2015/03/psychological-costs-of-austerity-briefing-paper-compressed.pdf

Mitchell, A., & Purtell, R. (2009). Community approaches, social inclusion and user involvement. In H. Beinart, P. Kennedy, & S. Llewelyn (Eds.), *Clinical psychology in practice* (pp. 364–376). London: Wiley–Blackwell.

Morss, J. (2000). Connecting with difference: Being critical in a postmodern world. In T. Sloan (Ed.), *Critical psychology: Voices for change* (pp. 103–111). New York: St Martin's Press Inc.

Newnes, C. (2016). *Inscription, diagnosis, deception and the mental health industry: How Psy governs us all*. Basingstoke, UK: Palgrave Macmillan.

Newnes, C., & MacLachlan, A. (1996). The anti-psychiatry placement. *Clinical Psychology Forum, 93*, 24–27.

Orford, J. (2008). *Community psychology: Challenges, controversies and emerging consensus*. Chichester, UK: John Wiley and Sons Ltd.

Parker, I. (1999). Critical psychology: Critical links. *Annual Review of Critical Psychology, 1*, 3–20.

Purtell, R.A., & Gibson, A. (2011). How to make health and social care research radical and really, really useful. In C. Lloyd & T. Heller (Eds.), *Long term conditions: Challenges in health and social care practice* (pp. 69–80). London: Sage.

Purtell, R.A., & Wyatt, K.M. (2011). Measuring something real and useful in consumer involvement in health and social care research. *International Journal of Consumer Studies, 35*, 605–608.

Rapley, M., Moncrieff, J., & Dillon, J. (2011). *De-medicalizing misery: Psychiatry, psychology and the human condition*. Basingstoke, UK: Palgrave Macmillan.

Reason, P. (2000). Action research as spiritual practice. Paper presented at the University of Surrey Learning Community Conference, 4–5 May. Retrieved on 25 February 2016 from www.peterreason.eu/Papers/AR_as_spiritual_practice.pdf

Rickard, W., & Purtell, R. (2013). Doing good carer-led research reflecting on past caring methodology. In P. Staddon (Ed.), *Mental health service users in research* (pp. 25–38). Bristol: Policy Press.

Smail, D. (1983). Psychotherapy and psychology. In D.Pilgrim (Ed.), *Psychology and psychotherapy*. London: Routledge & Kegan Paul.

7

TEACHING INDIGENOUS PSYCHOLOGY

A conscientisation, de-colonisation and psychological literacy approach to curriculum

Pat Dudgeon, Dawn Darlaston-Jones and Abigail Bray

For at least 20 years, Aboriginal and Torres Strait Islander peoples, leaders, educators and mental health workers have been calling on governments, institutions, professional bodies, educators and practitioners to embrace culturally appropriate methodologies of practice in order to address the significant social and health disparities experienced by Indigenous peoples. Psychology as a discipline of knowledge and as a profession has the capacity to be at the forefront of these endeavours. Despite much well-intended rhetoric and some important exceptions, to date, these calls have yet to be answered. In this chapter we argue that a seismic shift is required in the culture and practice of psychology whereby the definitions of knowledge construction and education are de-colonised, challenged and contested. This is articulated within theoretical frameworks offered by Foucault, and by Nakata's Cultural Interface Theory, situated within Freire's critical pedagogy. Evidence from the Australian Indigenous Psychology Education Project (AIPEP) and the de-colonised curriculum of the Bachelor of Behavioural Science at the University of Notre Dame, Australia (Fremantle Campus) demonstrates how psychology education can not only meet the needs of Indigenous students, but can address the unearned privilege of the non-Indigenous settler, and therefore deconstruct the truth claims that serve to reinforce racialised divisions that maintain social inequality.

Teaching indigenous psychology

> How many psychologists have an understanding of Aboriginal people? How many of you ... have an understanding of Aboriginal culture, history and contemporary issues? For many of you, this work is crucial given the social conditions and your work environment in such places as prisons and the welfare sector and where there are large numbers of Aboriginal clients. *It is your responsibility to seek that knowledge*

and understanding now, and to ensure that it is available for future generations of psychologists, in psychological training and education programs.

(Riley, 1997, pp. 15–16; emphasis added)

These powerful words were spoken on Wadjuk Nyungar land in Perth, Western Australia, by one of the nation's most influential Indigenous leaders. It was also the first time that the Australian Psychological Society (APS) had invited an Indigenous person to deliver a keynote address at the annual conference. This significant event was marked by Riley's call for psychologists to address the legacy of disadvantage and discrimination experienced by Aboriginal and Torres Strait Islander peoples by turning their focus and attention onto themselves. He argued that it was important for psychologists to understand how their perspectives, beliefs and assumptions, acquired via socialisation and context as well as through their education and training, contribute to the marginalisation and silencing of Aboriginal people. Inherent in this call is the recognition that psychology (as a discipline and profession) is complicit in creating and reinforcing problematic notions of deficit, which construct and frame the relationship between persons and groups. By calling for psychologists to examine their lack of knowledge and understanding of Indigenous history, Riley was challenging them to deconstruct their own identity; to bring into focus their sources of privilege and power within a colonised space and to understand what it means to be a member of the dominant, non-Indigenous group. This means recognising that psychology has been complicit in the domination over Aboriginal and Torres Strait Islander peoples and that this continues in the contemporary relationships between psychologists and Indigenous clients or groups (Dudgeon, Rickwood, Garvey, & Gridley, 2014). By definition, Riley's intention was for this critical self-reflexivity to transcend the individual psychologist; effectively, Riley called for a de-colonisation of the discipline and profession of psychology (Dudgeon, Darlaston-Jones, & Clark, 2011).

To accept this challenge requires de-colonising the epistemological and ontological foundations of the discipline and profession of psychology in relation to the individualised and universal laws imposed upon persons and groups (Dudgeon & Walker, 2015). Psychology must also strive for epistemological equivalence whereby Indigenous knowledges and practices are recognised and valued as making a contribution to the discipline and practice of psychology. Finally, there must be a deep reflexive analysis of the subjectivity of individual practitioners such that they identify their own positionality relative to Aboriginal and Torres Strait Islander peoples, and this includes analysis of the discourses surrounding colonisation and the resultant power and privilege accrued to non-Indigenous Australians (Foucault, 1977, 1980; Hook, 2007). Identifying the underlying mechanisms of thought is the central thesis in Foucault's (1972) treatise *The Archaeology of Knowledge*, in which he argues that hidden (unconscious) assumptions or rules dictate our understanding of and construction of knowledge. In an Australian contemporary context, this means identifying the legacy of privilege that accrues to the coloniser and which has been subsumed within therapeutic, policy and social spaces whereby the oppressor is positioned as the healer/saviour. The resultant binary relationship of the coloniser and the colonised is reflected in all aspects of social, political and economic engagement, including the psychological. The power dynamic that underpins this relationship is predicated on notions of white privilege and power and it is this foundational assumption that must be disrupted in order to provide the space and opportunity for mutually liberating praxis to emerge (Freire, 1970, 1998, 1999). In this context, recognition and inclusion of Aboriginal and Torres Strait Islander epistemologies, ontologies and practices as legitimate components of Australian psychology represent a core liberatory praxis.

Riley's call to de-colonise psychology is reflected in the 2015 Gayaa Dhuwi (Proud Spirit) Declaration, which in part requires Australian governments, mental health systems, educational institutions and practitioners to understand the long-term impacts on Indigenous peoples of living in a colonised space. The Declaration is part of an international movement of Indigenous leaders working in the mental health systems in neo-colonial countries calling for Indigenous partnerships and inclusion in mental health pertaining to Indigenous people. Specifically, it has its origins in the Wharerata Group of Indigenous mental health leaders from Canada, the United States, Australia, Samoa and New Zealand who developed the seminal Wharerata Declaration in 2010 (NATSILMH, 2015; Sones et al., 2010). Specific elements in the declaration require:

- all Australian governments in a bipartisan way, and in particular their health and mental health departments, to formally adopt and commit to supporting the *Gayaa Dhuwi (Proud Spirit) Declaration* by the 30th of June 2016 (p. 6).
- implementation of the *Gayaa Dhuwi (Proud Spirit) Declaration* by the 30th of June 2017.
- mental health professionals and professional associations, and educational institutions and standard-setting bodies that work in mental health (and also those in areas related to mental health, particularly suicide prevention) to formally adopt and commit to supporting the *Gayaa Dhuwi (Proud Spirit) Declaration* by the 30th of June 2016 (pp. 6–7).
- these bodies to develop an implementation component of the *Gayaa Dhuwi (Proud Spirit) Declaration* by the 30th of June 2017.

(Dudgeon, Calma, Brideson, & Holland, 2016)

While rhetorical commitment to such initiatives is both socially and politically desirable, this is just the first step; it is the effective implementation of the recommended strategies that is critical. Unless the public rhetoric of commitment is followed by implementation strategies, it does little to effect the social justice changes called for in the Declaration. Consequently, the Gayaa Dhuwi (Proud Spirit) Declaration contains key elements that can guide and structure the implementation process:

1. Building access to cultural healers and cultural healing.
2. Supporting the development of Aboriginal and Torres Strait Islander values-based social and emotional wellbeing and mental health outcome measures in combination with clinical outcome measures.

3. Developing, and resourcing the implementation of policies to ensure that Aboriginal and Torres Strait Islander people are trained, employed, empowered and valued to work (and, where appropriate, lead) across the mental health system; and
4. Developing, and resourcing the implementation of policies to ensure the Australian mental health system supports Aboriginal and Torres Strait Islander leaders to practice culturally informed concepts of leadership within that system, within their communities, and among their constituents.

(Dudgeon, Calma et al., 2016, p. 7)

The Declaration and its implementation framework echo Riley's call for education institutions, professional bodies and practitioners to authentically engage in a de-colonisation process. One way of understanding this process is through Cultural Interface Theory (Nakata, 2007a, 2007b), which argues that the interface between different persons/groups offers the opportunity for some form of exchange. Either the interaction can be oppositional in that each resists the influence of the other, often leading to further intensification of conflict/difficulties between the two; or it can result in productive dialogue based on aspects of similarity on which some form of mutual respect for difference might be achieved. In the context of a settler state, such interactions must be understood within the power differentials that have been constructed by the coloniser over the colonised person/group. While this power differential is readily seen by the colonised person/group, it often remains unseen by the coloniser (Suchet, 2007). In this context, the education and training of psychology students and practitioners becomes an essential component in the change agenda, and psychological literacy within a de-colonised and critical pedagogy framework offers the methodology to achieve it.

Psychological literacy is defined as the intentional application of psychological knowledge and skills in the pursuit of individual and societal goals (Cranney & Dunn, 2011). This includes understanding different cultures and a commitment to the human rights principles of social justice as well as a comprehensive awareness of how injustice is reproduced and contested (Dudgeon et al., 2011). By definition, this also means a critical understanding of how the discipline itself continues to contribute to social inequality (Dudgeon et al., 2011). Psychological literacy based on the principles of social justice and human rights would remain vigilantly self-reflexive, pedagogically innovative and dialogically responsive to the voices and lives of those who engage with the discourse both intellectually, as subjects or 'clients', and as co-healers, experts by experience and practitioners. A primary element is the de-naturalising of white privilege discourses and practices which privilege members of that social group by drawing attention to 'whiteness' as a social category. In so doing, the invisible power and privilege associated with being white can be identified and contested (Suchet, 2007; Walker, Schultz, & Sonn, 2014).

By making the invisible visible, it permits the construction of self/other dichotomies to be seen and challenged, which in turn provides the opportunity to dismantle the underlying power frameworks. Such deconstruction in relation to Indigenous issues is an exercise that should be practised by institutions as well as by the individuals who comprise them (Dudgeon et al., 2011). Indeed, building an *Indigenous* psychological literacy would go far in eradicating institutionalised and structural racism which often relies on prejudicial narratives about Indigenous peoples entrenched in Western psychological discourses of inferiority. Consequently, an Indigenous psychological literacy would see Indigenous knowledges, history, culture and ways of being embedded into a curriculum in such a way as to achieve epistemological equivalence, whereby both knowledge systems are regarded as equally relevant, important and synergistic such that each could benefit from the other and therefore co-construct new knowledges and interpretations of human functioning.

Mainstream psychology, and the epistemological and ontological foundations on which it is based, operates as a truth discourse about human consciousness, that describes and proscribes what is and is not 'normal' and 'pathological' (Foucault, 2004, 2008). Such constructions of what is and is not legitimised inform hegemonic understandings of difference, while masking political, social and economic investments in the policing of human behaviours. Therefore, this version of psychology operates as a truth regime which represents the interests of a minority of peoples (white, middle class and heterosexual), which is further limited by underlying ideas of individualism that are implicated in the colonial erasure of Indigenous culture, language, traditional healing and wisdom (Dudgeon & Walker, 2015; Hook, 2005). Consequently, Indigenous psychological literacy within a critical pedagogy framework would deconstruct these ethnocentric biases that naturalise the oppression of persons and groups, specifically Indigenous peoples in Australia (and elsewhere). An Indigenous psychological literacy would include, for example, a deep historical and cultural awareness of the social and emotional wellbeing impact of colonisation and the continuing contribution of racism, including how these patterns of historical oppression are played out in the local context. It would also work towards deconstructing the pathologising of Indigenous peoples which supports racist thinking. This deficit model – the entrenched prejudice that Indigenous people 'lack', across a range of competencies, abilities and capacities – would be replaced by a model which values the complex knowledge systems of Indigenous culture. Consequently, the position taken in this chapter is that Indigenous psychological literacy, in combination with Freire's concept of critical consciousness, and drawing on theoretical concepts such as Nakata and colleagues' Cultural Interface Theory (Nakata, M., Nakata, V., & Chin, 2008), might equip psychologists and psychology graduates to shift the oppositional binary discourse of deficit to one of capacity, strength and mutual respect (Dudgeon et al., 2011).

Background: a history of colonial dispossession

The British occupied Australia in 1788, and subsequently land was wrested from Indigenous peoples. Scholars have described this as "one of the greatest appropriations of land in world history" (Reynolds, 2013, p. 248). Indigenous Australians were decimated by the settlers, subjected to prolonged genocide, slavery and warfare, and had their children forcibly removed; they were relocated and contained in reserves and missions, and their culture, language, spirituality, land and communities were degraded, destroyed and outlawed (Gilbert, 1978; Reynolds, 2006, 2013). As a direct consequence, Indigenous peoples in Australia, like many in colonised spaces, have significantly reduced life chances, experience complex forms of intergenerational trauma, have poor health outcomes, and a youth suicide rate that is one of the highest in the world (Dudgeon, Milroy, & Walker, 2014). During the late 18th century, there were up to 250 language groups, but by the early 21st century, this had been reduced to approximately 150 (Dalby, 1998; Walsh, 1991). This loss of language is a signifier of the destruction of culture and the dramatic attrition is an indicator of the gravity of colonial dispossession. In contemporary times, Indigenous peoples represent only 3% of the Australian population and are still subjected to overt and covert forms of individual and institutionalised racism, including being imprisoned and dying in custody at far greater rates than their non-Indigenous counterparts (Cunneen, 2005).

In recognition of the disparities between Indigenous and non-Indigenous peoples' health, the Close the Gap: Indigenous Health Campaign was established in 2006 by the Commonwealth government in a bid to address these health and social inequities. However, parity between Indigenous and non-Indigenous Australians has yet to be achieved some 9 years later (Close the Gap, 2015). Despite a marginal improvement in the life expectancy of Aboriginal and Torres Strait Islanders (measured between 2010 and 2012) of 0.8 years for men and 0.1 for women, a life expectancy gap of roughly 10 years between non-Indigenous and Indigenous Australians still exists (Australian Bureau of Statistics, 2013a, p. 1). The level of psychological distress experienced by Indigenous peoples has increased from 27% (2004–2005) to 30% in the data period 2012–2013. Indigenous men and women experience approximately three times more intense psychological distress than non-Indigenous people (Australian Bureau of Statistics, 2013b). This augurs badly for individuals and communities overall because the impact of such widespread psychological distress can affect families and communities, not just the individual (Kelly, Dudgeon, Gee, & Glaskin, 2010). According to the *Overview of the Australian Indigenous Health Status 2013*, in "2012–2013, 69% of Indigenous adults experienced at least one significant stressor in the previous 12 months" (Australian Indigenous Health*InfoNet*, 2014, p. 22). Such stressors include death in the family, incarceration of members of a family, accidents, unemployment, homelessness, family breakdowns, reduced living arrangements and serious illness. These data indicate an even greater degree of disparity for those peoples located in regional and remote communities, due in part to the lack of services available and the lack of culturally responsive service delivery within those that do exist (Silburn et al., 2014).

Exposure to the death by suicide of someone in the community is also a significant stressor that is linked to increased risk of suicide and self-harm within the community. The small and close-knit nature of Indigenous communities means that every suicide has a widespread impact with ripples of loss, grief and mourning throughout the community and beyond – particularly where communities are highly interconnected. This can create layers of increased risk within affected communities during the grieving period, and in some situations, a 'suicide cluster' can form (Dudgeon et al., 2012, p. 45). Such communities are often already managing intergenerational trauma and chronic levels of psychological distress. The report *Overcoming Indigenous Disadvantage* showed that between 2004–2005 and 2012–2013, recorded hospitalisations for intentional self-harm increased by 48% (Productivity Commission, 2014, p. 1). Similarly, the rate of hospitalisation of Indigenous Australians for psychological and behavioural disorders rose at twice the level of that for non-Indigenous Australians between 2011 and 2012 (Australian Indigenous Health*InfoNet*, 2014, p. 33). Moreover, poisoning, injury, motor vehicle accidents, assaults, self-harm and falls were recorded as the second most common reasons for the hospitalisation of Indigenous people between 2012 and 2013 (Australian Institute of Health and Welfare, 2014).

The suicide rate for Indigenous peoples between 2001 and 2010 was more than *double* the rate for non-Indigenous people, making it the fifth leading cause of death for Indigenous peoples (Australian Bureau of Statistics, 2014). Indigenous men in the 25–29 age group have the highest rates of completed suicide, which is four times higher than for non-Indigenous men of the same group. Indigenous women in the 20–24 age group have the highest rates of completed suicide, which is in excess of five times higher than for non-Indigenous women in the same age group (Australian Bureau of Statistics, 2012–2013). Compared to non-Indigenous teens of the same age, Indigenous males between 15 and 19 years old are 4.4 times more likely to die from suicide, and Indigenous females of the same age group are 5.9 times more likely to die from suicide (Australian Bureau of Statistics, 2013a). Of concern are the significant data quality issues surrounding the statistics on Indigenous suicide which suggest that death rates are underestimated, thus highlighting the urgency of appropriate responses (Elliot-Farrely, 2004; Harrison, Miller, Weeramanthri, Wakerman, & Barnes, 2001; Silburn, Glaskin, Henry, & Drew, 2010, p. 92).

These health data are compounded by other social determinants such as lack of educational and employment opportunities, and inadequate housing, which in turn can contribute to allegations of anti-social behaviour and the entrenched racism that pervades the fabric of Australian society. The underlying racist assumptions about Aboriginal and Torres Strait Islander peoples make it harder for Indigenous people to complete their education, find employment or enter the housing market. Consequently, daily activities become a battle for inclusion and equity (Dudgeon, Cranney et al., 2016; Marmot, 2011; Zubrick et al., 2014).

These facts bring into sharp focus the urgency of Rob Riley's challenge to psychology in 1995 with which this chapter began. Throughout his life, Riley openly called attention to the significant lack of awareness within mainstream Australian psychology about Aboriginal people, history, spirituality and culture, and made it clear that it was urgent that educational training programmes for psychologists rectify this negligence. His speech was the first occasion on which an Indigenous leader addressed a national psychological organisation about the need to provide culturally safe and appropriate training for psychologists, and those who work with distressed Indigenous people. Around the time of and since Riley's ground-breaking address and his tragic death less than 12 months later, significant and powerful changes have occurred within the discourses and the institution of psychology in Australia. Such changes include the publication of landmark texts such as *Ways Forward: National Aboriginal and Torres Strait Islander Mental Health Policy National Consultancy Report* (Swan & Raphael, 1995), which moved away from individualist disease models towards models of collective health, wellbeing and community resilience; and later, the book *Working Together: Aboriginal and Torres Strait Islander Mental Health and Wellbeing Principles and Practice* (Purdie, Dudgeon, & Walker, 2010; Dudgeon, Milroy et al., 2014).

In 1997, the Australian Psychological Society (APS) Position Paper on racism, *Racism and Prejudice: Psychological Perspectives,* challenged sociobiological or social Darwinist ideologies about race as a biological fact and moved towards a recognition that the Western psychology had been (and still is) an instrument of colonial oppression (Bishop, Vicary, Mitchell, & Pearson, 2012). In doing so, it took the first step towards accepting the challenge laid down by Riley in his historic 1995 address. Later developments include the formation of the Australian Indigenous Psychologists Association (AIPA) in 2008, along with the release of the *APS Reconciliation Action Plan (RAP) 2011–2014.* Professor Pat Dudgeon, the co-chair of the APS RAP working group and inaugural chair of AIPA, in her statement in the *APS Reconciliation Action Plan* writes: "cultural safety and continuous, quality professional development are conceptual goals we plan to make achievable through targeted activities within the APS and in partnership with universities and colleges, our branches and key Aboriginal and Torres Strait Islander organizations" (APS, 2012, p. 6). Importantly, the APS acknowledged that there are

> significant knowledge gaps in the psychological and wider community about the diversity and wealth of Indigenous cultures and histories and the inequality between Aboriginal and Torres Strait Islander and non-Indigenous health and well-being remain[s] an alarming sign of how far we still have to go.
> *(APS, 2012, p. 4)*

The statement emphasises the harm done to Indigenous peoples through a violent and invasive colonisation, in particular the forced removal of children across generations (which has been recognised as an act of *prolonged* genocide) and how important it is, given the role that psychology and social services played in the forced removal of children from their families and other indignities and racist oppressions, that "political, legal and social strategies for the restoration of culture, individual human rights, privileges, and dignity are also pursued" (APS, 2012, p. 4).

Consequently, the APS, as the peak representative for psychology in Australia, acknowledged that to address the intergenerational trauma and disadvantage, and build on the strength and capacity that Indigenous peoples have demonstrated in resisting various oppressive regimes over the past 250 years, psychologists must work in partnership with Indigenous peoples to achieve sustainable change. Learning how to do this requires a range of individual and institutional strategies that include recognition of the legacy of power and privilege that non-Indigenous Australians experience; an understanding of the political and cultural aspects of the practice and education of psychology; and a genuine commitment to a sustainable agenda for social justice. As a result, in 2013, Dudgeon drew together a team of university investigators with the APS as a key industry partner to form the Australian Indigenous Psychology Education Project (AIPEP) to address the significant under-representation of Indigenous psychologists in Australia and create and support culturally safe and appropriate training for all professionals in the field. Aspects of this project will be discussed later in the chapter.

Psychology in Australia: institutionalised racism

While the ideological shifts discussed above are most welcome and signal a very different approach to working with Indigenous Australians, it is important to understand that this is just the first step in addressing psychology's role in the oppression of Aboriginal and Torres Strait Islander peoples. It is important to contextualise these recent changes in the history of psychology as a discipline and profession. Understanding that it is only in the late 20th century that the discipline began to shift from framing Indigenous peoples as specimens of a primitive culture to beginning to recognise the complexities of the oldest harmonious and equitable culture on earth is an essential step in moving the discipline and profession into a partnership relationship with Indigenous Australians.

Racism operates at multiple levels in society in both overt and covert ways. Individual racism can be manifest as personal attacks towards members of a marginalised group (overt); crossing a road to avoid contact, or standing on public transport rather than taking a vacant seat next to a member of the marginalised group (covert); or any number of other everyday actions. But institutionalised racism operates on a far broader and less easily identifiable level (Hook, 2007; Jones, 2002). Jones defines it as "the structures, policies, practices, and norms resulting in differential access to the goods, services, and opportunities of society by 'race'" (2002, p. 10). Jones makes the further subtle point, that while an institution might have seemingly addressed racism through, for example, affirmative action policies, if institutional practices result in marginalisation, then it is possible to argue that the institution is producing unintended racist *consequences* (Jones, 1972, 1997). That is, if the outcome of these policies is a "systematically advantaging to whites and disadvantaging to ethnic and racial minority groups, they represent a *standard of practice* criterion of institutional racism" (Jones, 1997, p. 439).

Institutional racism does not necessarily involve explicit exclusion and denial of access as was practised during the apartheid era in South Africa, for example; instead, it can be unconscious, hidden practices such as the unquestioning application of race-blind equality discourses. This is evident in the higher education sector because universities often apply an 'all students are equal' approach to students. For instance, failing to allow absence from class or extensions to assessment submission deadlines for Indigenous students who must follow cultural protocols associated with certain events (e.g. sorry business [mourning]) is an application of an equality discourse that adversely impacts one group of students on the basis of race. Similarly, not having one's cultural group represented in the curriculum is a form of institutionalised racism because, by definition, it privileges a certain group on the basis of race via the normative representation of white Western constructions of knowledge (Hook, 2007). In Foucauldian terms, both the archaeology (the foundational 'truths' that provide the basis for discourses to emerge) and the genealogy (the impacts of those discourses) need to be identified and understood in order to move beyond the constraints of that historical and social context (Foucault, 1972.) Therefore, it is the 'truths' – the events, practices and beliefs – that provide the unspoken backdrop associated with the creation and formation of racialised discourses about Aboriginal and Torres Strait Islander people. The discourses of racial difference and the hegemonic force associated with those discourses need not be expressed explicitly by powerful persons, groups and agencies (although this happens constantly) as such discourses are often normalised across generations. Racism occurs, often silently, by what is not said or done, to such an extent that racism becomes normalised to the point of invisibility (Darlaston-Jones, 2015b); it is unseen, but remains the 'truth' by which all action is shaped and influenced (Foucault, 1972, 1981; Giroux, 2011; hooks, 2002). It is this unseen structural racism that then pervades the unconscious of those who create the policies and practices which become the framework of institutionalised racism that pervades universities and the various disciplines that comprise them.

The declaration of Australia as *Terra Nullius* (no persons' land) by the early colonists established the foundation on which the relationship between Indigenous and non-Indigenous peoples was to be played out. By effectively relegating the inhabitants to the status of flora and fauna, the settlers established their cultural superiority over the native inhabitants; a position that was not formally addressed until the 1967 referendum which recognised Indigenous Australians as citizens in their own country. Closely associated with this act was the ideological position of the times based on social Darwinism that positioned persons of colour as being less intelligent and therefore less important than their white counterparts (Robinson, 2009). The impact of social Darwinism in naturalising racist prejudices about Indigenous peoples was profound and continues to influence contemporary evolutionary psychology and other branches of Western psychology which have affinities with sociobiology, especially those that are focused on intelligence and cognitive differences between so-called 'races' (Dudgeon & Bray, 2014).

The birth of psychology coincided with the emerging desire for 'scientific' forms of knowledge, which influenced the developing discipline to emulate the natural sciences in a pursuit of universal laws of human behaviour. Early adherents of phrenology, for instance, argued that the shape of the head and brain explained anything from sexual deviance and criminality to racial inferiority, and in Australia, phrenologists studied Indigenous skulls, arguing that the traditional custodians of the land were sub-human (Anderson, 2002; Anderson & Perrin, 2007). Racist stereotypes about the essential degeneracy of Indigenous people flourished in the journals of Western phrenology and psychology during the 1800s (Anderson, 2002; Anderson & Perrin, 2007). Significantly, the study and theorising of Indigenous Australians was used in the emergence of Western psychology as a dominant truth discourse; for example, a foundational Western psychology text, Spencer's *Principles of Psychology* (1855), discussed the 'savage' and 'primitive' mind of Aboriginal Australians. The emerging discipline often referred to the inferiority of Indigenous Australian peoples as evidence for establishing psychology as an evolutionary science (Ranzijn, McConnochie, & Nolan, 2009). This initial application of psychology with Indigenous Australians established the relationship by characterising them as "primitive, of low intelligence, ruled largely by instinct and genetically incapable of becoming civilized" (Ranzijn et al., 2009, p. 185), which by definition established the superiority of the white settler and legitimised the subsequent colonisation processes (Opotow, 1990) and contemporary attitudes and behaviours.

A key transformative event in the history of the relationship between mainstream white psychology and Indigenous peoples occurred in 1988 when the 24th International Congress on Psychology was held in Australia. The only Indigenous content in the conference was a small photographic exhibition called 'Indigenous Aspects of Australian Psychology', which was composed of photographs of Aboriginal skulls from the collection of craniometrists, anthropometrists and psychometrists (Turtle & Orr, 1989). Echoing the by then outdated prejudices of racist phrenologists, the exhibition caused concern among the international psychologists, but more importantly, it motivated sections within the APS to take action. As a consequence of this open display of racism, the APS Board of Community Psychologists (now the College of Community Psychologists) organised the first symposium on the 'Psychology of Indigenous People' at the 25th Annual Conference of the APS in Melbourne in 1990 where Tracey Bunda presented a paper by Aboriginal psychologist Pat Dudgeon and anthropologist Darlene Oxenham (1989) about Aboriginal identity. This symposium then led a group of 28 delegates to meet with Elders of the Maralinga Taruta community in the South Australian desert for a 7-day workshop event (Rickwood, Dudgeon, & Gridely, 2010) which linked to the fledgling Indigenous mental health movement. This event established an enduring connection between Indigenous rights and community psychology in Australia that is founded in critical social analysis and the pursuit of sustainable redress through participatory practices. Since then, Indigenous understandings of mental health have emerged.

Indigenous critical psychology is founded on Indigenous conceptions of health which, necessarily, challenge monolithic and monocultural narratives about Indigenous peoples, drawing attention to the complexities of different language groups, cultural practices and kinship networks. Indigenous psychology is also guided by models of participatory action research and a dynamic and dialogical process of culturally sensitive capacity building, grounded in the grass-roots needs of communities. Honouring the power of Elders to heal the cultural wounds inflicted by colonisation is of critical importance. This holistic construction of health recognises the importance of the interconnections between body, family, land, culture and spirituality (Gee, Dudgeon, Schultz, Hart, & Kelly, 2014) that embeds subjectivity within the collective, such that each is inseparable. Complex and dynamic interactions between subjectivity, land, culture, spirit and community within Indigenous communities are the foundations of the concept of Social and Emotional Wellbeing (SEWB). Within the holistic model of SEWB, subjectivity cannot be abstracted from a connection to family, land, spirituality and culture. Moreover, SEWB recognises that people have different experiences in different domains across their lives, which means that it is possible to experience strength and resilience in one aspect, and vulnerability and distress in another simultaneously. Similarly, different approaches to healing and care might be required at different times and in response to different issues.

The key point is that SEWB is founded on the socio-political concepts of self-determination and empowerment, and therefore becomes a central tool in the de-centring of the dominance of Western conceptions of racialised deficit and the associated (missionary) healer/saviour response. These key components of empowerment and self-determination are also central to the United Nations *Declaration on the Rights of Indigenous Peoples* (United Nations, 2008). Such a concept was argued as essential to the Indigenous mental health movement in that they envisioned dynamic autonomous mental health services designed and delivered by Indigenous people in continuous consultation with communities. So effective is such a response that The World Health Organization now frames all such interventions through this lens (Gee et al., 2014). However, to be successful, this approach to service provision and delivery requires the (usually non-Indigenous) decision makers to understand their role and voice, and for policy to be informed by the people and not by white experts. It is this aspect of critical self-reflexivity, which is the cornerstone of critical pedagogy, that is currently missing from the psychology curriculum (Darlaston-Jones, 2015a).

Indigenous psychological literacy in Australia: critical pedagogy and conscientisation

If psychology is to play a leading role in challenging and changing racist discourses about Aboriginal and Torres Strait Islander peoples and the power structures that benefit non-Indigenous Australians, then Indigenous knowledges and cultural responsiveness need to be embedded into the psychology curriculum at both undergraduate and postgraduate levels (Darlaston-Jones, 2005, 2015a; Darlaston-Jones et al., 2014; Dudgeon et al., 2011). To achieve this, though, requires deconstruction of the existing ontological foundations of the theory and practice of psychology and the construction of a new vision of the purpose and role of psychology that is founded on human rights and social justice (Darlaston-Jones, 2005, 2015a, 2015b; Darlaston-Jones et al., 2014; Dudgeon et al., 2011; Watkins & Shulman, 2008). Consequently, the education of students needs to reflect these values and principles, not only in the content of the curriculum but also through the pedagogical practice of educators (Giroux, 2011; hooks, 1996; Smyth, 2011).

Identifying and contesting the ontological basis of psychology practice is critical to its capacity to provide appropriate and effective responses to psychological distress (Kagan, Burton, Duckett, Lawthom, & Siddiquee, 2011; Martín-Baró, 1994). All actions, thoughts and practice are driven by underlying, often unconscious, values, beliefs and assumptions. The meaning that a person ascribes to experiences, events, thoughts, emotions and so forth, is dependent on a number of idiosyncratic factors that make each person unique. Indeed, it is the ability of the person to interpret his or her world and to derive meaning from it that is the foundation of psychology. The irony is that by ignoring this aspect of human consciousness, a particularly narrow view of social interaction is presented. That is, the nuances that differentiate between individuals as a result of the unique history of the person could not be examined, or even accepted to exist, based on the narrow positivist definitions of scientific research that dominate psychology (Breen & Darlaston-Jones, 2010). The social context of the person is deemed irrelevant in this version of psychology and so too are the individual values and biases that formed the basis for motivation and action within the social setting (Gergen, 1999). In contrast, critical psychologists argue for a more nuanced and textured understanding of human functioning; one that is situated within the interpretative spaces within and between the multiple identities, roles and realities we occupy (Darlaston-Jones, 2005). In this interpretation of psychology, the historical realities of dispossession, genocide, marginalisation and the subsequent intergenerational trauma derived from those experiences of Indigenous peoples become the relevant contextual lens through which behaviours and responses are interpreted. Parallel to this, though, must be the equally important understanding of the position of power and privilege afforded to the non-Indigenous educator/practitioner by virtue of the dualism created by the marginalisation of the 'other'. Failure to understand, recognise and then contest and deconstruct a racialised hierarchical self/other dichotomy leads to a false equivalency and race-blind claims of equality. In the teaching spaces, this fallacy leads to Indigenous narratives, history, culture and beliefs being invisible in the curriculum, and by default, being viewed as 'less than' the neoliberal, white, North American version of psychology that has permeated the globe. In the practice area, graduates are ill-prepared to meet the needs of a vulnerable client base because they lack the knowledge and understanding of the role that culture and history play in creating the subject positions occupied by both the 'client' and the 'practitioner'. This power resides in constructions of privilege situated in the notion of *being* the practitioner and therefore being assumed to be psychologically healthy and in a position to 'treat' or 'heal' the 'client' who, by definition, is not. This dynamic is further reinforced by the power inscribed through the advanced education of the practitioner as the 'healer' who then commands a certain level of income and social status by virtue of that education. In addition to this, the power associated with the position occupied by the non-Indigenous practitioner contributes to a saviour complex that is rooted in historical missionary definitions of benevolent intervention. The lack of representation of Aboriginal and Torres Strait Islander peoples within the mental health professions is symptomatic of the entrenched racist assumptions of academic deficit, as well as the lack of cultural relevance that these training programmes have for Indigenous peoples. The following sections demonstrate the importance of addressing the teaching and practice of psychology by drawing on evidence from AIPEP as well as an undergraduate curriculum founded on a de-colonised and critical theory framework.

Australian Indigenous Psychology Education Project (AIPEP)[1]

As discussed, Aboriginal and Torres Strait Islander peoples experience such high levels of psychological distress that it can be described as a mental health crisis. This disadvantage is also played out in all other aspects of social life with lower levels of educational achievement, high unemployment and poor life expectancy. However, in highlighting these disparities, it is essential not to ignore equally high levels of strength and resilience demonstrated by Indigenous peoples and communities, and the manner in which they have resisted and challenged the deficit discourses created by the dominant group. AIPEP draws on the perspectives of Indigenous and non-Indigenous stakeholders in order to develop guidance, support and recommendations for psychology training programmes that contribute to a social justice agenda based on commitment to human rights and Indigenous sovereignty. Specifically, AIPEP focuses on how psychology education and training can develop a more culturally responsive mental health workforce, and how the numbers of Aboriginal and Torres Strait Islander psychologists can be increased through recruitment to, retention on and graduation from both undergraduate and postgraduate programmes. More detail about the aims and outcomes of the project, including resources for educators and practitioners, can be accessed from the project website (www.Indigenouspsyched.org.au).

The project, which commenced in 2013, focuses on two priority areas identified by the APS – Cultural Responsiveness and Indigenous Education and Employment – and is funded through the Commonwealth government Office for Learning and Teaching (OLT). The project seeks to transform the curriculum of higher education psychology training in order to maximise the cultural responsiveness of non-Indigenous students and the engagement of Indigenous students in psychological education. Combining the understandings of Aboriginal and Torres Strait Islander staff, students, employers and psychologists, as well as non-Indigenous educators and employers, AIPEP has developed a curriculum framework which, if adopted by all Schools of Psychology, has the capacity to de-colonise the discipline and profession of psychology at both the theoretical and practical levels.

Data presented in the AIPEP 'Summary of Findings' (Dudgeon, Cranney et al., 2016) identified that there are around 103 Indigenous psychologists, a figure which represents approximately 0.5% of all psychologists in Australia (Health Workforce Australia, 2014, p. 14). In order to achieve parity, whereby at least 3% of psychologists are Indigenous, a further 500 Indigenous psychologists are needed. Identifying and then removing the barriers that prevent Indigenous students from choosing psychology as a career path is essential to achieving this goal. Consequently, AIPEP investigated the:

1. availability and range of Indigenous knowledges and pedagogies within Australian psychology programs at both undergraduate and postgraduate levels
2. barriers and facilitators to improving the curriculum, and student engagement and success
3. training experiences of Aboriginal and Torres Strait Islander psychologists
4. perspectives of mental health professionals working with Aboriginal and Torres Strait Islander peoples in relation to workforce competencies
5. representation of Aboriginal and Torres Strait Islander peoples in the psychology profession and psychology training programs.

Interviews were conducted with Heads of Schools and Departments of Psychology; key academics; Indigenous Education Centre Directors/Heads; and workforce representatives. In addition, four focus groups were conducted with Indigenous psychologists and students, and an online survey was developed for all members of the APS (see Table 7.1 for details).

Thematic analysis identified the following significant findings:

Professional and student representation

Due to the many limitations in how data are collected and reported, the availability and accuracy of information on the numbers of Indigenous psychology students/ psychologists are limited. The available data suggest that numbers are slowly rising, but that numbers are well below parity.

Recruitment and retention of students

A range of initiatives is needed to increase the recruitment of Indigenous students into psychology: a commitment at Vice Chancellor level that Indigenous education across the sector is in need of attention; an active cultural awareness and cultural safety programme; financial assistance; inclusion of Indigenous leaders and community members as cultural guides for the academy and as supports for the students; a focus

TABLE 7.1 Participants in AIPEP survey

Participant group	*Number of participants*
Aboriginal and Torres Strait Islander psychologists and psychology graduates	13 participants
Indigenous Education Centre (IEC) staff	15 participants
Psychology educators	33 participants
First-year psychology students (non-Indigenous)	30 participants
Psychologists and other mental health professionals	Symposium: 5 participants Interviews: 10 participants

Source: Dudgeon, Cranney et al. (2016)

on de-colonised curricula; and strong partnerships between the Indigenous Education Centres and the schools of psychology.

Curriculum

This emerged as a pivotal element in addressing the recruitment and retention of students; providing a culturally responsive workforce; and as a mechanism for addressing structural and institutional racism. Curriculum must include fundamental information on colonisation history and its impact on Aboriginal and Torres Strait Islander peoples, and self-reflection and reflexivity to enable the contextual framing and critique of majority views and perspectives. Work-integrated learning (WIL) is also recognised as an important learning opportunity for psychology students at all levels and an opportunity to form meaningful partnerships with Aboriginal and Torres Strait Islander organisations for two-way learning.

Professional competencies

Creating a culturally responsive workforce requires a shift in the philosophical lens through which the education of psychology graduates is conducted. This requires a curriculum focused on the three pillars of values, knowledge and skills. The synergistic relationship between these three elements creates the mode of practice such that the values one holds individually and as a cultural group influence the manner in which knowledge is created and applied; consequently, the skill development reflects the values. Psychology's commitment to value-free/neutral objectivity and the pursuit of universal laws of behaviour does not equip graduates to work effectively with Indigenous peoples and reinforces the oppositional binaries that exist between Indigenous and non-Indigenous Australians. It therefore represents a significant barrier to the recruitment of Indigenous students into psychology and fails to equip non-Indigenous students with the requisite knowledge and skills to work effectively with Indigenous persons and communities.

Findings from the AIPEP data indicate the need for significant reform in the education and training of psychology students in order to attract and retain Indigenous students and to (re)educate non-Indigenous students so that, at the very least, they do no harm when working with Indigenous clients and communities. They also echo Freire's calls (1998) for a conscientisation approach to education that explicitly emphasises the socially and historically situated identities and roles that students and educators bring with them into the teaching and learning space. This also aligns with Nakata et al.'s Cultural Interface Theory (2008) which argues that by coming together to share, debate and discuss in a mutual exchange of ideas and knowledge, each group not only has the chance to understand the unique differences that persons and groups have, but also the essential sameness that unites us. Such a process then allows for a cultural exchange to occur that respects and values the diversity in each group, but which invites a willingness to integrate knowledges from each group into the repertoire of the other within a scaffolded framework of unity. In order for Indigenous students to be attracted to studying psychology and becoming psychologists, it is critical that their knowledges, culture, history and ways of knowing are visible within the discipline and the classroom.

Focus group data from Indigenous psychologists continually showed that, as students, they were in a state of constant 'code switching' or 'translation' (Dudgeon, Cranney et al., 2016) in that every theory or protocol or piece of evidence that they were taught in the classroom needed to be converted to a culturally relevant mode of operation; the normative white, Western knowledge system had little or no relevance to Indigenous students. This additional burden – of continually converting content into something meaningful and relevant – places additional pressures on these students, which non-Indigenous students do not have to face. Potentially of greater concern, though, is the fact that none of this culturally relevant information was being shared with the non-Indigenous students. Therefore, the non-Indigenous students failed to learn that the imposition of Western normative assumptions, practices and interventions was potentially harmful for Indigenous persons and communities, and that therefore they were being trained unconsciously to work in an unethical manner which saw the cultural context as irrelevant to the practice of psychology.

Creating a more culturally relevant curriculum not only requires educators to understand their own positionality relative to their cultural space and what it means to be a non-Indigenous person in a settler context (Darlaston-Jones, 2015b); it also requires the discipline and the institution to do the same (Hook, 2007). Consequently, the de-colonisation project becomes a holistic integrated process that makes visible the unspoken 'truths' that operate at the unconscious as well as the conscious level of awareness to identify and eradicate institutionalised racism and exclusion (Freire, 1998; hooks, 1998; Giroux, 2011). Such an approach requires strong leadership which both empowers students and combats racist practices and policies. It also requires curricula which make visible Indigenous cultures and ways of knowing and which deconstruct hegemonic Eurocentric paradigms.

De-colonised psychology curriculum in practice

An example of a de-colonised curriculum can be seen in the Bachelor of Behavioural Science at The University of Notre Dame, Australia (Fremantle Campus; for a more complete discussion, see Darlaston-Jones, 2015a). The degree encompasses two complementary approaches. The first is at the instrumental level whereby Indigenous knowledges and practices are embedded within and between all subjects (units of study/courses) over the 3 years. In practice, this involves having guest speakers, using published Indigenous research, building relationships with Indigenous organisations and using Indigenous psychology in the classroom rather than promoting a dominant Western theory. A concrete example of this is the Model of Grief and Loss developed by Wanganeen (2010); this model captures the intergenerational trauma associated with grief and loss and the multifaceted responses and reactions to it across the spectrum of grief and loss experiences. It can be applied to death and dying, but it also allows for different types of grief and loss in a way that the more traditional mainstream theory offered by Kübler-Ross (2009) does not. Despite Wanganeen's model offering a far more holistic understanding of grief and loss, it is Kübler-Ross who retains dominance in undergraduate textbooks and classrooms.

Building relationships that are mutually beneficial between the academy and Indigenous organisations also offers the opportunity for staff/managers in those organisations to speak first-hand to psychology students about their role and that of the organisation, which helps to identify the funding and policy implications of service delivery. It offers a visible presence of Indigenous professionals that is missing from the discourses around Indigenous capacity, which enhances the learning opportunities for all students, but decentres the dominant Western norms. In addition, such relationships offer practical exposure though work-integrated learning (WIL) and internship opportunities for students.

Relationships also offer the opportunity to integrate SEWB, as well as aspects of Indigenous spirituality, into the professional development of psychology students. This is an area of human functioning that is often invisible in mainstream psychology classrooms and textbooks because it is conflated with religiosity and treated as a variable external to the functioning of the person. In contrast, SEWB views spirituality as an integral component of wellbeing which cannot be separated from the person or the context in which the person is situated. Indigenous conceptions of spirituality transcend the narrow confines of organised religion (although for some people the two concepts are related) and speak of a deep connection with land, culture and community (Gee et al., 2014). This connection needs to be understood in relation to the health and social inequities experienced by Indigenous peoples. For example, one of the authors of this chapter, Dawn Darlaston-Jones, who is a non-Indigenous academic, supported several groups of students in a cultural immersion programme in a remote community in the North West of Western Australia over an 18-month period. During one of these trips, she had a conversation with a senior Aboriginal man who shared his experience of his ancestors manifesting to him and guiding him throughout his life. During the conversation, she struggled to hear his story through his cultural lens rather than imposing the diagnostic frameworks of psychosis that she had been taught as part of her postgraduate education. The subsequent conversation between them allowed for the tensions she experienced to be discussed and navigated in a mutually respectful dialogue that allowed her to shift her understandings into a new framework. Examples such as this illustrate the importance of Indigenous knowledges and frameworks such as SEWB being taught because misunderstandings can contribute to misdiagnosis from service providers and clinicians.

The second component of the degree is arguably the most important as it makes visible the underlying socio-political and historic context (Darlaston-Jones, 2005; Freire, 1998; Foucault, 1980; Nakata et al., 2008) and explores not only the dispossession of Indigenous peoples as a function of colonisation, but the resultant privileging of white Western norms and ideologies (Dudgeon, Milroy et al., 2014). This de-colonisation approach moves from an oppositional binary and brings students to a space where new understandings of positionality can emerge. This draws on Nakata et al.'s (2008) Cultural Interface Theory which argues that it is at the interface, the coming together of two groups/persons, that opportunities exist. Once the hidden 'truths' are made visible, and the false foundation that these 'truths' have been created upon is available to be contested, it is possible to move into a third space (Dudgeon & Fielder, 2006) based on mutual respect, understanding and a recognition of the shared history as well as the differential outcomes of that shared history. One of the guiding frameworks that help to support this criticality comes from Tanaka (2002) who offers the five probes of *Voice, Power, Authenticity, Reflexivity* and *Reconstitution* to contest and challenge thoughts, beliefs and actions. The framework can be applied to any issue in any context, including the development of a single lecture, the construction of a unit of study, or indeed the architecture of an entire degree programme or a discipline. To illustrate this argument, the following questions, when applied in relation to each element of the framework, require the deconstruction of the educator's position and by definition the position of the 'other' as well as the 'truth' claims that are constructed as a result of these subject positions, relative to the discipline of psychology:

- *Voice*: whose voice is privileged in psychology and, by extension, who is silenced? Are students and educators able to be seen as having 'subject positions' in the discipline?
- *Power*: do we question the Eurocentric monocultural nature of psychological knowledge? Do we examine the ways in which such an approach positions Indigenous peoples and by extension the non-Indigenous person/group? Do we scrutinise the ways in which pedagogical theory and teaching practices reinforce the dominant perspectives and truth claims and so contribute to cultural hegemony?
- *Authenticity*: do educators and students identify their own cultural space, including issues of social, economic and political power?
- *Reflexivity*: is there an explicit examination of the subject positions that individuals occupy in society and their role in constituting the norms that contribute to inclusion or exclusion?
- *Reconstitution*: is psychology able to effect change and create a learning environment conducive to the development of an inclusive society?

Incorporating Indigenous psychology within a conscientisation (Freire, 1998) model of education offers a different set of opportunities, not only for the discipline but for its players, educators, students and practitioners as well as the persons and groups they engage with (Darlaston-Jones, 2015a; Darlaston-Jones et al., 2014; Dudgeon et al., 2011).

Conclusion

It is appropriate to end this chapter where we began; with the challenge issued specifically to psychologists and psychology by Riley, requiring that we identify and contest our constructed understandings of Indigenous peoples, and by definition, our understandings of ourselves. He urged the profession, its educators and practitioners to be courageous enough to look into the history of colonial oppression and recognise our complicity in creating the categories of segregation and legitimisation which led to the formation of the binaries of inclusion and exclusion and the resultant harms associated with such categorisations. Specifically, Riley called for a critical understanding of the methods by which these discourses were transmitted and reinforced; namely, the educational sites that privilege one set of values and norms over others and in doing so create the binary relationships that cause much of the disadvantage the profession is supposedly trying to address. Such reflexivity requires strength and willingness to unlearn the entrenched 'truths' that shape the psyche of Australia and the interactions between its peoples. It is also important to draw on the historically significant and recent Gayaa Dhuwi (Proud Spirit) Declaration which calls on governments as well as mental health professions, educational institutions, educators and practitioners to rapidly address systematic inequality within the mental health system and more broadly in society. In doing so, we emphasise that for at least 20 years Aboriginal and Torres Strait Islander peoples have been calling for the same thing: recognition that the significant levels of disadvantage experienced by Indigenous peoples is the result of 250 years of colonial history and the associated trauma. It is a call for recognition that the application of culturally inappropriate interventions and models of care further undermines the self-determination of Indigenous persons and groups as well as contributing to the ongoing trauma associated with the effects of that colonial history. It is also a call for recognition of the power and privilege accrued to the coloniser by virtue of that colonial history.

It is now time for psychology and psychologists to respond to those calls and to accept the challenge to work in partnership with Indigenous communities and leaders to address the mental health crisis and associated social, economic and educational disadvantages experienced by Aboriginal and Torres Strait Islander peoples. Drawing on the evidence from both AIPEP and the Bachelor of Behavioural Science degree at the University of Notre Dame, Fremantle Campus, we have demonstrated how such a response to the education and training of psychology students and practitioners might be framed. Guided by critical theory and situated within a critical pedagogy framework, psychology education can shift the cultural lens to one which is capable of producing a workforce that includes Indigenous peoples and enables non-Indigenous persons to work in an ethically and culturally responsive manner that contributes to social justice.

Note

1   The authors acknowledge the role of all members of the AIPEP team (Professor Sabine Hammond, Associate Professor Jacky Cranney, Associate Professor Judi Homewood, Professor Jeanie Herbert and Dr Jillene Harris as well as Ms Katrina Newnham, the Project Manager, and Dr Greg Phillips, Project Consultant) in the production of the data and the subsequent report. For the full report, please see the AIPEP website: www.Indigenouspsyched.org.au

References

Anderson, K., & Perrin, C. (2007). 'The miserablest people in the world': Race, humanism and the Australian Aborigine. *The Australian Journal of Anthropology, 18*(1), 18–39.

Anderson, W. (2002). *The cultivation of whiteness: Science, health and racial destiny in Australia.* Melbourne, Vic.: Melbourne University Press.

APS. (2012). *Reconciliation action plan 2011–2014.* Retrieved from www.psychology.org.au/Assets/Files/RAP-Booklet_Final_WEB.pdf

Australian Bureau of Statistics. (2012–2013). *Australian Aboriginal and Torres Strait Islander health survey: Updated results 2012–2013.* ABS Cat. No. 4727.0.55.006. Retrieved from www.abs.gov.au/ausstats/abs@.nsf/mf/4727.0.55.006

Australian Bureau of Statistics. (2013a). Life tables for Aboriginal and Torres Strait Islander Australians 2010–2012. ABS Cat. No. 3302.0.5.003. Retrieved from www.abs.gov.au/ausstats/abs@.nsf/mf/3302.0.55.003

Australian Bureau of Statistics. (2013b). *Aboriginal and Torres Strait Islander health survey: First results, Australia 2012–2013.* Table 7 (data cube). Canberra, ACT: Australian Bureau of Statistics.

Australian Bureau of Statistics. (2014). *Causes of death, Australia 2012.* ABS Cat. No. 3303.0. Canberra, ACT: Australian Bureau of Statistics.

Australian Indigenous Health*InfoNet*. (2014). *Overview of the Australian Indigenous health status 2013.* Available at www.healthinfonet.ecu.edu.au/key-resources/bibliography/?lid=28061

Australian Institute of Health and Welfare. (2014). *Australian hospital statistics 2012–13.* Canberra, ACT: Australian Institute of Health and Welfare. Retrieved from www.aihw.gov.au/publication-detail/?id=60129546922

Bishop, B.J., Vicary, D.A., Mitchell, J.R., & Pearson, G. (2012). Aboriginal concepts of place and country and their meaning in mental health. *The Australian Community Psychologist, 24*(2), 26–42.

Breen, L., & Darlaston-Jones, D. (2010). Moving beyond the enduring dominance of positivism in psychological research: An Australian perspective. *Australian Psychologist, 45*(1), 67–76.

Close the Gap. (2015). *Progress and priorities report.* Retrieved on 20 January, 2016 from www.humanrights.gov.au/sites/default/files/document/publication/CTG_progress_and_priorities_report_2015.pdf

Cranney, J., & Dunn, D. (Eds.) (2011). *The psychologically literate citizen: Foundations and global perspectives.* New York: Oxford University Press.

Cunneen, C. (2005). Racism, discrimination and the over-representation of Indigenous people in the criminal justice system: Some conceptual and explanatory issues. *Current Issues Criminal Justice, 17,* 329–346.

Dalby, A. (1998). *Dictionary of languages.* London: Bloomsbury Publishing plc.

Darlaston-Jones, D. (2005). *Evidence from the survivors: Factors affecting retention of undergraduate psychology students at a Western Australian university and implications for cultural change within higher education* (Unpublished doctoral dissertation). Edith Cowan University, Perth, Australia.

Darlaston-Jones, D. (2015a). (De)constructing paradigms: Creating a psychology curriculum for conscientisation education. *The Australian Community Psychologist, 27*(1), 38–48.

Darlaston-Jones, D. (2015b, August). White voices Black spaces: Authenticity, legitimacy and place in a shared decolonisation project. Keynote address presented at the New Zealand Psychological Society Conference, Hamilton, New Zealand, 26–31 August, 2015.

Darlaston-Jones, D., Herbert, J., Ryan, K., Darlaston-Jones, W., Harris, J., & Dudgeon, P. (2014). Are we asking the right questions? Why we should have a decolonization discourse based on conscientisation rather than Indigenising the curriculum. *Canadian Journal of Native Education, 37*(1), 86–104.

Dudgeon, P., & Bray, A. (2014). Disabling the First People: Re-scientized racism and the Indigenous mental health movement. *The Journal of Critical Psychology, Counselling and Psychotherapy, 14*(4), 226–237.

Dudgeon, P., & Fielder, J. (2006). Third spaces within tertiary places: Indigenous Australian studies. *Journal of Community & Applied Social Psychology, 16*(5), 396–409.

Dudgeon, P., & Oxenham, D. (1989). The complexity of Aboriginal diversity: Identity and kindredness. *Black Voices, 5*(1), 22–39.

Dudgeon, P., & Walker, R. (2015). Decolonizing Australian psychology: Discourses, strategies and practices. *Journal of Social and Political Psychology, 3*(1), 179–197.

Dudgeon, P., Calma, T., Brideson, T., & Holland, C. (2016). The Gayaa Dhuwi (Proud Spirit) Declaration: A call to action for Aboriginal and Torres Strait Islander leadership in the Australian mental health system. *Advances in Mental Health, 14*(2), 1–14.

Dudgeon, P., Cox, K., D'Anna, D., Dunkley, C., Hams, K., Kelly, K. . . . Walker, R. (2012). *Hear our voices: Community consultations for the development of an empowerment, healing and leadership program for Aboriginal people living in the Kimberley, Western Australia: Final research report*. Perth, WA: Telethon Institute for Child Health Research: Aboriginal Health.

Dudgeon, P., Cranney, J., Darlaston-Jones, D., Herbert, J., Hammond, S., Harris, J., & Homewood, J. (2016, September). *The outcomes and future directions of AIPEP: Increasing cultural responsiveness and Indigenous representation in psychology*. Paper presented at the Australian Psychological Society Congress, 13–16 September, Melbourne, Vic., Australia.

Dudgeon, P., Darlaston-Jones, D., & Clark, Y. (2011). Changing the lens: Indigenous perspectives on psychological literacy. In J. Cranney & D. Dunn (Eds.), *The psychologically literate citizen: Foundations and global perspectives* (pp. 72–90). New York: Oxford University Press.

Dudgeon, P., Milroy, H., & Walker, R. (Eds.) (2014). *Working together: Aboriginal and Torres Strait Islander mental health and wellbeing principles and practice* (2nd ed.). Canberra, ACT: Commonwealth of Australia.

Dudgeon, P., Rickwood, D., Garvey, D., & Gridley, H. (2014). A history of Indigenous psychology. In P. Dudgeon, H. Milroy, & R. Walker (Eds.), *Working together: Aboriginal and Torres Strait Islander mental health and wellbeing principles and practice* (2nd ed., pp. 39–54). Canberra, ACT: Department of the Prime Minister and Cabinet.

Elliot-Farrely, T. (2004). Australian Aboriginal suicide: The need for an Aboriginal suicidology? *Australian e-Journal of Mental Health, 3*(3), 1–8.

Foucault, M. (1972). *The archaeology of knowledge*. New York: Pantheon.

Foucault, M. (1977). History of systems of thought. In D.F. Bouchard (Ed.), *Language, counter-memory, practice* (pp. 139–164). New York: Cornell University Press.

Foucault, M. (1980). Powers and strategies. In C. Gordon (Ed.), *Power/knowledge: Selected interviews and other writings by Michel Foucault* (pp. 134–145). New York: Pantheon Books.

Foucault, M. (1981). The order of discourse. In R. Young (Ed.), *Untying the text: A post-structural anthology* (pp. 48–78). Boston, MA: Routledge & Kegan Paul.

Foucault, M. (2004). *Abnormal: Lectures at the Collège de France, 1974–1975*. New York: Picador.

Foucault, M. (2008). *Psychiatric power: Lectures at the Collège de France, 1973–1974*. New York: Picador.

Freire, P. (1970). *Pedagogy of the oppressed*. New York: Continuum.

Freire, P. (1998). *Pedagogy of freedom: Ethics, democracy, and civic courage.* Lanham, MD: Rowman & Littlefield Publishers Inc.

Freire, P. (1999). Making history and unveiling oppression. *Dulwich Centre Journal, 3,* 37–39.

Gee, G., Dudgeon, P., Schultz, C., Hart, A., & Kelly, K. (2014). Aboriginal and Torres Strait Islander social and emotional wellbeing. In P. Dudgeon, H. Milroy, & R. Walker (Eds.), *Working together: Aboriginal and Torres Strait Islander mental health and wellbeing principles and practice* (2nd ed.; pp. 55–68). Canberra, ACT: Commonwealth of Australia.

Gergen, K.J. (1999). *An invitation to social construction.* London: Sage.

Gilbert, K. (1978). *Living black: Blacks talk to Kevin Gilbert.* Ringwood, Vic.: Penguin.

Giroux, H. (2011). *On critical pedagogy.* New York: Continuum International Publishing Group.

Harrison, J., Miller, E., Weeramanthri, T., Wakerman, J., & Barnes, T. (2001). *Information sources for injury prevention among Indigenous Australians: Status and prospects for improvement.* Canberra, ACT: Australian Institute of Health and Welfare.

Health Workforce Australia. (2014). *Australia's Health Workforce series: Psychologists in focus.* Adelaide, SA: Health Workforce Australia. Retrieved from http://iaha.com.au/wp-content/uploads/2014/03/HWA_Australia-Health-Workforce-Series_Psychologists-in-focus_vF_LR.pdf

Hook, D. (2005). A critical psychology of the postcolonial. *Theory and Psychology, 15*(4), 475–503.

Hook, D. (2007). *Foucault, psychology and the analytics of power.* Basingstoke, UK: Palgrave Macmillan.

hooks, b. (1996). Teaching to transgress: Education as the practice of freedom. *Journal of Leisure Research, 28*(4), 316.

hooks, b. (1998). *Teaching to transgress: Education as the practice of freedom.* New York: Routledge.

hooks, b. (2002). *Rock my soul: Black people and self-esteem.* New York: Beyond Words/Atria Books.

Jones, C.P. (2002). Confronting institutionalised racism. *Phylon, 50,* 7–22.

Jones, J. (1997). *Prejudice and racism.* New York: McGraw-Hill Higher Education.

Jones, J.M. (1972). *Prejudice and racism.* Reading, MA: Addison Wesley Publishers.

Kagan, C., Burton, M., Duckett, P., Lawthom, R., & Siddiquee, A. (2011). *Critical community psychology.* Chichester, UK: Wiley–Blackwell.

Kelly, K., Dudgeon, P., Gee, G., & Glaskin, B. (2010). *Living on the edge: Social and emotional wellbeing and risk and protective factors for serious psychological distress among Aboriginal and Torres Strait Islander people.* Discussion Paper No. 10, Cooperative Research Centre for Aboriginal Health, Darwin, NT, Australia.

Kübler-Ross, E. (2009). *On death and dying: What the dying have to teach doctors, nurses, clergy and their own families.* London: Routledge.

Marmot, M. (2011). Social determinants and the health of Indigenous Australians. *The Medical Journal of Australia, 194,* 512–513.

Martín-Baró, I. (1994). Toward a liberation psychology. In A. Aron & S. Corne (Eds.), *Writings for a liberation psychology* (pp.17–32). Cambridge, MA: Harvard University Press.

Nakata, M. (2007a). *Disciplining the savage: Savaging the discipline.* Canberra, ACT: Aboriginal Studies Press.

Nakata, M. (2007b). The cultural interface. *The Australian Journal of Indigenous Education, 36,* 7–14.

Nakata, M., Nakata, V., & Chin, M. (2008). Approaches to the academic preparation and support of Australian Indigenous students for tertiary studies. *The Australian Journal of Indigenous Education,* h37(S1), 137–145.

NATSILMH (National Aboriginal and Torres Strait Islander Leadership in Mental Health). (2015). *Gayaa Dhuwi (Proud Spirit) Declaration. A companion to the Wharerata Declaration for use by Aboriginal and Torres Strait Islander peoples*. Retrieved on 24 January, 2016 from http://natsilmh.org.au/sites/default/files/gayaa_dhuwi_declaration_A4.pdf

Opotow, S. (1990). Moral exclusion and injustice: An introduction. *Journal of Social Issues*, 46(1), 1–20.

Productivity Commission. (2014). *Overcoming Indigenous disadvantage: Key indicators 2014*. Melbourne, Vic.: Productivity Commission. Retrieved from www.pc.gov.au/research/ongoing/overcoming-indigenous-disadvantage/key-indicators-2014

Purdie, N., Dudgeon, P., & Walker, R. (2010). *Working together: Aboriginal and Torres Strait Islander mental health and wellbeing principles and practice*. Canberra, ACT: Department of the Prime Minister and Cabinet.

Ranzijn, R., McConnochie, K.R., & Nolan, W. (2009). *Psychology and indigenous Australians: Foundations of cultural competence*. Sydney, NSW: Palgrave Macmillan.

Reynolds, H. (2006). *The other side of the frontier: Aboriginal resistance to the European invasion of Australia*. Sydney, NSW: UNSW Press.

Reynolds, H. (2013). *The forgotten war*. Sydney, NSW: NewSouth Publishing.

Rickwood, D., Dudgeon, P., & Gridely, H. (2010). A history of psychology in Aboriginal and Torres Strait Islander mental health. In N. Purdie, P. Dudgeon, & R. Walker (Eds.), *Working together: Aboriginal and Torres Strait Islander mental health and wellbeing principles and practice* (pp. 13–24). Canberra, ACT: Department of the Prime Minister and Cabinet.

Riley, R. (1997). *From exclusion to negotiation: The role of psychology in Aboriginal social justice*. Discussion paper, Curtin Indigenous Research Centre, No. 1/1997. Perth, WA: Gunada Press, Curtin University.

Robinson, L. (2009). *Psychology for social workers: Black perspectives on human development and behaviour* (2nd ed.). London: Routledge.

Silburn, S., Glaskin, B., Henry, D., & Drew, N. (2010). Preventing suicide among indigenous Australians. In N. Purdie, P. Dudgeon, & R. Walker (Eds.), *Working together: Aboriginal and Torres Strait Islander mental health and wellbeing* (pp. 91–104). Canberra, ACT: Department of the Prime Minister and Cabinet.

Silburn, S., Robinson, G., Leckning, B., Henry, D., Cox, A., & Kickett, D. (2014). Preventing suicide among Aboriginal Australians. In P. Dudgeon, H. Milroy, & R. Walker (Eds.), *Working together: Aboriginal and Torres Strait Islander mental health and wellbeing principles and practice* (2nd ed.; pp. 147–164). Canberra, ACT: Commonwealth of Australia.

Smyth, J. (2011). *Critical pedagogy for social justice*. New York: Continuum International Publishing Group.

Sones, R., Hopkins, C., Manson, S., Watson, R., Durie, M., & Naquin, V. (2010). The Wharerata Declaration: The development of Indigenous leaders in mental health. *International Journal of Leadership in Public Services*, 6(1), 53–63.

Spencer, H. (1855). *The principles of psychology*. London: Longman, Brown, Green and Longmans.

Suchet, M. (2007). Unravelling whiteness. *Psychoanalytic Dialogues*, 17(6), 867–886.

Swan, P., & Raphael, B. (1995). *Ways forward: National Aboriginal and Torres Strait Islander mental health policy national consultancy report*. Canberra, ACT: Department of Health and Ageing.

Tanaka, G. (2002). Higher education's self-reflexive turn: Toward an intercultural theory of student development. *The Journal of Higher Education*, 73(2), 263–296.

Turtle, A., & Orr, M. (1989). *The psyching of Oz*. Melbourne, Vic.: APS Ltd.

United Nations. (2008). *Declaration on the rights of Indigenous peoples*. New York: UN.

Walker, R., Schultz, C., & Sonn, C. (2014). Cultural competence – Transforming policy, services, programs and practice. In P. Dudgeon, H. Milroy, & R. Walker (Eds.), *Working together: Aboriginal and Torres Strait Islander mental health and wellbeing principles and practice* (2nd ed.; pp. 195–220). Canberra, ACT: Department of the Prime Minister and Cabinet. Available at https://aboriginal.telethonkids.org.au/globalassets/media/documents/aboriginal-health/working-together-second-edition/wt-part-3-chapt-12-final.pdf

Walsh, M. (1991). Overview of Indigenous languages of Australia. In S. Romaine (Ed.), *Language in Australia*. Cambridge: Cambridge University Press.

Wanganeen, R. (2010). Dealing with loss, grief and trauma: Seven phases to healing. In N. Purdie, P. Dudgeon, & R. Walker (Eds.), *Working together: Aboriginal and Torres Strait Islander mental health and wellbeing principles and practice* (pp. 267–284). Canberra, ACT: Department of the Prime Minister and Cabinet.

Watkins, M., & Shulman, H. (2008). *Toward psychologies of liberation*. New York & London: Palgrave Macmillan.

Zubrick, S.R., Shepherd, C.C.J., Dudgeon, P., Gee, G., Paradies, Y., Scrine, C., & Walker, R. (2014). Social determinants of social and emotional wellbeing. In P. Dudgeon, H. Milroy, & R. Walker (Eds.), *Working together: Aboriginal and Torres Strait Islander mental health and wellbeing principles and practice* (2nd ed.; pp. 93–112). Canberra, ACT: Department of the Prime Minister and Cabinet.

8
TEACHING WITHDRAWAL OF ANTIPSYCHOTICS AND ANTIDEPRESSANTS TO PROFESSIONALS AND RECIPIENTS

Peter Lehmann

Summary

Problems at withdrawal from neuroleptics ("antipsychotics") and antidepressants are well known from animal research and experiments in normal subjects. The existence of dependence is denied by the pharmaceutical industry and mainstream medicine. People withdraw with or without problems. Older studies did not distinguish between withdrawal problems and so-called true relapse. Meanwhile there is some knowledge about reducing risks in withdrawal, especially on the side of ex-users and survivors of psychiatry. But there is still a mass of open questions for physicians and natural healers, carers, therapists, social workers, jurists, pharmacologists, relatives and experts by experience. Until today, teaching withdrawal consists of passing on knowledge and experiences, but also teaching the open questions and staying involved in the decision processes of future research.

Introduction

Teaching withdrawal of neuroleptics and antidepressants to professionals and recipients is not easy. It seems easy for professionals to persuade people in emotional distress to take these drugs. Sometimes they use simple power and administer them by the use of violence. Sometimes they praise their drugs as harmless or the only available helpers in painful emotional states, (mis)using the trust they have as physicians. Sometimes people in emotional distress suffer so much that they would do nearly anything, or they do not care about the risks of the chemical substances they swallow, just to get some relief. And sometimes individuals have the experience that they cannot exist in their current life-conditions without taking these psychiatric drugs. The discussion always goes in the direction of intake, not of stopping. One might get the impression that, on the part of psychiatric mainstream professionals, there is no need for knowledge about withdrawal problems. This is wrong.

It has been evident since the introduction of neuroleptics and antidepressants into the "market", that withdrawal from both drug groups can be a serious problem. And with the passage of time, that there are receptor changes, supersensitivity problems, rebound problems, tolerance issues, physical and psychic dependence. It has also been well known for decades, that the benefit of longer-term use of psychiatric drugs, the basis of the development of drug dependence, has to be questioned. Following his long-term study in 1972, for example, psychiatrist Manfred Bleuler from Switzerland saw no indication of an improved course or outcome in patients following long-term treatment with neuroleptics. In fact, the opposite seemed to be the case; he wrote:

> Not one single patient who—healed or improved—lived outside the clinic over the years or permanently, has ever taken long-term drugs. The assumption, that the majority of improved schizophrenics would stay improved on the long term only under the influence of neuroleptic drugs, is an error. First of all, it is an error to assume that relapses after remissions could be avoided by neuroleptic drugs. There are many cases of permanent remissions and there are many cases of relapses under the influence of neuroleptics.
>
> *(Bleuler, 1972, p. 366)*[1]

By the way, the difference between neuroleptics and antidepressants is hard to define exactly. No standard criteria exist for the assignment of a single psychiatric drug to a group of substances. The classification of a drug can depend on its pharmaceutical basic schedule, biochemical mechanism, produced effects or the administrator's subjective intention. For example, oxypertine was marketed in the United States as an antidepressant, in the UK as a neuroleptic; flupentixol in the UK as a neuroleptic and antidepressant.

Animal research and experiences in normal subjects

It is known from animal studies that the sudden withdrawal of neuroleptics can be life threatening. For 6 months, Helma Sommer and Jochen Quandt (1970), two neurologists in the former German Democratic Republic (GDR), tested the neuroleptic prototype chlorpromazine on rabbits. After those animals which had received the highest dosage died after a brief fit of cramping (probably due to irreversibly blocked metabolic processes), they wrote that similar observations in human beings have been published in which death followed a brief stage of cramping. In a self-experiment with a 10-day regimen of thioridazine and following 3 weeks of administering chlorprothixene to tuberculosis patients, who were given it because of its antimicrobial effect, the sudden withdrawal caused, in all test persons, more or less severe reactions of lack of concentration and nervousness about their depressed mood, diarrhoea and lack of sleep, even leading to manic states which lasted up to 2 weeks (Hollister, Eikenberry, & Raffel, 1960; Degkwitz, 1964).

Janssen-Cilag (Switzerland) warns of eventually life-threatening withdrawal problems in newborns, when their mothers received neuroleptics:

> In neonates, whose mothers took antipsychotics (including haloperidol) during the third trimester of pregnancy, after birth there is the risk of extra-pyramidal symptoms and/or withdrawal symptoms. These symptoms in newborns may include agitation, abnormally increased or decreased muscle tonus, tremor, sleepiness, difficulty breathing or feeding problems.
> These complications may have a different severity. In some cases, they were self-limiting, in other cases the newborns required monitoring in the intensive care unit or a longer hospitalisation.
> *(Janssen-Cilag AG, 2016, n.p.)*

Self-experiments with antidepressants showed similar experiences. For her dissertation, the German Gisela Rautmann took the antidepressant prototype imipramine for 3 weeks, and reported on her withdrawal symptoms which were already noticeable 3 days after she stopped taking the drug:

> The subject of the trial responded with dizziness and dry mucous membranes of the mouth. Hot and cold feelings alternated rapidly with physical efforts. . . . While driving her car, she soon felt ill. She suffered from sweating; the tip of the nose remained constantly cold.
> *(Rautmann, 1964, p. 29)*

Other people, who undertook "long-term" self-experiments (1–3 weeks), reported loss of concentration, weight and appetite, restlessness, jumpiness, a bitter taste in the mouth, sweating and hot flashes, nausea, enlarged pupils, enhanced intestine activity and especially sleeping problems. Rautmann's colleague Gerhard Seuwen (1964) took amitriptyline for 2 weeks, and after stopping the drug, in his dissertation he reports heavy pain in the heart area, sweating, headaches, sleeping disorders and a continuously enhancing state of fear and restlessness, which only declined after 10 days (pp. 27–28).

Denial of dependence

Over the decades, the existence of dependence has been denied by the pharmaceutical industry and mainstream medicine (although there are some exceptions to this), as it was denied for decades in relation to benzodiazepines. Representative of many of his colleagues, the German pharmacologist Gerd Glaeske (1989, p. 25) justified the replacement of tranquilisers by neuroleptics and antidepressants, "because no problem of dependence can be expected in these drugs". Discussing dependence on neuroleptics and antidepressants often leads to reflex-like responses by physicians, that these drugs do not produce addiction, that only benzodiazepines produce dependence, that neuroleptics and antidepressants might have been misused, that, as the Royal College of Psychiatrists in the United Kingdom stated: "there is potentially overprescribing of these medications, particularly SSRIs, where there is no particularly strong clinical indication" (quoted in BMA, 2015, p. 25).

If a discussion starts at all, as initiated by the British Medical Association (BMA) in 2014, then perhaps it is discussed whether antidepressants might produce dependence; the potential of neuroleptics to produce dependence keeps being factored out (BMA, 2015) or starts to be addressed with a shudder and a delay of 65 years (Lehmann, 2016). In their guide for drug-dependent people and their relatives, the physician Wolfgang Poser, the social economist Dietrich Roscher and the psychiatrist Sigrid Poser describe the typical definition of dependence:

> There is drug dependence when a continuous medication or even increasing drug doses are required to suppress the symptoms sufficiently and to control the condition, and/or drugs-holidays lead to enforced occurrence of the initial and additional complaints. Signs of chronic intoxication become noticeable.
>
> *(Poser, W., Roscher, & Poser, S., 1985, p. 34)*

Referring to Heribert Czerwenka-Wenkstetten and colleagues from the University Clinic of Vienna, the term addiction is used for compulsive use of a substance

> for the adjustment of an unbearable state of body and mind, if necessary by rolling back all other aims and by overriding each hindering circumstance. As a criterion of an addictive drug, we see primarily the occurrence of withdrawal symptoms at withdrawal as well as the patient's inability to withdraw using their own will power, secondarily the euphoric effect and the mostly existing need for dose escalation to maintain the effect.
>
> *(Czerwenka-Wenkstetten, Hofmann, & Kryspin-Exner, 1965, p. 1013)*

Dependency and tolerance building is a dark area, not least because psychiatrists strictly deny its existence in public. In their own magazines, they speak differently, as the example of Rudolf Degkwitz, a former President of the German Association for Psychiatry and Neurology, and his colleague Otto Luxenburger shows, which stated already more than half a century ago: "We now know that it is extremely difficult, if not impossible, for many of the chronic patients to stop neuroleptics because of the unbearable withdrawal-symptoms" (1965, p. 175).

If there is no diagnosis of dependence, then there is no possibility to get refunds from health insurance companies for physicians, and there is no possibility for patients who become dependent on neuroleptics and antidepressants to receive rehabilitation facilities, therapy and compensation for damaged people. Drug companies and medical practitioners who do not inform patients about the risk of these drugs seem protected against criminal prosecution. No diagnosis of dependence also means no awareness about the problem, no education about this danger, no information, no warning of the patients. They let them run into their undoing.

According to Margrethe Nielsen and Peter C. Gøtzsche from the Nordic Cochrane Centre in Denmark and their colleague Ebba Holme Hansen from the Faculty of Pharmaceutical Sciences at the University of Copenhagen (Nielsen, Hansen, & Gøtzsche, 2012), the main reason for denial of the potential of antidepressants and neuroleptics to produce physical dependence is the dependence of the psychiatric system and its opinion leaders on the pharmaceutical industry. Nielsen and colleagues (2012) clarified the connection between the criteria for dependence on psychiatric drugs and the pharmaceutical industry's interest in selling their drugs optimally with the activities of the opinion leaders to change the criteria for drug dependence in the *ICD-10 (International Statistical Classification of Diseases and Related Health Problems*, 10th revision) and the *DSM III-R (Diagnostic and Statistical Manual of Mental Disorders*, 3rd edition) after disclosure of the dependence produced by benzodiazepines which led to the decline in their number of sales. Hans-Jürgen Möller, former Director of the Psychiatric University Clinic in Munich and Chair of the Pharmacopsychiatric Section of the World Psychiatric Association (WPA), is a splendid example of the connection of the pharmaceutical industry with the denial of the potential of their products to produce physical dependence, in this case from neuroleptics. This opinion leader stated: "Neuroleptics have the big advantage over benzodiazepines that they do not produce dependence. In particular, the problem that leads to the questioning of the broad application of benzodiazepines that way does thus not occur"(Möller, 1986, p. 386).

Möller (2009, p. 514) received money for research, lectures and membership on their Advisory Boards from AstraZeneca, Bristol-Myers Squibb, Eisai, Eli Lilly, GlaxoSmithKline, Janssen-Cilag, Lundbeck, Merck, Novartis, Organon, Pfizer, Sanofi-Aventis, Sepracor, Servier and Wyeth.

Withdrawal symptoms with use of neuroleptics

In principle, all kinds of phenomena of irritation can occur in the withdrawal from neuroleptics, including states of fear and confusion, hallucinations, withdrawal psychoses, sleep disorders, breaking out in a sweat, and much more. In their advertisement for Risperdal, Janssen Pharmaceutica Inc./SmithKline Beecham mentioned a "withdrawal syndrome" (1996), but without further description.

Psychological withdrawal symptoms like tension, restlessness, destructiveness, aggression, irritability and excitability, as well as outbreaks of sweating, racing heartbeat, inner restlessness, vomiting and diarrhoea, can trigger massive anxiety and may also develop into withdrawal psychoses and delirious states. In 1963, Helmut Selbach of the Psychiatric University Hospital in Berlin described the state of shock caused by the sudden withdrawal: "After cold turkey withdrawal from a high dose of neuroleptics (which produced extrapyramidal symptoms), extreme euphoria accompanied by a rapid pulse ('choc en retour' [backfire]) can be caused solely by the withdrawal, in contrast to the previous affective indifference" (Selbach, 1963, p. 67).

Fritz Reimer, for many years Chairman of the German Committee of Directors of Psychiatric Clinics, concluded the following concerning the possibility of post-withdrawal delirium that may last several days: "The ultimate factor in the delirium syndrome is certain to be the psychoactive pharmaceuticals. On the surface, it appears to compare to the withdrawal delirium of the alcoholic" (1965, pp. 446–447).

His American colleague George Brooks at the Vermont State Hospital in Waterbury reported "severe withdrawal reactions indistinguishable clinically from a moderate withdrawal reaction following long-term ingestion of morphine" (1959, p. 931). Degkwitz compared the withdrawal symptoms of psycholeptics (neuroleptics and antidepressants) with those from alkaloids; morphine belongs to this substance group. Sleeping pills are considered to work addictively, and it is well known that their withdrawal can go along with life-threatening convulsions. The psychiatrist wrote: "As described above, the reduction or withdrawal from psycholeptics leads to considerable withdrawal symptoms that cannot be distinguished from those symptoms occurring with the withdrawal of alkaloids and sleeping pills" (1967, p. 161).

Roy Lacoursiere and his colleagues at the Veterans Administration Hospital in Topeka, Kansas, explained how to distinguish withdrawal symptoms such as insomnia and restlessness from the original psychiatric symptoms. They optimistically assumed that the withdrawal symptoms subside more quickly; these "(1) tend to occur earlier after drug withdrawal than schizophrenic exacerbation, (2) may be accompanied by other medical withdrawal symptoms, and (3) usually clear up spontaneously or with supportive treatment within a few days" (Lacoursiere, Spohn, & Thompson, 1976, p. 292).

There are many reports in the medical literature about central nervous system withdrawal symptoms, such as headaches, insomnia, nightmare, feelings of numbness, disturbed taste, even convulsions. The vegetative withdrawal symptoms affect organ systems and functions and include feeling hot or cold, neuroleptic malignant syndrome (a syndrome with fever, muscle stiffness, impaired consciousness), dizziness, fainting, bingeing, pronounced sweating, heavy nasal discharge, excessive mucous and saliva secretion, anorexia (or a lesser loss of appetite), ravenous appetite, diarrhoea, gastritis, stomach ache, colic, nausea, vomiting, sebaceous gland discharge, cardiovascular (i.e. heart and circulatory system) problems such as a racing heartbeat and physical collapse. The symptoms can last, in some cases, for months. Thomas Gualtieri and colleagues from the North Carolina Neuropsychiatry Clinics in Chapel Hill described the vegetative withdrawal symptoms as anorexia, nausea and vomiting—symptoms that occurred during the reduction of neuroleptics or within 2 weeks after their complete cessation for the first time and that could not be attributed to other causes; for example, viral diseases or food poisoning (Gualtieri, Quade, Hicks, Mayo, & Schroeder, 1984, p. 21).

Withdrawal from neuroleptics can also cause various muscle and motor disturbances, so-called withdrawal dyskinesias. Known motor symptoms are: the inability to move, increased or initial tremor, joint pain, inner agitation, hyperkinesia and dystonia such as tongue-throat syndrome. Parkinsonoid disturbances caused by neuroleptics occur sometimes more frequently; neuroleptics not only trigger Parkinsonoid disorders—symptoms of the brain disorder resulting from the use of the neuroleptics—but also suppress their expression. Mental problems, which appear as a reaction to the muscular disturbance, are often interpreted as a relapse.

The withdrawal symptoms can lead relatives and physicians to believe that patients are suffering relapses. Brooks was concerned that the severity of the withdrawal symptoms may mislead the clinician into thinking that he is observing a relapse of the patient's mental condition (1959, p. 932). The patients themselves may believe in the need for maintenance treatment with neuroleptics. Degkwitz commented on such secondary dependence: "Such patients do not increase the dose but believe that they can no longer exist without the 'crutch' of the psychotropic. This is clearly not an addiction, but a medication dependence resulting from the patient's own insecurity" (1967, p. 162).

Similarly, the Swedish physician Lars Martensson looked at the mental consequences for the people around the patients:

> Neuroleptic drugs induce specific changes in the brain that make a person more psychosis-prone. It is like having a psychosis-inducing agent built into the brain. The effect of neuroleptic drugs may subside more or less with time if the drug is discontinued. But by then it may be too late. Because of psychotic symptoms, which are after effects of the drug, the conclusion has already been reached: 'He needs the drugs.' The trap has become a fact.
> *(Martensson, 1998, p. 107)*

The confusion can have fatal consequences, since withdrawal symptoms may be warning signs of permanent damage. The sudden occurrence of psychotic symptoms when reducing dosage could be an indication of developing supersensitivity psychoses, which then become chronic following the further administration of neuroleptics.

Receptor changes, supersensitivity, tolerance

Neuroleptic effects consist mainly in the disruption of the nerve impulse transfer with dopamine. The subsequent withdrawal problems are due to the changes in the nerve conduction system, a natural reaction to the disturbed nerve impulse transmission, and can trigger rebound, supersensitivity and withdrawal psychoses. Animal experiments have demonstrated that continuous administration of neuroleptics can lead to supersensitisation of the dopamine receptors, dopamine turnover and tardive dyskinesia. In other words, the animals have mobility impairments during the course of administration of neuroleptics, on their withdrawal or afterwards. The pharmacologist Guy Chouinard and his colleague Barry Jones at the University Clinic in Montreal did a lot of research and concluded:

> The authors suggest that dopaminergic supersensitivity also occurs in the mesolimbic region after chronic neuroleptic exposure, resulting in the development of a supersensitivity psychosis. . . . An implication of neuroleptic-induced mesolimbic supersensitivity is that the tendency toward psychotic

relapse in such patients is determined by more than just the normal course of the illness.

(Chouinard & Jones, 1980, p. 16)

Kenneth Davis and Gordon Rosenberg of the Veterans Administration Hospital in Palo Alto, California, tested fluphenazine and summarised the results of their study in *Biological Psychiatry*:

> Long-term administration of antipsychotic drugs to animals induces supersensitive mesolimbic [referring to nerve tracts from the midbrain to the cortex] postsynaptic dopamine receptors. It is possible that a similar process can occur in man. Following a reduction in the dose of antipsychotic medications, or their complete discontinuation, mesolimbic dopamine receptor supersensitivity could be reflected in rapid relapse of schizophrenic patients, the development of schizophrenic symptoms in patients with no prior history of schizophrenia, or in the necessity for ever-increasing doses of long-acting depot fluphenazine to maintain a remission.
>
> *(Davis & Rosenberg, 1979, p. 699)*

It has been known since the 1950s that neuroleptics can lead to tolerance of the so-called antipsychotic effects because of experience with chlorpromazine. In 1958, Stefan Hift and Hans Hoff of the University Hospital of Vienna explained: "A further key factor is the speed at which tolerance to the substance develops, which then becomes less and less efficacious, as is the case with chlorpromazine" (Hift & Hoff, 1958, p. 1046).

Development of tolerance cannot be avoided (Meyer, 1953, p. 1098). The dose has to be constantly increased to achieve a continuous effect; this is an indication of the dependence potential of psychiatric drugs. Tolerance occurs mostly with low-potency neuroleptics and also at relatively low doses (Haase, 1982, p. 214), including in non-psychiatric uses (Broglie & Jörgensen, 1954). As a reaction to the neuroleptic blockade, within a few weeks or months, the dopamine receptors form additional receptors, a response known as up-regulation.

As a result of the increased receptivity to psychotic reactions, supersensitivity psychoses, also known as breakthrough psychosis, can occur, and finally lead to tardive psychoses. Frank Tornatore and his colleagues at the University of Southern California's School of Pharmacy in Los Angeles warned of the development of supersensitivity psychoses:

> There is a worsening of the psychosis (delusions, hallucinations, suspiciousness) induced by long-term use of neuroleptic drugs. Typically, those who develop supersensitivity psychosis respond well initially to low or moderate doses of antipsychotics, but with time seem to require larger doses after each relapse and ultimately megadoses to control symptoms.
>
> *(Tornatore, Sramek, Okeya, & Pi, 1987, p. 44)*

Four years later, the same authors wrote: "Thus, a tolerance to the antipsychotic effect seems to develop" (Tornatore, Sramek, Okeya, & Pi, 1991, p. 53).

The frequent damage caused by typical neuroleptics like haloperidol arises from changes in dopamine-D_2-metabolism, observable as motor disturbances; the usual damage caused by "atypical" neuroleptics like clozapine, sertindole or quetiapine goes in the direction of changing the metabolism of special subtypes of dopamine receptors, dopamine-D_1 and -D_4, seen as producing or increasing mid- and long-term psychotic syndromes of organic origin.

In 1977, Urban Ungerstedt and Tomas Ljungberg at the Karolinska Institute in Stockholm published results of studies in which rats were administered the conventional neuroleptic haloperidol and as a comparison the "atypical" clozapine. They believe that "atypical" neuroleptics modify subtypes of specific dopamine receptors, produce their supersensitivity and contribute to the risk of new, increasing, or chronically powerful psychoses of organic origin, which can be understood as a "counterpart to tardive dyskinesia" (p. 199). Since then, medical journals have steadily published findings on supersensitivity, rebound and withdrawal psychoses. In particular, clozapine, the prototype of "atypical" neuroleptics, can cause irreversible psychoses (Chouinard & Jones, 1980, 1982; Ekblom, Eriksson, & Lindstroem, 1984; Borison, Diamond, Sinha, Gupta, & Ajiboye, 1988).

Withdrawal symptoms with use of antidepressants

When stopping antidepressants, massive withdrawal symptoms can be expected; they are rather similar to neuroleptics. The longer an antidepressant has been taken and the shorter its half-life is, the more likely that withdrawal symptoms can be expected; for example, gastrointestinal symptoms with or without anxiety, sleep disturbance, Parkinson-like disorders, convulsions, paradoxical activation, aggression or worsening of the underlying depression. Dilsaver and Greden clarified that anxiety, agitation or impending panic are common withdrawal symptoms with antidepressants (1984a, p. 240).

The *British National Formulary* listed more withdrawal symptoms:

> Gastro-intestinal symptoms of nausea, vomiting, and anorexia, accompanied by headache, giddiness, 'chills', and insomnia, and sometimes by hypomania [elevated mood below mania], panic-anxiety, and extreme motor restlessness may occur if an antidepressant (particularly an MAOI) is stopped suddenly after regular administration for 8 weeks or more.
>
> (BNF, 2008, p. 205)

In 2012, the register added movement disorders, muscle pain and manias, and noted:

> Withdrawal effects may occur within 5 days of stopping treatment with antidepressant drugs; they are usually mild and self-limiting, but in some

cases may be severe. Drugs with a shorter half-life, such as paroxetine and venlafaxine, are associated with a higher risk of withdrawal symptoms.

(BNF, 2012, p. 243)

In the case of newer antidepressants such as the serotonin-reuptake-inhibitors (SSRIs)—for example, paroxetine—and the serotonin-noradrenalin reuptake-inhibitors (SNRIs)—for example, venlafaxine—a special withdrawal syndrome has to be expected:

> Gastro-intestinal disturbances, headache, anxiety, dizziness, paraesthesia [sensation of tingling, burning, pricking, or numbness of a person's skin], electric shock sensations in the head, neck, and spine, tinnitus, sleep disturbances, fatigue, influenza-like symptoms, and sweating are the most common features of abrupt withdrawal of an SSRI or marked reduction of the dose; palpitation and visual disturbances can occur less commonly.

(BNF, 2012, p. 250)

In 2014, dependence is foreshadowed for the first time in the *DSM-5* (*Diagnostic and Statistical Manual of Mental Disorders*, 5th edition). According to the American Psychiatric Association, the "antidepressant discontinuation syndrome" has no other solution than permanent intake of antidepressants: "Symptoms are alleviated by restarting the same medication or starting a different medication that has a similar mechanism of action—for example, discontinuation symptoms after withdrawal from a serotonin-norepinephrine reuptake inhibitor may be alleviated by starting a tricyclic antidepressant" (Black & Grant, 2014, p. 412).

Receptor changes, supersensitivity, tolerance with antidepressants

Rebound phenomena and receptor changes are assumed as reasons for withdrawal symptoms in antidepressants. Eventually a sub- or supersensitivity of the postsynaptic receptors might have developed in the course of the drug administration. After the withdrawal, the altered sensitivity can trigger a relatively abrupt change of the neurotransmitters' effect—into the opposite direction (Mirin, Schatzberg, & Creasey, 1981; Dilsaver & Greden, 1984b, 1986). Dennis Charney and colleagues from the Psychiatric University Clinic, New Haven, Connecticut, discussed different models of receptor changes resulting from continued administration of antidepressants, which could cause the withdrawal symptoms (Charney, Heninger, Sternberg, & Landis, 1982). They also addressed rebound phenomena, which were proved in the nervous system of animals— for example, in rats and bear macaques after the administration of antidepressants (Svensson & Usdin, 1979; Sugrue, 1980)—and made responsible for fear reactions (Redmond & Huang, 1979). With remarkable similarity, such symptoms are found also in opiate withdrawal in humans.

In the early 1970s, physicians expressed the suspicion that antidepressants led to chronic depression (Irle, 1974, pp. 124–125). Now Paul Andrews (2011) and his team at the Department of Psychology, Neuroscience & Behaviour at McMaster University in Hamilton, Ontario (Canada), are finding that synthetic antidepressants interfere with the brain's natural self-regulation of serotonin and other neurotransmitters and that the brain can overcorrect once the medication is suspended. Thus, depression would be triggered. Andrews explains:

> We found that the more these drugs affect serotonin and other neurotransmitters in your brain—and that's what they're supposed to do—the greater your risk of relapse once you stop taking them. . . . All these drugs do reduce symptoms, probably to some degree, in the short-term. The trick is what happens in the long term. Our results suggest that when you try to go off the drugs, depression will bounce back. This can leave people stuck in a cycle where they need to keep taking anti-depressants to prevent a return of symptoms.
> *(Andrews, quoted in McMaster, 2011, para. 9)*

Andrews and colleagues conclude that it is important to inform patients about the risk of dependence before the administration of ADMs (antidepressant medications):

> Drugs that promote the risk of relapse or withdrawal upon discontinuation can cause dependence on the drug to prevent the return of symptoms. Consequently, such drugs must be managed carefully and patients must provide informed consent for their use. ADMs are sometimes prescribed to people with alcohol or illicit drug dependencies, because the use of such substances to medicate feelings of anxiety and depression is thought to play a role in the dependency. Ironically, the use of ADMs to help people wean off such substances might merely replace one dependency with another.
> *(Andrews, Kornstein, Halberstadt, Gardner, & Neale, 2011, p. 15)*

The reason for this dependence lies in the down-regulation of the serotonin and noradrenalin receptors as a reaction to the artificial levels of transmitters in the synapses caused by the antidepressants; the receptors become insensitive and degenerate. In 2012, Andrews and colleagues explained once more:

> It is a principle of evolutionary medicine that the disruption of evolved adaptions will degrade biological functioning. Because serotonin regulates many adaptive processes, antidepressants could have many adverse health effects. For instance, while antidepressants are modestly effective in reducing depressive symptoms, they increase the brain's susceptibility to future episodes after they have been discontinued. Contrary to a widely held belief in psychiatry, studies that purport to show that antidepressants promote neurogenesis are flawed because they all use a method that cannot, by itself, distinguish between neurogenesis and neuronal death. In fact, antidepressants

cause neuronal damage and mature neurons to revert to an immature state, both of which may explain why antidepressants also cause neurons to undergo apoptosis (programmed death).
(Andrews, Thomson, Amstadter, & Neale, 2012, n.p.)

Referring to the SSRIs, the Swiss physician and psychotherapist Marc Rufer warned: "In the long-term, the effect of serotonin is weakened. If the serotonin deficiency hypothesis of depression were correct, then the SSRI should cause very severe depression" (1995, p. 144).

Even with antidepressants, a development of tolerance that indicates a process of dependence is reported (Moldawsky, 1985; Tornatore et al., 1991, p. 108). With the example of Tofranil (imipramine), Selbach recommended in 1960 to solve the problem of tolerance building—without further ado, the administration of electroshocks:

> The effectiveness of Tofranil may decrease with [an] increasing number of depressive episodes. It is known that in the life-course, the amplitude will decrease, but the ill system often freezes for therapy resistance, and the ability for spontaneous or therapeutically provoked counter-regulation is lost or is greatly reduced. Here often only one or a few electroshocks can bring a relief of the counter-regulatory insufficiency, often with a strikingly fast homeostasis. Well, within seconds the seizure causes the same with extreme amplitude that Tofranil brings unspecifically with stretched and flat amplitude over a much longer time, but milder and more gently.
> *(Selbach, 1960, p. 267)*

Internally, psychiatrists address extensively the problem that withdrawal symptoms of antidepressants correspond with the withdrawal symptoms of street drugs. Although antidepressants do not have euphoric or subjectively pleasant and calming effects, withdrawal symptoms, tolerance building and psychological dependence would justify the term "dependence", as it is used with other addictive substances. Some psychiatrists were convinced of the necessity to expand the term "dependence" to a new type to make clear the problem of dependence on neuroleptics and antidepressants. As early as 1960, the antidepressants' pioneer Roland Kuhn wrote that withdrawal symptoms

> can look really turbulent, under certain circumstances bringing on severe headaches, profuse sweating, tachycardia attacks [racing heart beat], sometimes going along with vomiting, and disappear within a half hour of resuming the medication. This is a phenomenon that looks at least very similar to the 'withdrawal symptoms' of toxicomania [drug dependence].
> *(Kuhn, 1960, p. 248)*

Six years later, psychiatrist Chaim Shatan (1966) asked, using an example of the discussion of a case-report with imipramine in the *Canadian Psychiatric Association*

Journal, if the drug dependence definition of the World Health Organization used since 1950 should also be used for antidepressants, since there is development of tolerance, psychic and bodily dependence, as well as characteristic withdrawal symptoms. According to Shatan, it is remarkable that the withdrawal reactions in course and symptomatology are nearly indistinguishable from those following average opiate dependence.

Raymond Battegay from the University Hospital in Basel, Switzerland, explained (1966) that the term dependence needs to be expanded in order to clearly describe the problem of dependence on antidepressants and neuroleptics. Battegay referred to an article by John Kramer and colleagues (1961) of the Psychiatric Hospital in Glen Oaks, New York City, on the subject of antidepressants and tranquilisers. In a comparison of withdrawal symptoms with those of tranquilisers such as meprobamate or chlordiazepoxide, conducted at the hospital,

> the main difference lay in the fact that following withdrawal of the neuroleptic substances no craving was triggered . . . Furthermore the two groups differed from each other whereby in the case of the neuroleptics, in contrast to meprobamate, there was no muscle twitching in the withdrawal phase and no epileptic fits. . . . In those patients we examined who had been treated over months, or in most cases years, neuroleptics caused physical dependence as the occasional occurrence of abstinence symptoms demonstrated, but not psychological dependency. Withdrawal symptoms or rather physical dependency appeared especially with combined administrations of neuroleptics and anti-Parkinson drugs. . . . Going by the experience of Kramer et al., who observed similar symptoms during the withdrawal of imipramine which had been administered at high doses for over two months, the same criteria would apply also to antidepressant substances, so that one can speak of a neuroleptic/antidepressant type drug dependency.
> (Battegay, 1966, p. 555)

Frequency of withdrawal symptoms in use of neuroleptics and antidepressants

The medical and psychiatric literature includes widely varying information relating to the frequency of withdrawal symptoms associated with neuroleptics. According to diverse studies, up to 84% of the people withdrawing have vegetative, especially gastrointestinal, problems; 22% have withdrawal dyskinesias; and 60% have muscle pain (see Lehmann, 2017, pp. 421–455). Chouinard and Jones reported that they had found signs of supersensitivity psychoses among 30% of the 300 patients they studied, many of whom had not necessarily gone through an abrupt withdrawal (1982).

Withdrawal symptoms are to be expected for all neuroleptics. Low-potency neuroleptics tend to cause stronger vegetative effects, so withdrawal symptoms are expected here first. Since all neuroleptics can potentially cause receptor changes, there is always the possibility, if not the certainty, that withdrawal symptoms can occur. In their withdrawal study, Lacoursiere et al. (1976) could not identify a link between the drug dose and the severity of the withdrawal symptoms. Brooks had come to the same conclusion in his study in 1959: "There seemed to be no correlation of the intensity of the reaction with the level of dosage" (p. 932).

Dilsaver and Greden delivered an overview of the available literature on withdrawal symptoms with antidepressants. They came to the conclusion that withdrawal symptoms occur surprisingly often; namely, for 21% to 55% of adults. Some authors even claimed a frequency of 80%; the frequency found was connected with the diligence with which the investigation was conducted (Dilsaver & Greden, 1984a).

The current situation

Ever since the emergence of psychiatric drugs, many people who have taken prescriptions have made their own decision to quit. Many were able to quit the drugs successfully and were never seen again by physicians. As long ago as 1967, Degkwitz informed us: "Unquestionably, some patients tolerate the abrupt discontinuation of psycholeptics [neuroleptics and antidepressants] readily, while others experience considerable discomfort" (1967, p. 162).

What remains is a percentage of people who attract attention or ask for new psychotropic drugs and become patients again. I think it is safe to say that a great number of attempts to quit would have been more successful if those wishing to quit and those around them had been better informed as to the potential problems that might arise as well as means for preventing the often-prophesied relapse. How often are these withdrawal problems misdiagnosed as relapse into psychoses? Brigitte Woggon of the Zurich University Psychiatric Hospital, a strong proponent of psychiatric drugs, saw problems with the lack of differentiation made between withdrawal symptoms and the return of the original psychological symptoms: "Interestingly, in most studies on withdrawal, no position is taken on possible withdrawal symptoms apparently because the studies are not set up to deal with these findings" (1979, p. 46).

What was meant by "relapse" usually was not defined, or "relapse" was seen as a "return to active medication" or a "deterioration in performance". In addition, often there was no double-blind experimental design; that means, in open trials, the expectations of the physicians coined the results decisively.

Withdrawal with and without physicians

Mostly, physicians are not very helpful for patients who decide to withdraw. Single exceptions cannot hide this fact. Many consumers of psychiatric drugs are convinced that they need their physician's absolute agreement to withdraw. But people who stop taking psychiatric drugs against their physician's advice are just as likely to succeed as those who come off with physician agreement. This was the finding of the research project Coping with Coming Off, commissioned by the national organisation Mind in England and Wales. Funded by the UK Department of Health, a team of users-) and survivors of psychiatry carried out 250 interviews to investigate experiences with coming off psychiatric drugs. The forms of support found most helpful were: support from a counsellor, a support group or a complementary therapist; peer support; information from the internet or from books; and activities such as relaxation, meditation and exercise. Physicians were found to be the least helpful group to those who wanted to reduce or come off psychiatric drugs (Read, 2005; Wallcraft, 2007). Following this study, Mind changed its standard advice to patients—but only for a short period. Historically, their advice was not to come off psychiatric drugs without consulting a physician first. After the publication of the *Coping with Coming Off* study, people were reminded of the indoctrination of physicians by Big Pharma (Darton, 2005, p. 5) and advised to seek information and support from a wide variety of sources (Read, 2005).

Withdrawal on your own and eventually with competent support

Finally—now—it is time to begin with the overdue building of a network to support consumers of psychiatric drugs who claim their right to terminate the additional intake of these substances with words and deeds. On the basis of certain knowledge and with knowledge of existing uncertainties, all people involved in withdrawal processes should be enabled to deliver competent support.

Some stakeholders in the psychosocial field have, more or less isolated from each other, started as pioneers to offer aids in coming off psychiatric drugs. The time has come to gather knowledge as to how people came off these substances without ending up once again in the doctor's office and make it available for all. Mistakes and gaps in knowledge have to be identified. An overview on withdrawal symptoms from psychotropic drugs has to be built. Research on withdrawal problems and damage caused by dependence on psychotropic prescription drugs should be defined and suggested to foundations and universities as well as organisations of users and survivors of psychiatry for user-controlled research. Patients' experiences should be integrated into relevant programmes. Pilot projects showing how local organisations can accompany withdrawal and be financed and continued should be stimulated, and regular first-aid telephone hotlines should start without delay.

There is much knowledge already about reducing risks in withdrawal, especially on the side of ex-users and survivors of psychiatry. There are some publications by critical (ex-)users and survivors of psychiatry and their supporters with some tips for risk reduction at withdrawal (NAPA, 1984; Caras, 1991; Lehmann, 1998 [2004a]; Breggin & Cohen, 2000; AGIDD-SMQ & RRASMQ with ÉRASME, 2003; Breggin, 2012; Icarus Project & Freedom Center, 2012; DGSP, 2014).

Without question, there is a lot of good will on the side of ex-users and survivors of psychiatry and their supporters, but sometimes they offer problematic tips, too. For example, the German Federal Association of Users and Survivors of Psychiatry gives the information that if withdrawal problems arise, people can take a high dosage of neuroleptics spontaneously to "bring you down", but without warning about the enormous burden on the body through an extreme blood-level change and the risk of a delirium of organic nature (Krücke, 2014, p. 11). It is well known that rapid changes in dosage are a risk factor for deliria, and that such syndromes can end in a deadly fashion. Another example: a service provider in Berlin summarised the publication of a German psychiatrist about the high mortality of psychiatric patients, unwanted effects of neuroleptics, alternatives, risk-lowering ways of withdrawal, and the task of giving as low a dosage as possible for people who cannot do without neuroleptics, with the headline: "Neuroleptics can and must be administered in minimal dose" (Pinel, n.d.). Coming off, then, is no issue any more; the further intake of neuroleptics seems inevitable. To give drugs in doses higher than are required is a standard in mainstream medicine, psychiatry included. Some psychiatrists use the unwanted effects from antidepressants, dependence included, to praise electroshock as less dangerous—despite its effect of destroying brain nerves irreversibly. Enhancing the statistics for electroshock administration is one of the results of their way of dealing with drug dependence.

A mass of open questions

For medical practitioners and natural healers, carers, therapists, social workers, jurists, pharmacologists, relatives and experts by experience, a mass of open questions remains. It is especially the task of those listed last to raise the open, unpleasant and huge questions and to ensure that they do not lose the power to define the unresolved issues. All the knowledge and the answers to the open questions should lead to a curriculum and be used for education in the psychosocial field and in the self-help sector, and be offered to patients who decide for themselves to quit their psychotropic drugs and the relatives and friends who want to support them.

The emphasis, especially, should be on these topics:

- Psychiatric-medical aspects: which doctrines of the need for continuous administration of psychotropic drugs make it difficult for physicians, and in particular psychiatrists, to provide assistance in self-determined withdrawal from psychiatric drugs? How can physicians ensure support in coming off, as long as no appropriate diagnoses—except for the diagnosis of dependence on benzodiazepines—and therefore no billing codes exist? Which residential possibilities of support do exist? What risk factors require a residential support at withdrawal? Is there a sporadic, needs-adapted support at withdrawal?
- Which unwanted psychotropic effects require an immediate withdrawal? Which physiological and psychological withdrawal symptoms can be expected? How can you cope with them? Which withdrawal symptoms may occur, especially during the transition from mini doses to zero? In an insurmountable situation, is a so-called very low dosage useful, and if so, what residual risks does it include? Who makes and controls the decision on the need for a minimum dosage? As in alcohol dependence, can a premature offer of a minimum dosage jeopardise the decision to withdraw? Which check-ups are also useful with a

minimum dosage; which symptoms point to the development of long-term damage?
- How can one find competent and user-orientated physicians?
- Homeopathic aspects and aspects in natural healers' practice: which methods are used to relieve withdrawal symptoms, to stabilise users, particularly in the vulnerable period immediately after withdrawal? What are the options for detoxifying and use of "emergency pharmacies" in homeopathic or naturopathic practice?
- Aspects in social work, nursing, psychotherapy, service providers: how can psychotherapists, social pedagogues, social workers and psychiatric nurses be trained to give competent help? Are there psychotherapeutic methods especially suitable for monitoring withdrawal? What psychoeducational processes hamper aid at withdrawal? How can one find competent and user-orientated psychologists?
- Which opportunities and problems are faced by providers of community-based services, wards in hospitals and psychiatric clinics when offering support in coming off psychiatric drugs on a secure institutional and financial basis?
- Pharmacological and pharmaceutical aspects: how to withdraw combinations of drugs? What role do various forms of administration play in the gradual reduction? How can dosages be reduced beyond pre-determined product units? When can you use pill cutters? What if capsules contain pellets (balls, beads)? How can pellets be protected from breaking down in the stomach, if they require an intestinal absorption? How can doses be reduced by time stretching, and which psychotropics do not deliver this possibility? What is the ratio of half-lives for speed of withdrawal? Where do patients find practical advice if their physicians do not respect their wish to withdraw and deny any technical assistance in dose reduction? What do you do when, in the neuroleptic withdrawal process, the sensitivity returns faster than the suicidal tendencies disappear?
- Legal aspects: what risks do physicians have to face who—in spite of the occurrence of early warning symptoms which point to the development of long-term damage—do not initiate any step to reduce or withdraw? Can physicians who do not inform patients about the risk of dependency and withdrawal symptoms at the beginning of the administration, during its course and at the transition to long-term administration be prosecuted? What if they deny aid and do not want to treat patients if they demand assistance in gradual withdrawal? Which professional and civil rights risks do service providers, nurses and other psychiatric professionals have to face who assist patients in their withdrawal process, but without medical instruction or against it? What possibilities do the UN Convention on the Rights of Persons with Disabilities (United Nations, 2006), other human rights declarations, and laws deliver to enforce people's demands to withdraw from psychiatric drugs against the decision of their legal guardians?
- Self-help and family aspects: where can patients, their relatives and friends inform themselves in a balanced way about possibilities and problems at

withdrawal? What can they do if physicians do not support self-determined withdrawal, or if there is a lack of sufficient knowledge about the possibilities and problems at withdrawal on the part of the physician? How can they plan the withdrawal process, and which issues should they keep in mind? Where do patients who are alone find support? Which substances lower withdrawal symptoms? How useful and promising are advance directives to guarantee self-determination at least partially in case of withdrawal symptoms and relapses? Which environment, lifestyle, diet and physical activity support a successful withdrawal? How do patients cope with sleeping problems caused by the withdrawal? Which support options, but also which risks, can be expected in the self-help sector?

Drug companies make money by selling drugs; stock prices depend on new drugs in the pipeline. Profit maximisation does not always correspond with maximum ethical standards (Gøtzsche, 2013, 2016). To warn of dependence would lower profits, in the same way as warning about withdrawal problems or providing information on how to lower withdrawal risks would do. Then withdrawal outcomes would be more positive, people would be more likely to recover. Their bodies would be missed as a business market. As long as there is no general demand for the renunciation of toxic synthetic substances in nature, the living area, nutrition and medicine; as long as there is the illusion that psychiatry as a scientific discipline can do justice to the expectation of solving mental problems that are largely of a social nature; as long as there is no warning on blurbs about the risk of dependence from neuroleptics and antidepressants; as long as there is no duty for Big Pharma to pay for compensation and rehabilitation (comparable to the tobacco industry); as long as Big Pharma finances professionals, "self-help" groups like GAMIAN (Global Alliance of Mental Illness Advocacy Networks) and organisations of relatives to get them on board for PR strategies; and as long as there is no involvement of independent organisations of users and survivors of psychiatry in psychiatric drug registration, evaluation and monitoring, drug companies can go on undisturbed to merchandise their drugs and conceal the fact of physical dependence arising from neuroleptics and antidepressants.

Meaningful involvement in drug issues would require involvement in licensing processes in order to participate in decision-making about the granting and withdrawal of licences (Lehmann, 2004b). This involvement might be directly or via trusted experts and end with recommendations to governmental committees on the safety of medicines. Compared to other medical patients, a specific involvement of organisations of users and survivors of psychiatry would be required. This is due to the current discrimination and the lack of legislative changes to enable them to fight successfully for compensation in court for the damages sustained.

Teaching withdrawal: a task for decades

Until today, teaching withdrawal has been based on passing on knowledge and experiences, but also teaching the open questions and the need for participation of independent users and survivors of psychiatry in deciding the direction of future politics and research—a task for decades. Teaching withdrawal, too, is teaching alternatives beyond psychiatry and the need for co-operation of all organisations and people of good will, with the meaningful involvement of users and survivors of psychiatry at all levels. (It is questionable whether organisations and persons taking money from Big Pharma, even if they maintain that they deal critically with dependence arising from neuroleptics and antidepressants, can be assigned to the organisations and people of good will, especially when they do not uncover their financial enmeshment with the pharmaceutical industry.)

In the light of these many problems, the belief of stakeholders that withdrawal problems can be solved all alone, without the co-operation of competent experts and groups, does not seem a promising approach. Reflecting the lack of clear borders between black and white and the altering in convictions and beliefs in opinion leaders on all sides, who could arrogate to deliver a patent recipe on how to solve the problem of dependence from neuroleptics and antidepressants?

Note on quotations

1   Translations of quotations into English and explanations in text within square brackets within quotations are all by Peter Lehmann.

References

AGIDD-SMQ (Association des groupes d'intervention en defénse des droits en santé mentale du Québec) & RRASMQ (Regroupement des ressources alternatives en santé mentale du Québec), in collaboration with ÉRASME (Equipe de recherche et d'action en santé mentale et culture). (2003). *My self-management guide to psychiatric medication*. Montreal, QC: Self-publication.

Andrews, P.W., Kornstein, S.G., Halberstadt, L.J., Gardner, C.O., & Neale, M.C. (2011). Blue again: Perturbational effects of antidepressants suggest monoaminergic homeostasis in major depression. *Frontiers in Psychology, 2* (July), article 159. doi: 10.3389/fpsyg.2011.00159

Andrews, P.W., Thomson, J.A., Amstadter, A., & Neale, M.C. (2012). Primum non nocere: An evolutionary analysis of whether antidepressants do more harm than good. *Frontiers in Evolutionary Psychology, 3*, article 117. doi: 10.3389/fpsyg.2012.00117

Battegay, R. (1966). Entziehungserscheinungen nach abruptem Absetzen von Neuroleptica als Kriterien zu ihrer Differenzierung. *Nervenarzt, 37*, 552–556.

Black, D.W., & Grant, E. (2014). *DSM-5™ guidebook: The essential companion to the diagnostic and statistical manual of mental disorders* (5th ed.). Washington, DC & London: American Psychiatric Association.

Bleuler, M. (1972). *Die schizophrenen Geistesstörungen im Lichte langjähriger Kranken- und Familiengeschichten*. Stuttgart: Thieme.

BMA (British Medical Association). (2015, October). *Prescribed drugs associated with dependence and withdrawal—building a consensus for action. Analysis report.* Retrieved 14 April 2017 from www.smmgp.org.uk/download/others/other102.pdf

BNF. (2008, September). *British national formulary* (56th ed.). London: RPS Publishing.

BNF. (2012, March). *British national formulary* (63rd ed.). Basingstoke, UK: Pharmaceutical Press.

Borison, R.L., Diamond, B.I., Sinha, D., Gupta, R.P., & Ajiboye, P.A. (1988). Clozapine withdrawal rebound psychosis. *Psychopharmacology Bulletin, 24*, 260–263.

Breggin, P.R. (2012). *Psychiatric drug withdrawal*. New York: Springer Publishing Co.
Breggin, P.R., & Cohen, D. (2000). *Your drug may be your problem*. Cambridge: HarperCollins.
Broglie, M., & Jörgensen, G. (1954). Über die Anwendung von Phenothiazinkörpern in der Inneren Medizin. *Deutsche Medizinische Wochenschrift, 79*, 1564–1567.
Brooks, G.W. (1959). Withdrawal from neuroleptic drugs. *American Journal of Psychiatry, 115*, 931–932.
Caras, S. (1991). *Doing without drugs*. Santa Cruz, CA: Self-publication.
Charney, D.S., Heninger, G.R., Sternberg, D.E., & Landis, H. (1982). Abrupt discontinuation of tricyclic antidepressant drugs. *British Journal of Psychiatry, 141*, 377–386.
Chouinard, G., & Jones, B.D. (1980). Neuroleptic-induced supersensitivity psychosis. *American Journal of Psychiatry, 137*, 16–21.
Chouinard, G., & Jones, B.D. (1982). Neuroleptic-induced supersensitivity psychosis, the "Hump Course," and tardive dyskinesia. *Journal of Clinical Psychopharmacology, 2*, 143–144.
Czerwenka-Wenkstetten, H., Hofmann, G., & Kryspin-Exner, K. (1965). Tranquillizersucht und missbrauch. *Wiener Medizinische Wochenschrift, 115*, 1012–1016.
Darton, K. (2005). *Making sense of coming off psychiatric drugs*. London: Mind Publications.
Davis, K.L., & Rosenberg, G.S. (1979). Is there a limbic system equivalent of tardive dyskinesia? *Biological Psychiatry, 14*, 699–703.
Degkwitz, R. (1964). Zur Wirkungsweise von Psycholeptica anhand langfristiger Selbstversuche. *Nervenarzt, 35*, 491–496.
Degkwitz, R. (1967). *Leitfaden der Psychopharmakologie*. Stuttgart: Wissenschaftliche Verlagsgesellschaft.
Degkwitz, R., & Luxenburger, O. (1965). Das terminale extrapyramidale Insuffizienz-bzw. Defektsyndrom infolge chronischer Anwendung von Neurolepticis. *Nervenarzt, 36*, 173–175.
DGSP (Deutsche Gesellschaft für Soziale Psychiatrie e.V.). (Ed.) (2014). *Neuroleptika reduzieren und absetzen: Eine Broschüre für Psychose-Erfahrene, Angehörige und Professionelle aller Berufsgruppen*. Bonn: Self-publication.
Dilsaver, S.C., & Greden, J.F. (1984a). Antidepressant withdrawal phenomena. *Biological Psychiatry, 19*, 237–256.
Dilsaver, S.C., & Greden, J.F. (1984b). Antidepressant withdrawal-induced activation (hypomanic and manic). *Brain Research Reviews, 7*, 29–48.
Dilsaver, S.C., & Greden, J.F. (1986). Mania induced by antidepressant withdrawal. *Psychosomatics, 27*, 798–799.
Ekblom, B., Eriksson, K., & Lindstroem, L.H. (1984). Supersensitivity psychosis in schizophrenic patients after sudden clozapine withdrawal. *Psychopharmacology, 83*, 293–294.
Glaeske, G. (1989). Psychopharmaka: Zerstörung auf Rezept. *Psychologie Heute, 16*(1), 20–29.
Gøtzsche, P.C. (2013). *Deadly medicines and organised crime: How Big Pharma has corrupted healthcare*. London: Radcliffe Publishing Ltd.
Gøtzsche, P.C. (2016). *Tödliche Psychopharmaka und organisiertes Leugnen: Wie Ärzte und Pharmaindustrie die Gesundheit der Patienten vorsätzlich aufs Spiel setzen*. Munich: Riva Verlag.
Gualtieri, T.C., Quade, D., Hicks, R.E., Mayo, J.P., & Schroeder, S.R. (1984). Tardive dyskinesia and other clinical consequences of neuroleptic treatment in children and adolescents. *American Journal of Psychiatry, 141*, S. 20–23.
Haase, H.-J. (1982). *Therapie mit Psychopharmaka und anderen seelisches Befinden beeinflussenden Medikamenten* (5th ed.). Stuttgart & New York: Schattauer.
Hift, S., & Hoff, H. (1958). Die organische Therapie der Psychosen. *Wiener Medizinische Wochenschrift, 108*, 1043–1048.

Hollister, L.E., Eikenberry, D.T., & Raffel, S. (1960). Chlorpromazine in nonpsychotic patients with pulmonary tuberculosis. *American Review of Respiratory Diseases, 81*, 562–566.

Icarus Project, & Freedom Center. (2012). *Harm reduction guide to coming off psychiatric drugs and withdrawal* (2nd ed.). New York & Northampton, MA: Self-publication.

Irle, G. (1974). *Depressionen*. Stuttgart: Kreuz.

Janssen-Cilag AG (Switzerland). (2016, March 16). Haldol. Product information. In Arzneimittel-Kompendium Online. Basel, Switzerland: Documed AG. Retrieved on 19 August, 2016 from https://compendium.ch/mpro/mnr/3404/html/de?start=1#7450

Janssen Pharmaceutica, Inc./SmithKline Beecham (1996). Advertisement. *American Journal of Psychiatry, 153*(3), A15–A17.

Kramer, J.C., Klein, D.F., & Fink, M. (1961). Withdrawal symptoms following discontinuation of imipramine therapy. *American Journal of Psychiatry, 118*, 549–550.

Krücke, M. (2014). *Psychopharmaka absetzen. Ein Leitfaden von Psychiatrie-Erfahrenen für Psychiatrie-Erfahrene*. Booklet. Bochum: Bundesverband Psychiatrie-Erfahrener.

Kuhn, R. (1960). Probleme der praktischen Durchführung der Tofranil-Behandlung. *Wiener Medizinische Wochenschrift, 110*, 245–250.

Lacoursiere, R.B., Spohn, H.E., & Thompson, K. (1976). Medical effects of abrupt neuroleptic withdrawal. *Comprehensive Psychiatry, 17*, 285–294.

Lehmann, P. (Ed.) (1998). *Psychopharmaka absetzen: Erfolgreiches Absetzen von Neuroleptika, Antidepressiva, Carbamazepin, Lithium und Tranquilizern*. Berlin: Antipsychiatrieverlag [English edition 2004a. *Coming off psychiatric drugs: Successful withdrawal from neuroleptics, antidepressants, mood stabilizers, Ritalin and tranquilizers*. Berlin, Eugene, OR, & Shrewsbury, UK: Peter Lehmann Publishing (ebook in 2013)].

Lehmann, P. (2004b). PSY DREAM: Psychiatric drug registration, evaluation and all-inclusive monitoring. *Journal of Critical Psychology, Counselling and Psychotherapy, 4*, 233–241.

Lehmann, P. (2016). 65 Jahre nonchalantes Wegschauen: Diskussion um die unterlassene Hilfe beim selbstbestimmten Absetzen psychiatrischer Psychopharmaka im historischen Rückblick. Lecture given to the Psychose-Begleitung und Neuroleptika Conference of the Deutsche Gesellschaft für Soziale Psychiatrie, Bad Honnef, 3 June. Retrieved on 16 June, 2016 from www.antipsychiatrieverlag.de/artikel/gesundheit/ppt/lehmann-wegschauen-ppt.pdf

Lehmann, P. (2017). *Schöne neue Psychiatrie. Vol. 2: Wie Psychopharmaka den Körper verändern* (ebook). Berlin & Shrewsbury, UK: Antipsychiatrieverlag.

Martensson, L. (1998). Should neuroleptic drugs be banned? In The Voiceless Movement/ Les Sans-Voix (Ed.), *Deprived of our humanity: The case against neuroleptic drugs* (pp. 97–151). Geneva: Association Ecrivains, Poètes & Cie.

McMaster. (2011, July 19). Patients who use anti-depressants can be more likely to suffer relapse, researcher finds. *Science Daily*. Retrieved 24 January 2012 from www.sciencedaily.com/releases/2011/07/110719121354.htm

Meyer, H.-H. (1953). Die Winterschlafbehandlung in der Psychiatrie und Neurologie. *Deutsche Medizinische Wochenschrift, 78*, 1097–1100.

Mirin, S.M., Schatzberg, A.F., & Creasey, D.E. (1981). Hypomania and mania after withdrawal of tricyclic antidepressants. *American Journal of Psychiatry, 138*, 87–89.

Moldawsky, R.J. (1985). Tolerance to antidepressants. *American Journal of Psychiatry, 142*, 1519.

Möller, H.-J. (1986). Neuroleptika als Tranquilizer: Indikationen und Gefahren. *Medizinische Klinik, 81*, 385–388.

Möller, H.-J. (2009). Unipolare depressive Erkrankungen. *Nervenarzt, 80*, 513–514.

NAPA (Network Against Psychiatric Assault). (Ed.) (1984). *Dr. Caligari's psychiatric drugs*. Berkeley, CA: Self-publication.

Nielsen, M., Hansen, E.H., & Gøtzsche, P.C. (2012). What is the difference between dependence and withdrawal reactions? A comparison of benzodiazepines and selective serotonin re-uptake inhibitors. *Addiction, 107*, 900–908.

Pinel gemeinnützige Gesellschaft mbH (n.d.). Neuroleptika können und müssen in minimaler Dosis eingesetzt werden. Retrieved 30 March 2016 from www.pinel-online.de/index.php?id=573

Poser, W., Roscher, D., & Poser, S. (1985). *Ratgeber für Medikamentenabhängige und ihre Angehörigen* (6th ed.). Freiburg, Germany: Lambertus-Verlag.

Rautmann, G. (1964). *Langfristiger Selbstversuch mit Imipramin* (Unpublished dissertation). University of Frankfurt am Main, Germany.

Read, J. (2005). *Coping with coming off*. London: Mind Publications.

Redmond, D.E., & Huang, Y.H. (1979). New evidence for a locus coeruleus-norepinephrine connection with anxiety. *Life Sciences, 26*, 2149–2162.

Reimer, F. (1965). Das "Absetzungs"-Delir. *Nervenarzt, 34*, 446–447.

Rufer, M. (1995). *Glückspillen: Ecstasy, Prozac und das Comeback der Psychopharmaka*. Munich: Knaur.

Selbach, H. (1960). Klinische und theoretische Aspekte der Pharmakotherapie des depressiven Syndroms. 2. *Wiener Medizinische Wochenschrift, 110*, 264–268.

Selbach, H. (1963). Über regulations-dynamische Wirkgrundlagen der Psychopharmaka. In J.D. Achelis & H. von Ditfurth (Eds.), *Starnberger Gespräche 2* (pp. 53–74). Stuttgart: Thieme.

Seuwen, G. (1964). *Die Wirkung von Amitriptylin, Bellergal und Alkohol in langfristigen Selbstversuchen* (Unpublished dissertation). University of Frankfurt am Main, Germany.

Shatan, C. (1966). Withdrawal symptoms after abrupt termination of imipramine. *Canadian Psychiatric Association Journal, 11* (Suppl.), 150–158.

Sommer, H., & Quandt, J. (1970). Langzeitbehandlung mit Chlorpromazin im Tierexperiment. *Fortschritte der Neurologie, Psychiatrie und ihrer Grenzgebiete, 38*, 466–491.

Sugrue, M.F. (1980). Changes in rat brain monoamine turnover following chronic antidepressant administration. *Life Sciences, 26*, 423–433.

Svensson, T.H., & Usdin, T. (1979). Alpha-adrenoreceptor mediated inhibition of brain noradrenergic neurons after acute and chronic treatment with tricyclic antidepressants. In E. Usdin, I.J. Kopin, & J. Barchas (Eds.), *Catecholamines: Basic and clinical frontiers*. Vol. 1 (pp. 672–674). New York: Pergamon Press.

Tornatore, F., Sramek, J.J., Okeya, B.L., & Pi, E.H. (1987). *Reactions to psychotropic medication*. New York & London: Plenum Medical Book Co.

Tornatore, F., Sramek, J.J., Okeya, B.L., & Pi, E.H. (1991). *Unerwünschte Wirkungen von Psychopharmaka*. Stuttgart & New York: Thieme.

Ungerstedt, U., & Ljungberg, T. (1977). Behavioral patterns related to dopamine neurotransmission. *Advances in Biochemical Psychopharmacology, 16*, 193–199.

United Nations. (2006). *Convention on the rights of persons with disabilities – articles*. Retrieved from www.un.org/development/desa/disabilities/convention-on-the-rights-of-persons-with-disabilities/convention-on-the-rights-of-persons-with-disabilities-2.html

Wallcraft, J. (2007). User-led research to develop an evidence base for alternative approaches. In P. Stastny & P. Lehmann (Eds.), *Alternatives beyond psychiatry* (pp. 342–351). Berlin, Eugene, OR, & Shrewsbury, UK: Peter Lehmann Publishing (ebook in 2014).

Woggon, B. (1979). Neuroleptika-Absetzversuche bei chronisch schizophrenen Patienten. 1. Literaturzusammenfassung. *International Pharmacopsychiatry, 14*, 34–56.

9
PSYCHIATRY AND THE LAW

The Law Project for Psychiatric Rights' public education approach

Jim Gottstein

About the Law Project for Psychiatric Rights

The Law Project for Psychiatric Rights (PsychRights.Org) is a public interest law firm whose mission is to mount a strategic legal campaign against forced psychiatric drugging and electroshock in the United States akin to what Thurgood Marshall and the National Association for the Advancement of Colored People (NAACP) mounted in the 1940s and 1950s on behalf of African-American civil rights. The public mental health system is creating a huge class of chronic mental patients through forcing them to take ineffective, yet extremely harmful drugs.

Due to the massive growth in psychiatric drugging of children and youth and the targeting of them for even more psychiatric drugging, PsychRights has made attacking this problem a priority. Children are virtually always forced to take these drugs because it is the adults in their lives who are making the decision. This is an unfolding national tragedy of immense proportions. As part of its mission, PsychRights is further dedicated to exposing the truth about these drugs and the courts being misled into ordering people to be drugged and subjected to other brain- and body-damaging interventions against their will.

PsychRights believes that changing public attitudes is the most important task facing those who are seeking a truth-based, humane, and helpful approach to people whose behavior is disturbing and who get labeled as having a mental illness.

PsychRights' strategic approach

Figure 9.1 is a graphic of three key elements that PsychRights believes can interact synergistically to bring about beneficial system change. Having "Public Attitudes" at the top is deliberate. The fundamental reason why the mental health system does not rely on truth-based, humane, and helpful approaches is that the public doesn't

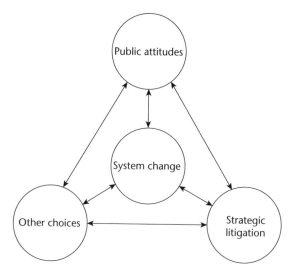

FIGURE 9.1 The Transformation Triangle

understand that the current standard care is against the evidence, counterproductive, and harmful. So, to the extent that public attitudes can be brought around to the truth, the public will support other choices. Going back the other way, to the extent that such other approaches can be implemented and their success publicized, it will change public attitudes to support these approaches.

The other sides of the triangle are based on United States' law, where people's right to the least restrictive (in the case of psychiatric imprisonment) or least intrusive (in the case of forced drugging) alternatives are violated as a matter of course.[1] The fundamental reason they are violated is that the judges deciding these cases, and the lawyers assigned to defend people faced with psychiatric imprisonment and/or forced drugging reflect public attitudes about the necessity of psychiatric imprisonment and forced drugging (or electroshock). In other words, they believe that if the person wasn't crazy, she would know it was good for her and therefore they do not let her pesky legal rights get in the way of what they think is for her own good. So, to the extent that the judges deciding the cases and the lawyers assigned to represent people understand the truth, the judges will be far more likely to respect their rights and the lawyers to put up a real defense.

Going back the other way is harder to see, but perhaps the best example is the 1954 United States Supreme Court decision in *Brown v. Board of Education*[2] overruling its 75-year-old decision holding that segregation of blacks from whites was constitutional so long as the segregation involved "separate but equal" facilities. Before *Brown*, there were wide swaths of the United States population who believed that segregation was acceptable. After all, the United States Supreme Court had ruled that it was. Today there is only a small percentage of people in the United States population who believe that racial segregation is acceptable. *Brown v. Board of Education* played a pivotal role in this change in public attitude. PsychRights believes that strategic litigation challenging psychiatric imprisonment and forced drugging, based on the faulty science and worse outcomes, can play a role in changing public attitudes. In fact, PsychRights' strategic litigation in Alaska has had at least some positive effect.

Down at the bottom of the triangle, people in the United States have the right to the least restrictive or least intrusive alternatives before psychiatric imprisonment or forced drugging (or electroshock) can be ordered by a court. In Alaska, this has been interpreted to mean that if there is a feasible less intrusive alternative to forced drugging, the state has to either provide it or let the person go. However, even though people have this legal right, to the extent that there is no less restrictive alternative in existence, judges are not likely to just let the person go. Instead, they will disingenuously find that there is no feasible less intrusive alternative. So, the existence of less restrictive/intrusive alternatives dramatically increases a person's chances of having that right honored. Going from right to left on the bottom, litigation establishing that there is a feasible less intrusive alternative creates pressure on the government to provide it.

Language

Before getting to the substance of PsychRights' information, it must be noted that one of the most important aspects of communication is the words used. Organized psychiatry, aided and abetted by Big Pharma, has occupied the field of language to the point where it is almost impossible to discuss the issues without resort to this biased language. However, it is important to do so as much as possible. For example, above, I used the much more accurate term "psychiatric imprisonment" [3] instead of the accepted, but euphemistic term of "involuntary commitment." At the same time, when I speak or write to the general public, I will usually use "involuntary commitment" because I don't want to lose people. However, I never use Electro-Convulsive Therapy or its acronym ECT because electroshock is not therapy and people accept the term "electroshock."

I never say that someone is a schizophrenic and try to never say that someone has schizophrenia. Instead I say that the person is diagnosed with schizophrenia. This is often referred to as "people who" language. PsychRights tries to be effective with its public education efforts and that means using words and phrases people will understand, and not using words and phrases that will destroy one's credibility. The careful use of language is very important.

Because of the much more pervasive use of forced drugging than electroshock, I will often refer to forced drugging without including forced electroshock even when electroshock is included. That is true in this chapter. At other times, forced drugging only refers to forced drugging and does not include electroshock. It is hoped that the context makes it clear. These conventions are used to keep the language from getting too cumbersome.

Content

PsychRights' education effort includes a large number of channels as described below and while the content is tailored for each audience, there are three main foci of the information. People's legal rights and how they are violated is, of course, a prime topic, but this is virtually always accompanied by information on the harm that the drugs (and electroshock) cause without any corresponding benefit for most people, and emphasizes that other approaches are far more helpful for most people without the harm, or at least usually much less harm. On the other hand, information about the harm of the drugs (and electroshock) and other approaches might be conveyed without any reference to violations of legal rights.

Psychiatric drugs

PsychRights teaches that psychiatric drugs (and electroshock) are very harmful without any real benefit for most of the people taking them. For example, people diagnosed with serious mental illness in the public mental health system in the United States have a life span that is 25 years shorter than that of the general population.[4] This contrasts with such people having normal life spans around 1900. After the first neuroleptic, chlorpromazine (Thorazine in the United States, Largactil in the UK), and the other phenothiazines, such as Haldol, Mellaril, and Stelazine, were introduced in the 1950s, people's life spans were decreased by 10–15 years. The advent of the second generation of neuroleptics, such as Zyprexa, Risperdal, and Seroquel, and the increasing use of polypharmacy where multiple psychiatric drugs are administered concurrently, are almost certainly the reasons for going from 10–15 years' early death to 25 years'. Contrary to the marketing hype, the second-generation neuroleptics are more harmful than the older drugs and just as ineffective. In fact, 74% of the patients in a study comparing first- and second-generation neuroleptics quit because the drugs were ineffective, or the effects were intolerable, or both.[5]

For most people, especially those who are not allowed to determine for themselves if, when, and how much to take, they are debilitating. In fact, long-term use of neuroleptics dramatically increases what is diagnosed as psychosis over the long term and decreases recovery rates.[6]

The SSRI (selective serotonin reuptake inhibitor) so-called antidepressants, such as Prozac and Paxil, are mostly no better than a placebo on the target symptoms, cause people to become manic and then get put on neuroleptics. They also cause suicide and violence, including homicide. They are addictive, with some people having great difficulty getting off. They also cause a large percentage of people to suffer sexual dysfunction.[7]

The anticonvulsants, misbranded as "mood stabilizers," cause hostility, aggression, depression and confusion, liver failure, fatal pancreatitis, severe skin disorders, and may cause cognitive impairment with long-term use.[8]

The benzodiazepines such as Valium, Xanax, Klonopin, and Ativan, are only effective for a few weeks, extremely addictive, and can also cause violence, including homicide.

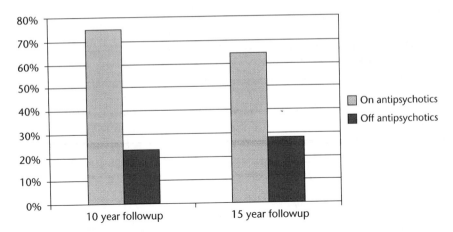

FIGURE 9.2 Psychotic symptoms

Note: The schizophrenia patients who stayed on antipsychotics long-term were much more likely to continue to suffer from psychotic symptoms.

Source: Martin Harrow and Thomas Jobe. Factors involved in outcome and recovery in schizophrenia patients not on antipsychotic medications: A 15-year multifollow-up study. *The Journal of Nervous and Mental Disease, 195* (2007): 406–414.

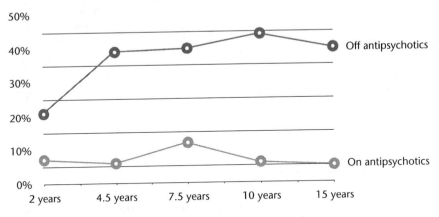

FIGURE 9.3 Long-term recovery rates for schizophrenia patients

Source: Harrow M. [and Jobe T.] Factors involved in outcome and recovery in schizophrenia patients not on antipsychotic medications: [A 15-year multifollow-up study]. *The Journal of Nervous and Mental Disease, 195* (2007): 406–414.

One result has been an explosion in the United States disability rate from 213 per 100,000 in 1955 to 1315 in 2007, more than a six-fold increase.

While not all of this is due to psychiatric drugs, a large proportion almost certainly is.

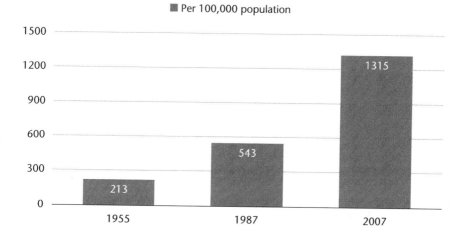

FIGURE 9.4   The disabled mentally ill in the United States, 1955–2007 (under government care)

Source: Silverman, C. *The Epidemiology of Depression* (1968): 139. U.S. Social Security Administration Reports, 1987–2007.

Other approaches

PsychRights' message regarding other approaches is that there are proven approaches that are far better at achieving recovery and are generally not harmful. The act of diagnosing someone with a mental disorder can be harmful in itself, sometimes very harmful. In addition, non-drug and non-electroshock therapies can also be harmful, but I would say the harm is at least an order of magnitude less. Both the Soteria House study in the 1970s[9] and the current Open Dialogue approach show that if neuroleptics are avoided if possible, about 80% of people can get through what becomes a temporary problem and on to a full life. The Open Dialogue statistics are shown in Table 9.1.

It is fair to contrast this 80% recovery rate with the 5% recovery rate in the Harrow [and Jobe] study (2007) for people who are maintained on neuroleptics as depicted in Figure 9.3. It is also fair to assume that the reason only 40% recovered in the Harrow [and Jobe] study for those who got off the drugs is that being put on these drugs dramatically worsens one's prospects.

With respect to children, rather than telling them something is wrong with them/their brain, that they have no control over their behavior, that it cannot be fixed, and they will have to take debilitating drugs for the rest of their diminished life, we need to be helping children be successful as well as helping parents be successful parents. We refer to and rely on Module 8 of the CriticalThinkRx.Com curriculum: Evidence-Based Psychosocial Interventions for Childhood Problems.[10] CriticalThinkRx was funded by a grant from the Attorney General Consumer and Prescriber Grant Program, from the multi-state settlement of consumer fraud claims

TABLE 9.1 Outcomes with selective use of antipsychotics

Patients (N=75)
Schizophrenia (N=30)
Other psychotic disorders (N=45)

Antipsychotic use	
Never exposed to antipsychotics	67%
Occasional use during five years	33%
Ongoing use at end of five years	20%
Psychotic symptoms	
Never relapsed during five years	67%
Asymptomatic at five-year follow-up	79%
Functional outcomes at five years	
Working or in school	73%
Unemployed	7%
On disability	20%

Note: Five-year outcomes for first-episode psychotic patients in Finnish West Lapland treated with Open-Dialogue therapy.

Source: Seikkula, J. Five-year experience of first-episode nonaffective psychosis in open-dialogue approach. *Psychotherapy Research, 16* (2006): 214–228.

regarding the marketing of the prescription drug Neurontin® and is extremely well researched.

Legal rights (United States)

In the United States, psychiatric imprisonment and forced drugging are by far most often imposed under state, rather than federal, law. While there are similarities, each state has its own statutes and case law interpreting the statutes. However, everyone in the United States has certain rights under the Due Process clause of the United States Constitution. The principal tenets of "procedural due process" are the right to meaningful notice and a meaningful opportunity to be heard. In other words, people have the right to know of what they are being accused, and the right to tell their side of the story.

Under "substantive due process" when a *fundamental right* is infringed by the government, (1) the governmental interest (reason for the infringement) must be compelling, (2) the means employed must be the least restrictive or intrusive, and (3) the infringement must be likely to achieve the governmental goal. Being locked up is clearly a deprivation of a fundamental constitutional right and the U.S. Supreme Court has so held.[11] In addition, under the United States Constitution, civil psychiatric imprisonment is only permissible when (1) it takes place pursuant to proper procedures and evidentiary standards, (2) there is a finding of "dangerousness either to one's self or to others," and (3) the proof of dangerousness is "coupled ... with the proof of some additional factor, such as a 'mental illness' or 'mental abnormality'."[12] Being unable to take care of oneself can constitute danger to self if the person is "incapable of surviving safely in freedom."[13]

These elements must be proven by "clear and convincing evidence," which is more stringent than "preponderance of the evidence" used in most civil (non-criminal) litigation, but less stringent than "beyond a reasonable doubt," which is the criminal standard. When the United States Supreme Court made this decision, one of the reasons it cited for not holding that "beyond a reasonable doubt" is required was that mental health professionals can never or virtually never testify that someone is a danger to self or others beyond a reasonable doubt: "The subtleties and nuances of psychiatric diagnosis render certainties virtually beyond reach in most situations."[14] The reality is that the best psychiatrists and other mental health professionals can achieve on predicting violence is about 50%, and then only when they rigorously use instruments developed for that purpose, which they rarely do.[15]

For forced drugging, there may be some doubt about whether it is an infringement of a fundamental right. The United States Supreme Court decision in *Sell v. United States*,[16] a case in which the government wanted to psychiatrically drug a dentist to make him competent to stand trial for Medicaid fraud, uses fundamental rights analysis without explicitly holding that it is a fundamental right. In *Sell*, the U.S. Supreme Court held that the government cannot drug someone against their will to make them competent to stand trial unless the court:

1. Finds that *important* governmental interests are at stake.
2. Concludes that involuntary medication will *significantly further* those concomitant state interests.
3. Concludes that involuntary medication is *necessary* to further those interests. The court must find that any alternative, less intrusive treatments are unlikely to achieve substantially the same results.
4. Concludes that administration of the drugs is *medically appropriate*, i.e., in the patient's best medical interest in light of his medical condition. The specific kinds of drugs at issue may matter here as elsewhere. Different kinds of antipsychotic drugs may produce different side effects and enjoy different levels of success.[17]

This is fundamental rights analysis, which is why I think it is fair to say that the right to be free of unwanted psychiatric drugs is a fundamental constitutional right, triggering a higher threshold for the government to infringe.

These legal principles are used in conjunction with the information about psychiatric drugs and other approaches in PsychRights' teaching efforts. In light of the truth about psychiatrists' and other mental health professionals' inability to predict violence, I estimate that no more than 10% of the people psychiatrically imprisoned in the United States actually meet the criteria. Because psychiatric drugs, especially the neuroleptics most often forced on people, are so harmful to all, without any real benefit for most, and there is almost always a feasible less intrusive alternative, forced psychiatric drugging can virtually never meet the constitutional criteria in my view.

Strategic approaches to the psychiatric drugging of children

PsychRights has developed two strategic litigation approaches to specifically address the massive psychiatric drugging of children in the United States, especially poor children who are given psychiatric drugs at much higher rates than other children for various reasons. Children in state custody, such as foster care, have the highest rates of psychiatric drugging of all children. The first approach is based on the fact that almost all of the psychiatric drugs being prescribed to poor children are paid for by the government under Medicaid or a related program and most of these are not covered under Medicaid. Off-label prescriptions are not covered under Medicaid unless there is "support" for the use in at least one of three specifically identified drug references called "compendia."

The government is paying for these drugs in spite of them not being covered, but the United States has a unique anti-fraud law, called the False Claims Act, which allows people to bring lawsuits on behalf of the government against people submitting or causing false claims based on non-public information and to share in the recovery, if any. The doctors writing these prescriptions are causing such claims when they write the prescriptions and the pharmacies are submitting them to the government for payment. Each offending prescription is a "false claim" and carries a minimum penalty of $5,500. Any prescriber is likely to have written at least 1,000 such prescriptions within the 6-year statute of limitations, which amounts to a minimum penalty of $5.5 million. The idea is that by winning even just one case, it will scare prescribers into stopping. PsychRights therefore has a Medicaid Fraud Initiative Against Psychiatric Drugging of Children with a model (form) complaint for people to use.[18] The model complaint also includes the pharmacy(ies) because the larger ones have enough money to make such lawsuits attractive to lawyers.

The second approach is based on the principle that children in state custody have the right not to be harmed by the government while in state custody, and that giving them psychiatric drugs is harmful. PsychRights has not been able to mount such a lawsuit due to resource issues, but is hopeful that it will in the future, or encourage someone else to do so.

Silos or stovepiping (preaching to the choir)

Before turning to the public education efforts of PsychRights, a word about silos or stovepiping, also known as "preaching to the choir," is in order. All of these terms refer to the phenomenon of people tending to get their information from sources with which they agree. In order to be successful in changing public attitudes, one must get beyond this choir. This is the biggest challenge.

Website

Historically, PsychRights' website (http://psychrights.org) has been its primary means of public education. It has a reputation for providing a vast amount of information, having tens of thousands of webpages and documents.

Psychiatry: Force of Law

The PsychRights website was launched with Psychiatry: Force of Law, which describes people's rights and how these rights are pervasively violated. This is achieved by witnesses not telling the truth, and lawyers not fighting for their clients, while the judges participate in the misuse of judicial force. As Professor Michael Perlin has put it:

> [C]ourts accept . . . testimonial dishonesty, . . . specifically where witnesses, especially expert witnesses, show a "high propensity to purposely distort their testimony in order to achieve desired ends." . . .
> Experts frequently . . . and openly subvert statutory and case law criteria that impose rigorous behavioral standards as predicates for commitment . . .
> This combination . . . helps define a system in which (1) dishonest testimony is often regularly (and unthinkingly) accepted; (2) statutory and case law standards are frequently subverted; and (3) insurmountable barriers are raised to insure that the allegedly "therapeutically correct" social end is met. . . . In short, the mental disability law system often deprives individuals of liberty disingenuously and upon bases that have no relationship to case law or to statutes.[19]

As set forth above, if the lawyers knew that psychiatric drugs are counterproductive and extremely harmful, they should be fighting more for their clients, including challenging this perjury, and finding and putting on the evidence rebutting the story told by psychiatry.[20]

Exposés

PsychRights has been the first to publish a number of important exposés. An example is the February 18, 2004 Food and Drug Administration (FDA) report by Andrew Mosholder, regarding the harm caused by antidepressants, that the FDA ordered was to be kept secret. PsychRights was provided with surreptitiously taken digital photographs of the report, converted them to Acrobat format, and posted the report on its website on July 26, 2004. Within a month, other copies had made their way to the Internet and the FDA was essentially forced to make the report public.[21] Similarly, PsychRights published Allen Jones's whistleblower report[22] about corruption in the development of the Texas Medication Algorithm Program, commonly referred to as TMAP. The TMAP called for the second generation of neuroleptics, marketed as "atypical antipsychotics," such as Risperdal, Zyprexa, and Seroquel to be tried before the older neuroleptics, such as Haldol and Thorazine. This was picked up by the *British Medical Journal*, in an article by Jeanne Lenzer.[23] The Allen Jones whistleblower report has been downloaded tens of thousands of times.

Forced Drugging Defense Package

On PsychRights' Home Page is the "Forced Drugging Defense Package," which is a generic set of legal papers to oppose court-ordered psychiatric drugging. It includes affidavits from Robert Whitaker and Dr. Grace Jackson that can be filed in court if one obtains certified copies from MindFreedom at a small cost.

Scientific Research by Topic

In its "Scientific Research by Topic" section, PsychRights posts exactly the type of evidence that the lawyers should use as well as making it available for everyone to influence public opinion. PsychRights generally posts full articles, asserting that it is a "fair use" under the copyright laws and therefore permissible. The Scientific Research by Topic section has the following categories:

- ADHD—Attention Deficit Hyperactivity "Disorder"—(& Stimulant "Treatment")
- Allostatic Load
- AntiDepressants
- Benzodiazepines
- Children & Youth
- Dangerousness
- Diagnosis
- Effective Non-Drug Treatments
- Electroshock
- Genetics
- Informed Consent
- Lobotomy
- Making Decisions for Presumed Incompetents
    - Forced Treatment
- Mental Illness Is Not a Brain Disease
- Miscellaneous
- "Mood Stabilizers"
- Neuroleptics and Chronic Mental Illness (research cited in *Mad in America*)
- Neuroleptics
    - Failure to Medicate Does Not Harm Patients

- Outpatient Commitment
- Peer Run Services from the National Empowerment Center
- Psychiatric Drugs
- Science for Sale
- Stigma.

Everyday Horrors of the Mental Health System

PsychRights' "Everyday Horrors of the Mental Health System" page carries first-hand accounts of people's experiences with the mental health system. It has grown from just a few accounts to more than 100 today. These first-hand accounts can be very compelling.

States/Countries

In its States/Countries section, PsychRights posts state- and country-specific information as well as information about the United Nations. For example, the Massachusetts webpage has a couple of memos about what is called "Rogers Orders," that suggest strategies to use existing law to prevent forced drugging. One of the target audiences was the lawyers. Similarly, a memo was written about community drugging orders in New York, euphemistically called "Assisted Outpatient Treatment," directed at recruiting *pro bono* (volunteer) attorneys to represent people.

While PsychRights' expertise is in United States law, it does have some information about other countries as well as the United Nations and the European Union. For example, the United Nations page has two Special Rapporteurs calling to eradicate all forms of non-consensual psychiatric treatment.[24]

Mainstream media

Exposure of the truth about psychiatry and its so-called "treatments" in the mainstream media is both the most important task and the hardest. Especially for the national media and television, in particular, it is hard to conclude anything except that the massive amount of drug advertising money results in suppression of negative news about drugs and the drug industry. Still, it is possible, as exemplified by the Zyprexa Papers. Also, in the United States, the horrific mass shootings have led to a scapegoating, witch-hunt environment against people diagnosed with mental illness, calling for even more forced drugging, even though the truth is that psychiatric drugs increase rather than decrease violence.[25]

The Zyprexa Papers

In late 2006, a series of stories in *The New York Times* reported on documents I had subpoenaed out of the consolidation for discovery and settlement purposes of around 30,000 lawsuits in the United States District Court in Brooklyn over Zyprexa (olanzapine) causing diabetes and other metabolic problems.[26] I had been contacted by an expert witness for plaintiffs in the case, Dr. David Egilman, who was so outraged by the serious harm to people's health that the documents revealed, and the prospect of these harms being kept secret through settlement, that he called me to see if I was willing to subpoena him for the documents. The reason he wanted me to subpoena them was because they were subject to a Secrecy Order by the Court. The reason he contacted me is that he became aware of the report *An Analysis of the Olanzapine Clinical Trials—Dangerous Drug, Dubious Efficacy*, by Dr. Grace Jackson (Jackson Report),[27] that had been filed in the *Myers v. Alaska Psychiatric Institute* case and uploaded to the Internet.[28]

Under the Secrecy Order, Lilly had to be given notice of the subpoena and a reasonable opportunity to object. I subpoenaed the documents on December 6, 2006, and received the Zyprexa Papers on December 11–12, 2006, after Dr. Egilman determined that Lilly had had an opportunity to object. I think it is fair to say that all hell broke loose after the first article in *The New York Times* came out on December 17, 2006. Lilly moved for an injunction against disseminating the documents, and threatened me with contempt and that they would file a complaint against me to the Alaska Bar Association, presumably to have my license to practice law suspended or revoked.

Lilly got an injunction in short order, but the Zyprexa Papers had already been uploaded by someone to Tor, an untraceable, distributed system on the Internet that could be thought of as a predecessor to Wikileaks. They were also uploaded to at least a couple of regular websites in the United States, and some locations outside the United States.

Lilly threatened a couple of psychiatric survivors who had obtained copies of the Zyprexa Papers and were disseminating them. One of them, Eric Whalen, was threatened three times by Lilly within 5 hours to take them down, which he understandably did in light of the Lilly Lawyer Blitzkrieg. My favorite response was from long-time activist, Pat Risser:

> Gosh, what a mess. I'm sorry but I wasn't aware of any court order at the time I downloaded the "secret zyprexa documents" so, I not only downloaded them but I made several copies (burned them to CDs) and distributed them. I mailed them to some family and friends as well as several newspapers (in Ohio and Oregon). Since I had some extra copies (about 40 or so) I also passed them out to folks who seemed interested as I stood outside of a shopping center store. I have no idea who these strangers were so I can't possibly get these CDs returned. I'm so sorry. I figured since you're making such a fuss over the thousands of copies that went over the internet, I'd better let you know that this "secret" has spread and I really can't help stop the spread at this point. Sorry.

TortsProfBlog law professor William Childs posted a blog about the situation, titled, "Judge Tries to Unring Bell Hanging Around Neck of Horse Already Out of Barn Being Carried on Ship That Has Sailed."[29]

According to *The New York Times*, the release of the Zyprexa Papers caused the government's investigation of Lilly's illegal promotion to "gain momentum," which ultimately resulted in a $1.4 billion payment by Lilly settling criminal and civil charges. The whistleblowers bringing the secret cases against Lilly received $79 million. I received none of this, instead ending up with just under $300,000 in attorney's bills to defend myself against Lilly. I still owe over $100,000, but am not being pressed to pay it.

There is little or no doubt that the release of the Zyprexa Papers had a great deal of impact. Certainly it exposed the extreme harm caused by the drug. I think it is fair to say it saved thousands of lives, maybe tens of thousands. It also had a positive impact on the practice of keeping documents secret as the price for settlement, with documents in similar cases, especially Seroquel, being released later. It resulted in a number of states suing Lilly for having to pay for treating diabetes and other metabolic problems caused by Zyprexa and receiving millions of dollars in settlements. Ironically, but also unsurprisingly, states still drug tens of thousands of people with Zyprexa against their will. The psychopharmaceutical juggernaut rolls on, and while the Zyprexa Papers episode was an important bump in the road, it was still just a bump in the road.

A final point which can be made from the Zyprexa Papers experience is that one never knows what will happen when material is posted on the Internet. The release of the Zyprexa Papers can be traced back to PsychRights posting Dr. Grace Jackson's report on Zyprexa, which led to Dr. Egilman calling me to see if I was willing to subpoena him.

Other print media

Other relatively noteworthy print stories in which I or PsychRights (or both) have appeared are:

- Feds pay for drug fraud: 92 percent of foster care, poor kids prescribed antipsychotics get them for unaccepted uses, by Art Levine, *The Huffington Post*, April 30, 2015.
- Predicting violence is a work in progress, by David Brown, *The Washington Post*, January 3, 2013.
- Alaskan tackles mental health care reform, by Lisa Demer, *Anchorage Daily News*, November 6, 2005

    – Companion article: Lawyer says patients don't get fair hearings.

- Woman fights order to take drugs: ANTI-PSYCHOTICS: Faith Myers says decision to take medicine should be hers, by Lisa Demer, *Anchorage Daily News*, April 7, 2003.

Television and radio

I have also been on local television and radio a number of times. Television appearances include:

- Patient rights vs. treatment: A complex question, KTVA Channel 11, February 28, 2014.
- Ritalin gone wrong: Alaska Community News-KACN, February 25, 2013.
- *The Dan Fagan Show*, Fox4/KTBY, October 5, 2012.
- *Mind Over Meds* (4-part series), KTUU Channel 2, May 7–10, 2012.
- Lawyer takes on psychiatric industry for over-prescribing foster children, KTUU Channel 2, February 10, 2010.

There are links to most of the mainstream media in which PsychRights is featured in its Media Center webpage.[30]

At this point, I am well enough known that I sometimes get called about stories.

E-mail

Over the years, PsychRights has compiled an e-mail list of 2,500 people. This has proven to be a very good way to get information out, although, again, it is primarily to the choir. We try not to overburden people's mailboxes and do not send out more than ten e-mails or so a year. While e-mail may seem passé at this point, I think this e-mail list is a quite effective communication method, albeit preaching to the choir.

Talks

Since forming PsychRights in 2002, I have spoken dozens of times, both inside and outside Alaska. Outlines for many of the talks, and videos of some since 2012, can be found by clicking on my *curriculum vitae*.[31] While there are common elements in most of my talks, I try to tailor them to the particular audience.

Right after forming PsychRights in 2002, I "crashed" the annual rights conference of the National Association for Rights Protection and Advocacy (NARPA) held in Portland, Oregon, by renting a room to give an off-agenda presentation titled "Unwarranted Court Ordered Medication: A Call to Action" and distributing flyers for it at the conference.[32] I also brought a bunch of copies of *Mad in America* to give away to people who came to my talk. It could have been awkward. MindFreedom International was selling copies of *Mad in America*, and PsychRights giving away copies had the potential for causing problems for MindFreedom. However, it worked out quite well. NARPA was very gracious and because my talk was at the end of the conference, everyone who wanted *Mad in America* and could afford it had already purchased it from MindFreedom, and those who couldn't afford it received a free copy from PsychRights.

Psychiatry and the law

Before that 2002 trip to NARPA, I had never participated outside Alaska in what in the United States is called the "C/S/X" movement (Mental Health **C**onsumers/ Psychiatric **S**urvivors/e**X** Patients) because I didn't feel I had anything in particular to add to what so many people were doing nationally, and my efforts were better spent focused on Alaska. However, when I read *Mad in America*, I saw it as a roadmap for litigation against forced drugging based on it not being in people's best interest. *Mad in America* author Robert Whitaker, Dr. Loren Mosher, whose Soteria House study was described in *Mad in America*, and law professor Michael Perlin, the icon of mental health disability law, were all speaking and I wanted to meet them and see if I could establish a relationship with them. This ended up being wildly successful.

Dr. Mosher gave tremendous testimony in the *Myers* case just a few months later, which was cited by the Alaska Supreme Court in its 2006 decision holding that Alaska's forced drugging statute was unconstitutional. These cases happen very fast and I e-mailed Dr. Mosher as soon as I took the case to see if he would testify by telephone, and when I hadn't heard back, I called him the day before the trial. He told me he had just got back from Germany, was very tired, didn't have time to prepare and couldn't do it. When I said, "I understand," he said, "Okay, I'll do it." He gave terrific and enduring testimony. My favorite part of his testimony is when he said, "I find that people who are psychotic and not medicated are among the most interesting of all the customers one finds." This was after he had testified that in all of his many years of practice, and having probably the most experience of anyone in working with people who are psychotic and not on drugs, he had never had to involuntarily commit anyone:

> Now, if because of some altered state of consciousness, somebody is about to do themselves grievous harm or someone else grievous harm, well then, I would stop them in whatever way I needed to. I would probably prefer to do it with the police, but if it came to it, I guess I would do it. In my career I have never committed anyone. It just is—I make it my business to form the kind of relationship that the person will—that we can establish an ongoing treatment plan that is acceptable to both of us. And that way you avoid getting into the fight around whatever. And, you know, our job is to be healers, not fighters.[33]

Dr. Mosher died of cancer in Germany while undergoing experimental treatment for his cancer in July 2004, just 16 months after his testimony. I realized then that he was already very sick and had just come back from being treated in Germany when he testified in the *Myers* case. This illustrates what a wonderful person he was and why he is revered by psychiatric survivors/(ex-)users around the world. I treasure my brief time knowing him.

Since 2002, I have given talks at close to a dozen NARPA rights conferences. I have also given talks to a similar number of conferences put on by the International Society for Ethical Psychology and Psychiatry (ISEPP), which used to be known as the International Center for the Study of Psychology and Psychiatry (ICSPP).

In 2005, I gave a talk at the Alternatives Conference in Phoenix, Arizona, titled "How the Legal System Can Help Create a Recovery Culture in Mental Health Systems," and used it to present a paper that lays out the problem and a strategic approach to changing the mental illness system.[34] The Alternatives Conference is funded by the United States government and brings together around 1,000 mostly former and current mental health "consumers," many of whom are employed by the mental illness system. I used that title to get past the government censors. The "Transformation Triangle" was first introduced in this talk and paper and while it is over 10 years old, I think the principles still hold up.

I have spoken numerous other times outside Alaska, most notably for Amalie Days in Oslo, Norway, in 2010, PsychOUT in New York City in 2011, and as the 2012 Honoree at the Annual Meeting of the United States Chapter of the International Society for Psychological and Social Approaches to Psychosis (ISPS-US) in Chicago, Illinois. The PsychOut and ISPS talks are on the PsychRights YouTube Channel.

In Alaska, among others, I have spoken at a Senior Center, the Libertarian Party's state convention, to the Bartlett Democratic Club in Anchorage, and at the Wilda Marston Theater. I have gone into the lion's den and spoken at a National Alliance for Mental Illness annual meeting. I have spoken at numerous "consumer" conferences. I have also given a number of guest lectures at college and university classes, including to graduate students. In my view, these classes and non-mental health audiences are the most important, and I have found to my surprise that the information I present seems to be accepted, even though it is so far from what people have been led to believe.

Social media

Social media quintessentially exemplifies the preaching to the choir problem, yet can still be useful, especially for organizing purposes. It also has the potential for reaching the general public, bypassing traditional media. The Holy Grail of social media is to have posts go "viral," with millions of people viewing and sharing them, but we have not been able to make that happen so far.

I do have over 4,000 Facebook Friends at this point; probably about half of them are not PsychRights-related so that when I post public education items on my Timeline, these people are also being exposed to the information. After Facebook started allowing organizations to have pages, PsychRights created one, and now has about 1,300 "likes."

The utility of Facebook for effective public education purposes has proven elusive. Part of it is that Facebook has become fairly passé, even though (or maybe because) there are over 1 billion users worldwide. There is also the illusion of having an impact by "liking" and "sharing" posts. These are pretty meaningless in my view, except to the extent that people who are not normally exposed to the information receive it.

I got a Twitter account and then one for PsychRights, and for a while tried to "reward" followers by tweeting before e-mailing or posting on Facebook. That has fairly gone by the wayside as I can't spend that much time on social media. Also, I frankly don't seem to understand how to use Twitter to maximum effect. I don't really "get" Twitter. I am not an Instagram user, whatever that is.

I do think social media can be used as *part* of protest organizing. In fact, I think it can be so useful for this purpose, it is addressed as a separate topic: Network Against Psychiatric Assault.

Local events

PsychRights also puts on community events. For example, in 2011/2012, PsychRights publicly screened Daniel Mackler's films, *Take These Broken Wings* (2008), *Open Dialogue* (2011), and *Healing Homes* (2011),[35] and then I gave a presentation titled, "The Mental Health System: Who's Crazy?" These events were free and we promoted them to the general public. In November 2015, PsychRights, with the financial support of the Alaska Mental Health Trust Authority, brought up Laura Delano to speak on "Recovering Myself: A Talk about Journeying through the Mental Health System and Coming Back to Oneself." With the same grant from the Trust Authority, Dr. Peter Gøtzsche spoke on "Forced Admission and Treatment in Psychiatry Are Violations of Basic Human Rights and Must Be Abolished" in June 2016. In all of these, attendance was okay, but not terrific. However, Ms. Delano's talk was videoed and has been viewed over 5,000 times as of this writing, and the video of Dr. Gøtzsche almost 6,000.[36]

In December 2002, PsychRights brought up *Mad in America* author Robert Whitaker to speak to the Alaska Mental Health Board, the psychiatric hospital staff, and the community mental health directors' association about what he had found regarding the lack of benefit—even counterproductive effect—and great harm caused by long-term use of neuroleptics. I was on the Alaska Mental Health Board at the time, which is why I was able to arrange the talk. The most interesting reaction was at the Alaska Psychiatric Institute, which had a number of psychiatrists in attendance. I would characterize the overall reaction as something like, "Even if we agree with what you are saying (and we pretty much do), we wouldn't be allowed to do as you suggest." At the time, the idea that doctors would abandon their oath to do no harm so readily was striking to me. This was right after I founded PsychRights, but by now my opinion of the entire U.S. medical profession, let alone psychiatry, has gotten so low that I don't expect anything different.

Educating attorneys and judges

I previously pointed out that the judges and lawyers involved in psychiatric force believe that if the person being accused of being mentally ill weren't crazy, she would know that what the mental health system wants to do to her is good for her, and therefore they don't let her pesky rights get in the way. Thus, teaching them that involuntary psychiatric interventions are not good for the person is very important.

In 2003, PsychRights brought up mental health disability law expert, Professor Michael Perlin, and acclaimed author Robert Whitaker to put on a 2-day seminar for lawyers, judges, clinicians, and users and ex-users of psychiatry. Robert Whitaker started it off with his analysis of the lack of benefit from the long-term use of neuroleptics and the great deal of harm they are doing, to set the stage for Professor Perlin going through people's rights. Lawyers, judges, clinicians, and (ex-)users of psychiatry did attend and, afterwards, Professor Perlin made a point of telling me how unique (and good) it was for all of those different groups to be involved in the same seminar.

In 2008, I published the law review article, "Involuntary Commitment and Forced Psychiatric Drugging in the Trial Courts: Rights Violations as a Matter of Course" in the *Alaska Law Review*.[37] The *Alaska Law Review* goes to every attorney in Alaska, including judges, so I felt it was a good outlet for trying to educate attorneys and judges in Alaska. In the article, I tried to weave the science, primarily Robert Whitaker's work, with the legal aspects and incorporating how legal coercion is experienced by those against whom it is directed. For example, I cited expert testimony from a New Zealand peer I know, Sarah Porter, who happened to be in town during one of my cases:

Q. Now, you mentioned—I think you said that coercion creates problems. Could you describe those kind of problems?
A. Well, that's really about the fact that [there is] growing recognition—I think worldwide, but particularly in New Zealand, that coercion, itself, creates trauma and further distress for the person, and that that, in itself, actually undermines the benefits of the treatment that is being provided in a forced context. And so our aiming and teaching is to be able to support the person to resolve the issues without actually having to trample ... on the person's autonomy, or hound them physically or emotionally in doing so ...
Q. And have you seen success in that approach?
A. We have. It's been phenomenal, actually. ... I had high hopes that it would work, but I've ... been really impressed how well, in fact, it has worked.[38]

The law review article has only been cited a couple of times in other law review articles, and never in an appellate opinion, so that is something of a disappointment.

I have also spoken to what are called sections of the Alaska Bar Association on "Forced Psychiatric Drugging in Alaska" and "Remedying Medicaid Fraud for Psychiatric Drugs Given to Children and Youth through the Federal False Claims Act."

The most persuasive teaching to lawyers and judges, though, is to win appellate cases. Trial judges are obligated to follow these decisions (although they often don't in this area of the law) and lawyers use them on behalf of their clients. My first PsychRights appellate victory, *Myers*,[39] invalidated Alaska's forced drugging statute which provided that if the person was found to be incompetent, the hospital could drug him or her any way they wanted. PsychRights argued that in order to be constitutional, the government had to at least prove (a) it is in the person's best interest; and (b) there are no less intrusive alternatives. The Alaska Supreme Court agreed, but added the word "available" to the least restrictive alternative requirement. In *Bigley*,[40] the Alaska Supreme Court held that "available" means "feasible" and if the less intrusive alternative is feasible, the government has to provide it or let the person go.

In *Wetherhorn*,[41] the Alaska Supreme Court held that a person cannot be involuntarily committed for being gravely disabled unless the condition makes that person not "capable of surviving safely in freedom."[42] In *Wayne B.*,[43] the Alaska Supreme Court invalidated the Superior Court's decades-long practice of ignoring the rule that when a case is referred to a Master for a recommendation to the Superior Court, a transcript has to be prepared and filed so the Superior Court can determine whether the Master's recommendation should be approved.

> We conclude that it was [reversible error not to file a transcript]. We take a strict view of the transcript filing requirement because, as we noted in *Wetherhorn v. Alaska Psychiatric Institute*, involuntary commitment for a mental disorder is a "massive curtailment of liberty." Given the nature of the liberty interest at stake, it was critical that the superior court have full knowledge of the evidence that was said to justify committing Wayne B. to a mental institution.[44]

The Alaska Supreme Court also held that an acceptable alternative to filing a transcript is for the Superior Court Judge to listen to the recording of the hearing.[45] The *Wayne B.* decision illustrates a couple of things. First, that appellate courts tend to be far more concerned about actually following the statutes and protecting people's rights than the trial courts. The second is that the courts often don't follow the law in this area. I am pretty sure that no transcripts are being filed (the proceedings are usually secret) and the Superior Court Judges are not listening to the recordings of the hearings. In fact, shortly after *Wayne B.*, a judge said so on the record.

Most recently, in *Heather R.*,[46] the Supreme Court held that before a judge can order a person to be picked up by the police and taken for an involuntary psychiatric evaluation, the screening investigation required by the statute must be conducted, including interviewing the person if reasonably possible.

Mad in America website

I also write for the Mad in America website (www.madinamerica.com), primarily on legal topics related to PsychRights' mission, but sometimes on alternatives to mainstream mental health "treatment."[47] To say that Mad in America is an extremely informative site is a gross understatement. At the same time, it is fair to say that Mad in America mainly reaches people who largely believe the same things about current psychiatric treatment as outlined here. In other words, its audience is mostly the choir. Still, it is good to get information out to the choir. Articles on Mad in America have included:

- Has the FDA Abandoned Its Off-Label Promotion Ban?
- Lessons from Soteria-Alaska
- PsychRights' Letter to the President's Task Force on Gun Violence
- The Illegality of Forced Drugging and Electroshock
- A Three Pronged Approach to Mental Health System Change.

Journals and book chapters

In addition to this chapter, I have written chapters for a couple of books as well as a few journal and newsletter articles:[48]

- Legal Issues Surrounding the Psychiatric Drugging of Children and Youth, in Sharna Olfman and Brent Dean Robbins (Eds.) (2012), *Drugging Our Children: How Profiteers Are Pushing Antipsychotics on Our Youngest, and What We Can Do to Stop It* (Childhood in America series), Santa Barbara, CA, Denver, CO, and Oxford: Praeger.
- Το χρήμα, τα δικαιώματα και οι εναλλακτικές. Απαίτηση νομικών δικαιωμάτων ως μέσον για την επέκταση μη ιατρικών εναλλακτικών. In Peter Lehmann, Peter Stastny, and Anna Emmanouelidou (Eds.) (2012), *Αντί της ψυχιατρικής – εναλλακτικές μορφές συνάντησης με τον ψυχικό πόνο* (pp. 264–276), Thessaloniki, Greece: Edition Nissides.
- Ethical and Moral Obligations Arising from Revelations of Pharmaceutical Company Dissembling, *Ethical and Human Psychology and Psychiatry, 12*(1), 22–29 (2010).
- Involuntary Commitment and Forced Psychiatric Drugging in the Trial Courts: Rights Violations as a Matter of Course, 25 *Alaska Law Review* 51 (2008).
- Rights and Alternatives: Enforcing Legal Rights as a Mechanism for Creating Non-Medical Model Alternatives, in P. Lehmann and P. Stastny (Eds.) (2007), *Alternatives Beyond Psychiatry* (pp. 308–317), Berlin, Eugene, OR, and Shrewsbury, UK: Peter Lehmann Publishing.
- Psychiatrists' Failure to Inform: Is There Substantial Financial Exposure?, *Ethical Human Psychology and Psychiatry, 9*(2), 117–125 (2007).

YouTube videos

I wanted PsychRights to produce and post videos for a long time, but I wouldn't do it until we were able to get good sound. For us, good sound is absolutely critical and I think it is pointless to post a video with bad sound. In fact, to me, for what PsychRights is trying to do, having good-quality sound is far more important than having good-quality video. In 2012, PsychRights was donated a modestly priced video camera with a remote microphone, and since then has produced about

80 videos that have almost 95,000 views. These consist mainly of talks I have given or that PsychRights has sponsored, and of people speaking at Network Against Psychiatric Assault protests.

Protests/Network Against Psychiatric Assault

Public protests can be an effective way to get our message out. PsychRights has supported such efforts since its inception, starting with the Fast for Freedom in Mental Health, also known as the Hunger Strike, organized by MindFreedom International in August 2003. MindFreedom challenged the American Psychiatric Association (APA), the National Alliance on Mental Illness (NAMI), and the United States Surgeon General to produce any reliable scientific evidence establishing, among other things, that what gets diagnosed as major mental illnesses are biologically based brain diseases. The Surgeon General didn't respond, but both the APA and NAMI foolishly did. The APA's response[49] was thoroughly debunked[50] and the APA then essentially admitted that in 100 years of looking, they hadn't found a biological cause, but are sure they will by continuing to look.[51] The NAMI's response was an attack on the Hunger Strikers.[52] Psychiatrist Duncan Double gave a presentation on the Hunger Strike at the 2004 ICSPP conference, titled "Biomedical Bias of the American Psychiatric Association."[53] The Hunger Strike was reported in *The Washington Post* and some local papers, but the media coverage wasn't what it might have been.

MindFreedom has also organized many protests at the annual meetings of the APA, which PsychRights supports as much as it can. I have participated in a number of them, with the 2012 protest resulting in some media coverage, including the first of a four-part series on the local NBC affiliate, called *Mind Over Meds*.[54]

For the 2012 APA protest, a number of organizations, including MindFreedom, PsychRights, the Freedom Center, the Center for the Human Rights of Users and Survivors of Psychiatry, and Speak Out Against Psychiatry formed an umbrella organization, now known as the Network Against Psychiatric Assault, to organize protests. The idea is to use Facebook to organize and document protests. It is designed for all of the protests against psychiatry around the world to be organized and aggregated. This way, it will show that there are a lot of protests, adding up to an impressive effort as well as a way for the international psychiatric survivor community to support local protests. It is possible to have more than a single organization hosting the same Facebook event, so that the sponsoring organization or person can organize and host it and gain the advantage from it also being a Network Against Psychiatric Assault event. There have been about 80 Network Against Psychiatric Assault events since it was launched in 2012, including 24 protests against electroshock on the same day, May 16, 2015, all over the world.

As with many things, the vitality of the Network Against Psychiatric Assault varies as people's efforts wax and wane. At this time of writing, the Network Against Psychiatric Assault has mostly devolved into a typical Facebook group with postings about psychiatric abuses, but the infrastructure is there to organize and document protests to the extent that people want to use it for its intended purpose. The list of protests and the documentation of the protests are pretty impressive in my view, demonstrating that it can work as intended.

Conclusions

In evaluating all of these efforts, two contradictory conclusions emerge. First, there is no doubt that many people have greatly benefited from these educational efforts. I have received a large number of communications attesting to it. This includes people who are greatly comforted in finding out that they are not alone in their views about psychiatry and being able to access scientific evidence to support what they have come to know. People have been given hope and found a way out of psychiatry. Second, at the macro level, the effort has fundamentally failed to break through to the mainstream. If psychiatry's murder of Rebecca Riley and Gabriel Myers (young children who died from psychotropic drugs) hasn't done it. If the medical kidnapping of Justina Pelletier (and others) hasn't done it. If the fact that these drugs are reducing the life spans of people in the public mental health system in the United States by 25 years hasn't done it. If the rate of disability of people diagnosed with mental illness increasing six-fold since the introduction of the supposed miracle drug Thorazine (chlorpromazine) in 1954 hasn't done it. If the massive psychiatric drugging of children, especially children in poverty, hasn't done it, I don't know what will. What I do know, is that we have to keep trying.

Notes

1 James B. Gottstein (2008). Involuntary Commitment and Forced Psychiatric Drugging in the Trial Courts: Rights Violations as a Matter of Course. 25 *Alaska Law Review* 51. Available on the Internet at http://psychrights.org/Research/Legal/25AkLRev51Gottstein2008.pdf
2 347 U.S. 483.
3 The definition of "inmate" is a person confined to an institution such as a prison or hospital.
4 National Association of State Mental Health Program Directors (2006, October). *Morbidity and Mortality in People with Serious Mental Illness.* Available on the Internet at http://psychrights.org/Articles/2006NASMHPDonEarlyDeath.pdf
5 Jeffrey A. Lieberman, T. Scott Stroup, Joseph P. McEvoy, Marvin S. Swartz, Robert A. Rosenheck, Diana O. Perkins . . . John K. Hsiao (2005). Effectiveness of Antipsychotic Drugs in Patients with Chronic Schizophrenia, for the Clinical Antipsychotic Trials of Intervention Effectiveness (CATIE) Investigators. *New England Journal of Medicine, 353*, 1209–1223.
6 The graphs and charts (Figures 9.2–9.4, Table 9.1) were supplied by Robert Whitaker, author of *Mad in America* (2nd ed.; Basic Books, 2010) and *Anatomy of an Epidemic* (Broadway Books, 2010).
7 Peter R. Breggin (2008). *Brain Disabling Treatments in Psychiatry.* New York: Springer Publishing Co. Robert Whitaker (2010). *Anatomy of an Epidemic.* New York: Broadway Books.
8 Peter R. Breggin (2008). *Brain Disabling Treatments in Psychiatry.* New York: Springer Publishing Co.

9 J. Bola and L. Mosher (2003). Treatment of Acute Psychosis without Neuroleptics: Two-Year Outcomes from the Soteria Project. *The Journal of Nervous and Mental Disease*, 191(4), pp. 219–229.
10 See: http://criticalthinkrx.org/module.asp?moduleid=12#
11 *Humphrey v. Cady*, 405 U.S. 504, 509 (1972) (involuntary commitment is a "massive curtailment of liberty").
12 *Kansas v. Crane*, 534 U.S. 407, 409–10, 122 S.Ct. 867, 869 (2002).
13 *Cooper v. Oklahoma*, 517 U.S. 348, 116 S.Ct. 1373, 1383 (1996).
14 *Addington v. Texas*, 99 S.Ct. 1804, 1811 (1979).
15 See James B. Gottstein (2008). Involuntary Commitment and Forced Psychiatric Drugging in the Trial Courts: Rights Violations as a Matter of Course. 25 *Alaska Law Review* 51, 90–93. Available on the Internet at http://psychrights.org/Research/Legal/25AkLRev51 Gottstein2008.pdf
16 539 U.S. 166 (2003).
17 539 U.S. at 180–181.
18 Information, including the model complaint, can be found on the Internet at http://psychrights.org/Education/ModelQuiTam/ModelQuiTam.htm
19 Michael L. Perlin (1993/1994). The ADA and Persons with Mental Disabilities: Can Sanist Attitudes Be Undone? 8 *Journal of Law and Health* 15, 33–34.
20 In reality, the lawyers assigned to represent people faced with forced drugging or electroshock are there to check off the box that the person has legal representation, not to zealously advocate for their clients' rights. This is a violation of lawyers' ethics rules.
21 For the Mosholder Report, see www.psychrights.org/Research/Digest/AntiDepressants/Mosholder/MosholderReportwo24.pdf (version "leaked" to PsychRights); and www.psychrights.org/Research/Digest/AntiDepressants/Mosholder/MosholderReport.pdf (the version that the FDA was forced to make public after it had been published by PsychRights [and others]).
22 For the Allen Jones Report, see www.psychrights.org/Drugs/AllenJonesTMAPJanuary20.pdf
23 J. Lenzer (2004). Whistleblower Removed from Job for Talking to the Press. *British Medical Journal*, 328, 1153.
24 See: www.ohchr.org/en/NewsEvents/Pages/DisplayNews.aspx?NewsID=16583&LangID=E
25 See Peter R. Breggin (2008). *Medication Madness*. New York: St. Martin's Press.
26 Links to the articles and other documents referred to in this section can be obtained from the Internet at http://psychrights.org/States/Alaska/CaseXX.htm#NYTimes
27 This can be found on the Internet at http://psychrights.org/States/Alaska/CaseOne/30-Day/ExhDGraceJacksonZyprexaAffidavit.pdf
28 Detailed information on the *Myers v. Alaska Psychiatric Institute* case, including other court documents, can be found on the Internet at http://psychrights.org/States/Alaska/CaseOne.htm
29 Available on the Internet at http://lawprofessors.typepad.com/tortsprof/2006/12/judge_tries_to_.html
30 See: http://psychrights.org/PR/PR.htm
31 See: http://psychrights.org/about/JGVita.pdf
32 This can be found on the Internet at www.psychrights.org/calltoaction.htm
33 Transcript of Record at 176, *In re Myers v. Alaska Psychiatric Inst.*, No. 3AN 03-277 P/S (Alaska Super. Ct. 2003), available at http://psychrights.org/States/Alaska/CaseOne/30-Day/3-5and10-03transcript.htm
34 The paper can be found at http://psychrights.org/Education/Alternatives05/RoleofLitigation.pdf
35 Daniel subsequently released a fourth film, *Coming off Psych Drugs* (2013). All Daniel Mackler's films were produced by himself in the United States.
36 See: https://youtu.be/R0dQSdoTrmY

37 James B. Gottstein (2008). Involuntary Commitment and Forced Psychiatric Drugging in the Trial Courts: Rights Violations as a Matter of Course, 25 *Alaska Law Review* 51. Available on the Internet at http://psychrights.org/Research/Legal/25AkLRev51Gottstein2008.pdf
38 Proceedings for 30-Day Commitment Hearing at 73–81, *In The Necessity for the Hospitalization of W.S.B.*, No. 3AN-07-1064 PR (D. Alaska Sept. 5, 2007), available at http://psychrights.org/states/Alaska/CaseXX/3AN-07-1064PS/070905TBBTranscript.pdf
39 *Myers v. Alaska Psychiatric Institute*, 138 P3d 238 (Alaska 2006), available on the Internet at http://psychrights.org/States/Alaska/CaseOne/MyersOpinion.pdf
40 *Bigley v. Alaska Psychiatric Institute*, 208 P3d 168 (Alaska 2009), available on the Internet at http://psychrights.org/States/Alaska/CaseXX/S13116/090522BigleyvAPIsp-6374.pdf
41 *Wetherhorn v. Alaska Psychiatric Institute*, 156 P.3d 371 (Alaska 2007), available on the Internet at http://psychrights.org/States/Alaska/CaseFour/WetherhornIsp-6091.pdf
42 In another place, the standard was described as being "a level of incapacity that prevents the person in question from being able to live safely outside of a controlled environment."
43 *Wayne B. v. Alaska Psychiatric Institute*, 192 P.3d 989 (Alaska 2008), available on the Internet at http://psychrights.org/States/Alaska/CaseSix/080829WayneBOpinion.pdf
44 *Wayne B. v. Alaska Psychiatric Institute*, 192 P.3d at 991, footnote omitted.
45 *Wayne B. v. Alaska Psychiatric Institute*, 192 P.3d at 991.
46 *In the Matter of the Necessity for the Hospitalization of Heather R.*, 366 P.3d 530 (Alaska 2016), available on the Internet at http://psychrights.org/States/Alaska/HR/160129Opinion.pdf
47 Links to my articles can be found on the Internet at http://www.madinamerica.com/author/jgottstein/
48 Links to most of these can be found in my *curriculum vitae* available on the Internet at http://psychrights.org/about/JGVita.pdf
49 Available on the Internet at http://psychrights.org/education/HungerStrike/030812APAResponse.txt
50 Available on the Internet at http://psychrights.org/education/HungerStrike/panel.pdf
51 The APA's response can be found on the Internet at http://psychrights.org/Education/HungerStrike/030926APAStatement.htm
52 This response can be found on the Internet at http://psychrights.org/education/HungerStrike/NAMIResponse.txt
53 Available on the Internet at http://psychrights.org/Articles/DuncanDoublebiomedicalbias.htm
54 *Mind Over Meds* can be found at https://youtu.be/9-1_4FjKuXU

10

HUMAN RIGHTS AND CRITICAL PSYCHOLOGY

Beth Greenhill and Laura Golding

> There are some things in our society, some things in our world, to which we ... must always be maladjusted if we are to be people of good will. We must never adjust ourselves to racial discrimination and racial segregation. We must never adjust ourselves to religious bigotry. We must never adjust ourselves to economic conditions that take necessities from the many to give luxuries to the few. We must never adjust ourselves to the madness of militarism, and the self-defeating effects of physical violence. ... There comes a time when one must take a stand that is neither safe, nor politic, nor popular. But one must take it because it is right.
>
> *(Martin Luther King, addressing the American Psychological Association, 1967)*

Human rights and clinical psychology

Clinical psychology as a discipline sails within complex, challenging and competing contextual waters. Against this background, human rights-based approaches can provide an anchor to enable trainee clinical psychologists to critically conceptualise legal, moral and regulatory currents and assist them to navigate disparate areas of policy and practice. Legally, most clinical psychologists in the UK have a 'positive obligation' to promote rights, through their employment by the National Health Service (NHS) or in services commissioned by other public authorities (Human Rights Act, 1998). Key legislative frameworks, such as the Mental Health Act (1983, amended 2007) and Mental Capacity Act (2005), are rooted in human rights principles (Department of Health, 2015). In terms of values, as for other professions, clinical psychology's code of ethics is informed by human rights (British Psychological Society, 2009). In addition, the regulatory body for the NHS, the Care Quality Commission (CQC), also takes a human rights-based approach (HRBA) to evaluating services (CQC, 2014).

Views differ on whether clinical psychology has a helpful or potentially damaging role in relation to human rights. For some, there is a sense that the underlying values of rights and psychology might be shared (Kinderman, 2007; Butchard & Greenhill, 2015; see also Mann, Lazzarini, Gostin, & Gruskin, 1997). While declared values alone may not be sufficient for psychologists to make a difference, progressive values are almost certainly a necessary precursor to progressive action (see Newnes, 1996). Psychological theory can be seen as an enabler of rights attainment through reducing the gap between law and practice (Kinderman & Butler, 2006). Other perspectives draw attention to the ways in which clinical psychologists have reinforced inequalities through uncritical practices which fail to challenge the social relations maintaining injustice and rights abuses:

> In their efforts to address the psychological impacts of injustices against humanity, clinical psychologists, often with the best intentions, have applied psychology in a way which has continued to ignore the relationship between the individual and the historical, political and social contexts which have shaped their lives and given rise to their distress.
>
> *(Patel, 2003, p. 16)*

Human rights as a construct in healthcare services occupy a broad and thought-provoking space; corporate enough for the adoption of an HRBA by some NHS Trusts (Dyer, 2015) and to act as the regulatory framework for the CQC, and yet sufficiently radical to challenge power relationships and to demand a reflexive, historical accounting of clinical psychology theory and practice. It is perhaps this fluidity and flexibility which allow rights-based approaches to provide a forum for ethical dilemmas and debates and to act as a particularly valuable framework for clinical psychology training that we will describe and explore in this chapter.

Human rights-based approaches for healthcare professionals

Human rights-based approaches aim to promote human rights through empowering rights holders to claim their rights and by holding organisations to account in delivering their human rights obligations. Taking an HRBA operationalises the core principles of complex legislative human rights frameworks at a practical level, both in terms of the human rights standards to be achieved and the processes through which this is facilitated. Although well-established within the field of international development, the explicit use of HRBAs within the UK healthcare system is relatively novel (Department of Health & British Institute of Human Rights, 2008; Curtice & Exworthy, 2010).

The basic principles of a human rights-based approach can be summarised through the 'PANEL' principles (British Institute of Human Rights, 2013). Within PANEL, 'p' represents participation, 'a' accountability, 'n' non-discrimination, 'e' empowerment and 'l' legality. These principles have been applied to service development and practice, acting as a filter to highlight where progressive changes are needed (Greenhill & Whitehead, 2011; Roberts et al., 2013; Montenegro & Greenhill, 2014). They have also been applied to policy. For example, the multi-agency guidance on reducing the use of restraint (Department of Health, 2014) applies the PANEL principles to positive behavioural support (Bailey, Ridley, & Greenhill, 2010). The principles can also be applied to review curricula and practice within professional healthcare training. So, for example, as human rights-based approaches emphasise citizen participation and empowerment, taking a rights-based approach to training favours a culture in which service users, carers and experts by experience actively shape the curriculum, research and clinical activities of the programme, within the constraints of regulatory body approval and professional body accreditation processes. Table 10.1 provides an example of this as applied to the training of clinical psychologists.

TABLE 10.1 Examples of the application of human rights principles in the delivery of UK clinical psychology training

Human rights principle	Description of principle	Application to clinical psychology training (examples)
Participation	Enabling meaningful participation of all key people and stakeholders	• Use of participatory learning methods in the taught curriculum • Increased involvement of experts by experience in all aspects of the programme through aiming to use co-production as a means to maximise participation and promote the most equal distribution of power • Focus on trainee representation in programme committee and structures • Actively seeking, and listening to, feedback from trainees on all aspects of the programme
Accountability	Ensuring clear accountability, identifying who has legal duties and practical responsibility for a human rights approach	• Historical accountability: an approach to the delivery of teaching which includes critiques of psychology as a discipline and acknowledges and describes the uses and abuses of power in the history of clinical psychology as a profession • Legal accountability: a focus on trainees understanding their legal responsibilities and on learning how to use the law and policy to support progressive and safe practice • Professional accountability: 'gate-keeping' such that applicants selected for training demonstrate human rights values and those who complete the programme are both 'fit to practise' and understand the importance of power, diversity and inclusivity to that practice

(continued)

TABLE 10.1 Examples of the application of human rights principles in the delivery of UK clinical psychology training *(continued)*

Human rights principle	Description of principle	Application to clinical psychology training (examples)
Non-discrimination	Discrimination avoided, attention paid to groups made vulnerable	• Widening access to clinical psychology training in selection • Promoting clinical psychology services which address health inequalities and issues of accessibility • A focus within the taught curriculum on the experience of specific groups and theories explaining inequality • Facilitating critical thinking about the theory base underpinning clinical psychology
Empowerment	Empowerment of staff and service users with knowledge, skills and commitment to realising human rights	• Creating links with community organisations. • Encouraging and enabling a community psychology approach • A focus on recovery and non-stigmatising approaches to mental health • Co-production with experts by experience
Legality	Expressly apply human rights laws, particularly the Human Rights Act	• Focussing on clinically relevant human rights-related topics in teaching. • Ensuring that trainees are competent in risk assessment, safeguarding, the Mental Health Act and Mental Capacity Act

Clinical psychology training at the University of Liverpool

This chapter draws on our experience as clinical psychologists and clinical psychology trainers at the University of Liverpool in the UK. It includes examples of how we are using a human rights-based approach to encourage and enable our students (trainee clinical psychologists) to think critically about psychology and to conceptualise the legal, moral and regulatory frameworks, enabling them to navigate disparate areas of policy and practice. To contextualise this, first we provide a summary of UK clinical psychology training, followed by a brief overview of the University of Liverpool Doctorate in Clinical Psychology training programme.

A recent estimate suggests that there are 11,889 clinical psychologists registered with the UK's Health & Care Professions Council (HCPC) (Longwill, 2015). Estimates suggest that there were fewer than 121 clinical psychologists working in England and Wales in 1950 (Hall, Pilgrim, & Turpin, 2015). In the UK, then, the profession of clinical psychology is relatively new and has rapidly expanded in numbers over several decades. A comprehensive account of the history of the profession is given by Hall et al. (2015) in their edited volume *Clinical Psychology in*

Britain: Historical Perspectives. It might be noted that Hall et al.'s edited book only makes one reference to human rights in its index. This is in the context of human rights and international solidarity, and focusses on the psychological implications of systematic human rights violations, referencing the work of Nimisha Patel (e.g. Patel, 2003) in a chapter by Melluish, Latchford and Marks (2015).

The roots of the profession of clinical psychology in the UK are closely linked to the creation and development of the NHS (Lavender & Turpin, 2015). Clinical psychology training in the UK today is funded by the NHS. The number of training places commissioned each year is, therefore, determined by workforce demands in the NHS. The first post-graduate clinical psychology training programme began at the Institute of Psychiatry in London in 1947. Development of the work of clinical psychologists from being primarily the administrators of psychological tests (though the Tavistock Clinic course focussed on psychoanalytic ideas) resulted in a training of 12 months that expanded to 2 years in response to the rapid development and expansion of the work of clinical psychologists who started to use behaviour therapy techniques which led to a substantial broadening of the psychologist's role. This resulted, in the 1950s and 1960s, in post-graduate training increasing to 2 years' duration and then to 3 years at doctorate level for all UK programmes in the early 1990s.

Pilgrim and Patel (2015) note the influence of British culture on the development of the profession of clinical psychology during the 20th century:

> [T]he peculiarities of the British context, for example, its empiricism, its faith in eugenics, its policy of 'muddling through' and its obdurate postcolonial white racism, were embedded in some universal processes. Psychology, the world over, is contested and so the diverse character of British clinical psychology has been in part about that universal feature of epistemological contestation.
>
> *(Pilgrim & Patel, 2015, p. 62)*

There are currently 32 clinical psychology training programmes in the UK. While every programme must meet the requirements of the standards of the Health & Care Professions Council (HCPC) and the British Psychological Society (BPS), each course has its own distinct flavour and focus.

The University of Liverpool's Doctorate in Clinical Psychology training programme is one of the oldest in the UK. It began in 1961 and, since then, approximately 700 qualified clinical psychologists have graduated from the programme. It began as a 2-year programme at Master's degree level and was subsequently re-established, in 1991, as a Doctorate in Clinical Psychology in response to a not uncontroversial national initiative led by the BPS to strengthen post-graduate training programmes in clinical psychology. The current 3-year doctorate programme is approved by the UK regulatory body for clinical psychologists, the HCPC, and accredited by the BPS.

As a programme with long roots at the university and one which took a relatively traditional approach to training, recent years have seen a shift towards a more critical approach with a particular emphasis on the involvement of experts by experience in all aspects of the programme. Consistent with this is the movement towards delivery of the programme within a human rights framework. We aim to co-produce much of the programme's content and delivery with experts by experience. This is consistent with the increasing emphasis on advocating more equal distributions of power for service users and carers in UK healthcare services in recent years. This has led to the promotion of services that are co-designed and co-produced (Boyle & Harris, 2009; Needham & Carr, 2009). Co-production is best understood as delivering public services in a way which works to reduce power inequalities in relationships between professionals and people using services, their families and their communities. This approach recognises people as assets, values capabilities differently, promotes reciprocity and aims to remove 'them' and 'us' distinctions (Needham & Carr, 2009).

Pedagogical approach

Human rights education is not often considered within the training of healthcare professionals, although there are honourable exceptions; for example, within occupational therapy (Crawford, Aplin, & Rodger, 2016) and some medical schools in the USA (Cotter et al., 2009). This is despite the fact that most of the professions allied to healthcare have made some commitment to human rights through the codes of their professional body (e.g. World Federation of Occupational Therapists, 2006; Royal College of Nursing, 2012). Recent attempts to develop human rights teaching resources for clinical psychologists (Butchard et al., 2016) and a review of the relevant literature suggest that pedagogical approaches to human rights education have a number of key features. Arguably, teaching on human rights should particularly demonstrate human rights values, not only in the content covered, but also in the pedagogical approach.

The pedagogy of human rights teaching is a hotly contested topic. Meintjies (1997, p. 65) describes human rights education as being "unique as a pedagogical objective goal" which "differs markedly from the goals of other areas of conventionally defined education", in empowering the participants through critical thinking. This requires an active, experiential learning model ("an empowering pedagogy" [p. 65]) with learners who are consciously involved in the creation and integration of knowledge and experience. For Meintjies, this also necessitates drawing upon Freire's (1993) concept of a 'problem posing education'. Freire argues that for education to be liberating for those without or with less power, it must include them as active agents in the educational process. For trainee clinical psychologists, this also requires taking a critical stance in relation to clinical psychology's history and purpose, and developing a deeper awareness of socio-cultural perspectives.

The literature suggests that human rights education involves several key elements: basic human rights literacy (history, core concepts, documents, substantive provision, knowledge about the institutions and practices of modern human rights); attitudinal change including promoting an attitude of solidarity; dialogue and reflection aimed to help students clarify values; developing an understanding of rights; and the teaching of programmes and techniques directed towards empowerment of others (Meintjies, 1997). Recommendations for human rights education for health include sharing a three-tiered model of the relationship between health and human rights, outlining how health policies and practices impact on human rights; how severe human rights violations impact on health; and the interplay between the promotion and protection of rights and of health (Mann et al., 1997; Patel, 2003). There is also a strong emphasis on an interdisciplinary and collaborative pedagogical approach, enabling participants with health expertise to liaise with human rights experts in their professional setting (Mann et al., 1997):

> So that each student knows the concepts of human rights thinking and so as to be capable of critical analysis of research and writing on human rights, to engage in a meaningful dialogue with persons working in human rights . . . and to know how to use human rights analysis to help identify and resolve problems.
>
> *(Mann et al., 1997, p. 335)*

There are two particular challenges and tensions within clinical psychology with regard to the pedagogical approach taken. Training is the gateway to a considerable change in the power and status of the trainee. While the flow of power between trainee and service users is complex (Smail, 2005), arguably, becoming a trainee, irrespective of the power attached to other aspects of trainees' multifaceted identities, elevates the trainee's structural power in relation to service recipients while in training. The curriculum, therefore, needs to acknowledge and encourage critical awareness and an examination of the power inequalities inherent in clinical psychology's disciplinary praxis (see Newnes, Chapter 3, this volume), from the beginning of the training programme. Power-mapping may be a way in which the ebb and flow of power can be brought more fully into awareness (Hagan & Smail, 1997). Despite the impact of the 'new public management' (Gruening, 2001) and service constraints on the freedom of professionals, trainees graduate from their training with the title 'Doctor', earn a good salary in the NHS compared to most non-medical NHS employees, and inevitably occupy positions of power, particularly with service recipients and many staff. The clinical psychology training curriculum, therefore, needs to engage with the potential conflict arising from the development of a professional identity and a consequent increase in personal and structural power. This shift has the potential to change the place of the developing professional in the power relationships, distancing them from the factors which promote a sustained attention to inequality and difference. The onus on the newly qualified clinical psychologist career-long is to use their power wisely, and to resist being seduced by power in ways that lead them to misuse their position (it might be noted here that Smail sees power as using *us* rather than *vice versa*: see, for example, Smail, 2005).

Our experience suggests that, as for all healthcare professionals, poor practice and abuse can arise both from acts of omission as well as acts of commission. The challenge for us, as trainers, is how to train clinical psychologists so they use their power wisely and are fully aware of the changes that occur, during and by dint of their training, in their relationship with power. This includes taking a critical stance to their profession and their work, and being critical activists and citizens in all senses, rather than passive deliverers of psychology within the healthcare system.

Related to this position, and unique to UK clinical psychologists, is the impact of entering a career in the NHS with the title 'Doctor'. There remain different perspectives regarding the utility and meaning of the title of 'Doctor' for clinical psychologists and a range of levels of comfort/discomfort with this. Providing space within clinical training to explore this, as an overt example of the shift in power, is crucial. This leads directly on to the second challenge that arises – that human rights education is often about self-empowerment. Thought, therefore, also needs to be given to how developing professionals engage with this without either resorting to paternalism or self-aggrandisement.

Arguably, a genuine commitment to co-production (Boyle & Harris, 2009) flows from the emphasis on empowerment and participation within a human rights-based approach (Roberts et al., 2013; Butchard & Greenhill, 2015; Montenegro & Greenhill, 2014) and has the potential to ground healthcare professionals in training, such as clinical psychologists, as their structural positioning changes. Co-production aims to disrupt the power relationships of service provider and service user, to involve both in equal partnerships of service design and delivery. Although originally advocated at least in part as a solution to cuts in statutory funding, co-production does offer a model of shared working which exceeds that (Needham & Carr, 2009) proposed by most other models of carer and service-user participation; for example, consultation, informing, partnership and delegation (Arnstein, 1969). Crucially, it also provides a basis for transcending the artificial 'them and us' divisions which can permeate and restrict the partnership between providers and users of services. The BPS and the HCPC both state that service-user involvement should be an integral part of the education and training of clinical psychologists (British Psychological Society, 2014; Health & Care Professions Council, 2014).

In summary, then, the optimum learning environment for human rights education emphasises empowerment through learner participation and critical thinking; praxis through problem-based methods – perhaps to the extent of activism; goes beyond cognitive learning and stresses lifelong learning and development through continuing professional development.

An example: human rights initiatives within the University of Liverpool's Doctorate in Clinical Psychology programme

Recent developments within the Liverpool programme have advanced the human rights-based approach through key, interwoven, strands. These include developing our capacity to work alongside experts by experience and developing our ability to better reflect as a profession on our own mental health and capacity to experience significant distress. This all enables us to explicitly work to promote rights, develop our capacity to reflect on power relationships, minimise stigma, promote multidisciplinary working and develop community links.

In general terms, in recent years, the Liverpool programme has been much more explicit about expressing its functions within a human rights framework. So, for example, the 'Annual Review' day hosted by the programme offers the opportunity to outline the direction of travel for the coming year, and to review, with experts by experience and NHS colleagues, the year that has passed. The 2015 Annual Programme Review Day had an explicitly human rights theme, involving a keynote speech from Nimisha Patel; a drama production about child sexual exploitation; a presentation from a clinical psychologist working locally with older people, Sarah Butchard, describing her work on human rights; and presentations from trainees involved in developing innovative human rights resources with the Equality and Human Rights Commission and the British Institute of Human Rights. All participants were asked to consider, whatever their role, three ways in which they would be taking the PANEL principles forward. Consistent with this direction of travel, the 2016 Annual Programme Review Day was focussed on community psychology, community connections and activism.

The Liverpool programme has also applied human rights-based approaches to the main functions of the programme (selection, clinical, academic and research), which are discussed in detail below.

Selection

The need for accountability is nowhere more evident than in selection processes for healthcare training. Following publication of the Francis Inquiry report (2013) which examined the causes of the failings in care at Mid Staffordshire NHS Foundation Trust between 2005 and 2009, NHS employers, including those in the training community, are mandated to include 'values-based recruitment' (VBR) in attracting and selecting potential candidates. The Liverpool programme took the opportunity presented by VBR to discuss our ethos, arriving at the values which seemed distinctive to the programme, including the 'PANEL' principles. Values-based recruitment is probably most effective in recruitment through structured interviews, selection centres using work exercises, and in situational judgement tests (Patterson et al., 2014) and so we have introduced human rights dilemmas as part of the interviewing process. Based on Kohlberg's famous moral reasoning tests (Kohlberg, 1984), the dilemmas, presented in the form of vignettes, aim to explore the quality of candidates' ethical reasoning in situations in which there is no clear 'right' answer.

We have also continued to build upon the involvement of service users and carers in selection interview panels. Although experts by experience have, for a long time, had an equal role on the programme in shortlisting, in developing the questions for interviews and in conducting the interviews, to date, the rating framework had been devised by psychologists. Members of our experts by experience steering panel were asked to define 'what makes a good psychologist'. Thematic analysis of their responses suggested that the attributes of psychologists which are valued by service users and carers include being 'trustworthy', 'friendly' and 'warm'. These attributes have since been incorporated into the rating sheets used by all panel members. Experts by experience also make a significant contribution to the new open day for potential applicants to the programme, and preliminary evaluation suggests that this has been identified by some attendees as significant in their decision to apply to the Liverpool programme.

Expert by experience involvement in the selection of staff has created interesting hurdles to straddle. Personal experience of distress is now included among 'desirable' experiences and through liaison with university human resources colleagues, recent staff interviews have included a service user or carer as an equal member of the panel.

Teaching and assessment

The academic component of teaching on the Liverpool programme has provided particularly exciting opportunities for change. While this remains a work in progress, across the curriculum, we have developed our capacity for participation through introducing systems for tracking levels of involvement and doubling the number of teaching sessions co-facilitated by experts by experience. The involvement of experts by experience in clinical assessment teaching has been carefully nurtured by colleagues who have integrated feedback from experts by experience into actor role plays to support trainees' developing interviewing skills. Guidelines for responding to co-facilitated teaching sessions have been adapted from colleagues at the University of Nottingham (Tickle, personal communication) to support trainees, staff and experts by experience in questioning their assumptions about identities and in respecting different sources of expertise within teaching sessions.

Participatory learning methods have been woven into the curriculum, again, with increased involvement of experts by experience, within a newly developed clinical health psychology Enquiry Based Learning (EBL) teaching unit. In addition, through funding from the Equality and Human Rights Commission, we were able to pilot an innovative educational toolkit using EBL methods to develop trainees' understandings of human rights in response to case studies (Butchard et al., 2016); this is now being delivered in the first year of training. Lectures by Dave Pilgrim exploring the history of the profession have helped to establish a tone of critical, reflexive thinking at the beginning of the first year. This progresses as a strong theme throughout the 3 years and is further developed by a day's teaching in the third year delivered by Craig Newnes on 'Clinical Psychology: A Critical Examination' (Newnes, 2014).

Research

Colleagues within the research team have worked with experts by experience to identify meaningful opportunities for increased involvement in the trainee research cycle (INVOLVE, 2016), consistent with calls from research funders, service users and carers to conduct more participatory, service-user- and carer-informed research. To date, developments include first-year trainees working with service users early on in their training to consult on their ideas for their doctorate research. This is now done very early on in the first year to enable meaningful participation and co-production. Further consultations follow, and trainees are required to describe what consultation has taken place with service users and carers in their DClin research proposals.

Since 2014, the programme's 'research fair', at which clinicians and academics present ideas for the major thesis to first-year trainees, has featured a keynote speaker with expertise in inclusive research and is attended by experts by experience involved in the programme. The research interests of members of the programme's service user and carer group (Liverpool Experts by Experience [LExE]) are mapped and shared with first years to create opportunities for consultation. Our first expert by experience research 'supervisor-in training' has been supporting a trainee for the last 2 years, making a unique contribution to the development of her research competencies. Experts by experience also attend the programme's annual research conference, sharing reflections and constructive thoughts about the completed major research projects of the third-year trainees.

Increasingly, the research topics of the major thesis as chosen by trainees are reflecting human rights themes. Examples of current research projects include a grounded theory approach to exploring disclosure and non-disclosure of psychological distress and mental health issues in trainees; an experimental study researching the impact of poverty on cognitive processes relevant to depression and anxiety; and a Q-sort investigating the nature of autonomy in dementia.

Some of the research conducted by staff is also aligned with human rights values and processes, such as involvement of experts by experience and co-production. Research colleagues in our team, in collaboration with colleagues at the Salomons Centre Doctorate in Clinical Psychology programme, Canterbury Christchurch University, have been successful in gaining funding from the BPS's Division of Clinical Psychology to develop a model for evaluating the impact of involving experts by experience in UK clinical psychology training.

Clinical

Involving experts by experience in all parts of clinical training can be particularly complex during clinical placements when the roles of service provider and service user are most explicit (British Psychological Society, 2008; Tickle & Davison, 2008; Kemp, 2010). Clinical placements, supervisor training and other supporting processes for the clinical elements of training have been developed to facilitate increased levels of participation and community engagement. Mid-placement reviews now routinely assess the opportunities for service-user involvement and co-production on trainees' clinical placements. We have also adopted the end-of-placement assessment form developed by colleagues at Lancaster University which assesses trainees' awareness of the social, economic, political and cultural contexts of their clinical work, their 'ethical decision-making', 'community engagement skills' and skills in 'working alongside service users'. There is also more of a focus on 'innovative placements' organised in partnership with the voluntary and third sectors, including local homelessness outreach services, which offer challenges to current clinical practice, opportunities for trainees to develop skills in community engagement, and a chance to work with groups who are often excluded from mainstream services.

With regard to encouraging and developing placement supervisors' engagement in co-production, the programme team has co-produced and co-delivered a supervisor training workshop on co-production run by the three North West Doctorate in Clinical Psychology courses (University of Manchester, University of Liverpool and Lancaster University) on 'Involving Experts by Experience in Supervision, Placement Evaluation and Service Delivery'. The workshop aimed to provide a forum to think about how feedback from experts by experience can be provided to trainees on their indirect and direct clinical work, to develop and exchange good practice in working alongside people to deliver services and to think jointly about some recommendations for future placement practice. Within the workshop, co-production on placement was articulated at three levels of involvement (British Psychological Society, 2008):

1. *therapeutic:* working collaboratively with service users and carers to evaluate satisfaction with sessions and gain feedback in relation to the therapeutic relationship;
2. *organisational:* using co-production or consultation with service users and carers to create organisational change within services; and
3. *mentoring:* service users and carers acting as mentors to enhance and develop trainees' skills and abilities.

Through a series of exercises, supervisor participants were asked to share good practice and consider how each of these elements could be taken forward within their own services. Feedback for the pilot suggested that supervisors enjoyed the space to think practically about how to develop co-production, but would have liked more theory to be included.

Experts by experience have consistently stressed their need for psychologists who have skills in influencing challenging systems and working effectively in multi-disciplinary teams (MDTs). Members of the DClinPsychol programme team are leading a University of Liverpool project on running Schwartz Rounds with pre-registration and pre-qualification healthcare students. Schwartz Rounds (Goodrich, 2012) are a multi-disciplinary forum designed for healthcare staff to come together once a month to discuss and reflect on the non-clinical aspects of caring for patients – that is, the emotional and social challenges associated with their jobs. The underlying premise for Rounds is that the compassion shown by healthcare staff can make the difference to a patient's experience of care, but in order to provide care with compassion, staff must, in turn, feel supported in their work. The project is multi-professional, involving students from a range of different pre-qualification/ pre-registration professional healthcare education programmes including medicine, clinical psychology, nursing, physiotherapy, occupational therapy, diagnostic radiography, radiotherapy and orthoptics.

Leadership and using power wisely is a strong theme in the professional issues teaching for third-year trainees. In addition, we have included a role play on MDTs for the second years in the forensic learning disability teaching this year, as well as the requirement for supervisors to directly observe two instances of non-direct clinical work; for example, working with a team while trainees are on each placement. Further teaching and role play on working in teams take place in Year 3 too.

The Liverpool programme has recently been awarded funding by the Higher Education Funding Council for England (HEFCE) for the 'Swapping Seats' initiative, a variant of the expert by experience mentorship schemes developed by the Surrey, Salomons (Canterbury Christchurch University) and Manchester programmes (Atkins, Hart, O'Brien, & Davidson, 2010; Cooke & Hayward, 2010). Following a teaching session on participatory learning for trainees, training for expert by experience mentors and the development of co-produced guidance for the scheme, each trainee within a particular NHS Trust will be mentored during their placement by an expert by experience. It is hoped that this will allow trainees to experience alternative opportunities to learn from service users and carers. The initiative will be extended to other post-graduate professionals within the Trust, which we hope will further extend the opportunities for MDT learning.

In Liverpool, each trainee is allocated an 'academic advisor', a member of the course team who meets with them throughout their 3 years on the programme to support their learning and clinical development. Advisors complete an annual review with trainees, which reviews their progress in all areas of the course. The annual review includes an assessment of how each trainee has demonstrated the core values of the programme, including the 'PANEL' principles, over the previous year. So, for example, trainees are asked to show how they have used human rights thinking explicitly in their role, what evidence they have of non-discriminatory practice and of encouraging service-user and carer participation.

Plans for the programme

The overall vision developing for the Liverpool Doctorate in Clinical Psychology programme is one in which human rights and the related themes of community engagement are both highlighted explicitly and deeply woven into the fabric of the training course.

More than ever there is a need for psychologists to be engaging in public debates about mental health, health inequalities and the psychological wellbeing of our communities. Our digital identity as a programme is vital to our ability to intervene. We want to make sure our human rights values are clear in all of our communications and in externally facing events. Our website will often be the first point of contact that many service users and potential trainees have with the programme. It needs to act as a progressive resource for the community and clearly reflect our values. We are currently updating our website to ensure that our representations of clinical psychologists and trainees reflect diversity. We also want to make clear that service-user inclusion is integral to our approach through proper representation on our website, through continuing to have an emphasis on LExE as part of our open day, and through making community links and blogs available on the website. We hope to include a statement around mental health stigma and links to the BPS's 'Only Us' (rather than 'Us and Them') and other relevant campaigns. We also want to make sure that the voices of our trainees come across in all of those arenas; for example, through quotes and vignettes on the website, and trainees taking part in the open day.

To promote human rights-based thinking and processes, we hope to build on our current equalities and LExE work through an 'Inclusivity and Human Rights' working group, including services users and trainees, which will drive through innovative projects and adaptations to routine course processes and functions. A human rights 'impact assessment', using a structured framework to review core processes against the 'PANEL' principles, is one method of identifying areas for development as part of a systematic and coherent strategy. Impact review would also allow us to consider whether developments from other DClin programmes and professional post-graduate programmes might be effectively integrated. We have much we can learn, for example, from many social work courses that are more advanced than clinical psychology in integrating radical ideas.

Mechanisms for promoting equality and human rights issues which are widespread in secondary education – such as using LGBT (lesbian, gay, bisexual and transgender) history month and Black history month to focus on particular diversity themes – are also being considered by the programme team. Such initiatives might involve working in partnership with other faculties using the arts and culture to promote emotionally and relationally resonant learning; for example, through film.

Integrating an explicit focus on human rights values into staff personal development plans would allow space for individual staff members to consider how the course values fit with their own roles and job plans.

Recruitment and selection

One of the key challenges faced by training programmes is around non-discrimination and widening access (Scior, Williams, & King, 2016), which is particularly salient given possible changes to funding models for pre-registration healthcare education and training in England (Department of Health, 2017). There is a view held by many that the current funding strategy for clinical psychology training promotes more equal access to education and training than self-funding models (Scior et al., 2016). We currently monitor applications in relation to diversity and, after profiling this, will aim to target under-represented groups in clinical psychology. This could be achieved through linking in with 'diversity role models' and similar organisations which go into schools to promote LGBT awareness. Feedback from experts by experience has suggested they would welcome the use of fewer interview-based recruitment methods in selection and a move towards more group and interpersonally based tasks. Other avenues which could be explored are greater involvement of trainees in the process of selection, which would have a number of other benefits. It would also be valuable to canvass opinion from trainees about how and whether to change selection processes. While this is complex to implement, our accountability in selection might be strengthened by making the selection process more transparent.

Mentoring

Anecdotally, some of us in the programme team have reflected that some trainees seek out relationships with supervisors and staff which might consolidate the development of their professional identities in the context of other aspects of their sense of self. For example, LGBT trainees might gravitate towards 'out' team staff as research supervisors in order to feel supported not just with their doctorate thesis, but also with the task of integrating their personal and professional identities. While the team's capacity for this is limited, a more diverse range of relationships is potentially available through the programme's mentoring scheme. This matches clinical psychologists with first-year trainees. Alongside proactive attempts to encourage mentors from diverse backgrounds, it is possible that prompting trainees to consider diversity (including experience of significant mental health distress), and taking this into account when thinking about their preferences, might provide more opportunities for support.

Teaching

A human rights-based approach to teaching suggests scope for enhancing both the process and content of teaching in ways which fit with the emphasis on improving the quality of teaching and the student experience within the academy.

In terms of process, we aim to increase the use of participatory methods such as Enquiry Based Learning (EBL), and are investigating other teaching methods. We feel it would be useful to have a widely circulated statement of our philosophy of teaching which explicitly embraces rights, Freire (1993) and other progressive educationalists, and which contains a commitment to question the neutrality of dominant psychological theory. We plan to continue to develop the number of teaching sessions which feature service-user participation, with some sessions being led solely by service users. We also want to develop co-produced teaching units, which will be reviewed by experts by experience from that specialism, through working in partnership with teaching unit convenors who are experts by experience. There are plans to pilot this with the learning disability unit. Identifying the human rights themes in teaching unit descriptions might also support trainees to recognise how rights are integrated into the curriculum. Community activism skills workshops led by community facilitators might complement the skills traditionally gained on programmes; for example, in bid-writing or organising media campaigns.

In relation to content, our aspirations are to develop a curriculum which explicitly reflects key human rights issues and which makes the links apparent to trainees – perhaps through conceptualising disparate sessions more as a coherent strand which spans the 3 years (see Table 10.2). One dilemma in teaching critical approaches is how to pitch induction teaching in a way which begins a process of critical engagement with clinical psychology, but which is also within the zone of proximal development for first-year trainees. The development of Cromby, Harper and Reavey's (2013) undergraduate textbook provides an articulation of an alternative radical view of mental health which might be built upon in the first-year curriculum. This focusses the experience of distress in a historical, biologically embodied social and cultural context (Cromby et al., 2013) and considers the Midlands Psychology Group's Draft Manifesto (2012) as a counterpoint to dominant diagnostic narratives and psychological models based on insight not 'outsight' (Moloney, 2013). As part of this, we could develop the contribution that members of LExE make to the induction teaching in a more theoretical direction, with a co-produced history of service user movement(s), the radical currents within this such as Italy's Psichiatria Democratica, and the impact of user movements upon services. It could also include a session on benefits, austerity and the links to mental health issues.

Once the foundations of conceptual frameworks have been laid, further sessions which make the historicised and ideological contexts of clinical psychology explicit might be added. This could complement David Pilgrim's teaching on the history of the profession. It might examine the history of psychiatry and progressive movements/trends in psychiatry; for example, Joanna Moncrieff's work (2008). This curriculum would need to acknowledge the history of mental health, considering briefly how concepts of psychological distress before the Industrial Revolution evolved, including understandings based on Greek philosophy and medicine, those viewed through the prism of theology and more recently through 'humours'. The rise and nature of the asylums would comprise a central feature of this, as would understanding the rich legacy of radical approaches developed by Goffman (1961), Laing (1969), Szasz (1974), Vygotsky (1978), Sedgewick (1982) and Newnes (2014, 2016).

Assessment

For the future, we will explore the scope for service-user involvement in assessment – particularly in formative pieces of work. For example, following the clinical assessment teaching in which experts by experience give feedback to trainees, the trainees are asked to submit their own reflective notes on the exercise. This could be an area in which increased participation of services users and carers could be integrated into our assessment functions. In addition, we plan to review our marking guidance notes to ensure that human rights themes are reflected and markers are prompted to consider service-user perspectives.

TABLE 10.2 Suggestions for specific taught areas of the curriculum based on the articles of the Human Rights Act

Articles of the Human Rights Act relevant to healthcare	Related teaching areas to integrate into the curriculum
Article 2 – Right to life:	• Inequalities in healthcare for relevant groups ('Do not resuscitate orders', euthanasia, advanced directives, death through negligence, including coverage of the Mazars report [2015] and issues in dementia care) • Inclusion of key theoretical frameworks for understanding health inequalities, ranging from 'Psychosocial theorists' (e.g. The Spirit Level – Wilkinson & Pickett [2010]) to neo-materialists (e.g. Friedli, 2009)
Article 3 – Right to be free from torture and inhumane and degrading treatment:	• Trauma-informed care • Physical and psychological abuse, sexual abuse • 'Positive and proactive' (Department of Health, 2014) – reducing use of excessive force, and restraint • Safeguarding and risk assessment • Working with historical disclosures • Torture and working with responses to torture (Patel, 2007) • Female genital mutilation
Article 4 – Right to be free from slavery and enforced labour:	• Modern-day slavery • The history of slavery and resistance
Article 5 – Right to liberty:	• Considering mental health law and how the Mental Health Act and Mental Capacity Act are underpinned by the Human Rights Act • Including Deprivation of Liberty Safeguards, informal detention, delays in mental health review tribunals, and excessive restraint
Article 6 – Right to be free from punishment without law:	• History of the asylum (Rogers & Pilgrim, 2010)
Article 7 – Right to a fair trial:	• Including mental health review tribunals
Article 8 – Right to home correspondence, private and family life:	• Situating consent within the legal framework of the HRA • Closure of hospitals, privacy onwards, care homes • Sexuality and relationships issues including forced marriage • Understanding how therapeutic approaches can support Article 8 rights to psychological integrity

(continued)

TABLE 10.2 Suggestions for specific taught areas of the curriculum based on the articles of the Human Rights Act (*continued*)

Articles of the Human Rights Act relevant to healthcare	Related teaching areas to integrate into the curriculum
Article 14 – Right to non-discrimination:	Sessions on working with significant issues for minoritised groups, including: • Working positively with gender and understanding gender discrimination • Working with refugees and asylum seekers • Working with people who identify as lesbian, gay, bisexual, transgender, queer and intersex (LGBTQi) • Race and culture • Mental health stigma • Poverty, class, austerity and food banks • Islam and religion • Working with translators • Intellectual disability • Physical disability • Hearing and other sensory impairment • Constructively critical approaches to theoretical perspectives on diversity and difference; e.g. privilege theory

Research

In research, existing developments could be extended through exploring both how we might apply, and how trainees might understand, the different approaches of consultation, collaboration and user-controlled research (Sweeney, Beresford, Faulkner, Nettle, & Rose, 2009). A co-delivered theoretical teaching session to trainees on service-user involvement in research might help to facilitate this. We hope to further progress the involvement of experts by experience across the rest of the research cycle (commissioning, designing and undertaking research). Further ideas for future developments include greater integration of service-user involvement into service-related clinical research; exploring options for citizen research within clinical psychology training programmes to develop community engagement; linking with community partners concerning the issues they would like to see being explored; and more emphasis on social justice in trainees' major research projects. We have established a human rights research group with the intention of developing the research undertaken in NHS trusts on developing practical resources to integrate human rights thinking into clinical practice, and to support a wider programme of trainee research on related themes.

Clinical

In thinking about how our clinical activities might develop a more human rights-based focus, we are concentrating on a number of areas. Our advanced supervisor workshop programme, offered jointly with the Manchester and Lancaster programmes, might offer workshops on working inclusively with diversity and difference, and on thinking about how to support supervisors to nurture their own and trainees' psychological wellbeing. We are also extending the range of innovative placements we offer (in partnership with NHS placements) and, for the future, we want to offer international placements. Future work will include an audit of trainees' clinical assessment forms that would allow us to develop a picture of the opportunities for service-user involvement on placement, and to think strategically about how to develop these. The 'Trainees' Assessment of Placement' (TAP) forms also need to be revised to be more consistent with the progressive emphasis of the supervisor's assessment forms which include community engagement. Both trainee and supervisor placement assessment documents could be reviewed to more explicitly include human rights aspects. Dependent on the outcomes of our Community Mentoring project, we may also consider extending this mentoring scheme in partnership with local third sector organisations to consolidate community links.

Moving forward in uncertain times

We began this chapter with a quote from Martin Luther King addressing the American Psychological Association in 1967. At the time of writing, the global political context arguably means that we must redouble our efforts as psychologists to be radical. The political impact of the UK 'Brexit' referendum result, the election of Donald Trump as president of the United States, and the grim realities of the experiences of those fleeing war-torn parts of the world highlight, indeed, Martin Luther King's imperative of never adjusting to injustice and serve as a reminder of every individual's human rights. The necessity of the huge movement of people across parts of the world as they fear for their lives and flee to safety has resulted in the construction of hugely damaging narratives which were woven through the UK referendum on leaving the EU and the Trump campaigns and are scarily reminiscent of other times in history which have led to dire consequences. This 'othering' and alienation have very real negative consequences in people's everyday lives.

Against such a global context, we believe that within the field of our work as clinical psychology trainers, using a human rights-based approach as the framework within which we deliver our programme enables us to challenge power relationships. This approach demands a reflexive, historical accounting of clinical psychology theory and practice, and helps to create a culture in which differences of opinion can be safely debated. We have described how, despite making significant progress as a programme in recent years to teach with a more critical focus throughout the programme, this remains work in progress. There are some who would argue that a liberal HRBA is not sufficiently radical or critical; ultimately, it does not challenge the economic status quo. We do not offer it here as a panacea to cure all ills, but we do believe its social and relational basis to be important in enabling a diversity of critical responses and in offering an effective antidote to the toxicity of the medical model and the fantasy of 'therapy as prescription'. As trainers, and paid staff, we are mindful of the power that is inherent in our work roles and know the tension that exists in 'working with good authority' when trying to promote more democratic learner-led structures. This presents challenges and complexities, but we are making real changes, and doing this collaboratively with services users and carers, trainees and staff. Members of LExE frequently challenge us to train clinical psychologists who are not, as they put it, "so nice", but who will assertively challenge the mental health system in multi-disciplinary team meetings and ward rounds, will champion a psychological understanding of human distress, and within that, will advocate meaningfully for service users' human rights. This involves teaching and conversations throughout the 3 years' training about power and the ethics of power and the fact that harm can be done as much through acts of omission as acts of commission. We believe that a human rights-based approach provides a framework within which we can do this. The EU Agency for Fundamental Rights has recommended that all healthcare professions include human rights training in pre-qualification training, so this supports our direction of travel. Although Brexit is likely to challenge the application of EU legislation, this recommendation currently stands, as does the context of international rights law.

We began this chapter by saying that clinical psychology as a discipline sails within complex, challenging and competing contextual waters. Health, in all of its dimensions, is a human right, not a commodity. Within such a choppy and uncertain context, human rights-based approaches can provide an anchor to enable trainee clinical psychologists to critically conceptualise legal, moral and regulatory currents and assist them to navigate disparate areas of policy and practice. It is an approach within which critical psychology can be taught and practised actively, and can reduce social inequalities and promote social justice.

Psychologists generally have a tendency to underestimate the importance of social movements in securing change. Just as progressive social movements gained and maintain our human rights, regressive political forces can legally and practically erode them. Trainees who are agnostic about the social or who wish to hide in their therapy rooms are unlikely to sustain hope and resilience as austerity bites ever harder into services, and exacts its human toll. As clinical psychology trainers, we must ensure that we are doing everything we can to teach and train a future workforce that actively addresses "the relationship between the individual and the historical, political and social contents which have shaped their lives and given rise to their distress" (Patel, 2003, p. 16).

Acknowledgements

The authors would like to thank all of the experts by experience who have been involved in the University of Liverpool's Doctorate in Clinical Psychology programme from whom we have learnt so much, and in particular, the members of the Liverpool Experts by Experience Group. We would also like to acknowledge the Liverpool trainee clinical psychologists whose enthusiasm, humanity and ability to constructively challenge give us hope for the future of the profession. Thanks, too, go to our colleagues on the programme team, for their creativity, critical thinking and sustained commitment to developing the space for progressive, humanist values within the Liverpool programme. We would have liked to have modelled co-production in the process of writing this chapter; however, all of the recent developments in the programme, and many of the ideas for future developments featured in this chapter, are based on discussion and the involvement of our experts by experience colleagues, trainees and staff for which we are very grateful. Finally, we would like to thank Amanda Roberts for her helpful comments on an earlier draft of this chapter.

References

Atkins, E., Hart, L., O'Brien, C., & Davidson, T. (2010). Service-users and carers as placement advisors: Part 2 – personal reflections on novel relationships. *Clinical Psychology Forum, 209*, 23–27.

Arnstein, S. (1969). A ladder of citizen participation. *Journal of the American Planning Association, 35*(4), 216–224.

Bailey, S., Ridley, J., & Greenhill, B. (2010). Challenging behaviour: A human rights-based approach. *Advances in Mental Health and Intellectual Disabilities, 4*(2), 20–26.

Boyle, D., & Harris, M. (2009). *The challenge of co-production: How equal partnerships between professionals and the public are crucial to improving public services*. Discussion Paper. London: New Economics Foundation & NESTA. Available at www.nesta.org.uk/publications/challenge-co-production (accessed 27 February 2015).

British Institute of Human Rights. (2013). *The difference it makes: Putting human rights at the heart of health and social care*. Retrieved from www.bihr.org.uk/differenceitmakes

British Psychological Society. (2008). *Good practice guidelines: Service user and carer involvement within clinical psychology training*. Leicester: British Psychological Society.

British Psychological Society. (2009). *Code of ethics and conduct*. Leicester: British Psychological Society.

British Psychological Society. (2014). *Standards for doctoral programmes in clinical psychology*. Leicester: British Psychological Society.

Butchard, S., & Greenhill, B. (2015). Human rights: Giving clinical psychology a backbone, *Clinical Psychology Forum, 276*, 16–22.

Butchard, S., Cameron, A., Donald, A., Dowling, C., Forde, E., Eames, C. . . . Roberts, B. (2016). *Human rights in clinical psychology: Enquiry Based Learning resources for training clinical psychologists in human rights decision-making, leadership and evaluation*. London: Equality and Human Rights Commission.

CQC. (2014). *Human rights approach for our regulation of health and social care services*. Retrieved from www.cqc.org.uk/sites/default/files/20150416_our_human_rights_approach.pdf

Cooke, A., & Hayward, M. (2010). Service-users and carers as placement advisors: Part 1 – getting started. *Clinical Psychology Forum, 209*, 21–22.

Cotter, L.E., Chevrier, J., El-Nachef, W.N., Radhakrishna, R., Rahangdale, L., Weiser, S.D., & Iacopino, V. (2009). Health and human rights education in U.S. schools of medicine and public health: Current status and future challenges. *PLoS ONE, 4*(3): e4916. doi:10.1371/journal.pone.0004916

Crawford, E., Aplin, T., & Rodger, S. (2016). Human rights in occupational therapy education: A step towards a more occupationally just global society. *Australian Occupational Therapy Journal*. doi:10.1111/1440-1630.12321

Cromby, J., Harper, D., & Reavey, P. (2013). *Psychology, mental health and distress*. Basingstoke, UK: Palgrave Macmillan Education.

Curtice, M.J., & Exworthy, T. (2010). FREDA: A human rights-based approach to healthcare. *The Psychiatrist, 34*(4), 150–156.

Department of Health. (2014). *Positive and proactive care: Reducing the need for restrictive interventions*. London: The Stationery Office.

Department of Health. (2015). *Mental Health Act 1983: Code of practice*. London: Department of Health. Retrieved from www.gov.uk/government/uploads/system/uploads/attachment_data/file/396918/Code_of_Practice.pdf

Department of Health. (2017). *NHS bursary reform*. Policy paper. Retrieved from www.gov.uk/government/publications/nhs-bursary-reform/nhs-bursary-reform

Department of Health, & British Institute of Human Rights. (2008). *Human rights in healthcare: A framework for local action* (2nd ed.). London: Department of Health. Retrieved 20 April 2017 from http://webarchive.nationalarchives.gov.uk/20130107105354/http://www.dh.gov.uk/prod_consum_dh/groups/dh_digitalassets/@dh/@en/documents/digitalasset/dh_088972.pdf

Dyer, L. (2015). A review of the impact of the Human Rights in Healthcare Programme in England and Wales. *Health and Human Rights Journal, 17(2)*, 111–122.

Francis, R. (2013). *Report of the Mid Staffordshire NHS Foundation Trust public inquiry*. London: The Stationery Office. Available from www.midstaffspublicinquiry.com/report

Freire, P. (1993). *Pedagogy of the oppressed* (new revised 20th anniversary ed.). New York: Continuum.

Friedli, L. (2009). *Mental health, resilience and inequalities*. Copenhagen: World Health Organization Regional Office for Europe.

Goffman, E. (1961). *Asylums: Essays on the social situation of mental patients and other inmates*. London: Penguin.

Goodrich, J. (2012). Supporting hospital staff to provide compassionate care: Do Schwartz Centre Rounds work in English hospitals? *Journal of the Royal Society of Medicine, 105*, 117–122.

Greenhill, B., & Whitehead, R. (2011). Promoting service user inclusion in risk assessment and management: A pilot project developing a human rights-based approach. *British Journal of Learning Disabilities, 39*(4), 277–283.

Gruening, G. (2001). Origin and theoretical basis of New Public Management. *International Public Management Journal, 4*, 1–25.

Hagan, T., & Smail, D. (1997). Power-mapping – 1. Background and basic methodology. *Journal of Community and Applied Social Psychology, 7*(4), 257–267.

Hall, J., Pilgrim, D., & Turpin, G. (Eds.) (2015). *Clinical psychology in Britain: Historical perspectives*. Leicester: British Psychological Society.

Health & Care Professions Council. (2014). *Standards of education and training guidance*. Retrieved from www.hcpc-uk.org/assets/documents/1000295EStandardsofeducationandtraining-fromSeptember2009.pdf

Human Rights Act. (1998). London: The Stationary Office. Retrieved from www.legislation.gov.uk/ukpga/1998/42/section/2

INVOLVE. (2016). Briefing note eight: Ways that people can be involved in the research cycle. Retrieved from www.invo.org.uk/posttyperesource/where-and-how-to-involve-in-the-research-cycle/

Kemp, P. (2010). The creative involvement of service users in the classroom. In J. Weinstein (Ed.), *Mental health, service user involvement and recovery*. London: Jessica Kingsley Publishers.

Kinderman, P. (2007). Human rights and applied psychology. *Journal of Community & Applied Social Psychology, 17*(3), 218–228.

Kinderman, P., & Butler, F. (2006). *Implementing a human rights approach within public services: An outline psychological perspective.* Department for Constitutional Affairs. Retrieved from http://old.mhe-sme.org/assets/files/Human%20Rights%20committee/Implementing_a_Human_Rights_Approach_within_Public_Service.pdf

Kohlberg, L. (1984). *The psychology of moral development: The nature and validity of moral stages (Essays on moral development, Volume 2).* San Francisco, CA: Harper & Row.

Laing, R.D. (1969). *The divided self.* London: Penguin.

Lavender, T., & Turpin, G. (2015). The development and training of the clinical psychological workforce: From probationers to practitioner doctorates. In J. Hall, D. Pilgrim, & G. Turpin (Eds.), *Clinical psychology in Britain: Historical perspectives.* Leicester: British Psychological Society.

Longwill, A. (2015). *Clinical Psychology Workforce Project.* Division of Clinical Psychology UK (Unpublished report). The British Psychological Society's Division of Clinical Psychology, Leicester, UK. Retrieved from www.bps.org.uk/system/files/Public%20files/Policy/final_draft_cliical_psychology_workforce_report.pdf

Mann, J., Lazzarini, Z., Gostin, L., & Gruskin, S. (1997). Teaching human rights education to public health practitioners. In G.J. Andreopoulos & R.P. Claude (Eds.), *Human rights education for the twenty-first century* (pp. 334–344). Philadelphia, PA: University of Pennsylvania Press.

Mazars. (2015). *Independent review of deaths of people with a learning disability or mental health problem in contact with Southern Health NHS Foundation Trust April 2011 to March 2015.* London: Mazars.

Meintjies, G. (1997). Human rights education as empowerment: Reflections on pedagogy. In G.J. Andreopoulos & R.P. Claude (Eds.), *Human rights education for the twenty-first century* (pp. 64–79). Philadelphia, PA: University of Pennsylvania Press.

Melluish, S., Latchford, G., & Marks, S. (2015). The international context of British clinical psychology. In J. Hall, D. Pilgrim, & G. Turpin (Eds.), *Clinical psychology in Britain: Historical perspectives* (Chapter 24). Leicester: British Psychological Society.

Mental Capacity Act 2005 (c.9). London: The Stationery Office.

Mental Health Act 1983 (amended 2007) (c.25). London: The Stationery Office.

Midlands Psychology Group. (2012). Draft manifesto for a social materialist psychology of distress. *Journal of Critical Psychology, Counselling and Psychotherapy, 12*(2), 93–107.

Moloney, P. (2013). *The therapy industry: The irresistible rise of the talking cure, and why it doesn't work.* London: Pluto Press.

Moncrieff, J. (2008). *The myth of the chemical cure.* Basingstoke, UK: Palgrave Macmillan.

Montenegro, M., & Greenhill, B. (2014). Evaluating "FREDA Challenge": A co-produced human-rights board game in services for people with intellectual disabilities. *Journal of Applied Research in Intellectual Disabilities, 28,* 223–237.

Needham, C., & Carr, S. (2009). *Co-production: An emerging evidence base for adult social care transformation.* Research briefing 31. London: SCIE.

Newnes, C. (1996). The development of clinical psychology and its values. *Clinical Psychology Forum, 95,* 29–34.

Newnes, C. (2014). *Clinical psychology: A critical examination.* Ross-on-Wye, UK: PCCS Books.

Newnes, C. (2016). *Inscription, diagnosis, deception and the mental health industry: How Psy governs us all.* Basingstoke, UK: Palgrave Macmillan.

Patel, N. (2003). Clinical psychology: Reinforcing inequalities or facilitating empowerment? *The International Journal of Human Rights, 7*(1), 16–39. doi:10.1080/714003792

Patel, N. (2007). The prevention of torture: Role of clinical psychology. *International Journal of Critical Psychology, Counselling and Psychotherapy, 7*(4), 229–246.

Patterson, F., Kerrin, M., Ashworth, V., Prescott-Clements, L., Murray, H., & Fung, K. (2014). *Evaluation of Values Based Recruitment (VBR) in the NHS: Literature review and evaluation criteria*. London: Health Education England. Retrieved from www.hee.nhs.uk/sites/default/files/documents/VBR%20literature%20review.pdf

Pilgrim, D., & Patel, N. (2015). The emergence of clinical psychology in the British post-war context. In J. Hall, D. Pilgrim, & G. Turpin (Eds.), *Clinical psychology in Britain: Historical perspectives* (Chapter 4). Leicester: British Psychological Society.

Roberts, A., Townsend, S., Morris, J., Rushbrooke, E., Greenhill, B., Whitehead, R. . . . Golding, L. (2013). Treat me right, treat me equal: Using national policy and legislation to create positive changes in local health services for people with intellectual disabilities. *Journal of Applied Research in Intellectual Disabilities, 26*(1), 14–25.

Rogers, A., & Pilgrim, D. (2010). *A sociology of mental health and illness*. Maidenhead, UK: Open University Press.

Royal College of Nursing. (2012). *Human rights and nursing: RCN position statement*. Retrieved 28 February 2015 from www.rcn.org.uk/__data/assets/pdf_file/0003/452352/004249.pdf

Scior, K., Williams, J., & King, J. (2016). Is access to clinical psychology training in the UK fair? The impact of educational history on application success. *Clinical Psychology Forum, 289*, 17.

Sedgewick, P. (1982). *Psychopolitics*. London: Pluto Press Limited.

Smail, D. (2005). *Power, interest and psychology: Elements of a social materialist understanding of distress*. Ross-on-Wye, UK: PCCS Books.

Sweeney, A., Beresford, P., Faulkner, A., Nettle, M., & Rose, D. (Eds.) (2009). *This is survivor research*. Ross-on-Wye, UK: PCCS Books.

Szasz, T. (1974). *The myth of mental illness: Foundations of a theory of personal conduct*. New York: Harper & Row.

Tickle, A., & Davison, C. (2008). Sowing the seeds of change: Trainee clinical psychologists' experiences of service user and carer involvement on placement. *The Journal of Mental Health Training, Education and Practice, 3*(1), 33–41.

Vygotsky, L. (1978). *Mind in society*. Cambridge, MA: Harvard University Press.

Wilkinson, R.G., & Pickett, K. (2010). *The spirit level: Why greater equality makes societies stronger*. New York: Bloomsbury Press.

World Federation of Occupational Therapists. (2006). *Position statement on human rights*. Available from www.wfot.org/ResourceCentre.aspx (accessed 28 February 2015).

11

CHILDREN'S EXPERIENCES OF DOMESTIC VIOLENCE

A teaching and training challenge

Jane Callaghan, Lisa Fellin and Joanne Alexander

In this chapter we explore the complexities of training and teaching students and practitioners about children's experiences of domestic violence. The research conducted on children's experiences has tended to focus on negative outcomes, representing these children as damaged and vulnerable (Callaghan & Alexander, 2015; Øverlien, 2013). Such research suggests that these children have elevated life-long risk of mental health difficulties (Bogat, DeJonghe, Levendosky, Davidson, & von Eye, 2006; Lamers-Winkelman, Willemen, & Visser, 2012; Stover, 2005); interpersonal difficulties (Baldry, 2003; Holmes, 2013; Renner & Slack, 2006); educational difficulties and educational drop out (Byrne & Taylor, 2007); and physical health problems (Bair-Merritt, Blackstone, & Feudtner, 2006). Despite this research representation of children as vulnerable and damaged, services for children who experience domestic violence are often underdeveloped and underfunded (Statham, 2004; Willis et al., 2010), typically additional to adult domestic abuse services; for instance, as part of the services offered in family shelters.

In contrast to the established narrative, which positions children as passive witnesses to domestic violence, and as inevitably pathologised, our research on domestic violence (in common with the work of Katz, 2015; Øverlien, 2014; Øverlien & Hydén, 2009) has focused on children as agents who *experience* domestic violence (Callaghan & Alexander, 2015). The Understanding Agency and Resistance Strategies project (UNARS) was a two-phase research project, funded by the European Commission and developed in four European countries (Italy, Greece, the UK and Spain). The first phase of the project had two aims: to build an understanding of children's experiences of domestic violence, with a particular focus on exploring their capacity for agency and resistance; and to develop an understanding of the service and policy landscape that provided a social context for young people's experiences. In this phase, our researchers spent time embedded in domestic violence services and related contexts, and conducted interviews with 107 children and young people, as well as focus groups with adult carers and with professionals who worked with children and young people, and a policy analysis, focused at the regional, national and European level.

This research explored children's capacity for agency and their ability to resist the controlling and coercive practices inherent in family life when domestic abuse occurs (Callaghan, Alexander, Sixsmith, & Fellin, 2016a). In addition, we explored how children who experience domestic violence challenge the normative presumptions of developmental psychology and its applications to practice (Callaghan, Fellin, & Alexander, 2017). Their capacity to care-take for others (Callaghan, Alexander, Sixsmith, & Fellin, 2016b), their ability to manage physical and emotional pain (Callaghan, Alexander, & Fellin, 2016), their monitoring and management of abusive familial dynamics (Callaghan, Alexander, Sixsmith et al., 2016a), and their complex emotional responses (Callaghan, Fellin, Alexander, Mavrou, & Papathanasiou, 2017) exceed our assumptions about 'normal' childhood (Burman, 2016). Based on the material generated in this phase, in the second phase, we developed and evaluated two interventions: one to provide a therapeutic programme, rooted in young people's experiences, focused on building their existing strengths and supporting their understanding of themselves as agentic, meaning-making and creative; the second to provide a training intervention for practitioners who worked with families who had experienced domestic violence and abuse.

When training and teaching this material to students and to professionals who support families affected by domestic violence, we found that several obstacles and challenges 'got in the way' of facilitating students' recognition of children's capacity for agency and their complex experience of domestic violence and abuse. The first obstacle to understanding children's experiences was the presumption that domestic violence occurs within the intimate adult dyad. This dyadic construction underestimates the relational, community and social context of domestic abuse, feeding into the second challenge we faced in training. This understanding of domestic violence is inscribed in policy descriptions, in dominant media representations and in professional practice (Callaghan, Alexander, Sixsmith et al., 2016a; Houghton, 2015; Katz, 2016). The construction necessarily excludes children as potential victims or participants in domestic abuse. When dominant professional and policy discourses do focus on children who experience domestic abuse, they focus on children's trauma and its impact, positioning children as silent, passive and damaged.

The second challenge we faced was the common presumption of children's developmental inability to understand/see/hear/experience the full impact of domestic violence on themselves and their family, or to understand its consequences. This belief feeds into a representation of children as unable to speak about, plan or reflect on their experiences, assuming that children were unable to make meaning of their own experiences.

A related third challenge is the assumption of children's vulnerability. This construction relies on a normative understanding of children as 'innocent', and abusive family interactions are seen as necessarily violating that innocence (see

Burkett, 2015). By positioning children who experience violence as perpetually fragile, and in need of adult protection, professionals and carers justify gatekeeping practices that effectively silence children and young people (Eriksson, 2012). This notion of vulnerability is underpinned by a biomedical discourse which presumes that children who experience early trauma are neurologically damaged by that experience, and that such children are also more likely to reproduce intergenerational patterns of violence because of this experience (Black, Sussman, & Unger, 2010; Bridgett, Burt, Edwards, & Deater-Deckard, 2015; Ehrensaft & Cohen, 2012; Ehrensaft et al., 2003; Stith et al., 2000). These ideas that children are damaged and doomed to repeat cycles of violence are pervasive in domestic violence research and practice, and become taken for granted and difficult to challenge in training and teaching. In training contexts in particular, it can be difficult to overcome a sense of powerlessness in professionals who work in domestic violence practice, because of the lack of good-quality services for children. Further, professionals express feelings of becoming deskilled and loss of capacity to bring about change, because they have not been trained to intervene with and support children and young people. This is fuelled by the last two assumptions of incompetence and damage: children are not regarded as reliable witnesses, and professionals fear that speaking about their experience will re-traumatise the children.

Getting children's needs met is also very challenging in a service landscape where they are treated like parcels passed back and forth between education, social services and Child and Adolescent Mental Health Services (CAMHS). In addition, UK practitioners are working in a landscape of austerity politics and service constriction, where competition between previously collaborative organisations is actively encouraged through commissioning processes. Consequently, working in partnership is strained, and the service landscape becomes a hostile space, where it is difficult to find appropriate support for children who experience domestic violence.

In this chapter, we describe how we trained professionals and groups of students to respond more positively and critically to the experiences of children who have lived with domestic violence. We then outline in detail the specific challenges that the academic and service landscape offers to critical scholars teaching in this area.

The presumption of adult victims

The service and policy context in which practitioners work with survivors of domestic violence is oriented towards an understanding that domestic abuse is a phenomenon taking place within the intimate dyad, between two adult actors – an adult victim (typically female) and an adult perpetrator (typically male). This is evident in the legal definitions of domestic violence that guide policy. The UK Home Office (2013, p. 2) defines domestic violence as: "Any incident of threatening behaviour, violence or abuse (psychological, physical, sexual, financial or emotional) between adults who are or have been intimate partners or family members, regardless of gender or sexuality."

Similarly, the Istanbul Convention on the Prevention of Violence Against Women and Girls (Council of Europe, 2011) defines it as:

> all acts of physical, sexual, psychological or economic violence that occur within the family or domestic unit or between former or current spouses or partners, whether or not the perpetrator shares or has shared the same residence with the victim.
>
> *(Council of Europe, 2011, p. 3)*

These kinds of definitions are typical of the policy context across the world (with a few notable exceptions, like Australia) in shaping a legal and practice context in which the victim of domestic abuse is explicitly an *adult* victim. In this context, children are implicitly framed as 'not-victims' – as people affected by domestic violence, but not as directly experiencing it. For instance, the Istanbul Convention indicates that European states must introduce measures "based on an integrated approach which takes into account the relationship between victims, perpetrators, children and their wider social environment" (Council of Europe, 2011, p. 7), suggesting that children are 'others' in the domestic violence context. They are excluded discursively from the category of victim. Children's needs are considered in their role as 'witnesses to violence' (in the Children Act, HM Government, 2004) as a separate child protection issue. However, this effectively positions children as "collateral damage" (Callaghan, Alexander, Sixsmith et al., 2016a, p. 5), not as victims, not as people in their own right, who, as family members living in a violent household, do experience and live with domestic abuse.

Such legal frameworks render children's experiences of domestic violence as secondary, and make them relatively invisible in, for instance, prevalence rates for victims of domestic violence. By focusing on domestic violence as an event that occurs between two adults in an intimate dyad, the child's victimisation within a home and family that are permeated with control, coercion and abuse can be obscured. By obscuring children's experiences as victims of domestic violence, and by positioning them as mere (mostly unreliable) witnesses, there is no substantial policy imperative to respond to their experiences. They are framed as additional to the main domestic violence services offered by specialist shelters, social services and police, crime and justice. This positioning of children's support as a bolt-on to specialist domestic violence services means that when services for women victims stop, support for children generally stops too. Further, because support services for women focus on risk management (e.g. getting the woman to a place of safety, and managing her 'risk' of violence), the limited services that are available for children usually disappear once the family is deemed to be 'safe'. This occurs despite the reality that children's emotional and social difficulties continue or often only emerge once their families have resettled post-separation (Morrison, 2015). The only exception to this would be if the children are labelled with a diagnostic category, granting them access to CAMHS. Even so, they would receive treatment linked to their 'disorder', not support that specifically focuses on their experience of violence and its personal and relational impact.

Domestic violence is typically framed as an act of violence against women. In the sense that domestic violence, particularly when repeated over time, is predominantly a crime of patriarchal power and control, we agree. However, this framing reduces the importance of the other common victims of patriarchal power and control – children. This has many additional unintended consequences. For instance, boy children as young as 14 can be excluded from women's shelters, because they are not defined as the *victims* of domestic abuse. The gender-based account of power and control that underpins many women-only services has been under attack in recent years, particularly by members of the men's rights movement, who argue against women-only services and for a prioritisation of male victims (Straus, 2012). As a consequence of these kinds of assaults, a call to recognise children as equal victims to women can be perceived as a further attack on women-only services. When training and teaching around this issue, it is important therefore for us to address and maintain a gender-sensitive account of domestic violence and abuse, while also arguing for a widening of the definition of the victim to incorporate children and men.

In teaching and training contexts, we have worked with this issue by focusing on the idea that recognising the familial nature of domestic violence does not necessarily mean losing a gendered analysis. We have explored the roles of masculinities and femininities in constituting children's experiences in predominantly heterosexual nuclear families.

Challenging the presumption of vulnerability

As we have already noted, children who experience domestic violence are described in literature as vulnerable, damaged and passive (Callaghan, Alexander, Sixsmith et al., 2016a, 2016b; Callaghan, Fellin, Alexander, Mavrou et al., 2017; Katz, 2016; Øverlien, 2009). While we certainly agree that it is important to emphasise the harmful impact of domestic violence on children, their positioning as passive and damaged witnesses, in academic literature, in policy and in practice leaves little space for children to articulate their capacity for resilience, resistance and agency in the context of domestic violence. It also leaves very little room for intervention and change, positioning carers and professionals as equally powerless. Children, however, can and do act when violence occurs in their homes: they maintain their capacity to care (Callaghan, Alexander, Sixsmith et al., 2016b; Katz, 2015; Mullender et al., 2003), they have complex strategies for maintaining their own and their families' safety (Callaghan, Alexander, & Fellin, 2016; Callaghan, Alexander, Mavrou et al., in press; Øverlien, 2016; Swanston, Bowyer, & Vetere, 2014), and for managing their emotional responses (Callaghan, Fellin, Alexander, Mavrou et al., 2017). The emphasis on children as damaged and passive in most psychological and social work literature on domestic abuse underestimates their capacity for conscious meaning-making within the relational context of the family and the material spaces they inhabit (Alexander, Callaghan, Fellin, & Sixsmith, 2016; Ugazio, 2013).

The policy and research emphasis on child 'witnesses' tends to overlook children's contextually located experience, with the effect of reducing the consequences of violence largely to 'passive' behavioural reactions. This is evident when considering the limited range of therapeutic interventions offered to children and young people, most of which are psychoeducational, and focus on teaching social skills, anger management (Holmes, 2013), and emotion coaching (Katz & Windecker-Nelson, 2006). These approaches all share an underlying presumption that children are incompetent subjects, who require training, psychoeducation or modelling to compensate for presumed deficits. Training professionals and volunteers to provide emotionally and socially focused support to children can be challenging in a context where children are largely positioned as reactive behavioural units rather than responsive and agentic semantically oriented beings.

The description of children as vulnerable, passive witnesses is frequently repeated and even amplified by professionals and volunteers who support families affected by domestic abuse. In focus groups, professionals reiterated this passive construction of children:

> P3: It is young, this creature is so innocent (Greece – Professional Focus Group 2)
>
> P5: The abilities of the children at that age are non-existent (Spain – Professional Focus Group)
>
> P3: This is a very, very frightened child, lost in space (Greece – Professional Focus Group 3)

Professional discourses, and particularly the language of safeguarding and child protection, focus on the notion of the child as vulnerable, helpless and in need of adult protection. Through this choice of language, the child is constructed as a helpless, passive object whose most immediate protectors failed to provide him/her with the kind of environment psychologists regard as necessary for normal development (Burman, 2016). In one organisation, our Italian partners reported direct resistance and anger about the idea that the child might have some sense of resilience, as professionals felt that this would challenge the emphasis on the child as vulnerable and damaged, and it was unthinkable to see children who had experienced violence in any other way. Being protected is enshrined as one of the fundamental rights of the child, and protecting your child is seen as a basic, necessary and highly valued part of the parental and family role. Professionals often describe the child as 'unprotected' and the parent as 'failing to protect'. In this sense, the child victim comes to embody and reflect the parents' failure to meet the principal requirements of parenthood such as providing a safe environment. This reiterates broader patterns of 'mother blaming' in academic literature, and in practice in social services, criminal and family court contexts.

The child is seen here as entirely dependent on parents, and without receiving appropriate parenting practice, the child is doomed to be 'damaged'. This focus on the apparent rescuing power of good parenting perhaps unwittingly reproduces the kind of mother-blaming discourse that is seen in much academic literature on domestic violence. This discourse positions the child's wellbeing as the responsibility of mothers, occluding the role of the perpetrator's violence, and of contextual and socio-economic factors in producing developmental challenges for children (Callaghan, 2015). This mother-blaming discourse is seen strongly in the following quote: "P3: No, no, because a lot of the mums don't want to know the truth that it was the domestic violence that's made the impact on the child" (UK – Professional Focus Group 1).

This representation of the mother as 'wilfully blind', not admitting to the impact of violence on her children, is a common construction. It contributes to discourses of mother blaming in domestic abuse support, in that mothers are positioned as complicit in offering poor care and insufficient protection to the 'vulnerable children', whose wellbeing is often described as being entirely the responsibility of victim mothers.

Professionals express their concern about the intergenerational transmission of violence (Black et al., 2010). Children who grow up in homes affected by domestic violence were seen as observing and repeating violence, and as passively absorbing the behaviours they observed. Professional knowledge of children who experience domestic violence rests heavily on the notion of intergenerational transmission: "P1: They will either adopt the role of the abused or the role of the abuser" (Greece – Professional Focus Group 4).

In this frame of reference, domestic violence is seen as a modelling context, in which children acquire a model of conflict-solving which leaves the child with no individual problem-solving skills or capacity for emotional competence. In this context, professionals suggest that aggressive behaviour is learned as the only effective way of reacting.

> P3: [I]t's learned behaviour isn't it, if they've seen it every day and dad's talking to mum, you know, talking her down and we've had some children that have come in who don't call mum "mum", who will call her "it" or "she" because that's what dad calls her or will say, "Mum, you're stupid," all the time and, "you can't do that 'cause you're stupid," . . . because that's what dad says all the time. (UK – Professional Focus Group 1)

Similarly: "P2: [I]t cannot be otherwise. If the child has learned to live under these codes, why would he/she think there is something else besides that" (Greece – Professional Focus Group 4).

Children are described here as being without choice in imitating and reproducing the behaviours that they see at home. This is the route by which professionals suggest that violence becomes 'normalised' for children. Children whom professionals see as 'damaged' in this way are also seen as lacking in their own capacity for healthy resilience. For this, professionals suggest they need professional intervention and support: "P4: They don't, they haven't got coping strategies when they come into refuge have they?" (UK – Professional Focus Group 1).

Children's experience of domestic violence is broadly accepted by the professionals as having damaged extensively major domains of life. They accept the normative view that children are inevitably harmed by domestic abuse and that such harm has a long-term (or permanent) effect.

The emphasis on the child as inevitably damaged, fragile and doomed to repeat abusive cycles reproduces the child who experiences domestic abuse as helpless and inert, a representation that is further underscored by child protection discourses. While we would not dispute that children have the right to be protected, when this right is framed in relation to the child's perceived helplessness and inherent vulnerability, the effect of this is to make it difficult to conceptualise children who experience domestic abuse as anything other than passive recipients of violence, whose agency is highly constrained, and who are damaged by the violence they experience. In reproducing these discourses, the adults whose role it is to support children reiterate self-fulfilling prophecies of helplessness and intergenerational transmission, instead of recognising children's complex and located coping strategies (Callaghan, Alexander, & Fellin, 2016; Callaghan, Fellin, Alexander, Mavrou et al., 2017), and using these strategies as a base from which to create more flexible and self-affirming conduct. This produces a subjugating dominant narrative that forecloses on positive possible futures, and offers no room for change for the child or for the parents.

Training students and professionals to work effectively with families who have experienced domestic abuse requires some deconstruction of dominant child protection discourses. There is a need to recognise children's right to live free from violence and abuse, while at the same time untangling this from the notion that children are 'innocents', naïve, passive and helpless. To support children who have lived with domestic abuse, it is important to recognise their ability to maintain some sense of self as agentic and capable, and to respect their capacity to act and to cope. If we do not recognise their located and contextually specific coping strategies, there is a risk that we disrespect their actual experiences. This is particularly clear in the way that professionals often problematize children's caregiving behaviour as 'parentification' and frame it as a problem to be removed. However, children's own experiences of this are more typically that their caregiving enables them to hold on to some sense of power in an oppressive set of family relationships (Callaghan, Alexander, Sixsmith et al., 2016b). We would argue that these kinds of coping strategies offer children a foundation for recovery post-violence, and need to be understood in their own right, not removed in the pursuit of an idealised notion of the restoration of 'normal' childhood through the assertion of children's proper place as passive and cared for, not as caring.

Challenging biomedical orthodoxy in trauma

The impact of trauma is increasingly understood as producing neurological damage for children who live with domestic violence. The orthodox account suggests that the developing brain of the traumatised child is flooded with cortisol, creating challenges for the child's developing nervous system and predicting long-term difficulties with cognitive and emotional functioning (Choi, Jeong, Polcari, Rohan, & Teicher, 2012). This is part of a broader turn to focus on 'adverse childhood events' and their neurological impact on children, which has found particular purchase in policy linked to criminal justice and child protection, where it has been seen as heralding a new era in prevention science. The promise here is that early neural screening of children who have experienced adverse childhood events might enable the identification of those who might be at risk of becoming involved in violence and abuse themselves (Rigterink, Katz, & Hessler, 2010).

In the domestic violence field, this is particularly expressed as a concern with children's capacity for emotional regulation, which is seen as associated with the impact of violence on neurological development, and particularly on the 'emotional centres' of the brain (Rigterink et al., 2010). Reducing children's experiences of violence down to damaged neural networks, however, risks obscuring the relational and socio-economic context within which that violence occurs. It also underestimates children's capacity for resistance to oppressive familial relationships, their attempts to improve these relationships and their potential for recovery after domestic abuse.

Nonetheless, these biomedical accounts predominate in social work and voluntary sector organisations which respond to families affected by domestic abuse. In training contexts, we were often explicitly asked to comment on the impact of domestic abuse on the developing brain. These biomedical accounts can be very seductive, because they offer such apparently 'certain' responses to the complexity of the relational world of children living with abuse. This biomedical orthodoxy supports a culture in which children's capacity for agency, resilience and resistance is almost unthinkable. It entrenches the positioning of children who experience domestic abuse as always and inevitably damaged, and forecloses any possible articulation of spaces for children to step outside abuse patterns. In contrast, children's capacity for resistance, resilience and agency is highly located, specific and subtle, not lending itself to easy or certain formulations. The complexity of children's lives does not easily fit into the needs of staff in highly pressurised service contexts to provide simple and generalisable solutions in the shape of pre-packaged manuals or formulaic service responses.

Passing the parcel: getting needs met

Child survivors have significant difficulty in getting mental health needs met. Co-ordinated Action Against Domestic Abuse (CAADA, 2014), drawing on their extensive database of domestic abuse cases in the UK, found that only half of the children were known to social services, while only 11% received help from specialist CAMHS. Given the documented elevated risk of mental health difficulties among children and young people exposed to domestic violence, this is a surprising phenomenon.

In our focus groups with parents, some reported an experience of constantly having to "battle" for services for their children. They suggested that support was available for their *parenting* and to manage children's behaviour, but that there was little available to deal with the emotional fallout of living in abusive households. This reflects the already described construction of children's difficulties as learned behaviour, reproducing a sense of them as behavioural units, rather than as reflexive, meaning-making and agentic human beings. In the UK, even the limited service that is available to support children and young people tends to be withdrawn once they are no longer on the Children in Need register. This is a reflection of the focus in the UK on delivering services that are geared towards reducing *risk*, with risk narrowly defined as risk of further exposure to physical violence. However, the emotional needs of children who experience violence in the family are often not evident while the family is unsettled: rather these difficulties are often expressed once the family is safer and more settled. Because children's risk is seen as a bolt-on to mothers' risk, and because mothers' risk is reduced to physical risk, the complexity of what it means to be 'in need' is underestimated. Services are not offered when the child perceives a need, but instead are offered when the child is deemed 'at risk'. Further, services offered through CAMHS are only really accessible if the child is diagnosed with a specific (and sufficiently severe) mental health difficulty. This hinders an agile preventative response to emerging mental health difficulties. Because of the tendency to reduce children's distress to individualised 'mere behaviour', they are more likely to receive diagnoses of ADHD (attention-deficit hyperactivity disorder) and conduct disorder (not really amenable to CAMHS therapeutic interventions), than mental health diagnoses that would give them access to emotional and therapeutic support.

In addition to the difficulties associated with inappropriate and inaccessible services, professionals in all four countries expressed a strong concern about the lack, or the deterioration, of some kind of coordinating or collaborative centre that could organise the action of those working to support families affected by domestic violence.

> P4: A good organizational model, to treat all cases of abuse, has been lacking in [our locality] for these years. (Italy, Umbria – Professional Focus Group 1)

> P1: [E]ven if many of the mentioned services are activated, there is a lot of confusion and lack of dialogue . . . every one of us starts with the best of intentions, that is to say to help victims of violence . . . but each present service does not communicate with the other! (shouts) . . . Everybody [wants] to be the "number one", but, at the end of the day, they are just cultivating their own little garden. (Italy, Puglia – Professional Focus Group 1)

> P3: [T]hat's the problem [–] each one has their own protocol, there isn't coordination. (Spain – Professional Focus Group)

> P2: I also agree that the most important thing, apart from understaffing, is the lack of coordination. (Greece – Professional Focus Group 1)

> P3: Since there was a split between Social and Health[,] a problem has emerged and internal divisions . . . one hand does not know what the other is doing and the staff does not want to intervene because they defend themselves. (Italy – Professional Focus Group 1)

This lack of coordination and collaboration presents problems in dealing with serious cases and diminishes the quality of service provision. Professionals feel that people affected by domestic violence do not get the help they need due to these deficiencies. In the UK, competitive commissioning practices in the charitable sector are seen as breaking down partnership working, making it more challenging for organisations to work together. Added to this is a concern about the privatisation and closure of many state and local authority organisations, which, in turn, places greater service demands on charitable sector organisations.

Many professionals suggested that working with children affected by domestic violence was something that needed to be embedded in schools, and that educational professionals needed to take some responsibility for what was described largely as prevention work.

> P10: The educational community has to be aware that it is up to them . . . but they are not prepared to do it. (Spain – Professional Focus Group)

> P3: Because it's domestic abuse and they don't want us in there. . . . They'd rather not know it's happening and a lot of schools will say they don't have domestic abuse in their school. (UK – Professional Focus Group 1)

> P1: I was invited to do a session at a secondary school in [name of town omitted] and it had to be entitled 'Healthy Relationships', wasn't allowed to call it 'domestic abuse', even though the subject matter was domestic abuse. (UK – Professional Focus Group 1)

These participants were concerned about what they saw as a lack of engagement with issues relating to domestic violence in schools, and saw this as a direct obstacle to working to raise awareness and ensure good-quality prevention and intervention for children and young people. They saw the resistance offered by schools as undermining integrated working and preventing good services for children who experience domestic violence.

With schools and CAMHS not offering specialist support for children affected by domestic abuse, social services and domestic abuse services experiencing rapid service cuts under 'austerity' policies, and an additional lack of an overarching coordinating response to children's experiences of domestic abuse, we are left with a situation where children's emotional distress is not really acknowledged and supported anywhere. This creates real challenges in training and supporting staff to offer support that recognises children's capacity for resistance and resilience, since they do not appear to be recognised as needing support anywhere within the service landscape.

Generally, professionals described an impoverished service landscape, impacted by austerity and cuts:

> P5: I know one size doesn't fit all . . . but there does need to be a restructure and streamlining around, and I think that is going to be happening around the commissioning. Money's a lot tighter, but it should be an opportunity to make it more effective and . . . I don't know, there's got to be some improvement there. (UK – Professional Focus Group 2)

> P3: And actually these children are the next generation and we need to get in there don't we and help them [?] (UK – Professional Focus Group 2)

Professionals in Greece also identified service cuts and austerity measures as contributing to and producing difficulties with service provision:

> P4: [T]hen, in the old times, then in our years (laughs)
>
> P3: [T]hen we had money (laughs)
>
> P4: [I]t was much more easier. (Greece – Professional Focus Group 3)

For some, the constriction of the service landscape associated with austerity cuts is placing children's services at significant risk. This intensifies the lack of support for children, making access to existing services more challenging, placing some of the limited services available at risk. For others, it highlights the need for more effective services, using the neoliberal discourse of the current UK government to reframe austerity measures as an "opportunity". However, this suggestion trails off ("I don't know") as it is clear that the individual does not have a sense of what this "more effective" alternative might be. This is perhaps related to the competitiveness inherent to austerity and a service landscape rooted in commissioning:

> P4: Unfortunately it all does come down to money at the end of the day. You know, everybody in the county is fighting for survival at the minute, to find out, you know, if domestic abuse services are going to be carried on and . . . you know, who's going to be cut. (UK – Professional Focus Group 1)

This extract highlights a fundamental flaw in the logic of the market and commissioning. When austerity discourses function so as to constantly justify service cuts, these services are positioned as constantly under threat. This sense of threat combined with increased competition to provide limited services in regional authorities where funding is very limited, has significantly undermined collaboration and cooperation between voluntary sector organisations. This undermines rather than strengthens the likelihood of the development of innovative solutions for the provision of appropriate and accessible services for children who experience domestic abuse. Further, the use of commissioning as a dominant funding model for service provision is inherently hostile to responses to children's needs that recognise complexity. The practice of competitive commissioning for services prioritises services for children and families as pre-packaged 'products' that can be purchased as units – reductionist solutions to complex problems. How do we train professionals who are hamstrung by a service landscape that is in constriction, riddled with creeping privatisation and in which professionals and organisations are forced into competition by commissioning structures?

A critical and reflexive teaching and learning strategy

As we have argued above, professionals often have a desire to provide better support for children and young people, but reproduce quite problematic and pathologising understandings of children who experience domestic violence. To effect any change in the way that children are positioned in domestic violence policy and practice, it was important to intervene in this arena, by sharing the insights of our work with children with professionals who work with them. Drawing on the insights built up throughout the programme, training was offered to professionals and voluntary sector workers who supported families who had experienced domestic violence. In particular, our focus was on communicating to professionals the importance of treating children who experience domestic violence as individuals with agency, as meaning-making beings who were just as much the victims as the adult targets of domestic violence.

A range of professionals were trained, including social services staff, psychologists, teachers, police officers, GPs, nurses, domestic violence support workers and family support workers. The training structure generally involved one training day, with varying patterns of follow-up training. Northampton had one training day, and four follow-ups, which allowed some facilitation of integration of acquired material. Some partners (Thessaloniki, Northampton and Puglia) had arranged for ongoing support for contact between the research team and trainees, to ensure follow-through of the project in each site. Training was well received, and there was a strong perception of a need for more training in all regions.

Consistent with our social-constructionist and systemic perspective, we adopted a collaborative and dialogical approach to teaching and learning (Vygotsky, 1978), to enable a learning environment in which our perspectives co-evolved and were co-constructed in the interactions with the professionals and students with whom we worked. We also assumed that reflective and inclusive practice was a necessary meta-competence, especially when training such a diverse group of learners. We aimed to foster a community of learners, researchers and practitioners and respect individual learners and diverse learning communities across different regions and countries (Lave & Wenger, 1990).

By reflexivity as a core competence, we mean that every knowledge in the domestic violence field is contextualised in the wider (socio-political) context, self-reflexive and grounded from the very start. Systemic thinking emphasises the importance of understanding individuals and their experience within the broader context and its multiple interlocking layers; that is, historical, cultural, socio-economic, political. According to Bateson (1979), second-order learning (or learning how to learn) denotes the reflexive ability to adapt, transfer and apply knowledge to different phenomena and contexts.

This reflective self-appraisal is pivotal to develop critical understanding on such a controversial and complex topic as domestic violence. As trainers, we needed to be reflexive on multiple aspects of our interaction with a specific audience:

1. methods – techniques and language employed, presentations, fora strategies drawing on students' experience, background and learning needs;
2. co-learners – one's own and others' stance, assumptions and safety;
3. context – the variety of internal and external factors influencing the learning and teaching experience.

In order to foster a sense of learning community, we adopted a flexible and experiential teaching style: reading and discussion groups, structured debates, seminar presentations. We especially valued visual methods, embodied and creative techniques that engaged diverse learners into a shared process by blending verbal with non-verbal communication. Materials like photos, videos, collages and other media (real case studies) employed in the UNARS project, as well as embodied techniques (genograms, role plays, sculptures) were essential to familiarise learners with powerful and empowering research and therapeutic tools, and to facilitate 'hands on' learning and critical appraisal. When teaching university students, we also used virtual learning environments and encouraged networking.

To promote learners' engagement and experience, we constantly linked the training content to their professional and personal experience and their transferable skills. At the same time, we supported learners' critical appraisal by providing an arena in which to evaluate, reflect and act upon the role played by social, institutional and legislative cultures in shaping, developing and evaluating services and therapeutic interventions for children in situations of domestic violence. We also worked with participants to overcome identified barriers and to re-evaluate and further develop existing theories.

Our learning strategy was both centred on children's lived experience and learners' needs. We also ensured that the training we offered did not just focus on learning skills or developing an intellectual understanding of the impact of domestic violence. Children's voices and their artistic and creative products were present throughout the training sessions; these were prioritised and explicitly given centre stage in all our learning. The impact of this was significant, and enabled a context in which our reflexive work was not (just) intellectual, but was worked through emotionally with the material that children had offered in the interviews we completed with them. Learners were also encouraged to use embodied techniques like family sculpture and an exploration of the embodied experience of power, and to reflect on the impact of these experiences on their understanding of the spatial, material and relational context of domestic violence. This facilitated a greater emphasis on integrated and participative activities that made the learning experience contextualised, reflective and accessible. This learning context was designed to facilitate not mere acquisition of knowledge and skills, but through liminal moments, to facilitate a transformation of learners' identities (Meyer & Land, 2005) by deconstructing taken-for-granted understandings of children as 'witnesses' and as damaged 'victims' and repositioning them to listen more closely to children's experiences in a way that enabled children's capacity for agency and resistance to be recognised.

In their post-training feedback, trainees generally reported that they found the training helpful and supportive, and that they had learned a great deal that they could apply in practice. Trainees valued collaborative working, and the provision of a quiet working environment in which they could build and develop networking opportunities with other professionals. In terms of knowledge and skills acquired, trainees reported that they found the emphasis on listening to the child, and giving proper attention and priority to their needs, rather than just focusing on the involved adults, very important. As one trainee commented: "I need to show I am available to listen, reassuring them[,] but not pressuring them to tell their accounts". They highlighted the importance of avoiding re-traumatisation, while at the same time providing space for children to express their experiences and to reflect. The training emphasised a range of techniques to enable this – particularly using creative and embodied approaches – which participants found useful.

They felt able to transfer their learning to their working environment, and many trainees made comments like: "I feel I am more confident to help children and young people". In particular, they felt they had acquired new skills and tools to assist them in their work with children and young people who have experienced domestic violence. They were enthusiastic about applying techniques, with one respondent saying, "The ecomap I will be able to use, and effectively I have already started using [it]", and another saying, "I can't wait to use the materials!".

Some trainees had secured institutional support for adopting new ways of working based on the training, saying, "Our work place environment want us to use the training in our everyday work"; "I have shared my experience with my manager who has supported me integrating skills learnt into my practice"; and "My workplace [is] embracing my need to apply principles of the training to my practice". They also offered useful insights into perceived barriers to working in a way that listens to children, takes them seriously as victims of domestic violence, and enables their agency to be recognised. They noted that institutional models of practice were hardy, and often resistant to change. This interpretation was also extended to them as individuals, as they emphasised that they too had their own 'cognitive categories' that could box children in, and that needed to be challenged. They also highlighted the lack of adequate organisations to respond to children's needs. Further, they noted that younger children (under 10 years old) might face communication challenges in expressing their experiences. They also noted that policy and legal frameworks present a barrier in taking children seriously: "The law safeguards and implements intervention addressed to women, but not to children or any other victim of domestic violence". They suggested that those on the frontline who work with children who experience violence often lack the skills to listen to children's accounts, and that while they recognise the violence directed to women, often do not see its effect on children.

The future

There is an urgent need for services to support children who have experienced domestic abuse. Training existing staff in social services, domestic abuse organisations, policing and mental health contexts is overdue. However, in engaging with training in these contexts, it is necessary to be aware of the dominant discourses in circulation that make it difficult to explore less pathologising ways of talking about children. In this chapter, we have highlighted how children who experience domestic abuse are often framed in service contexts as passive, helpless and damaged, leaving little space for the articulation of a child with capacity for agency, resistance and resilience. The lack of recognition of children as people and as victims in their own right removes the impetus to provide a coherent response to their needs, and much of the provision for them is ad hoc and additional to services for the adult intimate dyad that is conceptualised as victim and perpetrator in these relationships. Services are reliant on two dominant discourses to make sense of children's experiences of domestic abuse: an intergenerational transmission discourse, which positions children as having no choice but to be the passive inheritors of their parents' violence and victimisation; and a biomedical discourse that describes children as inherently damaged by the abuse that they 'witness'. Because children's sense of self as capable and resistant to oppressive relational practices is located and contextually specific, it is impossible to develop generic and universal models to apply to families affected by domestic abuse. However, this is precisely the kind of response demanded in commissioned services. Commissioning practices and austerity ideology commodify services for families affected by domestic abuse, encouraging services to respond with pre-packaged products that can easily be bought as units. This practice is hostile to the development of complex service responses that provide the time and contextually sensitive support needed by children who experience domestic abuse.

Training professionals and volunteers in this kind of landscape requires more than 'content' on children's responses to domestic abuse. Rather, training needs to enable professionals to work with understandings of children as people in their own right (Wells & Montgomery, 2014), not as dependent, passive and helpless. This requires a critical engagement with cultural discourses of childhood itself (Burman, 2017), and resources to challenge the orthodox account of the psycho-social and neurological impact on children of 'witnessing' domestic abuse. Reframing children's experiences in a manner that enables their capacity for agency and resistance requires the construction of accounts of children's lives that are relationally and socio-economically located (Callaghan & Alexander, 2015; Callaghan, Alexander, & Fellin, 2016; Callaghan, Alexander, Sixsmith et al. 2016a; Callaghan, Fellin, & Alexander, 2017). This kind of account is difficult to hear and apply in a UK service context limited by the commodification of services associated with austerity cuts and commissioning frameworks. Challenging these socio-economic practices is not easy when competitive commissioning and ideological practices of austerity produce a sense of constant tenuousness and threat for services that support families. As trainers and as academics, we must work with services to challenge the socio-economic conditions that place their work under such strain, if we are to provide more appropriate, accessible and responsive services for children who experience domestic abuse.

References

Alexander, J.H., Callaghan, J.E.M., Fellin, L.C., & Sixsmith, J. (2016). Children's corporeal agency and use of space in situations of domestic violence. In J. Horton & B. Evans (Eds.), *Geographies of children and young people. Play, recreation, health and well being* (pp. 523–543). Singapore: Springer.

Bair-Merritt, M.H., Blackstone, M., & Feudtner, C. (2006). Physical health outcomes of childhood exposure to intimate partner violence: A systematic review., 117, e278–290. doi:10.1542/peds.2005-1473

Baldry, A.C. (2003). Bullying in schools and exposure to domestic violence. *Child Abuse & Neglect, 27,* 713–732. doi:10.1016/S0145-2134(03)00114-5

Bateson, G. (1979). *Mind and nature.* New York: Dutton.

Black, D.S., Sussman, S., & Unger, J.B. (2010). A further look at the intergenerational transmission of violence: Witnessing interparental violence in emerging adulthood. *Journal of Interpersonal Violence, 25,* 1022–1042. doi:10.1177/0886260509340539

Bogat, G.A., DeJonghe, E., Levendosky, A.A., Davidson, W.S., & von Eye, A. (2006). Trauma symptoms among infants exposed to intimate partner violence. *Child Abuse & Neglect, 30,* 109–125. doi:10.1016/j.chiabu.2005.09.002

Bridgett, D.J., Burt, N.M., Edwards, E.S., & Deater-Deckard, K. (2015). Intergenerational transmission of self-regulation: A multidisciplinary review and integrative conceptual framework. *Psychological Bulletin, 141,* 602–654.

Burkett, M. (2015). Constructing innocence and risk as a rationale for intervention. In C. Newnes (Ed.), *Children in society: Politics, policies and interventions* (pp. 33–49). Monmouth, UK: PCCS Books.

Burman, E. (2016). *Deconstructing developmental psychology* (2nd ed.). London: Routlege.

Burman, E. (2017). *Deconstructing developmental psychology* (3rd ed.). London: Routledge

Byrne, D., & Taylor, B. (2007). Children at risk from domestic violence and their educational attainment: Perspectives of education welfare officers, social workers and teachers. *Child Care in Practice, 13,* 185–201. doi:10.1080/13575270701353465

CAADA. (2014). *In plain sight : Effective help for children exposed to domestic abuse.* Cardiff, UK: CAADA.

Callaghan, J.E.M. (2015). Mothers and children? Representations of mothers in research on children's outcomes in domestic violence. *Psychology of Women Section Review, 16.* 2–5.

Callaghan, J.E.M., & Alexander, J.H. (2015). *Understanding agency and resistance strategies: Children's experiences of domestic violence.* Report. Available at www.unars.co.uk

Callaghan, J.E.M., Alexander, J.H., & Fellin, L.C. (2016). Children's embodied experiences of living with domestic violence: "I'd go into my panic, and shake, really bad." *Subjectivity, 9,* 399–419. doi:10.1057/s41286-016-0011-9

Callaghan, J.E.M., Alexander, J.H., Mavrou, S., Fellin, L.C., & Sixsmith, J. (in press). Practices of telling, and not telling: The management of disclosure in children's accounts of domestic violence. *Journal of Child and Family Studies.*

Callaghan, J.E.M., Alexander, J.H., Sixsmith, J., & Fellin, L.C. (2016a). Beyond "witnessing": Children's experiences of coercive control in domestic violence and abuse. *Journal of Interpersonal Violence*. doi: 10.1177/0886260515618946

Callaghan, J.E.M., Alexander, J.H., Sixsmith, J., Fellin, L.C. (2016b). Children's experiences of domestic violence and abuse: Siblings' accounts of relational coping. *Journal of Clinical Child Psychology and Psychiatry, 21*, 649–668.

Callaghan, J.E.M., Fellin, L.C., & Alexander, J.H. (2017). Beyond vulnerability: Working with children who have experienced domestic violence. In C. Brownlow, L. O'Dell, & H. Bertilsdotter-Rosqvist (Eds.), *Different childhoods*. London: Routledge.

Callaghan, J.E.M., Fellin, L.C., Alexander, J., Mavrou, S., & Papathanasiou, M. (2017). Children and domestic violence: Emotional competencies in embodied and relational contexts. *Psychology of Violence*. doi: http://dx.doi.org/10.1037/vio0000108

Choi, J., Jeong, B., Polcari, A., Rohan, M.L., & Teicher, M.H. (2012). Reduced fractional anisotropy in the visual limbic pathway of young adults witnessing domestic violence in childhood. *Neuroimage, 59*, 1071–1079. doi:10.1016/j.neuroimage.2011.09.033

Council of Europe. (2011). *Convention on preventing and combating violence against women and domestic violence*. CETS No. 210. Strasbourg, France: Council of Europe.

Ehrensaft, M.K., & Cohen, P. (2012). Contribution of family violence to the intergenerational transmission of externalizing behavior. *Prevention Science, 13*, 370–383. doi:10.1007/s11121-011-0223-8

Ehrensaft, M.K., Cohen, P., Brown, J., Smailes, E., Chen, H., & Johnson, J.G. (2003). Intergenerational transmission of partner violence: A 20-year prospective study. *Journal of Consulting and Clinical Psychology, 71*, 741–753. doi:10.1037/0022-006X.71.4.741

Eriksson, M. (2012). Participation for children exposed to domestic violence? Social workers' approaches and children's strategies. *European Journal of Social Work, 15*, 205–221. doi:10.1080/13691457.2010.513963

HM Government. (2004). Children Act 2004. London: The Stationery Office Ltd.

Holmes, M.R. (2013). Aggressive behavior of children exposed to intimate partner violence: An examination of maternal mental health, maternal warmth and child maltreatment. *Child Abuse & Neglect, 37*, 520–530. doi:10.1016/j.chiabu.2012.12.006

Home Office. (2013). *Information for local areas on the change to the Definition of Domestic Violence and Abuse*. London: Home Office/AVA.

Houghton, C. (2015). Young people's perspectives on participatory ethics: Agency, power and impact in domestic abuse research and policy-making. *Child Abuse Review, 24*, 235–248. doi: 10.1002/car.2407

Katz, E. (2015). Domestic violence, children's agency and mother–child relationships: Towards a more advanced model. *Children & Society, 29*, 69–79. doi:10.1111/chso.12023

Katz, E. (2016). Beyond the physical incident model: How children living with domestic violence are harmed by and resist regimes of coercive control. *Child Abuse Review, 25*, 46–59. doi:10.1002/car.2422

Katz, L.F., & Windecker-Nelson, B. (2006). Domestic violence, emotion coaching, and child adjustment. *Journal of Family Psychology, 20*, 56–67. doi:10.1037/0893-3200.20.1.56

Lamers-Winkelman, F., Willemen, A.M., & Visser, M. (2012). Adverse childhood experiences of referred children exposed to intimate partner violence: Consequences for their wellbeing. *Child Abuse & Neglect, 36*, 166–179.

Lave, J., & Wenger, E. (1990). *Situated learning: Legitimate peripheral participation*. Cambridge: Cambridge University Press.

Meyer, J.H.F., & Land, R. (2005). Threshold concepts and troublesome knowledge (2): Epistemological considerations and a conceptual framework for teaching and learning. *Higher Education, 49*, 373–388. doi:10.1007/s10734-004-6779-5

Morrison, F. (2015). "All over now?" The ongoing relational consequences of domestic abuse through children's contact arrangements. *Child Abuse Review, 24*, 274–284.

Mullender, A., Hague, G., Imam, U.F., Kelly, L., Malos, E., & Regan, L. (2003). *Children's perspectives on domestic violence.* London: Sage.

Øverlien, C. (2009). Children exposed to domestic violence: Conclusions from the literature and challenges ahead. *Journal of Social Work, 10*, 80–97. doi:10.1177/1468017309350663

Øverlien, C. (2013). The children of patriarchal terrorism. *Journal of Family Violence, 28*, 277–287. doi:10.1007/s10896-013-9498-9

Øverlien, C. (2014). "He didn't mean to hit mom, I think": Positioning, agency and point in adolescents' narratives about domestic violence. *Child & Family Social Work, 19*, 156–164. doi:10.1111/j.1365-2206.2012.00886.x

Øverlien, C. (2016). "Do you want to do some arm wrestling?": Children's strategies when experiencing domestic violence and the meaning of age. *Child & Family Social Work.* doi:10.1111/cfs.12283

Øverlien, C., & Hydén, M. (2009). Children's actions when experiencing domestic violence. *Childhood, 16*, 479–496.

Renner, L.M., & Slack, K.S. (2006). Intimate partner violence and child maltreatment: Understanding intra- and intergenerational connections. *Child Abuse & Neglect, 30*, 599–617. doi:10.1016/j.chiabu.2005.12.005

Rigterink, T., Katz, L.F., & Hessler, D.M. (2010). Domestic violence and longitudinal associations with children's physiological regulation abilities. *Journal of Interpersonal Violence, 25*, 1669–1683. doi:10.1177/0886260509354589

Statham, J. (2004). Effective services to support children in special circumstances. *Child: Care, Health and Development, 30*, 589–598. doi:10.1111/j.1365-2214.2004.00472.x

Stith, S.M., Rosen, K.H., Middleton, K.A., Busch, A.L., Lundeberg, K., & Carlton, R.P. (2000). The intergenerational transmission of spouse abuse: A meta-analysis. *Journal of Marriage & the Family, 62*, 640–654.

Stover, C.S. (2005). Domestic violence research: What have we learned and where do we go from here? *Journal of Interpersonal Violence, 20*, 448–454. doi:10.1177/0886260504267755

Straus, M.A. (2012). Blaming the messenger for the bad news about partner violence by women: The methodological, theoretical, and value basis of the purported invalidity of the Conflict Tactics Scales. *Behavioural Sciences & the Law, 30*, 538–566.

Swanston, J., Bowyer, L., & Vetere, A. (2014). Towards a richer understanding of school-age children's experiences of domestic violence: The voices of children and their mothers. *Clinical Child Psychology and Psychiatry, 19*, 184–201. doi:10.1177/1359104513485082

Ugazio, V. (2013). *Semantic polarities and psychopathologies in the family: Permitted and forbidden stories.* London: Routledge.

Vygotsky, L.S. (1978). *Mind in society: The development of higher psychological processes.* Cambridge, MA: Harvard University Press.

Wells, K., & Montgomery, H. (2014). Everyday violence and social recognition. In K.Wells, E. Burman, H. Montgomery, & A. Watson (Eds.), *Childhood, youth and violence in global contexts* (pp. 1–15). Basingstoke, UK: Palgrave MacMillan.

Willis, D., Hawkins, J.W., Pearce, C.W., Phalen, J., Keet, M., & Singer, C. (2010). Children who witness violence: What services do they need to heal? *Issues in Mental Health Nursing, 31*, 552–560. doi:10.3109/01612841003721461

12

SUPERVISION

A principles-based approach

Sara Tai

This chapter aims, primarily, to describe a range of supervisory experiences subsequent to many years of both participating in and mostly providing supervision, in a range of contexts, modalities and for a variety of purposes. My experiences as a supervisor have been mostly, but not exclusively, in the context of working with therapists practising Cognitive Behaviour Therapy (CBT). The supervision has taken place across a number of different countries with considerable cultural diversity; for both psychologist and non-psychologist professionals working in a variety of clinical contexts; in one-to-one and group settings; in person on a face-to-face basis and also using alternative formats of web-based or telephone technologies. This chapter will describe some of these activities with reference to potential benefits and challenges that different formats of supervision might hold. In particular, it will describe a range of supervision methods and training activities aimed at encouraging therapists to take a responsive, flexible and client-led approach to working therapeutically. This chapter will provide some examples of supervision as a potential means to promoting diverse, stimulating, fun and inspiring learning and reflective experience for both supervisor and supervisees. A central theme is consideration of the underlying theoretical assumptions and evidence upon which psychological treatments and supervision are founded. This speaks to the question: how do we know what it is we should be doing in supervision? In response, I will describe a principles-based approach to psychological therapy and supervision, using a theoretical framework known as Perceptual Control Theory (PCT; e.g. Powers, 1973). This theory has informed my practice as a therapist and supervisor, but the intention here is to provide an illustration of one potential way in which it is possible to link theory, research and practice to supervision. Finally, this chapter will offer a brief reflection on a second essential question about supervision – how do we know if what we do in supervision is effective? It is acknowledged that the necessary data to provide empirical evidence for effectiveness of the experiences described in this chapter do not currently exist, and some reflection on how such evidence might be accrued will be offered. The principles that have influenced the supervision I provide will be outlined first, as these offer the rationale for the critical approach to providing and teaching supervision; followed by a description of the methods of supervision used.

Supervision in clinical psychology

Within clinical psychology, supervision is considered to be an essential element of clinical practice through which theory and research become woven into practice, subsequently developing the skills a psychologist possesses and improving their practice. Milne (2007, p. 440) conducted a systematic review of the literature and developed an evidence-based definition of supervision as "the formal provision, by approved supervisors, of a relationship-based education and training that is case-focused and which manages, supports, develops and evaluates the work of junior colleagues". Supervision has become a mandatory component within training and regulation (Holloway & Neufeldt, 1995) in order to practise in the UK as an applied psychologist in accordance with, for example, the Care Quality Commission's *Essential Standards of Quality and Safety* (2010), the Health and Care Professions Council's *Standards of Proficiency* (section 4.6) (2015), and the British Psychological Society, Division of Clinical Psychology's (2014) policy on supervision. For the most part, this is the accepted position internationally, with equivalent local guidance and policies requiring that psychologists seek regular supervision. This obligation is based on an assumption that supervision will enhance knowledge, competency-based practice, and most importantly, the quality of care that psychologists provide. Yet the evidence base for this assumption is relatively weak (for reviews, see, for example, Wheeler & Richards, 2007; Milne et al., 2010). Existing research on supervision has tended to focus on the process of supervision and the effects on the supervisee; and whether it actually changes what clinicians do. The paucity of research examining if what therapists do, in turn, benefits patient outcomes is partly explained by the challenges of conducting research that could possibly demonstrate such a causal link. Also, the content and structure of supervision are usually determined by the therapeutic orientation that informs the model of supervision, as well as clinical context; both of which vary considerably.

Model-specific supervision

Models of supervision tend to be specific to the model of therapy being practised; with the same theoretical framework and principles underlying the therapy being applied to guide supervision. As such, the supervisory relationship, to some degree, is expected to reflect that of a therapist and client relationship. The format of supervision might involve a similar structure to the therapy, and the supervisor usually illustrates many of the treatment's model-specific techniques and procedures. For example, in Cognitive Behaviour Therapy approaches, the supervision session would begin with the agreement of a specific agenda and the supervisor might use techniques such as Socratic questioning directly with the supervisee to address the problem at hand or the supervisory 'question' (e.g. Milne & Reiser, 2014). In model-specific approaches, the theoretical framework underlying the therapy provides the guiding principles for what a therapist does, making the assessment of therapist adherence to the model clear. Similarly, in psychodynamic supervision, the dynamics between the therapist and client are seen to be re-enacted within the supervisory relationship, whereby the problems experienced by the therapist in supervision are thought to reflect that of the client's problem (Binder & Strupp, 1997). Supervision therefore becomes a parallel process to therapy, conducted in a very similar manner.

While there might be some clear benefits to this, there are also some potential limitations. Supervisor–therapist relationships have some fundamental differences to therapist–patient relationships and some supervisees might not find a 'therapy style' approach conducive to some of the key goals of supervision; particularly those who might prefer a less directive approach to be provided by their supervisor in CBT, or perhaps, a more directive approach within psychodynamic therapy. Also, specific treatment models usually have quite clear specifications for what the therapist should *do*; posing a potential risk of becoming too focused on methods and techniques.

If supervision ultimately aims to improve the effectiveness of what therapists do, it seems reasonable to first have some clear notion of what it is therapists should be doing; what it is that is therapeutic, and why. It is currently estimated that between 250 and 1000 different treatment models and techniques exist (Duncan, Hubble, & Miller, 2004), with each model proposing a slightly different explanation of psychological distress along with its own novel therapy techniques. For example, schema therapy, Dialectical Behaviour Therapy (DBT), Acceptance and Commitment Therapy (ACT), behavioural therapy, CBT and metacognitive therapy each describes a novel perspective on what causes anxiety. Consider, for example, a scenario where six people with six different kinds of anxiety seek treatment. Statistically speaking, it would be almost impossible that the person with schema-model-type anxiety would just happen to be allocated to schema therapy, the person with DBT anxiety would get to see a DBT therapist, the person with CBT anxiety is allocated the CBT therapist, and so on. It is much more likely that there is some common element to all therapies that makes it possible for the six different people to reduce their psychological distress regardless of which type of therapy they receive. This has been referred to as the Dodo effect: as with the character in *Alice in Wonderland*, all therapies, regardless of the specific methods and techniques, produce equivalent outcomes (Rosenzweig, 1936). There is, of course, a growing literature on the ineffectiveness of therapies, particularly in their impact on the external and environmental factors in distress (see, for example, Smail, 2005).

Subsequently, questions such as "What is it that makes a therapist effective?" and "What is the mechanism of therapeutic change?" spring to mind. The answer to these questions also forms the foundations of clinical supervision. Having a plausible understanding of what works and when seems fundamental, along with understanding why these things don't work from time to time. And yet, when it comes to discussion of psychological treatments, mechanisms of action have rarely been specified at all. Alan Kazdin (2007) commented that despite the amount of research on psychological therapies, we still have no evidence-based explanations for how or why therapies produce change. So how can we be so confident about what we do in supervision? Kazdin also highlighted that the consequence of a mechanism of action is frequently confused with the mechanism itself. For example, within the literature on Cognitive Behaviour Therapy (CBT), there is a wide evidence base for an association between therapeutic alliance, cognitive change and therapeutic outcome. Researchers have commonly cited therapeutic alliance and cognitive change as putative mechanisms of change and while both are clearly explanations of what might have changed, they are not accurate explanations of how that change occurred (Carey, 2011). A plausible explanation for how therapeutic alliance or cognitive change can arise would also need to relate mechanisms of change to the internal biological correlates of that change. Yet, there is almost no research on psychological treatments that has provided such an explanation. Instead, models of psychological treatments are largely hypothetical explanations of psychological distress that postulate pathology and abnormality. In this sense, they are not really 'models' in the same way that a working model of a car or a diagrammatic model of an electronic circuit offers a representation of how something actually functions, which would lend itself directly to being empirically tested.

An alternative model: Perceptual Control Theory (PCT)

If supervision is about increasing therapist effectiveness, and therapist effectiveness is about creating the conditions that make whatever it is that brings about therapeutic change more likely to happen, then knowing how that change occurs seems essential. Within my own clinical practice as both a therapist and supervisor, I have utilised Perceptual Control Theory (PCT; Powers, 1973, 2005, 2008; Powers, Clark, & McFarland, 1960). Perceptual Control Theory is a theory of everyday human behaviour that integrates three key principles (control, conflict and reorganisation) evidenced in the literature to understand how psychological distress and psychological change occur. As a functional model that does indeed specify how change is mapped onto biological correlates, it meets the criteria for being a real functional 'model' that can be empirically tested. There is multidisciplinary evidence for the theory derived from simulations and modelling of human behaviour (e.g. Marken, 2001; Powers, 1989, 1999). As a general theory of human functioning as opposed to one based on 'pathology', it can also be applied to understanding the therapist–patient relationship and also the supervisor–supervisee relationship. An overview of the three principles of PCT will be provided here, in order to describe how these principles might inform therapy and, thus, what we do in supervision. The three principles have been applied directly to working therapeutically with people experiencing mental health difficulties, using an approach known as the

Method of Levels (Carey, 2006, 2008; Carey, Mansell, & Tai, 2015). For detailed descriptions and reviews of PCT and the Method of Levels (MOL), please see, for example, Marken and Mansell (2013) and Carey, Mansell and Tai (2014, 2015).

Control

From a PCT perspective, the survival of all living organisms is dependent on being able to control preferred states (Powers, 2008). The importance of control is well documented in mental health literature, although the term 'control' is often substituted with terms such as regulation and self-determination. Control is the process by which we make something just the way we want it to be. As you read this, you might have just had the background thought – "Isn't that just selfish?" The term control is most commonly understood to have these kinds of negative connotations, but here, we are talking about an essential process of life. Homeostasis is a good example of control, whereby we manage to maintain our body temperature at a 'just right' state. But we also control many other 'just right states', from how sweet we like our tea to taste; how close to the middle of the road we stay when driving the car; how safe we want to feel; to how clever or empathic or helpful we want our clients to perceive us as being, and so on. As behaviour is the means by which we make things the way we need them to be, all behaviour can therefore be understood as being goal- or 'just-right-state'-directed. This has major implications, as it means that we do not plan and control our behaviour, as is the prevalent assumption in psychology. Instead, we control our experience or 'perception' of our just right states. So, to use the example of the therapist who wants their client to perceive them as helpful, the therapist might attend to the willingness of the client to engage in the therapy process; the number of times the client says, "That was helpful"; the extent to which the client reports a reduction in their distress; or even the way in which the client smiles and gives a nod of the head in grateful acknowledgement. The therapist is highly unlikely to be planning and monitoring the number of helpful suggestions they attempt to make across the course of therapy; the frequency in which they use their "I want to help" tone of voice; or the number of times they ask the client what would be useful. Control is a process of negative feedback through which we perceive a current just right state, compare it to how we want it to be, and then act to reduce the discrepancy between the two. Our behaviour is a means to minimising any disturbance the environment creates on the preferred states we are trying to maintain. In other words, we control the effect our behaviour has on the way we experience our environment, not the behaviour itself. So, a client who does not engage with the therapist, report that therapy is helping, or give eye contact to encourage the therapist's efforts to help, is a disturbance on that therapist's just right state of the client perceiving them as helpful. In response, the therapist's behaviour is the means by which they increase their sense of being helpful.

Psychological distress is understood to result when there is a difference between our current experience of a just right state and the way we want it to be. Now, of course, there are plenty of times in life when things are not quite as we want them to be and we don't necessarily become distressed. The process of reducing discrepancy will be described later when outlining the principle of reorganisation. The causes of chronic loss of control that lead to mental health difficulties will also be described later. However, for the moment, let us apply the basic principle of control to thinking about what the utility of clinical supervision might be.

When a client seeks help for a problem, we can assume that their distress, which may present in various forms, results from them having lost the ability to control something in their life in order to make it the way they want it to be. It is reasonable to suggest that the most useful role of the therapist is to facilitate that client in finding a solution to making their just right state, just right. However, this would mean that the goal of the therapist would be to help direct the client's attention to what it is that they, the client, wants. Furthermore, what the client needs could only be relevant if understood from the client's perspective. The therapist might also help the client consider solutions deemed to be appropriate; again, 'appropriate' being defined from the client's perspective. Depending on the client, the means used by the therapist to achieve this end will, by necessity, vary considerably (Carey, Kelly, Mansell, & Tai, 2012). Traditionally in supervision, we ask supervisees to focus on their behaviours as a therapist and plan what they will do in accordance with whichever model-specific treatment they are using. From a PCT stance, however, supervision is about helping a therapist focus on the client's experience and what it is the client might be trying to control. Rather than assessing what the therapist did as a means unto itself – for example, the precision with which the therapist used a particular style of questioning or modelled a particular problem-solving strategy – principles-based supervision helps the therapist reflect on the degree to which they acted to facilitate the client being able to talk freely about a problem and focus their awareness on comparing current perceptions to just right states. Now, here's where things get a little more complicated because although resolving psychological distress is about reducing discrepancy between the way things are and the way we want them to be, understanding why this doesn't immediately happen for our clients is important. Reducing discrepancy between current experience and just right states is what all of us do quite successfully most of the day through. What we are not saying here is that our clients are somehow different or have some kind of pathology that prevents them doing this. The most common cause of loss of control is conflict, the second key principle in PCT.

Conflict

Conflict is also well evidenced within the psychological literature, incorporating terms such as incompatible goals and dilemmas. Within PCT, conflict is used to formulate psychological distress as resulting from wanting two incompatible just right states at the same time (Carey, 2008; Carey & Mullan, 2008; Powers, 2005). Subsequently, control over either state becomes compromised. All of us have countless just right states we are trying to realise simultaneously, making conflict inevitable. Resolution of conflict and re-establishing control usually happens spontaneously through a process of reorganisation, which is described in the next section of this chapter. Unresolved conflict can lead to mental health problems. An alternative way of thinking about conflict is in terms of 'relativity'. Thoughts, experiences or feelings are only problematic relative to co-existing thoughts, experiences or feelings. Tim Carey (2009, p. 168) suggested that "the value we attribute to a particular thought is always determined by the way in which it measures up to other thoughts, ideas, goals, and beliefs that we have". For example, anxiety about social situations is only distressing when a person simultaneously has a need to enter into social situations. To provide an illustration relative to a real supervisory context, imagine a therapist who aims to help a client address painful emotions, but who also holds a simultaneous just right state of not causing people upset. It would be no surprise to observe that the client, for whom approaching specific topics of conversation evokes difficult emotions, changes the focus of the conversation to something less salient whenever they start to feel any increase in painful emotions. The goal of the therapist might be to help the client maintain focus on the challenging topic and explore what makes it difficult. While the therapist might hold this goal in awareness, they are likely to be far less aware of the simultaneous just right state to not cause people any upset. Such a conflict for the therapist could lead to a scenario where they are observed to alternate arbitrarily between actions associated with both just right states – raising emotionally salient topics with the client, but then not managing diversions away from the topic and allowing the therapy to 'drift'. Thus, the therapist has little success in achieving either just right state and may have little awareness of the underlying motivations driving the situation. It is not uncommon that the therapist would 'formulate' this type of situation solely in terms of the client's behaviour, describing the client as "avoidant" or "treatment resistant". Within a principles-based approach to supervision, the role of the supervisor would be to help direct the therapist's attention to the just right states driving their (the therapist's) actions, thereby promoting awareness of the incompatibility of their own goals. From a PCT perspective, most difficulties that arise in therapy, often referred to as alliance ruptures, resistance, counter-transference, and so on, are most likely the result of an incompatibility of goals, either for the client, or between the client and therapist. This is described in detail by Carey, Kelly, Mansell and Tai (2012), who, in a paper exploring what is therapeutic about the therapeutic relationship, describe the interaction between a client and therapist as both control for their own just right states. Figure 12.1 is reprinted from that paper, illustrating a generic model of the interaction of two people conceptualised as control systems. The very same principles can be applied to understanding the supervisory context. Figure 12.2 illustrates the example described above, whereby the therapist is seeking supervision to facilitate a process of self-reflection and a supervisor is wanting to help the therapist reflect. Of course, if the goals held by both parties were not compatible, if the therapist in this case, for example, aimed to convince the supervisor that the client was "treatment resistant", a situation of conflict would be likely to arise.

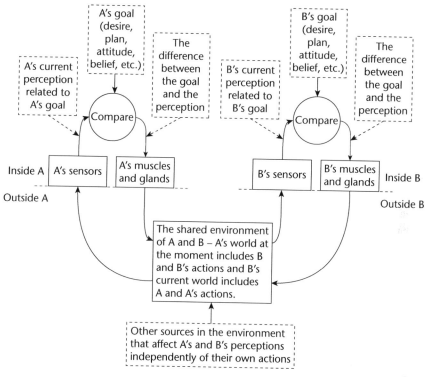

FIGURE 12.1 Generic model of the interaction of two people conceptualised as control systems

Source: Adapted from Carey et al. (2012)

Reorganisation as the mechanism of therapeutic change

Perceptual Control Theory states that when there is discrepancy between a just right state and a current perception of that state, we make changes to our behaviour to minimise the discrepancy. This mechanism of change is a basic, innate learning process known as reorganisation (Marken & Carey, 2015) – the third key principle. Decision-making, planning of behaviour, analysis of the pros and cons of behaviours potentially required, are not involved; the process of reorganisation is far less complex. Reorganisation basically consists of generating random changes to behaviour and then monitoring the effects of that change. Reorganisation is incessant and will continue to generate behavioural change until discrepancy reduces, in which case the change remains. As we all have complex hierarchical systems of just right states that are interacting with ever-changing environments, in reality, reorganisation is likely to be constant. Powers (2008) described how reorganisation takes place wherever mental awareness or 'consciousness' is focused; hence our attention is always drawn to areas of discrepancy. From this perspective, what makes any psychotherapy effective in creating therapeutic change is whether it facilitates

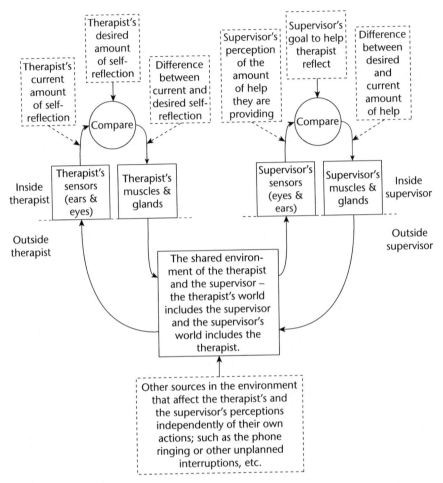

FIGURE 12.2 Model of a therapist seeking to self-reflect and a supervisor wanting to help the therapist reflect

Source: Adapted from Carey et al. (2012)

the mobility of awareness within a hierarchy of just right states being controlled so that reorganisation takes place at the right level (Carey et al., 2012). Reorganisation is referred to in the general psychology literature as a process of therapeutic change through which new perspectives, insights and solutions are generated. Reorganisation is not a neat, planned and systematic process – it is spontaneous and just keeps going unless a person succeeds in fulfilling and balancing multiple just right states. From this point of view, any successful therapy is one that helps a client focus on their problem long enough to develop awareness of conflict between just right states and generate new perspectives, thus maximising the chances of them making changes where required (Carey, 2011). Subsequently, many elements considered to be important in model-specific therapies, such as completing structured assessments and history taking, specific methods for alliance building, or giving homework, may not be useful.

Applying the very same principles to supervision, the focus becomes the goal of the therapist as opposed to planning specific techniques and strategies. Understanding the process of therapeutic change in terms of reorganisation has a number of implications: therapeutic change is unpredictable and does not occur in a linear fashion. The time needed for effective change will vary considerably from client to client as the first solutions generated will not necessarily be the best ones. Furthermore, sometimes things might get worse before they get better. Perceptual Control Theory provides a framework in which to understand psychological distress and how therapeutic changes occur. This principles-based approach thus informs the very purpose and process of supervision.

A principles-based approach to supervision in practice

Using a principles-based approach to supervision in my own practice has translated into some key goals as a supervisor. First, having a clear problem focus, as determined by the supervisee, in each supervision session is essential. This might include a specific question that the supervisee wishes to address or a problem they wish to solve. The problem might be related directly to a therapeutic issue with a client, or a problem within the workplace; for example, a conflict with another colleague. As a supervisor, my goal is to help the supervisee describe the issue in detail with the aim of directing the supervisee's awareness to the related just right states and potential conflicts. In doing so, this promotes reorganisation, whereby just right states might be re-prioritised or other novel solutions can be generated as a way of balancing competing demands. Sometimes, that solution might involve a need to acquire specific skills or knowledge that the supervisee does not currently feel proficient in, and supervision may then take on a role of training. For example, there may be specific procedures regarding risk that the supervisee may be required to learn. In the main part, using curious questioning is an efficient way of drawing out information about the supervisee's perspective and helping them to explore and seek out their own solutions, rather than making assumptions about what is needed and then being overly directive or giving advice.

There is some evidence that people who are more junior prefer more directive supervision as opposed to unstructured supervision, as do those who might be more experienced but are learning a specific new skill or dealing with a complex or crisis situation (Spence, Wilson, Kavanagh, Strong, & Worrall, 2001). Specific learning needs from supervisees can be viewed in terms of just right states, and principles-based supervision is about helping people become aware of these needs and the most appropriate means, from the individual's perspective, by which to address these needs. The following excerpt provides a brief example of how curious questioning might look:

SUPERVISOR: What would you like to focus on today?
THERAPIST: Well, I've seen the same client we discussed before and I still feel I'm doing it all wrong.

SUPERVISOR: What makes you say you're doing it all wrong?
THERAPIST: Well . . . er . . .
SUPERVISOR: What's crossing your mind right now as you think about that?
THERAPIST: Well, I was remembering how she said she still finds it difficult to get out of bed . . . so I'm clearly getting it all wrong.
SUPERVISOR: And so do you have an idea of what would be happening if you were getting it right?
THERAPIST: That she would be back at work.
SUPERVISOR: So, is getting back to work the goal you agreed with the client?
THERAPIST: No, she says she hates work. (Therapist laughs)
SUPERVISOR: So what makes you laugh about that?
THERAPIST: Because I just realised that getting back to work is what I want and I'm not even sure I know what she wants.
SUPERVISOR: How might you find that out?
THERAPIST: Well, I know I need to ask, but I don't feel that my questions come out in the way I need them to. I think I need some help with that.
SUPERVISOR: Do you have any specific thoughts on what I might do that would be most helpful to you?
THERAPIST: I've found it really helpful in the past when I have been able to role-play the client and you demonstrate some questions.
SUPERVISOR: Is that what you would like to do today?
THERAPIST: Yes.

The above dialogue also provides further demonstration of how the principles of control and conflict underlie the problem identified by the supervisee in this scenario of "feeling they were doing it all wrong". The curious questions are focused very much on the present-moment experiences of the therapist with an emphasis on encouraging exploration of how things seem now, how the therapist wants them to be, and how this also fits with other just right states held simultaneously. The supervisor also draws attention to indications that the supervisee might be experiencing background thoughts (e.g. the laughter) and directs attention to these to mobilise awareness to other perspectives.

Watkins and Milne (2014) describe a generic approach to supervision, in which they describe key objectives for all supervision to include normative, restorative and formative types of supervisor response. The example in the dialogue may meet the criteria for all three objectives in that the supervisor's behaviour provides an inherently empathic and 'normalising' response; it is restorative in that the confidence of the therapist is being directly addressed in a way that is encouraging and accepting; and formative in the way the needs of the therapist are immediately addressed through a 'training' opportunity. The principles-based approach is not at odds with more generic models of supervision, although specific techniques and methods advocated by such approaches as core to all supervision might not be regarded as always essential in principles-based supervision. In the next section of this chapter,

I will provide a description of some of the different methods and formats in which I have practised this approach.

Personal experiences of principles-based supervision

I have facilitated supervision in various formats, including on a one-to-one basis and in groups in a number of different countries or regions including North America, China, Australia, Scandinavia and Ireland. Some of this supervision has occurred within randomised clinical trials where the goal of supervision has been more tightly specified to focus on specifically training therapists to deliver a model-specific therapy such as Cognitive Behaviour Therapy (CBT). In these circumstances, there is usually more emphasis on engaging clients, conducting assessments, and employing rigorous procedures for assessing fidelity to the therapeutic model. Other supervision has been within routine clinical practice with a much more pragmatic focus that spans not just what happens therapeutically with the client, but the role of a psychologist within multidisciplinary teams and the range of additional complexities this brings. This role may include managing service demands and expectations of other team members, supervision, and work with non-psychology mental health professionals. Principles-based supervision is compatible with a range of model-specific therapeutic approaches. There have been a variety of modalities used for the supervision I have provided, including web-based video-conferencing and telephone.

Supervising people in different countries

Providing supervision in a country that is not where you are based brings a range of challenges. Obviously, there are regulatory formalities to investigate and fulfil; such as completing any licensing and insurance requirements, and engaging in mandatory training according to local policies where the people you are supervising are based. I regularly listen to audio-recordings of supervisees' therapy sessions, and so ethical and data protection issues related to data transfer and storage between countries need to be addressed. Also, the role of clinical psychologists varies internationally, so having a clear understanding of what the objectives of a supervisee are and thus what they are wanting from supervision might take a more detailed exploration compared to when working in more familiar territory (although I try to avoid making assumptions).

Here, I shall focus on some of the cultural differences experienced. Cultural 'norms' from a principles-based perspective are considered 'just right states'. They can commonly lead to conflict between the supervisor and supervisee if left out of awareness and unaddressed, negatively affecting the relationship and effectiveness of achieving the supervisory goals. I recall an example of working with a group of clinicians based at an adult in-patient unit where one of the female therapists was trying to engage a woman in discussion around what was assumed to be a 'delusional' state involving 'pathological jealousy' regarding her husband. The client's assumed delusion involved believing her husband was having an affair. There was additional information regarding this patient, which gave rise to my personal suspicions that domestic abuse might be involved and that the husband might have fabricated information to have his wife compulsorily detained. As it turned out, this was indeed the case and the woman was being detained in the absence of any diagnosable delusion.

However, within the supervisory context, this raised conflicts on all sorts of levels. For me, potential conflict involved wanting to act in the client's best interest, but by the nature of my indirect involvement, needing to be closely allied with the therapist to achieve that aim. Yet cultural differences presented a potential disturbance to both my goals – it was culturally unacceptable to discuss issues such as domestic abuse and marital infidelity; have a female clinician challenge the integrity of a man (the husband); have a supervisor question the 'formulation' developed by the therapist which might indicate the therapist had not been competent. In circumstances such as these, it has been useful to understand this as a number of competing just right states, and use sensitive but searching curious questions in supervision to increase awareness of these. By doing so, the potential dilemmas can be acknowledged gradually, as led by the supervisee, who then also leads in generating potential solutions. In the current example, it involved helping the therapist acknowledge her dilemma of wanting to consider a range of perspectives to accurately formulate the client's situation, but simultaneously wanting to avoid discussing culturally taboo perspectives; this enabled a focus on ways around this conflict that might otherwise have been problematic.

As an 'external' supervisor invited into a supervisory contract, I have experienced other challenges, including cultural expectations for supervisees to appear respectful and show gratitude at having benefitted from my input. The just right state of needing to 'flatter' the supervisor impedes the ability to utilise supervision as a safe space to talk. Alternatively, I have also experienced being asked to work as an external consultant with organisations where the culture has been more autocratic, where people have been instructed to participate in supervision and training in a specific model of therapy, which they are resistant to. Again, I have found that an approach aimed at inquiring curiously about what the just right states of supervisees are has been useful. For example, "Does it bother you to be expected to use a therapeutic model you don't believe is effective?" "Is that something you would like to use supervision to discuss?" Wherever possible, helping people to become aware of what their just right states are and explicitly aiming to help them achieve these in supervision has proved a useful way of working cross-culturally. This is often easier to do when meeting face-to-face with people, although running supervision using other modalities will now be discussed.

Using different modalities for conducting supervision

With significant advancements in technology, it is becoming more commonplace to work remotely and utilise web-based and telephone-facilitated modalities for supervision meetings. I have used Skype and also other web-based software to provide supervision for both one-to-one and group-based supervision. Generally, as the years pass by, the efficiency of these modalities is improving fast. VSee, UberConference, GoToMeeting, Webex, Voca, Viber, ooVoo and Zoom meeting are all examples of web-based communication platforms that vary in the availability of features such as video-conferencing for groups, attendees being able to share their screen with other attendees, using chat over text, and so on. In particular, I have utilised software provided by Google, including Google Docs, which allows group access to working documents such as Microsoft Word and PowerPoint slide presentations. These all enable supervision to involve the provision of more formal training in addition to discussion. So, it is possible to share formulations, for example, and other documents in a 'virtual' way where multiple users can access the document at the same time. In the case of Google Hangouts, it is possible to chat over text, video or VoIP call; you can also do group video chats with up to ten members, all free of charge.

This technology has made it possible to run group-supervision meetings with attendees who are vastly dispersed geographically in a way that would otherwise be impossible. There are some significant advantages, including having diverse groups with a range of experience and expertise. I have facilitated peer-supervision groups whereby the attendees are located across the globe and, other than coordinating time zones, the process has required very little effort and resource. Time-zone differences do require some consideration in order to agree mutually convenient call times. Calls to countries – for example, Australia and China – where the time difference with the UK can be in excess of 9 hours, have involved at least one party scheduling a call either very early in the morning or late at night. Attention and concentration might not be optimal. Furthermore, when participating in web-based meetings, a suitable quiet space is required to make the call, and being at home when there might be competing demands such as family interruptions is not ideal.

There are a number of potential pitfalls with web-based conferencing. Confidentiality is always a potential cause for concern, and it is important to check with the regulations at your own institution as to which web-based platforms are acceptable. Certainly, secure transfer of any data and audio-recorded files using web-based conferencing facilities cannot be guaranteed. There are other solutions to data management, using a variety of encrypted data transfer tools now available. Again, these are best organised through your own institution to avoid any breaches of ethical guidelines and data protection, particularly when operating on an international basis.

There are also many practical limitations. Unless all users have an Internet connection with sufficient bandwidth speed, calls can be severely disrupted. When sound quality is poor and intermittent, the fluidity of any conversation is badly affected. Supervision is often a process that involves discussion of sensitive issues and often a complex interplay of emotions within the interpersonal interactions taking place. This can all be compromised using modalities apart from face-to-face supervision; with a potential for causing miscommunication and interpersonal conflict. I have had experiences where the Internet connection has failed every other minute and this makes the meeting untenable. Where possible, I use video as well as audio as most supervision is likely to be more beneficial when, as a supervisor, you can access the non-verbal cues of the person you are working with. This is especially important when conducting group supervision as these cues help to guide turn-taking in conversation and facilitate spontaneous and productive discussion. This also relates to earlier points regarding cultural differences, where differences in conversational rules and etiquette are much harder to navigate unless the sound and vision in calls are of high quality.

In group settings, especially if the attendees have not met previously, establishing supervisory group rules (e.g. turn-taking, what it is OK to speak about, how much to speak, and so on), can initially feel awkward. It is advisable to dedicate specific and sufficient time to addressing these directly with the group so that common ground rules are clear and mutually acceptable. As a supervisor, it is common to also act as the group facilitator, although it is equally possible to nominate a chair or ask the group to operate on the basis of having a rolling chair. I have done this, particularly for supervisees who have wanted to develop skills in chairing group meetings. Nonetheless, having someone chair the session is much more important for web-based conferencing in order to avoid the conversation being stilted. As the group becomes more familiar, this does get easier, but it is probably one of the biggest barriers to running supervision with web-based conference calling. The chair can ensure that individuals in the group all have an opportunity to contribute and can provide prompts to coordinate interactions where the usual social cues are less obvious. For example, in a face-to-face group discussion, it is easier to direct a question to the group, whereas on video-conferencing facilities, people are less likely to respond unless a question is directed at them personally. It can also be more challenging to detect visual cues indicating that someone is not engaging or struggling with an interpersonal issue.

I recommend asking that attendees try and commit to having at least one face-to-face meeting, where possible, in the first instance, to become acquainted before commencing 'virtual' meetings. Also, requesting that attendees all commit to ring-fencing the supervision time to be in front of a computer for supervision is important. Otherwise, some people join by telephone with no video or try and participate while engaging in other activities (e.g. driving to another meeting), so they are distracted. This is not conducive to group cohesion and fostering positive group dynamics and is likely to exacerbate any existing problems of engagement with and commitment to the group. It is also advisable to have agreed a focus or agenda for the supervision meeting ahead of time as coordinating group consensus on conference calls is more challenging than in face-to-face meetings. The pace of conversation in conference calls is always slower and, if possible, allocating slightly longer for meetings than one would allocate for a face-to-face meeting might be considered. All these points are applicable to web-based conference calling whether on a one-to-one basis or group basis. Telephone conference calls are of a similar nature, with the disadvantage of having no video.

A key message I hope to convey is one of positivity and 'nothing ventured, nothing gained'. I advocate encouraging people to engage in supervision as much as possible and so any means by which this can happen is worth trying. When trying anything new, it has to be done on a trial-and-error basis. Initially, using new technology to conduct supervision can feel so inferior to face-to-face meetings, one hardly sees the point. But, with practice, it is surprising how productive supervision can become. In the next section, I will describe some of the methods and activities I have used in supervision. Obviously some activities may only be possible in a face-to-face meeting, but with some creative engineering, anything is possible!

Different methods used in supervision

The activities described here are just some examples of the methods I have used within supervision rather than an exhaustive list. The activities reflect my aim to help supervisees direct their attention to the just right states they have for: their goals as a therapist; level and range of skills; preferred learning styles; knowledge base; access to support; engagement in reflective practice and so on. Subsequently, wherever possible, I endeavour to facilitate supervisees in reducing discrepancy between these preferred states and their current experience. Most commonly, supervisees want to use supervision to close the gap between their desired and current levels of competence as a therapist, and so a number of the activities described here are aimed at serving this purpose. This is in keeping with the 'regulatory' or 'monitoring' function of supervision to ensure that minimum standards of proficiency are adopted by therapists.

Discussion and curious questioning

As with most model-specific supervision approaches, discussion and reflection remain a fundamental part of principles-based supervision. Discussion, however, is not 'aimless', as there is a required focus on specific question(s) or problem(s) as determined by the supervisee. The dialogue provided earlier in the section "A principles-based approach to supervision in practice" gave an example of how curious questions can be used to help therapists discuss typical issues that arise in supervision, with the aim of considering the matter from a range of perspectives in order to generate potential solutions. In group formats, all supervisees are encouraged to ask their peers curious questions with a focus on present-moment experiences, so that a range of perspectives and fruitful discussion are facilitated. This also assists in helping supervisees develop supervisory skills. When discussing clients, there is usually some focus on using available information to consider what just right states the client might be controlling for and the potential conflicts they might experience. However, speculation and assumptions are not encouraged and the aim is to consider what the therapist could do to try and help the client talk about this, and direct awareness to the just right states in conflict that might be driving their distress.

Reviewing audio- and video-recordings

Reviewing audio- and video-recordings of therapy sessions is an extremely useful exercise in supervision, both one-to-one-based supervision and groups.

Video-recordings, especially, provide the perfect means to reflect on the process of therapy. Therapists can select specific sections of recordings they would like to reflect on or the session can be played from the beginning. When supervising, I use this activity in a number of different ways:

- To provide specific feedback to therapists on what they did, including both positive feedback and constructive critique.
- To observe what happened during the session with a view to reflecting on how what the therapist did reflected the three main principles of PCT. This might involve pausing the recording to ask the therapist to reflect on what their goal had been in that moment.
- Pausing the tape randomly to focus the discussion on a specific utterance of the client and what the therapist might do next. We pay particular attention to utterances made by the therapist and the intention behind this.

Role-plays

Role-plays are an excellent way of helping therapists build confidence, practise managing pertinent issues that they face with clients and develop skills. They can be used to practise specific scenarios, skills or more complete sessions. Often the therapist is the best person to role-play a client as they know the client. It provides an opportunity for the supervisor or other supervisees, if it is group supervision, to model providing therapy. I particularly value the opportunity to do this as a supervisor as, if anything, it provides a message of "nobody's perfect". It might also be possible to use volunteers or actors to role-play clients. When delivering MOL therapy, the aim is to access current experiences for the client. This makes it difficult to role-play as it is necessary to access real thoughts as they occur spontaneously and naturally. Therefore, frequently in supervision, we take turns in being the 'client', but have people identify an experience they are willing to talk about that is real.

Obviously supervisees discussing real issues can experience real emotions and how to manage this within the supervision group will need some careful consideration and discussion. Informed consent and confidentiality are particularly important to bear in mind, although I do encourage participants in this activity to talk about fairly benign issues, which can still provide ample opportunity for valuable practice. It is also possible to bring in volunteers who are willing to discuss something that is real for them, or use actors. Role-plays can be used in a whole range of creative ways and here are some examples of how I have utilised them:

- One-to-one role-plays with one person role-playing a client and another acting as the therapist. This can be done with or without an observer. The role-play can be run as a real therapy session, continuing as long as required; or it is possible to stop and start the exercise to maximise feedback.
- Group role-plays have involved one person acting as the 'client' and then all other supervisees acting as the therapist, taking it in turns to ask questions.

This 'round robin' style of therapy can either involve each supervisee being 'therapist' for a few minutes before swapping to the next person, or just asking one question before moving to the next therapist. This has the advantage of everyone benefitting from hearing each other's questions and experiencing how the same principle might be achieved in therapy through a variety of means. Supervisees can provide mutual encouragement and feedback, which although initially could be anxiety-provoking, can be a great way of building confidence.

- For MOL therapy, there is a focus on the process of therapy as opposed to exploring the content and detail of a problem. In accordance with the principles of PCT, the aim is to get a client to speak about their problem and use curious questions to direct their attention to background thoughts, thereby mobilising their awareness to conflicting goals associated with the problem. This is a rather crude summary of MOL, which is described more sufficiently elsewhere (e.g. Carey et al., 2015). However, one particularly fun and creative role-play for groups, to help focus on using curious questions, is to have multiple therapists in a 'round robin'. The supervisees get into pairs consisting of one therapist and one client. They form two lines where each therapist–client dyad is facing one another. They begin to role-play therapy, but after approximately 5 minutes, the therapist at the end of the line moves to the opposite end to face a new client. All therapists move along one place so each is facing a new client. The clients then continue to discuss their problems and the therapists continue to ask relevant questions. This exercise is aimed at developing skills of asking detailed questions about present-moment experiences as opposed to content.

Using model-specific fidelity assessments

I have frequently used model-specific fidelity assessments in supervision as a way of helping therapists develop model-specific skills and also provide constructive feedback to one another. Fidelity measures such as the Cognitive Therapy Rating Scale – Revised (Blackburn et al., 2001) and the MOL Session Evaluation Form – Revised (Carey & Tai, 2012) clearly state what it is that the therapist is meant to be doing in therapy, and this can facilitate much discussion to promote learning and skill development for supervisees. I recommend using audio- and/or video-recordings of therapy to rate the adherence of the therapist to the model using the scale.

There are many more activities that can be used to facilitate supervision and I encourage supervisees to add to our ever growing repertoire of supervisory methods.

The effectiveness of supervision

In this chapter, PCT has been used as one possible framework for understanding psychological distress and therapeutic change, and informing clinical supervision. While there is a solid evidence base for the theory of PCT itself and its application as an effective therapy in the form of Method of Levels, currently there is no empirical evidence that a principles-based approach to supervision is effective. My own supervisory practice based on this approach has involved requesting feedback directly from supervisees and employing therapy fidelity measures to provide some indication of supervisees' ability to deliver interventions in accordance with model-specific principles (e.g. the Cognitive Therapy Rating Scale – Revised [Blackburn et al., 2001] and the MOL Session Evaluation Form – Revised [Carey & Tai, 2012]). Feedback from both sources suggests that supervision is indeed useful from the perspective of supervisees, and also might help therapists to develop their skills and deliver model-compliant therapy, as evidenced by improved scores on fidelity measures. Demonstrating a causal link between supervision and therapist effectiveness or client outcome is problematic. For a more detailed discussion on the need to demonstrate the effectiveness of supervision and developing the 'acid test' in which to do so, I would recommend the Special Issue of *The Cognitive Behaviour Therapist* on clinical supervision (published online in October 2016) and, more specifically, the paper by Reiser and Milne (2014).

Conclusion

In summary, this chapter has presented a potential principles-based theoretical framework (PCT) to inform clinical supervision. This approach to supervising therapists has the potential to be used regardless of the therapeutic orientation of the supervisee. Some suggestions of activities that might be used to facilitate supervision have been provided as well as discussion of the strengths and limitations of various modalities and formats of supervision. The evidence base for principles-based supervision requires further exploration, but informal feedback from supervisees suggests that this is an acceptable and informative approach, which they perceive to be beneficial.

References

Binder, J.L., & Strupp, H.H. (1997). Supervision of psychodynamic psychotherapies. In C.E. Watkins (Ed.), *Handbook of psychotherapy supervision* (pp. 44–62). New York: Wiley.

Blackburn, I.M., James, I.A., Milne, D.L., Baker, C., Standart, S., Garland, A., & Reichelt, F.K. (2001). The revised cognitive therapy scale (CTS-R): Psychometric properties. *Behavioural and Cognitive Psychotherapy, 29*(04), 431–446.

Care Quality Commission. (2010). *Essential standards of quality and safety*. London: Care Quality Commission.

Carey, T.A. (2006). *The method of levels: How to do psychotherapy without getting in the way*. Hayward, CA: Living Control Systems Publishing.

Carey, T.A. (2008). *Hold that thought. Two steps to effective counseling and psychotherapy using the method of levels*. St. Louis, MO: Newview.

Carey, T.A. (2009). Dancing with distress: Helping people transform psychological troubles with the Method of Levels two step. *The Cognitive Behavioural Therapist, 2*(3), 167–177.

Carey, T.A. (2011). Exposure and reorganization: The what and how of effective psychotherapy. *Clinical Psychology Review, 31*(2), 236–248.

Carey, T.A., & Mullan, R.J. (2008). Evaluating the method of levels. *Counselling Psychology Quarterly, 21*(3), 247–256.

Carey, T.A., & Tai, S.J. (2012). MOL Session Evaluation Form – Revised. In W. Mansell, T.A. Carey, & S.J. Tai, *A transdiagnostic approach to CBT using Method of Levels therapy* (pp. 137–141). London: Routledge.

Carey, T.A., Kelly, R.E., Mansell, W., & Tai, S.J. (2012). What's therapeutic about the therapeutic relationship? A hypothesis for practice informed by Perceptual Control Theory. *The Cognitive Behaviour Therapist, 5*(2–3), 47–59.

Carey, T.A., Mansell, W., & Tai, S.J. (2014). A biopsychosocial model based on negative feedback and control. *Frontiers in Human Neuroscience, 8,* 94.

Carey, T.A., Mansell, W., & Tai, S. (2015). *Principles-based counselling and psychotherapy: A Method of Levels approach.* London: Routledge.

Division of Clinical Psychology. (2014). *DCP policy on supervision.* Leicester: British Psychological Society.

Duncan, B.L., Hubble, M.A., & Miller, S.D. (2004). Beyond integration: The triumph of outcome over process in clinical practice. *Psychotherapy in Australia, 10*(2), 32–41.

Health and Care Professions Council (HCPC) (2015). *Standards of proficiency: Practitioner psychologists.* London: HCPC.

Holloway, E.L., & Neufeldt, S.A. (1995). Supervision: Its contributions to treatment efficacy. *Journal of Consulting and Clinical Psychology, 63*(2), 207–213.

Kazdin, A.E. (2007). Mediators and mechanisms of change in psychotherapy research. *Annual Review of Clinical Psychology, 3,* 1–27.

Marken, R.S. (2001). Controlled variables: Psychology as the center fielder views it. *The American Journal of Psychology, 114*(2), 259–281.

Marken, R.S., & Carey, T.A. (2015). Understanding the change process involved in solving psychological problems: A model-based approach to understanding how psychotherapy works. *Clinical Psychology & Psychotherapy, 22*(6), 580–590.

Marken, R.S., & Mansell, W. (2013). Perceptual control as a unifying concept in psychology. *Review of General Psychology, 17*(2), 190–195.

Milne, D. (2007). An empirical definition of clinical supervision. *British Journal of Clinical Psychology, 46*(4), 437–447.

Milne, D.L., & Reiser, R.P. (2014). SAGE: A scale for rating competence in CBT supervision. In C.E. Watkins, Jr. & D.L. Milne (Eds.), *Wiley international handbook of clinical supervision* (pp. 402–415). Oxford: Wiley–Blackwell.

Milne, D., Reiser, R., Aylott, H., Dunkerley, C., Fitzpatrick, H., & Wharton, S. (2010). The systematic review as an empirical approach to improving CBT supervision. *International Journal of Cognitive Therapy, 3*(3), 278–294.

Powers, W.T. (1973). *Behavior: The control of perception.* New York: Aldine.

Powers, W.T. (1989). *Living control systems: Selected papers of William T. Powers.* Gravel Switch, KY: Control Systems Group.

Powers, W.T. (1999). A model of kinesthetically and visually controlled arm movement. *International Journal of Human-Computer Studies, 50*(6), 463–479.

Powers, W.T. (2005). *Behavior: The control of perception* (2nd ed.). New Canaan, CT: Benchmark.

Powers, W.T. (2008). *Living control systems III: The fact of control.* Bloomfield, NJ: Benchmark.

Powers, W.T., Clark, R.K., & McFarland, R.L. (1960). A general feedback theory of human behavior: Part I. *Perceptual and Motor Skills, 11,* 71–88.

Reiser, R.P., & Milne, D.L. (2014). A systematic review and reformulation of outcome evaluation in clinical supervision: Applying the fidelity framework. *Training and Education in Professional Psychology, 8*(3), 149–157.

Rosenzweig, S. (1936). Some implicit common factors in diverse methods of psychotherapy. *American Journal of Orthopsychiatry, 6*(3), 412–415.

Smail, D. (2005). *Power, interest and psychology: Elements of a social materialist understanding of distress.* Ross-on-Wye, UK: PCCS Books.

Spence, S.H., Wilson, J., Kavanagh, D., Strong, J., & Worrall, L. (2001). Clinical supervision in four mental health professions: A review of the evidence. *Behaviour Change, 18*(03), 135–155.

Watkins, C.E. Jr., & Milne, D.L. (Eds.) (2014). *Wiley international handbook of clinical supervision.* Oxford: Wiley–Blackwell.

Wheeler, S., & Richards, K. (2007). The impact of clinical supervision on counsellors and therapists, their practice and their clients: A systematic review of the literature. *Counselling and Psychotherapy Research, 7,* 54–65.

13

TRAINING THAT DOMESTICATES OR EDUCATION THAT LIBERATES?

Tensions and dilemmas related to teaching critical psychology in the context of UK clinical psychology training

Anne Cooke

Before taking up my current academic post, I worked as a clinical psychologist in a community mental health team in inner-city London. Partly because of that experience, I became aware of the potential for mental health services to do harm as well as good. I also observed how dominant discourses and practices socialise trainee mental health professionals from various disciplines, sometimes appearing to blind them to this potential for harm (Foucault, 1967; Newnes, 1990; Coles, Diamond, & Keenan, 2013). I became interested in critical perspectives on psychology and, in particular, on psychosis (e.g. Pilgrim & Treacher, 1992; Johnstone, 2000; Bentall, 2003) and began writing in this area (e.g. Kinderman & Cooke, 2000; Cooke, 2008). As an academic, I am currently active in promoting professional and public debate about 'taken for granted' (Barrett, 1996) ideas in mental health (e.g. Cooke & McGowan, 2013; Cooke, Gilchrist, & McGowan, 2014; Cooke & Kinderman, in press). My current role at Canterbury Christ Church University, UK, includes teaching on a doctoral programme that trains clinical psychologists to work in the British National Health Service (NHS). This chapter describes some of the tensions inherent to teaching critical psychology in such a context. It also outlines the ways that colleagues and I have managed these tensions and developed teaching in this area such that the programme's critical 'edge' is now one of the aspects most valued by trainees (Chatfield, 2016).

In the UK, the profession of clinical psychology has evolved within the British NHS (Newnes, 2014; Hall, Pilgrim, & Turpin, 2015). Until the 1990s, many clinical psychologists were trained 'on the job' as part of 'in-service' training schemes run by the NHS (Lavender & Turpin, 2015). These in-service programmes gradually moved to higher education institutions. Currently all clinical psychology training is governed by universities and takes the form of a 3-year postgraduate professional doctorate.

As with other university-based professional training programmes – for example, nursing (e.g. Grant, 2014) – there is an inherent tension between the requirements of different stakeholders. On the one hand, the NHS requires workers to deliver the currently mandated interventions. For clinical psychology programmes, the pressure is to provide therapists trained and accredited to deliver standardised 'evidence based', 'empirically validated' or 'NICE compliant' therapies (NICE being the National Institute for Health and Care Excellence: see www.nice.org.uk) (Crits-Christoph, Frank, Chambless, Brody, & Karp, 1995; Court, Cooke, & Scrivener, 2016). Indeed, the standards for the accreditation of UK clinical psychology programmes have recently been revised to place more emphasis on this (British Psychological Society, 2014). This requirement to provide skilled-up workers is sometimes in conflict with an aim of higher education to teach critical, reflexive thinking and to encourage students to question orthodoxies and taken-for-granted ideas (Grant, 2014). This tension could perhaps be paraphrased as a conflict between the imperative to *train* and the imperative to *educate*. It also speaks to an ongoing debate about the nature and purpose of clinical psychology.

Theoretically, clinical psychologists have been valued for their knowledge of, and ability to appraise critically, a wide range of psychological ideas and theory. This wide knowledge and critical ability should make it possible to formulate unique problems at both an individual and a systemic level, in collaboration with those affected, thus enabling complex clinical decision-making. This was the conclusion of an influential review of the profession in the 1980s (Management Advisory Service to the NHS, 1989) and has been widely promulgated since (Gilbert, 2009; Pilgrim, Turpin, & Hall, 2015). Of course, the review was commissioned by the Division of Clinical Psychology and was unlikely to conclude that clinical psychology was mainly an expensive version of counselling. There has, however, been a recent turn towards the privileging of standardised, protocol-based 'evidence based treatments' (Marks, 2015). Critics of this development have argued that by attempting to standardise clients (by means of allocation to diagnostic categories) and approaches to helping (protocol-based 'brand name' therapies), clinical psychology has sold its birthright (Hall & Marzillier, 2009). On a conceptual level, Pilgrim (2011) argues that this development marked a change from an 'idiographic' to a 'nomothetic' approach to human difference in a powerful and visible section of the profession:

> ... the uncritical acceptance of the ontological status of diagnostic categories drawn from psychiatry. The discourse ... for psychologists not just psychiatrists became one of selectively treating particular reified disorders, such as "major depression", "anxiety disorders" "social anxiety disorders" "personality disorders" etc.
>
> *(Pilgrim, 2011, p. 122)*

In terms of application, some argue that clinical psychology may prove to have contributed to its own demise by reducing applied psychology to a set of techniques that managers can then arrange to be delivered by cheaper workers (Court et al., 2016). Diamond (2006, p. 6) argues that 'Clinical psychology is at risk of putting all its eggs in the basket of therapeutic techniques'.

This chapter takes the example of a teaching unit (module) in the third year of the Doctoral Programme in Clinical Psychology at Canterbury Christ Church University, UK. The module is compulsory for all students (known in this context as trainees) on the programme and takes place in their final year. By that point, trainees have had extensive experience of NHS services: practice placements (internships) run alongside lectures throughout the programme, so in the third year, trainees are on their fourth or fifth placement. The unit in question is entitled 'Psychology and Society'. It invites trainees to take a step back and reflect critically on the role played by psychology – both the academic discipline and the profession – in our society, together with the role played by mental health services more generally. The latest accreditation standards for clinical psychology programmes issued by the British Psychological Society state that graduates need to understand 'social approaches to intervention; for example, those informed by community, critical, and social constructionist perspectives' (Committee on Training in Clinical Psychology, 2014, p. 23). Accordingly, our programme's 'Psychology and Society' unit exposes trainees to various critiques and invites them to consider their own position relative to the different debates and to think about 'the type of psychologist they want to be'. While much of clinical psychology training could be seen as 'domesticating' (Wellington & Austin, 1996), in the sense that tutors are passing on accepted ways of going about things within the profession, this unit aims to be 'liberating' (Wellington & Austin, 1996) in that its aim is to enable trainees to engage with various critiques of clinical psychology as usually practised. I 'top and tail' the unit with an introduction and then a final half-day reflective session, but most teaching is delivered by visiting contributors. I see it as a priority to involve critical thinkers who have publicly articulated their ideas. Those involved change from year to year, but have included: Diana Rose, David Smail, Lucy Johnstone, Guy Holmes, Jennifer Clegg, Peter Kinderman, Odi Oquosa, David Pilgrim, Rufus May, Joanna Moncrieff, Bob Diamond, David Fryer, Jay Watts, Clare Crestani (Mad Hatters of Bath), Lucy Clarke (Special Yoga), Uma Dinsmore-Tuli and Nirlipta Tuli (Yoga Nidra Network), SAGE (Salomons Advisory Group of Experts, our programme's service survivor group), and Psychologists Against Austerity. The aim is to create the opportunity for genuine dialogue with original thinkers. Students value hearing the arguments direct 'from the horse's mouth' rather than mediated by me. Engaging in real dialogue also lends ecological validity (Bronfenbrenner, 1979) to the sessions. I brief contributors about the aims and objectives of the block and give them a copy of the questions that trainees discuss in the introductory session (see boxed material, p. 264). Having done this, I leave them with freedom to structure their session (a day or half a day) as they choose.

The unit was used as a case example of innovative practice by the Mental Health in Higher Education Project, an initiative of the Higher Education Academy, which aimed to improve teaching about mental health within universities (Higher Education Academy, n.d.; Cooke, 2004). It is complemented by other units on community psychology and 'service user and carer perspectives' which have sympathetic aims and often draw on some of the same theoretical ideas (McGowan, 2015; Lea, Holttum, Cooke, & Riley, 2016).

As expressed in the programme handbook (McGowan, 2015), the aim of the unit is for trainees to be able to practise in a manner mindful of the debate about the function of clinical psychology and other professions within society. Its objectives are:

- To have an awareness of sociological, political and cultural perspectives on clinical psychology and related institutions.
- To have a thorough understanding of the debate about the role of psychology in our society.
- To have a detailed knowledge of ethical dilemmas for the profession.
- To develop a conceptual framework to examine issues of power and social inequalities and their relevance to clinical psychology knowledge and practice.

(McGowan, 2015, p. 49)

The topics covered include:

- Anthropological and sociological perspectives on British clinical psychology.
- Historical influences on the development of the profession, and how they affect current values and practice.
- Political interests and social forces that shape psychological theory and research, and how they are presented.
- The relationship between psychology and social policy.
- Power, discrimination and disenfranchised groups/minorities.
- Abuse by social systems, institutions and organisations (including psychology).
- The psychologisation of society, and therapy as 'the opium of the people'.
- Clinical psychology and the media.
- Alternatives to traditional mental health/psychology services.
- The interface between the personal, the professional and the political.

(McGowan, 2015, p. 49)

The unit evolved from a previous one entitled 'Models of Psychopathology'. In 2003, I was asked to design it in response to a recognition that there was insufficient space on the programme for trainees to reflect on the place of psychology within society or to familiarise themselves with, and consider their responses to, critiques of clinical psychology and other mental health professions. The relevant critiques emanate both from within the discipline and profession (e.g. Pilgrim & Treacher, 1992: Newnes, 2014) and from elsewhere, notably from disciplines such as philosophy, anthropology, sociology and from the service user/survivor movement (e.g. Spandler, Anderson, & Sapey, 2015). My brief then was to contribute to making the programme more critical, and to invite trainees to be 'questioning' clinical psychologists (Coles et al., 2013). The focus is on mental health, although many of the issues also apply in other settings where clinical psychologists work, such as physical health or learning disabilities.

Meyer and Land (e.g. Meyer & Land, 2003; Land, Meyer, & Smith, 2008; Meyer, Land, & Baillie, 2010) have put forward the idea of 'threshold concepts': core concepts that, once understood, transform perception of a given subject. There are several ideas discussed in the unit which have the potential to be threshold concepts for trainee clinical psychologists. These include:

1. *The role of the social environment in distress and 'mental illness':* the suggestion that clinical psychology, as commonly practised, tends to focus disproportionately on intrapersonal factors in explaining distress ('psychocentrism') and to pay relatively less attention to the events and circumstances of people's lives (Midlands Psychology Group, 2012; Cooke, 2014).
2. *The potential for professions to do harm as well as good, despite good intentions* (e.g. Moloney, 2013; Kinderman, 2014).
3. *The contested nature of mental health and professional practice* (e.g. Kinderman, 2014; Loewenthal, 2015).
4. *The potential value of 'not knowing'* as opposed to having to be an 'expert' (Anderson & Goolishian, 1992).
5. *The often unseen and unacknowledged role of vested interests in maintaining the status quo* (Smail, 2005).

In approaching this unit, my aim was to expose trainees to critiques of clinical psychology as commonly practised. This creates space for them to engage with these critiques and to voice their own questions and doubts, and, it is hoped, come to some resolution about the kind of clinical psychologist they aspire to be. I took as a starting point those questions that my own experience of both training and clinical practice had thrown up. My philosophy of teaching (Pring, 2000) draws on the following (overlapping) principles and these are reflected in my approach to this unit.

- A critical realist approach to knowledge (Dragonas, Gergen, McNamee, & Tseliou, 2015). Critical realism is a 'halfway' position between realism (the idea that our perception is an accurate reflection of a knowable and measureable reality) and social constructionism (the idea that knowledge is constructed by discourse) (Fleetwood, 2013).
- The value of 'not knowing' (Anderson & Goolishian, 1992). Based on critical realism, this approach conceptualises the role of the therapist or educator as primarily one of facilitation rather than one of imparting 'expertise'.
- A humanistically informed adult learning model (Knowles, 1990). Humanistic approaches (e.g. Rogers, 1961; May, 1969) assume that (like plants) humans have an innate potential for growth and development, given the right conditions. The role of the therapist or educator is not so much to impart wisdom as to help create these conditions. The adult learning approach, also known as andragogy

(Knowles, 1990), values and tries to capitalise on the existing knowledge that adults bring to a learning situation. It is problem-based and collaborative rather than didactic, and emphasises more equality between teacher and learner, commitment to 'education' and specifically to the development of critical thinking, over 'training' in the sense of passing on accepted ways of going about things (Grant, 2014).

- Reflective practice (Schön, 1991, 2009). This approach suggests that practitioners learn and develop by continually reflecting on their actions and practices, and on the values and theories that inform them. It is a popular approach in clinical psychology (Lavender, 2003) and is an explicit tenet of our programme: we aim to train 'reflective practitioners' able to learn continuously in this way even after they qualify (Salomons Centre for Applied Psychology, 2015).
- A growth mindset (Dweck, 2000): talents and abilities are not fixed, but can be developed through effort, good teaching and persistence, including learning from failures.

I first generated a list of questions (see below), drawn from critiques of psychology, and then revised it on the basis of feedback from a range of people including academics, clinicians, service users and those who prefer to be called 'survivors'. I circulate the questions to the trainees at the beginning of the unit and host a session where they debate them in small groups. In the second, plenary part of the session, each group facilitates a debate in the wider group on their particular question.

CANTERBURY CHRIST CHURCH UNIVERSITY – DOCTORAL PROGRAMME IN CLINICAL PSYCHOLOGY – THINKING ABOUT THE ROLE OF PSYCHOLOGY IN SOCIETY

Anne Cooke

Possible topics for group discussion

1. Epistemological, historical, political and cultural perspectives on clinical psychology and related institutions
    - What have the historical influences been on the development of the profession, and how do they affect current practice?
    - How might anthropologists view British clinical psychology?
    - Why are the majority of our clients women, while men are 'over-represented at the sharp end of psychiatry – admissions, detentions, secure and forensic services' (Rose, 2001, n.p.)?
    - Why are black people 'often denied the softer therapies of psychologists' (Rose, 2001, n.p.)?

- To quote Kutchins and Kirk (2003, p. 21):

  > As you reflect on conversations you have had during recent weeks, you recall that your cousin, a young stockbroker, complained of not sleeping well; . . . a colleague at work, who is single, appears to always choose to be alone after work; a close friend confided that she has almost no sexual desire for her husband; your supervisor's 10-year-old is in trouble at school; . . . your partner has been feeling blue and your sister can't stop obsessing about a former boyfriend. In addition, you are really worrying about an upcoming speech. According to DSM-IV, each of the behaviours above is listed as a criterion for one or more mental disorders.

  Has our society's increasing tendency to medicalise the ups and downs of everyday life gone too far?

2. The debate about the role of psychology in our society

   - Oprah Winfrey syndrome: has society's psychologisation gone too far?
   - To what extent are we just 'modern day priests', hearing confession?
   - Is psychological therapy just 'the opium of the people'?
   - Are we part of the solution or part of the problem?
   - If we agree with Kenneth Gergen (1990) that concepts of 'healthy functioning' are suffused with moral and cultural assumptions, what might this mean for our practice?

3. The debate about whether efforts directed at changing individuals would be better directed at changing society

   - David Smail (1993, 1996) has argued for an environmentalist psychology in which therapy is a secondary part to socio-political change and ordinary relationships. He argues (1996) that rather than seeing people as 'manipulable deviants from unassailable norms', we should see them as 'characters in search of public structures which are generous enough to accommodate them, . . . honest enough to acknowledge their private pain and take account of the lesson it teaches'. To what extent do you agree with him?
   - Rachel Perkins (2000, n.p.) advocates de-emphasising therapy in favour of a rights-based approach:

     > The wider disability movement did not reject medicalisation in favour of a nicer therapeutic approach. They rejected it in favour of rights – to employment, to be educated, to travel, to vote, to

stand as a politician ... But still the mental health world puts most of its energies into debating which treatments and services people should have – rather than the rights that could transform our lives so much more profoundly.

What do you think?

- A press release by the UK Community Psychology Network (2007) about the IAPT initiative made the following statement:

  Cognitive Behaviour Therapy and associated approaches are comprehensively problematic ... Moreover, these treatments individualise social problems, draw attention away from the more important social economic and material causes of distress and position individual cognitive dysfunction as both the cause of the person's problem and the locus for intervention. It is bad enough to be depressed because of difficult living circumstances or to be anxious because you are subjected to regular domestic violence, without being told your depression or anxiety are caused by your own dysfunctional cognitions. Blaming the victim like this imposes irrelevant therapeutic rituals on top of societal oppression.

  To what extent do you agree?

4. The debate about ethical dilemmas for the profession

   - How might we negotiate the interface between the personal, the professional and the political in our work?
   - Harper (1999, n.p.) wrote:

     There is a need for therapists and professionals to be more honest about the essentially arbitrary and contingent nature of their language, concepts and even treatments ... to be more openly pragmatic with users rather than pretending there is some secret expert knowledge.

     If we don't make this claim, are our high salaries justified?

   - Do you agree with Diana Rose (2001) that the usual discourse of the clinical psychology profession is 'self-congratulatory'? If so, why do you think this is?
   - Clinical psychologists often work as part of wider systems (e.g. institutions) that are arguably damaging to clients. Is it best to work

for change from within or to leave and work elsewhere? If the former, how can we avoid becoming part of 'the problem'?

5. The politics of theory and research

- Is theory 'used as a gloss on application which has been undertaken for quite different reasons' (Potter, 1982, p. 46)? Does it matter?
- 'Researchers need to locate the interests that may have shaped their own research and need to refuse funding by drug companies' (Harper, 1999, n.p.). What might some of the interests and forces be that shape our research as clinical psychologists in the NHS?
- Do you agree with David Pilgrim and Andy Treacher (1992) that clinical psychologists' practice is more influenced by discussions with colleagues and experience than by published research, and that many see research as nothing more than a rhetoric of professional legitimisation?
- Mary Boyle (2000, n.p.) argues that

    > research is always potentially influential. Whether we approve it, intend it or are even aware of it, our work will have influence in so far as particular psychological ideas become part of the construction of reality, which is then drawn on by policy makers to frame both social problems and their perceived solutions. . . . For example, the idea that we all have personalities and that these personalities can become disordered.

    If we accept her argument, what might its implications be?

6. Debates about clinical psychology, social responsibility and service user critiques of clinical psychology

- 'For damaging ideas to flourish requires only that those who know better remain silent' (based on Burke, quoted in Coleman, 2016). We frequently see examples of unhelpful media coverage about mental health problems, and sometimes hear politicians making misinformed statements. Should clinical psychologists contribute to the public debate about our areas of expertise? In the media? In the political debate?
- Carla Willig (1998, p. 96) argues that

    > we find ourselves within a context in which things are always already going on or being done. Within this context it is impossible to abstain from involvement since inaction is always a form of

action. Thus, we can only ever argue for or against, support or subvert particular practices or causes but we can never disengage ourselves from them.

If we accept her argument, what might its implications be?

- According to Harper (1999, n.p.):

  In this apparently post-modern world of ours the old overarching grand narratives have broken down and it is possible for the practitioner to either feel so paralysed by competing ideas that they cannot move forward, or feel the only way to do anything is to ignore many critical voices and instead simply engage with the individual client. The harder choice is to enter that ambiguous terrain where we act strategically to do what is possible in our individual positions whilst continuing to question dominant ideas and practices.

  What might this mean in practice?

- How might the current limited dialogue between clinical psychology and those who use its services be developed? What changes might clinical psychologists be able to make to their thinking, practice and professional structures as a result?
- Foucault (1967, p. xii) observed that for centuries there has been a 'monologue of reason about unreason'. Similarly, Peter Campbell (2001) comments that while professionals are gradually accepting the idea that 'consumers' might be able to comment on the services that they use, there is greater reluctance to accept users and survivors as agents able to reflect on their mental distress and to provide valuable understandings of it. He notes (p. 201) that 'what many service providers seem to hanker after is raw evidence, uncontaminated by reflection'. Diana Rose (2001, n.p.) comments that 'power is at stake because dominant discourses and practices will always try to undermine us by pathologisation and exclusion'. How can we contribute to the evolution of the monologue into a dialogue with those traditionally positioned as 'unreason'?
- What aims might we have in common with those of the user/survivor movement? How might we be able to work together in pursuit of those aims?

Source: Adapted from Cooke (2015).

Following the sessions by the external speakers, I facilitate a final reflective session where trainees are invited to consider the following three questions:

1. Which ideas have most resonated with you in this unit?
2. What have you found most difficult/challenging?
3. How, if at all, has your thinking changed about the type of clinical psychologist you want to be?

Reflection on the unit

The unit appears successful: it is consistently highly evaluated by students, has survived a number of curriculum reorganisations since its inception in 2001, and I have managed to continue to persuade busy and high-profile people to come and teach on it! Importantly, given its inherent critical stance, it has consistently been supported by other members of the programme team. The programme is known for its invitational stance towards critical perspectives (British Psychological Society, 2016) and trainees often cite this as a reason for having applied to us in particular (Chatfield, 2016). Our educational philosophy is articulated in the *Programme Handbook* (Salomons Centre for Applied Psychology, 2015):

> A broad theoretical/knowledge and experience base underpins the Programme. The Programme is based on a growing body of psychological knowledge, which draws on a range of theories considered of relevance to the work of clinical psychologists including behavioural, cognitive, psychoanalytic, systemic, humanistic, social constructionist, community, critical and biological. The Programme aims to provide trainees with the experience, knowledge and skills necessary to conceptualise a problem from a number of different theoretical viewpoints and to use the practice associated with this range of models.
>
> Whilst psychology is the main knowledge base for practice, the importance of integrating contributions from other bodies of knowledge, including sociology, politics, organizational theory, ethics, philosophy, education, management, legal/judicial, informatics, economics and anthropology is also recognised. Training, therefore, aims to provide input from these bodies of knowledge when relevant to practice.
>
> The Programme . . . aims to integrate three models of clinical psychology practice . . . the scientist practitioner, the reflective practitioner and the critical practitioner . . . A critical approach places value on challenging the construction of knowledge and practice to promote emancipation and social justice and reduce the risk of harm.
>
> *(Salomons Centre for Applied Psychology, 2015, p. 10)*

Trainees' responses to the unit

I had been concerned that the students might feel oppressed by exposure to – sometimes quite damning – critiques of clinical psychology. I have not found that to be the case. Trainees value the contact with people who hold passionate opinions and who are prepared to speak openly about their views. They enjoy the opportunity to debate amongst themselves, on occasions continuing heated discussions over breaks. The inclusion of a final session devoted entirely to structured reflection, discussion and debate seems to be particularly appreciated. A typical piece of feedback was:

> The structure allowed us the space to think and express ideas that were in development in the previous teaching but were not discussed there. We greatly enjoyed the session and would really like to have a lot more of this . . . it was a really good experience having the opportunity . . . to get together and discuss the ideas raised in teaching the day before. This left people wanting more of this, so the year group is asking if a half day debate or seminar at the end of each teaching unit can be incorporated into the teaching schedules.

This approach to teaching provides opportunities for trainees to voice doubts and questions which have arisen in their clinical placements, and to begin to theorise them and to think about how they personally want to practise. A 'learning cycle' (Kolb, 1984) is thus set up. They seem to appreciate my acknowledgement that many of the questions discussed in the unit are ones thrown up by my own experience of working as a clinical psychologist in the NHS. They benefit from the chance to synthesise ideas and consider the kind of practitioner they want to be. I have been struck by how new some of the ideas have been to some of them, even after 3 years with us. The teaching seems well placed in the third year of the programme, by which time trainees have been exposed to a number of placement settings on which to reflect.

Challenges

The first challenge has been the obvious one: the inherent tension between two of the aims of NHS-funded clinical psychology programmes. On the one hand, programmes need to provide workers able to deliver the 'evidence based practice' that NHS organisations are currently mandated to provide. On the other hand, the programmes also aim to educate creative, critical thinkers which I would argue the NHS urgently needs. The profession has to balance its different commitments to the NHS. The first is to meet immediate service demands, which in the present context are often for 'doers' rather than thinkers. For example, many current posts are linked to the provision of a particular 'brand name therapy'. This has to be balanced with a parallel commitment to thoughtful practice under the rubric of the profession's 'scientist practitioner', 'reflective practitioner' and 'critical practitioner' models. The traditional model informing NHS clinical psychology provision was one of generic mental health services employing professionals with a broad training, able to draw on theoretical first principles to provide individualised treatment based on a collaborative formulation. However, this is increasingly being replaced by one of therapy model-specific services employing therapists with a shorter training in one, NICE-approved, model only, and offering predetermined, short packages of care to people with a particular diagnosis (Cooke & Watts, 2016). Commentators have linked this development to the current dominance of 'naïve modernism' in the intellectual sphere (Bohart & House, 2008; Faris & van Ooijen, 2011), an anxiety-driven and vain quest for 'safe certainty' on the part of clinicians and managers (Mason, 1993; Court, Cooke, & Scrivener, 2016), and in the political sphere of market capitalism, 'austerity' measures and privatisation of public services (Cooke & Watts, 2016). My own programme is exposed to this pressure along with the others, and I have sometimes had to 'argue my corner' to avoid some of my teaching time being diverted to other activities such as therapy skills training.

The second challenge in providing this teaching unit has been financial: the use of external contributors, many of whom are self-employed and come from far afield, places some strain on the programme budget. On the basis of student feedback, I have been able to convince budget holders of the excellent value for money this input represents.

A third challenge has concerned the relative scarcity of related practice placements. I have found it fairly easy to find people to talk about conceptual critiques of clinical psychology, but increasingly hard to identify local practitioners able to base their practice wholly or mainly on such ideas. Recently we have begun to make links with third-sector organisations engaged in more critically informed community practice (see, for example, Rhodes, 2016).

What makes it possible despite the challenges?

In thinking about what enables such a currently counter-cultural teaching unit to survive and thrive, three factors come particularly to mind.

The first is the consistently positive evaluation by students (not to mention the willingness of the speakers to travel long distances to do this teaching, for which I am eternally grateful!).

Second, in revising its accreditation standards for programmes (British Psychological Society, 2014), the British Psychological Society's Committee on Training in Clinical Psychology, while still responding to the current focus on 'model-specific' therapy skills, has managed to withstand the pressure to squeeze out the more critical elements. The way this tension is managed in the current guidelines reflects the rich debate about the 'evidence based practice' approach within the profession (see, for example, Pilgrim et al., 2015; Court et al., 2016).

Third, the support for critical approaches within the university (e.g. Lavender, 2003), school (Burns, 2014), programme leadership and team (see above), has been enormously helpful. I can certainly think of other universities and departments where a unit like this might be much harder to introduce and sustain.

Does it make any difference?

Trainees really appreciate not only this particular teaching, but also the exposure to critical ideas in the wider programme. Comments about the programme in *The Alternative Handbook for Postgraduate Training Courses in Clinical Psychology* (British Psychological Society, 2016, p. 86) include, in response to the question: 'What would you say is your favourite aspect of your course?'

- The course teaches you to be very critical in your thinking and encourages you to develop your own opinions and viewpoints.
- I like the emphasis on critical psychology and social constructivism.
- Its critical and reflective stance on mental health.
- I particularly like the critical focus of the course and the emphasis on lived experience.
- The exposure to a wide range of content. It really does challenge your ways of thinking (irrespective of your positioning) allowing for awareness of alternative views.
- It is the type of course that builds you into an extremely competent practitioner while allowing you to maintain your sense of self.
- Very reflective; this can be the most challenging and best part of it. Don't think you can just take training super casually on the chin.
- The focus on values, which the course has above any particular therapeutic model.

(British Psychological Society, 2016, p. 86)

And my particular favourite: 'If you like the idea of spending a lot of time thinking about complex questions which might not have any answers, this is the course for you' (British Psychological Society, 2016, p. 86).

Feedback from clinical placement supervisors (some of whom take trainees from a number of courses) is also generally that they value Salomons' trainees' critical thinking, values-based practice and willingness to engage in debates and tolerate uncertainty. It is harder to judge the extent to which engaging in these discussions during training actually makes a difference to the way trainees subsequently practise post-qualification. Some have gone on to found their own third-sector organisations (e.g. MAC-UK: www.mac-uk.org) or to be active in social movements such as Psychologists Against Austerity (https://psychagainstausterity.wordpress.com). Most, though, are in NHS jobs where the opportunities to put this critical thinking into practice vary widely. Many provide placements to current trainees, so programme staff have an opportunity to visit them. Often what we hear is that they are able to find some ways to practise in accordance with their beliefs and values, partly shaped by the thinking they encountered on the programme, even when these are at odds with the current culture of the NHS. A recent research project provides some evidence of this. Court et al. (2016) interviewed local clinical psychologists, many of whom will have trained on our programme. We found that as a result of the pressure to be 'NICE-compliant' (Murphy, 2013), clinical psychologists sometimes describe their work in terms of particular 'brand-name' therapies while actually conducting much more sophisticated interventions. These draw on a range of psychological theory, including critical ideas, and are based on an individualised formulation co-constructed with the service user. I like to think that hidden in local NHS services, among the uniform plantations of 'NICE-compliant therapy providers', there lurk some 'guerrilla thinkers' doing thoughtful, democratic, client-centred work and being comfortable with 'not-knowing' (Anderson & Goolishian, 1992).

Despite the challenges and the questions, organising this unit remains one of the most satisfying elements of my role: a chance to engage trainees in debates that I think are vital not only to the profession, but more importantly, to those whom we are aiming to help.

Acknowledgement

I am very grateful to Sarah Strohmaier for help with referencing and generally shaping up this chapter.

References

Anderson, H., & Goolishian, H. (1992). The client is the expert: A not-knowing approach to therapy. In S. McNamee & K. Gergen (Eds.), *Therapy as social construction* (pp. 25–39). London: Sage.

Barrett, R. (1996). *The psychiatric team and the social definition of schizophrenia: An anthropological study of person and illness.* Cambridge: Cambridge University Press.

Bentall, R. (2003). *Madness explained: Psychosis and human nature.* London: Penguin.

Bohart, A.C., & House, R. (2008). *Against and for CBT: Towards a constructive dialogue.* Ross-on-Wye, UK: PCCS Books.

Boyle, M. (2000). Science and social influence. M.B. Shapiro Award Lecture, British Psychological Society Annual Conference, 14 April.

British Psychological Society (Partnership & Accreditation). (2014). Standards for Doctoral programmes in Clinical Psychology. Retrieved from www.bps.org.uk/system/files/Public%20files/PaCT/dclinpsy_standards_approved_may_2014.pdf

British Psychological Society (Division of Clinical Psychology Pre-Qualification Group). (2016). *The alternative handbook for postgraduate training courses in clinical psychology: 2016 entry.* Retrieved from https://www.bps.org.uk/system/files/user-files/Division%20of%20Clinical%20Psychology/public/alternative_handbook_2016.pdf

Bronfenbrenner, U. (1979). *The ecology of human development: Experiments by nature and design.* Cambridge, MA: Harvard University Press.

Burns, J. (2014, April). A political-representational crisis: A response to the draft manifesto for a social materialist psychology of distress. Special issue: *Clinical Psychology Forum, 256.*

Campbell, P. (2001). The service user/survivor movement. In C. Newnes, G. Holmes, & C. Dunn (Eds.), *This is madness: A critical look at psychiatry and the future of mental health services.* Ross-on-Wye, UK: PCCS Books.

Chatfield, S. (2016). *Summary report and thematic analysis of feedback from departing third years, Doctoral Programme in Clinical Psychology*. Canterbury Christ Church University, Salomons Centre for Applied Psychology (internal report, October).

Coleman, D. (2016). *Open Culture*. Retrieved from www.openculture.com/2016/03/edmund-burkeon-in-action.html

Coles, S., Diamond, B., & Keenan, S. (2013). Clinical psychology in psychiatric services: The magician's assistant? In S. Coles, S. Keenan, & B. Diamond (Eds.), *Madness contested: Power and practice*. Ross-on-Wye, UK: PCCS Books.

Committee on Training in Clinical Psychology. (2014). *Standards for the accreditation of doctoral programmes in clinical psychology*. Leicester: British Psychological Society.

Cooke, A. (2004). *What sort of practitioner do you want to be? Promoting critical reflection about clinical psychology*. MHHE case studies of learning and teaching. Case study available from former project manager Jill Anderson (j.anderson@lancaster.ac.uk).

Cooke, A. (2008). Problems associated with the use of the concept of mental illness. In T. Stickley & T. Basset (Eds.), *Learning about mental health practice* (pp. 329–346). Chichester, UK: Wiley. Retrieved from https://docs.google.com/viewer?a=v&pid=sites&srcid=ZGVmYXVsdGRvbWFpbnxqb2hubWNnYXJjGl2ZXxneDo2NDBmYzY4ZGY5OTAwYzM

Cooke, A. (2014). So what do we need to do? *Clinical Psychology Forum, 256*.

Cooke, A. (2015). Teaching materials for Psychology and Society Unit, Doctoral Programme in Clinical Psychology, Canterbury Christ Church University.

Cooke, A., & Kinderman, P. (in press). But what about real mental illnesses? Alternatives to the disease model approach to 'schizophrenia'. *Journal of Humanistic Psychology*.

Cooke, A., & McGowan, J. (2013, September 5). Is life a disease? *Discursive of Tunbridge Wells*. Retrieved from http://discursiveoftunbridgewells.blogspot.co.uk/2013/09/is-life-disease.html

Cooke, A., & Watts, J. (2016, February 17). We're not surprised half our psychologist colleagues are depressed. *The Guardian*. Retrieved from www.theguardian.com/healthcare-network/2016/feb/17/were-not-surprised-half-our-psychologist-colleagues-are-depressed

Cooke, A., Gilchrist, A., & McGowan, J. (2014, August 18). Robin Williams, depression and the complex causes of suicide. *The Guardian*. Retrieved from http://www.theguardian.com/science/blog/2014/aug/18/robin-williams-depression-causes-suicide

Court, A.J., Cooke, A., & Scrivener, A. (2016). They're NICE and neat, but are they useful? A grounded theory of clinical psychologists' beliefs about and use of NICE guidelines. *Clinical Psychology and Psychotherapy*. doi: 10.1002/cpp.2054 (published online ahead of print).

Crits-Christoph, P., Frank, E., Chambless, D.L., Brody, C., & Karp, J.F. (1995). Training in empirically validated treatments: What are clinical psychology students learning? *Professional Psychology: Research and Practice, 26*(5), 514–522. doi: 10.1037/0735-7028.26.5.514

Diamond, B. (2006, June). Reflections on the practice of clinical psychology. *Clinical Psychology Forum, 162*, 5–8.

Dragonas, T., Gergen, K., McNamee, S., & Tseliou, E. (2015). Education as social construction: An introduction. In T. Dragonas, K. Gergen, S. McNamee, & E. Tseliou (Eds.), *Education as social construction: Contributions in theory, research and practice*. Chagrin Falls, OH: Taos Institute. Available at www.taosinstitute.net/education-as-social-construction-contributions-to-theory-research-and-practice

Dweck, C. (2000). *Self-theories: Their role in motivation, personality, and development*. Hove, UK: Psychology Press.

Faris, A., & van Ooijen, E. (2011). *Integrative counselling and psychotherapy: A relational approach*. London: Sage.

Fleetwood, S. (2013, 20 September). What is (and what isn't) critical realism? Seminar presentation, Centre for Employment Studies Research, Bristol, UK.

Foucault, M. (1967). *Madness and civilisation: A history of insanity in the age of reason*. London: Tavistock.

Gergen, K.J. (1990). Therapeutic professions and the diffusion of deficit. *The Journal of Mind and Behavior, 11*, 353–368.

Gilbert, P. (2009, May). Moving beyond cognitive behaviour therapy. *The Psychologist, 22*, 400–403. Retrieved from https://thepsychologist.bps.org.uk/volume-22/edition-5/moving-beyond-cognitive-behaviour-therapy

Grant, A. (2014). Neoliberal higher education and nursing scholarship: Power, subjectification, threats and resistance. *Nurse Education Today, 34*(10), 1280–1282.

Hall, J., & Marzillier, J. (2009, May). Alternative ways of working. *The Psychologist, 22*, 406–407.

Hall, J., Pilgrim, D., & Turpin, G. (Eds.) (2015). *Clinical psychology in Britain: Historical perspectives*. London: British Psychological Society.

Harper, D.J. (1999). *Deconstructing paranoia: An analysis of the discourses associated with the concept of paranoid delusion* (Unpublished PhD thesis). Manchester Metropolitan University, Manchester, UK.

Higher Education Academy. (n.d.). *The Mental Health in Higher Education Project*.

Johnstone, L. (2000). *Users and abusers of psychiatry: A critical look at psychiatric practice*. London: Routledge.

Kinderman, P. (2014). *A prescription for psychiatry*. London: Palgrave Macmillan.

Kinderman, P., & Cooke, A. (2000). *Recent advances in understanding mental illness and psychotic experiences: A report by the British Psychological Society Division of Clinical Psychology*. Leicester: British Psychological Society.

Knowles, M.S. (1990). *The adult learner: A neglected species* (4th ed.). Houston, TX: Gulf Publishing.

Kolb, D.A. (1984). *Experiential learning: Experience as the source of learning and development*. Englewood Cliffs, NJ: Prentice-Hall.

Kutchins, H., & Kirk, S.A. (2003). *Making us crazy: DSM: The psychiatric bible and the creation of mental disorders*. New York: Simon & Schuster.

Land, R., Meyer, J.H.F., & Smith, J. (2008). *Threshold concepts within the disciplines*. Rotterdam: Sense Publishers.

Lavender, T. (2003). Redressing the balance: The place, history and future of reflective practice in clinical training. *Clinical Psychology, 27*, 11–15.

Lavender, T., & Turpin, G. (2015). The development and training of the clinical psychological workforce: From probationers to practitioner doctorates. In J. Hall, D. Pilgrim, & G. Turpin (Eds.), *Clinical psychology in Britain: Historical perspectives* (pp. 93–110). London: British Psychological Society.

Lea, L., Holttum, S., Cooke, A., & Riley, L. (2016). Aims for service user involvement in mental health training: Staying human. *Journal of Mental Health Training, Research and Development, 11*(4), 208–219. doi: http://dx.doi.org/10.1108/JMHTEP-01-2016-0008

Loewenthal, D. (2015). *Critical psychotherapy, psychoanalysis and counselling: Implications for practice*. London: Palgrave Macmillan.

Management Advisory Service to the NHS (1989, May). *Review of clinical psychology services*. Retrieved from www.mas.org.uk/uploads/articles/MAS%20Review%201989.pdf

Marks, S. (2015). Psychologists as therapists: The development of behavioural traditions in clinical psychology. In J. Hall, D. Pilgrim, & G. Turpin (Eds.), *Clinical psychology in Britain: Historical perspectives* (pp. 194–207). London: British Psychological Society.

Mason, B. (1993). Towards positions of safe uncertainty. *Human Systems, 4,* 189–200.

May, R. (1969). *Love and will.* New York: Norton.

McGowan, J. (Ed.) (2015). *Academic programme handbook for the Doctoral Programme in Clinical Psychology.* Tunbridge Wells, UK: author.

Meyer, J.H.F., & Land, R. (2003). Threshold concepts and troublesome knowledge: Linkages to ways of thinking and practising. In C. Rust (Ed.), *Improving student learning: Theory and practice – ten years on.* Oxford: OCSLD.

Meyer, J., Land, R., & Baillie, C. (2010). *Threshold concepts and transformational learning.* Rotterdam: Sense.

Midlands Psychology Group. (2012). Draft manifesto for a social materialist psychology of distress. *Journal of Critical Psychology, Counselling and Psychotherapy, 12*(2), 93–107.

Moloney, P. (2013). *The therapy industry: The irresistible rise of the talking cure, and why it doesn't work.* London: Pluto Press.

Murphy, D. (2013, 26 February). Psychotherapy guideline compliance: Fact or fiction? *Psychotherapy and Everyday Life* (blog). Retrieved 23 April 17 from https://personcentred psych.wordpress.com/2013/02/26/psychotherapy-guideline-compliance-fact-or-fiction/

Newnes, C.D. (1990). The harm that services do. Special issue: *Changes, 8*(1).

Newnes, C. (2014). *Clinical psychology: A critical examination.* Ross-on-Wye, UK: PCCS Books.

Perkins, R. (2000, March 15). I have a vision . . . Beyond deficit and discrimination. Paper presented at Meeting the Challenges of the 21st Century. Millennium Mental Health Conference, Nottingham, 15 March 2000. BRIJ consultancy.

Pilgrim, D. (2011). The hegemony of cognitive-behaviour therapy in modern mental health care. *Health Sociology Review, 20*(2), 120–132. doi: 10.5172/hesr.2011.20.2.120

Pilgrim, D., & Treacher, A. (1992). *Clinical psychology observed.* London: Routledge.

Pilgrim, D., Turpin, G., & Hall, J. (2015). Overview: Recurring themes and continuing challenges. In J. Hall, D. Pilgrim, & G. Turpin (Eds.), *Clinical psychology in Britain: Historical perspectives* (pp. 365–378). London: British Psychological Society.

Potter, J. (1982). '. . . Nothing so practical as a good theory.': The problematic application of social psychology. In P. Stringer (Ed.), *Confronting social issues.* London: Academic Press.

Pring, R. (2000). *Philosophy of educational research.* London: Continuum.

Rhodes, E. (2016, March 31). Be the grit in the oyster. *The Psychologist.* Retrieved from https://thepsychologist.bps.org.uk/be-grit-oyster

Rogers, C. (1961). *On becoming a person: A therapist's view of psychotherapy.* Boston, MA: Houghton Mifflin.

Rose, D. (2001). *Madness strikes back* (Unpublished book proposal).

Salomons Centre for Applied Psychology (2015). *Programme handbook for the Doctoral Programme in Clinical Psychology.* Tunbridge Wells, UK: Canterbury Christ Church University.

Schön, D.A. (1991). *The reflective practitioner: How professionals think in action* (new ed.). Surrey, UK: Ashgate Publishing Limited.

Schön, D.A. (2009). *Educating the reflective practitioner.* San Francisco, CA: Jossey-Bass.

Smail, D. (1993). *The origins of unhappiness: A new understanding of personal distress.* London: HarperCollins.

Smail, D. (1996). Environmental cause and therapeutic cure: The impotence of insight. *British Psychological Society Psychotherapy Section Newsletter, 19,* 4–16.

Smail, D. (2005). *Power, interest and psychology: Elements of a social materialist understanding of distress*. Ross-on-Wye, UK: PCCS Books.

Spandler, H., Anderson, J., & Sapey, B. (2015). *Madness, distress and the politics of disablement*. Bristol, UK: Policy Press.

UK Community Psychology Network. (2007, 16 October). Changing politicians' minds about changing our minds? (Press release). Retrieved 23 April 2017 from www.compsy.org.uk/changing%20minds.pdf

Wellington, B., & Austin, P. (1996). Orientations to reflective practice. *Educational Research, 38*(3), 307–316.

Willig, C. (1998). Social constructionism and revolutionary socialism: A contradiction in terms? In I. Parker (Ed.), *Social constructionism, discourse and realism*. London: Sage.

NAME INDEX

Aristotle (384–322 BCE) ix
Augustine, St (354–430) 48

Blair, A. 60
Breggin, P. 40, 83, 86, 93, 95

Clarke, L. 261
Clegg, J. 261
Crestani, C. 261

Deleuze, G. 20
Derrida, J. 30, 45
Diamond, B. 260
Dinsmore-Tuli, U. 261
Dudgeon, P. 130–3

Foucault, M. xvii, 2, 11, 20, 38, 39, 123–4, 268
Freire, P. xvi, 2, 17, 69, 74, 82, 86, 94, 97, 114, 123, 127, 138, 141, 200
Fryer, D. 53, 261

Gesell, A. (1880–1961) 37, 56

Heisenberg, W.K. (1901–1976) 85
Holmes, G. 56

Jesus xix
Johnstone, L. 40, 261

Kinderman, P. 261
King, Martin Luther (1929–1968) 195, 213

Martín-Baró, I. (1942–1989) xix, xxi
May, R. 261
Moncrieff, J. 210

Newnes, C. 40, 84, 112

Oquosa, O. 261

Perec, G. (1936–1982) 45
Perkins, R. 265
Pessoa, F. (1888–1935) 53
Pilgrim, D. 199, 204, 260, 267
Plato (428–347 BCE) 90

Rapley, M. 47
Riley, R. (1954–1996) 124–142
Rose, D. 261–8
Rose, N. 2, 12, 56, 264

Smail, D. 31, 44, 201, 261, 265
Squires, G. 83, 84
Szasz, T. 210

Thatcher, M. 29
Trump, D. 78, 213
Tuli, N. 261

Vonnegut, K. 49
Vygotsky, L.S. (1896–1934) xvi, 30, 231

Watts, J. 271
Wittgenstein, L. (1889–1951) 45
Wolfensberger, W. 47, 54, 56

SUBJECT INDEX

Aboriginal and Torres Strait Islanders x, 123–142
Acceptance and Commitment Therapy (ACT) 240
activism 6, 67, 107, 202, 209; disability 72; social 120
addiction 151; denial of 150; to prescription 41
adult learning model 263
agency 219–234
Alternative Handbook 272
American Psychiatric Association (APA) 157, 191
American Psychological Association (APA) 213
analysology 53
andragogy 263
antidepressant 148–166, 173, 179; dependence 151, 165; discontinuation syndrome 156 antipsychiatry/ antipsychology placement (internship) 40
antipsychotic 148–156; long-term use of 155; *see* neuroleptic
Attention-Deficit Hyperactivity Disorder (ADHD) 28, 37, 56, 83, 85, 90–2, 180, 228; and fear 95
austerity xxi, 8, 67, 119, 221, 230, 271–2; and the voluntary sector 234
Australian Indigenous Psychology Education Project (AIPEP) 123–142
autism spectrum disorders (ASD) 83–5

banking education 2, 86
Beck Depression Inventory (BDI) 43

benighted misconceptions xv
Brexit 213–4
Bridges Project 116
British Institute of Human Rights 196
British Psychological Society 103, 200–8; *Guidelines on Professional Practice* 43
Brothers of the Christian Schools 38
bumper sticker 38, 48
Butler Education Act 84

capital: human xviii
capitalism 7, 26, 56, 77, 271
Capitalist Realism 20
Care Quality Commission 195, 239; *Essential Standards of Quality and Safety* 239
champagne socialism 41
childhood 220, 226–7
children 84–96; and domestic violence 219–235; drugging of 175, 178; forced removal of 128, 130; looked after 117
China 249, 251
Citizens' Commission for Human Rights (CCHR) 48
Closed Circuit Television (CCTV) 43
cognitive behaviour therapy (CBT) 42, 48, 103, 238–241
Cognitive Therapy Rating Scale 255–6
colonisation 31, 124–140
compulsion 22, 261
compulsory: able-bodiedness; 71, 77; able-mindedness 71; education 71, 84, 95; heterosexuality 71, 77; model for training 103; reading 3, 44

conflict 241–253; of interest 52; solving 225
consent 43, 47, 158, 180, 211, 254
control 9–16, 55, 151, 222, 241–8
Coping with Coming Off 161–2
co-production 200, 202, 206
council estate 90
counselling 1, 260; staff 40–2
crip theory 67
critical: consciousness xxi, 127; educators xxi; pedagogy xxi, 64, 66, 123, 134; practitioner 43, 269–70; realism 263; thinking 4–5, 15, 33, 105, 200, 202, 264
critically informed teaching 29, 70
cultural: capital 44, 50; difference 90, 249–252; diversity 238; healing 125; -historical activity theory (CHAT) xvi; norms 24–9, 78
culture xviii, 26, 27, 34, 72, 134–9; consumer 30; oralist 66

de-colonisation 123–140
death-making 56n1
debate as an educational method 120, 262, 270
Department of Health (UK) 162
depression 6, 45, 65, 157–9, 175, 266
depressive hedonia 20
diagnosis 56, 83–95; of dependence 151, 163; peculiarity of 29
disability: affirmative theories of 67; childhood 78, 84; individualisation of 65; intellectual 67–8; medicalisation of 65, 265; physical 71; psychologisation of 65; social model of 8, 9, 65, 75; studies 25, 67–78
disablism 75–6
discipline 14, 23, 32, 38–9, 48–56, 121, 123–141
diversity 23, 72, 104, 110, 130
Division of Clinical Psychology (DCP) 46, 49, 102, 113, 117, 205, 239, 260
domestication vs liberation 261
dominant ideas and praxis 2, 11–16, 24, 65, 71–7, 103, 133, 140–1, 209, 220, 226, 234
Duluth model 8

ecological: injustice xvii; validity 261
electroconvulsive therapy (ECT) 49, 172 *see also* electroshock
electronic record 43
electroshock 159, 163, 171–3 *see also* ECT; protest 191

Enquiry Based Learning (EBL) 204, 209
entertainment 30, 40, 53–4
ethical dilemma 196, 262, 266
EU Fundamental Rights Agency 214
evidence: base for supervision 239, 255–6; -based treatments 260, 270
expert by experience 103, 204–7

Facebook 38, 52, 54, 186, 191
feedback 6, 10, 14, 34, 55–6, 87, 197, 271–2
feminism 75–7
flavourless carrots 19
fluphenazine 155
fundamental rights analysis 177

gaze 39, 42–56, 65
genital mutilation 211
genthanasia 46
German critical theory 26
Gladiator 54
Gobelins school 38, 58
governmentality xvii, 9–11, 56
growth mindset 264
guerrilla: tactics 47; thinkers 273

Happy Valley 41
Health and Care Professions Council (HCPC) 199, 239
heteronormativity 71
heteronym 53
Higher Education Funding Council for England (HEFCE) 23, 207
human rights 134, 164, 187, 195; Act (1998) 211–2; Award (CCHR) 48; -based approach 195–214; education 200; violation 199
Humble Pie 55

idiographic vs nomothetic approach 260
inscription *see* diagnosis
Institute of Psychiatry 42, 199
interdisciplinary 75, 116, 201
interpassivity 32
intersectionality 74
interview panels 40, 203
irreverent heresies xvi
Islam 212

Journal of Polymorphous Perversity 44

knowledge construction xv, 123

language 31, 45, 84, 88, 103, 128, 172, 224; and context 53; neutral 95; sign 66

Latin America xv, xix, 52
leadership 47, 111, 117, 207, 272
learners 64, 120–1, 231–3
learning 69, 89, 101–21, 207, 247; context 52; environment 141, 231–2; experiential 200; objectives (sigh…) 4, 10, 21, 55; strategy 231; theories of 64; un- 69; work integrated 138
leather trousers 50
lesbian, gay, bisexual and transgender (LGBT) 208–12
liberation theology xvi, xix

Machiavellianism 37
Mad Hatters of Bath 261
male privilege 7–8
Manassas 44
marijuana 21
market Stalinism 20
Marxism 7
Marxist-humanist xvi
mechanism of therapeutic change 240, 245
Mental Capacity Act (2015) 198, 211
Mental Health Act (1983/2007) 195, 198
mentoring scheme 209, 213
Method of Levels (MOL) 242, 255; Session Evaluation Form 255–6
mobile phones 44
mortality of psychiatric patients 163

naïve modernism 271
name calling *see* inscription and diagnosis
National Health Service (NHS) 102, 195, 259; and electronic record 43; Institute for Health and Care Excellence (NICE) 260
National Student Survey 21, 27
Nazi psychiatry 54
neoliberalism xvii, 7
neuroleptic 173–80; dependence 148–66, 188; withdrawal symptoms 152–4, 160–3
neuroscience 24–5, 69
normality 66–78, 127; in childhood 220, 227
norms 25–9, 71–8; Western 140
not-knowing approach 273

Open Dialogue approach 175

PANEL principles 208
panopticon 39–49
participatory learning methods 204, 207
partnership 101, 111–121, 125, 131, 138, 202, 206–13

pastis 44
pedagogy: decolonial xvi; eco- xvi; revolutionary critical xvi-xx
Perceptual Control Theory (PCT) 238–256
personal file 43
poison *see* antidepressant, antipsychotic, fluphenazine, neuroleptic
political: correctness xv; demagoguery xv
positivism 12
post-colonial perspective 2
poststructuralism 2
power: distal 37, 50, 53; mapping 50, 59n14, 201; proximal 37, 53; relations 16, 22, 196, 203, 213; social 9, 50
professional: identity 105–15, 201, 209; training 259
Program Assessment of Service Systems (PASS) 54
psy discourse 65, 103, 126–7, 225, 234, 259, 266
Psychiatric Times 52
psychiatry: survivors of 6–7, 39, 162, 165
psychocentrism 263
Psychologists Against Austerity 119, 261, 272
psychology: clinical 46, 195, 214, 259–60; doctoral programme in 40, 42, 52, 100, 102–21, 197–214, 259–272; *Forum* 45, 49; individual focus of 8, 101, 107, 263; supervision 239; critical 101, 113; community 113; environmentalist 265; indigenous 123, 133, 139
Pulp 20, 22

Quality and Assurance Agency 4
queer theory 76–7
questioning: curious 35, 247, 253; ethos 204; Socratic 240

racism 8, 75, 131–8, 199
rebound problem 149, 154–7
receptor changes 154–60
recruitment 137–8; values-based 203
reflective practice 49, 106, 119, 231, 253, 264–72
reflexive impotence 21
religion 11, 65, 140, 212
reorganization 243, 245–7
research 8–16, 40, 180, 204–5, 212; animal 149; base for supervision 238; emancipatory disability 78; indigenous 139; participatory 101, 111, 113–5, 133; politics of 166, 223; strategy 20, 40; user-controlled 113, 162, 212
resistance 3, 14, 219, 227

restraint 88
re-subjectification 3
rights-based approach 196–202, 214, 265
Rockin the Fillmore 55

safe uncertainty/tolerating uncertainty 111
Salomons Advisory Group of Experts (SAGE) 261
Schwartz Rounds 206
scientism 32
self-aggrandisement 202
seminars 58; on record keeping 43; virtual 29–30; writing 49
sensibilities 22, 34
service: recipient 40, 47, 51; survivor 40, 261; user 40, 100, 103, 118, 198, 203–6, 261, 267
shyness 47
sighchology 45
slavery 128, 211
social: and emotional wellbeing (SEWB) 125, 134; constructionism 12, 263; context 101, 132, 219; inequality 102, 126; injustice xvii, 120; justice xx, 14, 101–2, 120, 125–6, 212, 214, 269; responsibility 267
sophiacide xix
special: educational needs (SEN) 83; yoga 261
Standards and Testing Agency 88
subjective possibility spaces 21–2
subjectivity 12–13, 22, 53, 134; and social power 9; reconstituted 7
supersensitivity psychosis 154–60

supervision 250–3; lack of evidence of effectiveness 238; principles-based 243, 249–53
surveillance 9–16, 20, 33, 38
systemic thinking 231

taken for granted ideas 10
teaching: Excellence Framework 21, 27; violence 73; *see* entertainment
temper tantrum 37, 56; *see* vodka
therapeutic alliance 241
therapy: brand name 270; outcome 43
threshold concept 263
tolerance building 151–9
trainee *see* learners
trauma: informed care 211; intergenerational 128–39

Underwood Report 84

value production xvii, xx
values: -based practice 272; British 97; teaching 103–6
violence: domestic 8; interpersonal 71; presumptions concerning 220–2; and vulnerability 223; teaching strategy 231–3
vodka 56

warfare 38, 128
We're Not Mad, We're Angry 41
whiteness 126
withdrawal symptoms: antidepressant 156–60
wounds: cultural 133; service 41, 47

Yoga Nidra Network 261